Turbo C®++ DiskTutor, Second Edition

Turbo C®++ DiskTutor, Second Edition

Greg Voss and Paul Chui

Osborne **McGraw-Hill**

Berkeley New York St. Louis San Francisco
Auckland Bogotá Hamburg London Madrid
Mexico City Milan Montreal New Delhi Panama City
Paris São Paulo Singapore Sydney
Tokyo Toronto

Osborne **McGraw-Hill**
2600 Tenth Street
Berkeley, California 94710
U.S.A.

Osborne **McGraw-Hill** offers software for sale. For information on software, translations, or book distributors outside of the U.S.A., please write to Osborne **McGraw-Hill** at the above address.

This book is printed on recycled paper.

Turbo C® ++ DiskTutor, Second Edition

1234567890 DOC 9987654321

ISBN 0-07-881737-4

GMV

For Robert and Mary Voss

PC

For Sam and Michelle Chui

Contents at a Glance

Contents

Acknowledgments

Many hands deserve credit for this work. We thank Jeff Pepper, Emily Rader, and Judith Brown of Osborne for gentle, but firm guidance and tireless effort throughout revisions. John Sieraski of Borland gave careful reading of text and analysis of programs. His suggestions and explanations were always on the mark. Jim Turley lent a critical eye, which set straight typographical errors and improved organization. Nan Borreson of Borland kept us in constant supply of updated software and manuals and was instrumental in dialogs affecting the design of DiskTutor software. Priscilla kept things in perspective.

Melissa Milich provided consultation, research, administrative, and editorial services. Special thanks to Brad Gaiser of Athena for the introduction to C++ and nurturing us through early phases of frustration. Steve Kilgore's skillful programming made possible the core functions on which the DiskTutor User Interface library is based. David Intersimone has been a constant inspiration. We thank him for companionship as well as information and critical insights that shaped our thoughts in the early stages of design.

Introduction

The Turbo C++ DiskTutor is an interactive tutorial complete with working C++ example programs. Throughout the book, we emphasize the whole rather than the parts. It is far more important to understand the concepts of object-oriented programming than it is to memorize a list of rules regarding syntax and new language features. Once you understand classes, objects, inheritance, and polymorphism, filling out your knowledge of C++ language features will come naturally. You can easily fit the details into the broader framework of a new way of programming and thinking.

This book teaches object-oriented programming as practiced with the C++ programming language. The Turbo C++ DiskTutor will work with either Turbo C++ or Borland C++. The DiskTutor tutorial also walks you through Borland's integrated programming environment. Hands-on guidance with the mouse-oriented editor, debugger, clipboard, and hypertext help system will flatten your learning curve.

Every example program in this book is provided on disk. As you read through the examples, you will load, compile, and run each program. This keeps your focus where it should be: on reading and programming rather than typing. The compilers and the example programs follow the complete AT&T 2.0 specification for C++. You can experiment by changing the programs in any way you see fit.

Knowledge of C++ and object-oriented programming will open many doors: new skills, new projects, interesting jobs. Whether you ultimately plan to work with DOS, UNIX, OS/2, Microsoft Windows, or any operating environment that supports C++ programming, the skills you build by working through the tutorial in this book will put you ahead of the competition.

How this Book Is Organized

This book divides naturally into three parts. Part One (Chapters 1 through 5) introduces the DiskTutor programming environment and reviews the C programming language. Part Two (Chapters 6 through 9) introduces object-oriented programming and shows how to build classes and create objects. Part Three (Chapters 10 through 14) shows how OOP builds on the work of others through construction and reuse of class libraries.

Chapters 1 and 2 will get you through installation of the DiskTutor example programs and a quick introduction to Borland's editor, compiler, and debugger. Chapters 3 and 4 review C at a quick pace and get you to a point of familiarity with C so you are ready for the new features introduced by C++.

Chapter 5 presents new features of C++ in the context of procedural programming. You do not need to approach C++ as an object-oriented programming language. C++ can simply be regarded as a better C; that is, a C with strict type checking, better syntax, and better error detection.

Object-oriented programming, introduced in Chapter 6, requires a new way of thinking. The broad overview of classes, objects, messages, and methods covered here provides a framework for the remainder of the book. Chapters 6 through 9 work through specific examples in building reusable classes. In object-oriented programming, classes become the modular components from which software systems are built.

While Chapters 6 through 9 provide the core tools for object-oriented components, Chapters 10 through 14 show how to build systems based on reusable components. The aim of these chapters is to build and reuse class libraries. The notions of inheritance, multiple inheritance, and polymorphism allow flexibility in the reuse of code in ways not possible with standard C and Pascal libraries.

Extensible class libraries introduce the single greatest lever realized by object-oriented programming. In Chapters 10 through 14, you'll see a dramatic demonstration of how class libraries boost productivity and minimize source code complexity. Recent focus on the features and availability of class libraries neglects the most important question: what do you do with class libraries once you've got them?

What good are bags, sets, and dictionaries? What makes object-based stacks, lists, and queues different from similar data structures and their companion functions in typical C libraries? The final chapter of the book shows the ease with which complex software is built when based on well-designed class libraries.

How to Work with DiskTutor

To use the DiskTutor tutorial, you first need to install either Turbo C++ or Borland C++ and set the appropriate PATH environment variable. Refer to the installation guides provided by Borland. Next, install the DiskTutor example programs (see Chapter 1). For IBM compatibles, you will need 640K of memory and a hard disk. Each time you begin a new chapter, make sure the disk directory associated with the chapter is the current working directory. For example, before beginning Chapter 1, change to the directory with the following DOS command:

```
cd c:\dt\ch1
```

This assures that DiskTutor software has been installed in the default directory on drive C in a directory called \DT. Prior to beginning work on subsequent chapters you would type

```
cd c:\dt\ch2
cd c:\dt\ch3
.
.
.
cd c:\dt\ch14
```

Once you have entered the proper directory, invoke the C++ programming environment. If you are using Turbo C++, type

```
tc
```

If you are using Borland C++, type

```
bc
```

As you read through the text, you will be asked to perform tasks on your computer: load a program, compile and run a program, edit a file, and step through program execution with the debugger. The following font indicates program source code:

P6-1

```
// C++ program listing
#include <conio.h>

class Point
{
      int x, y;
public:
      Point(int u, int v) { x=u; y=v; }
      void print() { cprintf("x->%5d  y->%5d\r\n", x, y); }
};

main()
{
      Point p1(3,10);
      p1.print();
}
```

Whenever you see a program listing that has a symbol at the upper left, such as P6-1 in the previous listing, it means the program is available on disk. In the case of the above listing, the name of the program is P6-1.CPP and is the first program you are asked to load and compile in Chapter 6.

In most cases you are explicitly told to load and study the program as you read the text. You may also want to skip around the book in an ad hoc fashion looking for programs of interest. When you find something that strikes you, look for the program name, load the program, and give it a try. Some people work best in this manner. Others will want to work through the chapters in linear fashion loading each of the programs as they go.

Required Experience

This book assumes previous experience with C. It is possible to work through the entire book, loading and running each program, with no knowledge of C. You probably will be able to grasp some of the major concepts, particularly if you already understand the notions of loops, conditional execution, variables, and data structures such as arrays and records (C structs). However, you will get the most benefit from this book if you know how to code each of these abstract concepts (loops, structs, and so forth) in C. If this is not the case, we suggest a couple of weeks with a good C tutorial. By the way, it is possible to compile both C and C++ programs with the Borland C++ compilers. Simply use .C rather than .CPP for the filename extension, and C rather than C++ syntax rules are applied to program compilation. All programs in this book use the .CPP extension.

It's important not to get bogged down. If you're struggling to understand a program, try moving on to another example and come back after you've gained some insight. Most important: enjoy yourself. Learning is tough. But a tough road is more easily traveled if you remember to have fun.

The NIH Class Library

Chapter 13 programming examples are built on a radically altered version of Keith Gorlen's NIH class library. The NIH class library is in the public domain and available through USENET and various electronic bulletin boards. Keith Gorlen's work has advanced understanding of class libraries for the general C++ community by inestimable degrees. The availability of this library has promoted seminal study, analysis, and debate about the structure and purpose of class libraries among C++ practitioners.

Conventions Used in this Book

Program listings, C++ code fragments, and program output appear in a monospace font.

```
// Program Listing
```

Filenames for programs, header files, and projects appear in all uppercase letters: P10-3.CPP, POINT.H, CARDGAME.PRJ.

Boldface is used for class names (**Point**), variables (**i**, **aPoint**), function and method names (**printf**, **Point::print**), and C++ keywords (**char**, **float**, **if**, **for**, **while**). Note that in programs and text we have adopted the Smalltalk convention of starting class names with uppercase letters (**Rectangle**), while starting object names (instances of classes) with lowercase letters (**r1**, **aRectangle**).

Keys that appear on your keyboard are printed in a special uppercase font:

ESC, RETURN, UP ARROW, DOWN ARROW, PGUP, PGDN

Italics are used to introduce new concepts (*scope, resolution, operator*) and highlight text deserving special attention.

C++ as a Better C

Part One

1 Getting Started

To get you running DiskTutor example programs as quickly as possible, this chapter contains information on the following:

- Making a backup disk
- Installing Turbo/Borland C++
- Setting the DOS path
- Customizing Turbo C++ for DiskTutor
- Installing DiskTutor example programs
- Working with DiskTutor examples
- Accessing the README file

Throughout this chapter, it is assumed that you are familiar with DOS.

Making Backup Disks

The DiskTutor example program disk is not copy-protected. Before beginning, you should use the DOS DISKCOPY command to back up the DiskTutor disk. Put a blank formatted disk into drive A and type

```
diskcopy a:
```

Follow the instructions printed to the screen, or refer to the DISKCOPY command in the MS-DOS reference guide.

Put the original disk in a safe place and use the working copy of the disk for the installation.

Preparing to Use DiskTutor

Before you can begin using the Turbo C++ DiskTutor tutorial, you must install both the C++ compiler and the DiskTutor example programs on your hard disk. You must also edit the directory specifications that tell the compiler where to look for the DiskTutor class library and header files. For Turbo C++ you should change the default filename extension for program files from .C to .CPP.

It's best to perform these tasks in the following order.

1. Install your Borland C++ compiler.
2. Customize the compiler to work with DiskTutor.
3. Install Turbo C++ DiskTutor example programs.

Installing the Turbo/Borland C++ Compiler

The DiskTutor C++ tutorial will work with any of the three currently available C++ compilers shipped by Borland.

- Turbo C++ 1.0
- Turbo C++ 2nd Edition

- Borland C++

Refer to the installation guide provided with your compiler for specific instructions. Be sure to set the DOS path environment variable before you use your Borland C++ compiler with the DiskTutor C++ example programs.

The default installation directory for Turbo C++ 1.0 or Turbo C++ 2nd Edition is C:\TC. The default installation directory for Borland C++ is C:\BORLANDC. Therefore, the executable compiler is normally placed in either C:\TC\BIN or C:\BORLANDC\BIN. After installation is complete, you must set the DOS path variable to the directory containing the executable compiler. You should edit your AUTOEXEC.BAT to contain a path setting that includes this directory.

Turbo C++ example:

```
PATH=C:\DOS;C:\UTIL;C:\TC\BIN
```

Borland C++ example:

```
PATH=C:\BORLANDC\BIN
```

Also, your CONFIG.SYS file should contain the line

```
FILES = 20
```

Before operating your C++ compiler you should reboot the computer to make sure the PATH and FILES specifications take effect.

Customizing Turbo C++ for DiskTutor

Your Borland C++ compiler can be customized to work with Turbo C++ DiskTutor example programs by performing two modifications made inside the integrated development environment (IDE). After the modifications the configuration is saved to either TC.EXE or BC.EXE.

- Modify INCLUDE and LIB directory specifications.
- Set the default file extension to .CPP (Turbo C++ only).
- Save the compiler configuration.

These customizations can be performed by running the IDE provided by the Borland C++ compilers. For Turbo C++ 1.0 and Turbo C++ 2nd Edition the name of the IDE is TC.EXE. For Borland C++ the name is BC.EXE. To start the IDE, first log to the BIN directory, which contains the executable compiler and utility programs. Assuming that you have not changed the default installation directory, for Turbo C++ 1.0 and Turbo C++ 2nd Edition, you would type

```
CD \TC\BIN
```

For Borland C++ you would type

```
CD \BORLANDC\BIN
```

Now start the IDE. For Turbo C++ 1.0 and Turbo C++ 2nd Edition type

```
TC
```

For Borland C++ type

```
BC
```

The top-level menu for the installation utility appears.

Modify INCLUDE and LIB Directory Specifications First change the INCLUDE and LIB specifications that tell the C++ compiler where to look for C++ *header* (INCLUDE) and *class library* (LIB) files. Select the Options menu entry by pressing ALT-O. A submenu appears. Select the Directories menu entry from the submenu by pressing D. A dialog box appears containing three text input fields. You will modify two of these fields: Include Directories and Library Directories. Make the text field for Include Directories active by pressing ALT-I If you installed the C++ compiler in the default directory and you are using either Turbo C++ 1.0 or Turbo C++ 2nd Edition, the text in this box will be

```
C:\TC\INCLUDE
```

(Borland C++ substitutes BORLANDC for TC in the above pathname.)

Press the END key on your keyboard to move the cursor to the end of this line. Append the following text to specify an additional INCLUDE directory.

```
;C:\DT\INCLUDE
```

This assumes that you plan to install the DiskTutor example programs in C:\DT. The above path specification must be altered if you plan to use a different directory. The entire line should now read

```
C:\TC\INCLUDE;C:\DT\INCLUDE
```

Now perform a similar edit for the LIB specification. Make the text field for Library Directories active by pressing ALT-L.

```
C:\TC\LIB
```

(Borland C++ substitutes BORLANDC for TC in the above pathname.)

Press the END key on your keyboard to move the cursor to the end of this line. Append the following text to specify an additional LIB directory.

```
;C:\DT\LIB
```

This assumes that you plan to install the DiskTutor example programs in C:\DT. The above path specification must be altered if you plan to use a different directory. The entire line should now read

```
C:\TC\LIB;C:\DT\LIB
```

Press RETURN to accept the modifications.

Setting the Default File Extension to .CPP (Turbo C++ Only) By default Borland C++ uses .CPP as the default file name extension for loading source code files into the program editor; this modification is only necessary for Turbo C++. If you are installing Turbo C++, activate the Options/Environment/Editor menu from the top-level menu. Press ALT-O EE. Next select Default Extension by pressing D. A text edit box appears. Edit this text so that it reads

```
CPP
```

Press RETURN.

Saving the Configuration Select Options/Save from the top-level menu by pressing ALT-O S. A dialog box appears. Make sure there is an X in the Environment check box. Press RETURN and your modifications are saved as permanent settings for the IDE. After your Borland C++ compiler is properly installed you are ready to install the example programs provided with the Turbo C++ DiskTutor. To quit the IDE, select Files/Quit from the top-level menu (ALT-F Q).

Installing Turbo C++ DiskTutor Example Programs

Create a directory where you intend to install the DiskTutor sample programs. The recommended name for this directory is C:\DT. You can use whatever name you like, but these instructions assume you will install the DiskTutor example programs on drive C in the directory C:\DT. Make sure you are logged in to the appropriate drive. For example, if you plan to install the DiskTutor example programs on drive C type

```
C:
```

To create the DiskTutor directory, type the following command at the DOS prompt.

```
MD \DT
```

Next change to the newly created directory.

```
CD \DT
```

You are now ready to copy the installation files from the DiskTutor examples disk to the newly created directory. First insert the DiskTutor example program diskette in your floppy drive. Assuming this is drive A and assuming that your currently logged directory is C:\DT, you can now copy all files on the diskette to the DiskTutor directory with the DOS COPY command:

```
COPY A:*.*
```

This will copy four files to the DiskTutor directory:

```
INSTALL.BAT
DT.EXE
README.COM
README
```

DT.EXE is a self-extracting archive. Running the INSTALL batch program (INSTALL.BAT) will cause the self-extracting archive to create all the subdirectories required for the DiskTutor example programs. Next, each of the example programs is extracted from the archive and placed in the proper directory. This is all accomplished by typing the following command from the DOS prompt when you are logged into the DiskTutor directory on the hard disk (C:\DT):

```
INSTALL
```

You will now see the name of each example program file printed as it is extracted from the archive and copied to the hard disk. When the installation is through, you will have many subdirectories within the parent directory, \DT:

```
\DT
\DT\CH2
\DT\CH3
\DT\CH4
\DT\CH5
```

```
\DT\CH6
\DT\CH7
\DT\CH8
\DT\CH9
\DT\CH10
\DT\CH11
\DT\CH12
\DT\CH13
\DT\CH14
\DT\INCLUDE
\DT\LIB
```

The install program creates a unique directory for each chapter in the DiskTutor book starting with Chapter 2. The default directories for example programs correspond to chapter numbers as follows:

```
\DT\CH2
\DT\CH3
. . .
\DT\CH14
```

Before beginning work on a chapter, switch to the appropriate directory. For example, before beginning work in Chapter 2 type

```
CD \DT\CH2
```

DiskTutor is an interactive tutorial. You'll be asked to type in example programs as you work through the book. In addition, sample programs are provided on the disk. You can run many of these programs without reading the DiskTutor book. However, the more complex programs require *project files*. Project files are discussed in the second chapter, which also introduces the integrated programming environment. You are encouraged to work through Chapter 2 before experimenting with programs on the disk. You'll find the tutorial speeds along at a pace quick enough to satisfy the impatient. In order to conserve space on the distribution disks, project files are not provided. However, instructions for creating project files for a given program are supplied in the DiskTutor book.

Accessing the README file

The README file contains changes to the DiskTutor disks that may not have been made to the book. README also has a list of the files on the

DiskTutor disks and a description of each file.

To see the README file, follow these steps:

1. Type **cd \dt** and then press RETURN.

2. Type **readme** and press RETURN.

3. Use the cursor keys PGUP and PGDN to scroll through the README file.

4. Press P if you want to echo the output of the README screen to your printer.

5. When you have read the file, press ESC.

You are now ready to start using DiskTutor. As you read through this book you can call up the programs from the disk and work along with the book. If you choose not to do so, you will be able to follow the book without the disks.

Borland C++ versus Turbo C++

The DiskTutor tutorial will work with either Turbo C++ 1.0, Turbo C++ 2nd Edition, or Borland C++. Turbo C++ 1.0 was the first release of a C++ compiler by Borland. Turbo C++ 2nd Edition is a more recent release of the same product, which substitutes a more comprehensive and powerful on-line help system for the Library reference manual that came with Turbo C++ 1.0. Turbo C++ 2nd Edition would be a good choice if your main purpose were to learn C++ and object-oriented programming. Borland C++ is a professional C++ development package complete with a stand-alone debugger, a profiler, and an assembler. In addition, Borland C++ will let you develop programs for Microsoft Windows.

All example programs supplied with Turbo C++ DiskTutor run with either Turbo C++ or Borland C++. The main difference to keep in mind while working with DiskTutor example programs is the way you will invoke the Integrated Development Environment. If you are using Turbo C++ 1.0 or Turbo C++ 2nd Edition, invoke the Integrated Development Environment by typing

```
tc
```

If you are using Borland C++, invoke the Integrated Development Environment by typing

```
bc
```

Small Memory Model

All programs in the Turbo C++ DiskTutor should be compiled using the small memory model compiler option. The small memory model is the default compiler memory model option that is set automatically for Turbo C++ as well as Borland C++ when you install the compiler. Unless you have changed this default option since you installed your compiler you do not need to do anything. Actually, only the programs that link to either the DiskTutor container class library (DT.LIB) or the DiskTutor user interface class library (DTUI.LIB) will not work properly if the small memory model is not selected when compiling and linking programs. It's best however simply to leave the compiler memory model option set to the small memory model for all DiskTutor example programs.

Conserving Disk Space

Periodically, you may want to delete disk files in one or more of the chapter directories. The OBJ and EXE files generated by the Borland C++ compilers can be quite large. For example, the combined disk space occupied by these files for Chapter 13 is 2.5 megabytes. Chapter 14 generated files take up 1.4 megabytes. If you find yourself running low on disk space, and you're through working in a given directory, delete these files. For example, if you want to make space in Chapter 13, you would execute the following three commands:

```
CD \DT\CH13
DEL *.EXE
DEL *.OBJ
```

Be sure that you don't do this in \TC\BIN or \BORLANDC\BIN or you will destroy the compiler and be forced to reinstall your C++ compiler.

2 The Borland C++ Integrated Development Environment

All programs in this book assume you are working with the Integrated Development Environment (IDE) provided by Turbo C++ or Borland C++. Whenever you see the term *Borland C++* or the *Borland C++ IDE*, the reference applies to both Turbo C++ and Borland C++ compilers or development environments. More recently, the term Integrated Development Environment has been changed to *Programmer's Platform* in documentation provided by Borland C++. This book uses the more general terms *programming environment, development environment,* and *IDE* when explaining how to build and run programs with Borland C++.

The concept of the Integrated Development Environment (IDE) was pioneered by Borland years ago. Early IDEs consisted of an editor, simple menus, and the ability to run the program without leaving the system. The Borland C++ IDE is Borland's most powerful development to date. Among other features, this IDE has pull-down menus, dialog boxes, multiple windows, and integrated help.

As with any powerful system, it may take a little time getting used to all the commands. This chapter will give you hands-on experience with the IDE, without involving too much C++. You are encouraged to work through the examples in this chapter before working through the rest of the book.

Many commands have shortcuts, which will be pointed out along the way. After you have learned the basics, the shortcuts will be obvious.

Starting the DiskTutor IDE

After you have installed the DiskTutor as described in Chapter 1, type

```
cd \dt\ch2
```

to go to the working directory for this chapter.

NOTE The rest of the book will assume that you have activated the correct directory before beginning the exercises in each chapter.

Start DiskTutor by typing

```
tc
```

for Turbo C++ or by typing

```
bc
```

for Borland C++.

The first time that the Borland C++ IDE is activated, it displays a version number and copyright for the software. Press any key. The copyright will disappear and you will see the screen shown in Figure 2-1.

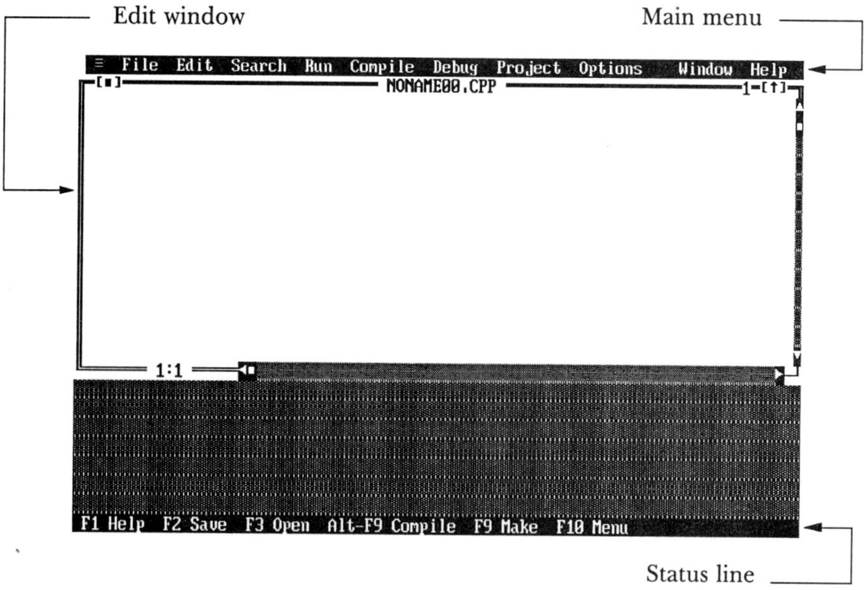

Figure 2-1. *The Borland C++ IDE*

The Main Menu

The top line on the screen is the main menu. This menu contains the most general commands available in the Borland C++ programming environment. You can access the main menu by pressing the F10 key. When the main menu is active, you can press the highlighted letter, or use the LEFT ARROW and RIGHT ARROW keys to select a submenu and then press RETURN to activate that submenu. Alternatively, you can press the ALT key combinations to activate a submenu. For example, to activate the File submenu, press ALT-F.

MOUSE If you have a mouse, you can click on a command in the main menu instead of using the keyboard. (In general, clicking on an item means clicking the left mouse button. The right mouse button always brings up a Help window on the item that you clicked on.)

Each command on the main menu actually invokes another menu. In general, menu commands can perform an action, invoke another menu, or call up a dialog box. Figure 2-2 shows a couple of typical menus.

The Status Line

The status line located on the bottom of the screen (see Figure 2-3) is actually an abbreviated help system. As the name indicates, the status line displays Borland C++ status information. In addition, the status line may list some available shortcuts (also called *hot keys*), or give hints about certain Borland C++ commands. The content of the status line depends on what is active in the IDE.

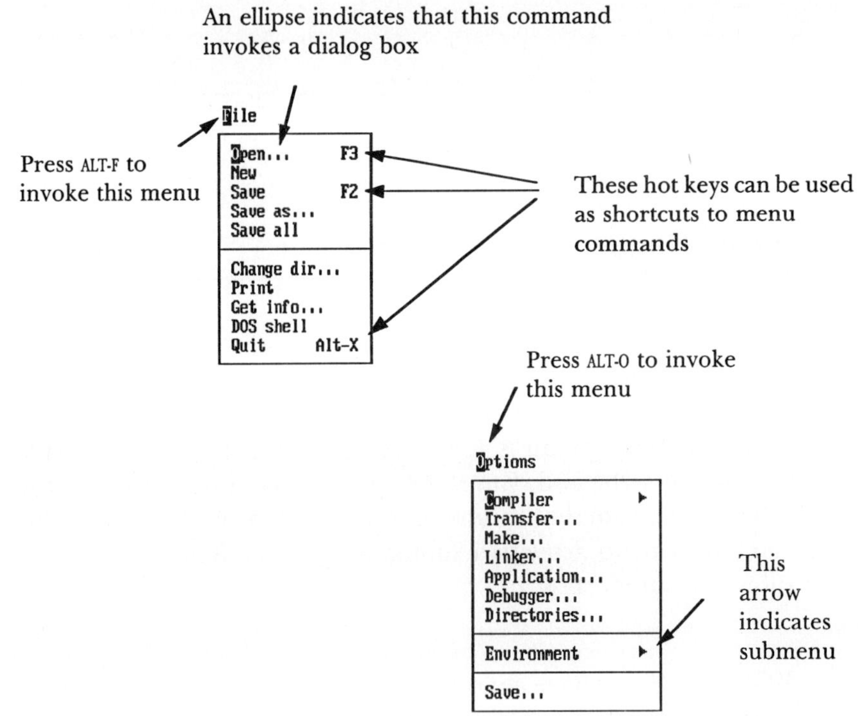

Figure 2-2. *The File menu and the Options menu*

Figure 2-3. *A typical status line*

MOUSE You can click on a hot key in the status line to invoke the command.

Controlling and Managing Windows

Initially, there is one Edit window displayed on the screen titled NONAME00.CPP. The window's border features a number of controls and status indicators (see Figure 2-4).

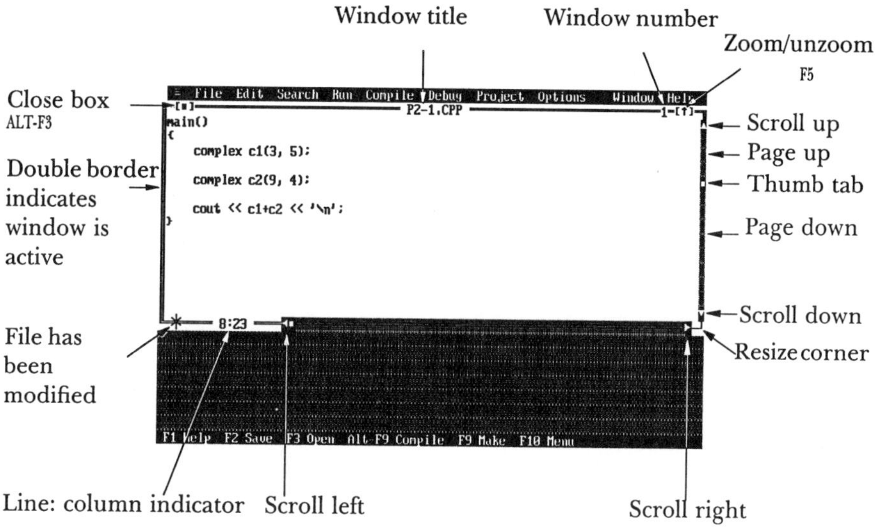

Figure 2-4. *An Edit window*

The title of the Edit window is centered on the window's top border and contains the name of the file that is being edited. The number of windows that the Borland C++ programming environment can open is limited only by the amount of memory your computer has, but only one window may be active at any time. Each window has a unique window number, which is displayed in its upper-right corner. The NONAME00.CPP Edit window is window number 1. A double border around this window indicates that it is the active window.

Each Edit window displays its current cursor position in *line:column* format in the lower-left corner. If the contents of the window have been modified since it was last saved on disk, an asterisk (*) will appear next to the line:column indicator.

Another type of window—the Message window—tracks information like compiler and linker errors. It operates similarly to the Edit window, but the Message window is a read-only window. Unlike Edit windows, you can only open one Message window.

Open the Message window by pressing ALT-W to invoke the Window menu. Then press **M** to select **M**essage. Notice that the newly created Message window (window 2) becomes active and has a double border, while the double border around the Edit window has changed to a single border. Pressing ALT and a window number activates that window. Reactivate the NONAME00.CPP Edit window by pressing ALT-1.

MOUSE Clicking on a window is another way to activate a window.

Another feature of Borland C++ windows is zooming and unzooming. A zoomed window covers the entire screen, letting you see more information without scrolling. Unzooming reverts a window back to its previous size. Press F5 to zoom the NONAME00.CPP Edit window. Press F5 again to unzoom it.

MOUSE Click on the [↑] symbol to zoom a window. When a window zoomed, the [↑] turns into a [↕]. Click on it to unzoom the window.

To move and resize the window, the window must be put into move/resize mode. Set move/resize mode by pressing CTRL-F5. A single border around the Edit window tells you that move/resize mode is active.

Use the cursor keys to move the Edit window around the screen. Don't be afraid to overlap the Message window with the Edit window.

Now hold down the SHIFT key and use the cursor keys to resize the Edit window. When you are finished, try setting the window back to its original size and position. Press ESC to end move/resize mode.

MOUSE To move a window, click and hold on the window title. Move the mouse to move the window. To resize it, click and hold on the resize corner (lower right) and then move the mouse.

Dialog Boxes

The IDE uses dialog boxes to let you set options and answer questions. Dialog boxes may contain text entry fields, command selector buttons, check boxes, radio buttons, and lists. A typical dialog box is shown in Figure 2-5. To see this dialog box press ALT-S F.

Dialog boxes are different from other windows in that you cannot select another window while a dialog box is active. You must answer the dialog box by selecting **[OK]** or **[Cancel]** to proceed. The selector button that is highlighted is the command that the dialog box will issue when RETURN is pressed. The **[OK]** selector is usually the default.

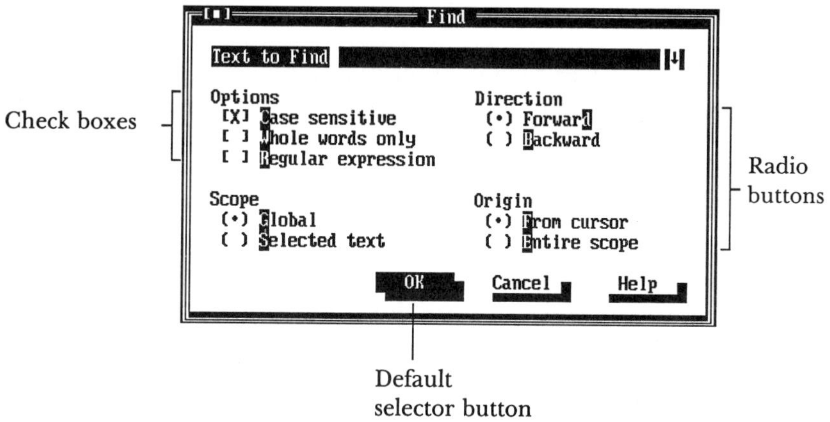

Figure 2-5. *The Find dialog box*

To move to a field or issue a command, press ALT and the highlighted key of the field or selector button. For example, to signal **OK** in the Find dialog box, press ALT-K. To cycle forward through the fields and buttons, press TAB. Press SHIFT-TAB to cycle backward.

The spacebar toggles radio button and check box options. Radio buttons let you select exclusive options within a group. For example, in the Find dialog box in Figure 2-5, you can set Direction to either Forwar**d** or **B**ackward. Check boxes let you select multiple options; for example, you can set the Find Options to both **C**ase sensitive and **W**hole words only.

MOUSE You can click on the fields, check boxes, and radio buttons to activate them. Clicking on a selector button invokes the command.

Press ESC to cancel the Find dialog now.

ALT-F3 closes a window. Close the NONAME00.CPP Edit window—you won't need it anymore.

MOUSE To close a window with a mouse, click on the close box.

Working with DiskTutor Programs

The program files in each chapter are named P*x*-1.CPP, P*x*-2.CPP, and so forth. This chapter contains only three program files and two programs. The files P2-2.CPP and P2-3.CPP are combined into one program as you will see later. For now, open the first program in the book, P2-1.CPP. This program adds two complex numbers together and prints the result to the screen. Don't be concerned with how this program works, because you are still exploring the IDE in this chapter.

To open a file, press ALT-F and then press **O**. Alternatively, you can use the F3 key as a shortcut. This should open the Load a File dialog box as shown in Figure 2-6. This dialog box is partitioned into several fields and has four command selector buttons. The highlighted **[Open]** selector button is the default.

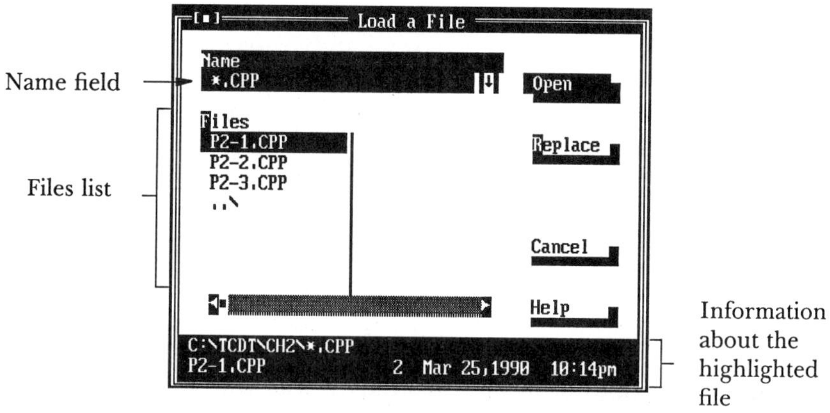

Figure 2-6. *The Load a File dialog box*

The Name field in this dialog box is set to "*.CPP" by default. The Files list contains files that match the file specification in the Name field. A file information section at the bottom of the window shows the current file's size in bytes, and the date and time. To load P2-1.CPP, type **P2-1.CPP** in the Name field. Press RETURN to invoke the default **O**pen command. The IDE should open a new window (as window 1) with program P2-1.CPP in it.

P2-1

```
#include <iostream.h>
#include <complex.h>

main()
{
    complex a(3,5);
    complex b(9,4);

    cout << (a + b) << '\n';
}
```

Another way to load a file is to select it from the Files list. To selectively load a file from the dialog box, press TAB (or ALT-F) to go from the Name field to the Files list; then select P2-1.CPP with the UP ARROW and DOWN ARROW keys, and press RETURN.

Online Help

The Borland C++ online help is a handy reference for the C++ language and functions as well as a good guide to IDE commands. Help is available anywhere in the IDE and is context-sensitive to the active window, menu, or dialog box.

If you want more information about editor commands, for example, make sure the P2-1.CPP Edit window is active by pressing ALT-1; then press F1. Help gives you information relevant to the active window, in this case the editor. You can then use the TAB key to move a highlight bar to help keywords. Pressing the RETURN key with a help keyword highlighted displays help information for the associated keyword. For example, requesting help on the editor will produce screens with information about editing keys such as those shown in Table 2-1. If you have used other Borland editors or WordStar, these keys should be familiar to you.

MOUSE You can also use the mouse to move the cursor in the Edit window. A mouse click moves the cursor to the point where you clicked it. You can click on the scroll bars to scroll the window.

You can zoom the window or scroll through it to look at the entire topic.

Press F5 to zoom the Help window. The main Help screen explains how the Help system works. Press F1 again to get the main Help screen. Several topics are listed at the bottom of this screen. You can call up any of these topics simply by moving the cursor to one of the highlighted items and pressing RETURN.

Place the cursor under one of the help keywords (explaining menus or the editor, for example) in the Help window and press RETURN. The IDE will display general help on menus or on the editor. To get back to the previous topic, press ALT-F1.

One of the most useful features of the Help system is Topic Help. To see how this works, you must first close the Help window. Press ALT-F3 to close the Help window. The P2-1.CPP Edit window should now be reactivated.

Move the cursor under the word "complex" on line 6. Press CTRL-F1 to invoke Topic Help if you are using Turbo C++. If you are using Turbo

Command	Key
Miscellaneous Commands	
Main menu	CTRL-K D or CTRL-K Q
Save and edit	CTRL-K S or F2
New file	F3
Tab	CTRL-I or TAB
Tab mode	CTRL-O T or CTRL-Q T
Autoindent on/off	CTRL-O I or CTRL-Q I
Restore line	CTRL-Q L
Set place marker	CTRL-K *n*
Find place marker	CTRL-Q *n*
Language help	CTRL-F1
Character prefix	CTRL-P
Find	CTRL-Q F
Find & replace	CTRL-Q A
Abort operation	CTRL-U
Repeat last find	CTRL-L
Cursor-Movement Commands	
Character left	CTRL-S or LEFT ARROW
Character right	CTRL-D or RIGHT ARROW
Word left	CTRL-A or CTRL-LEFT ARROW
Word right	CTRL-F or CTRL-RIGHT ARROW
Line up	CTRL-E or UP ARROW
Line down	CTRL-X or DOWN ARROW
Scroll up	CTRL-W
Scroll down	CTRL-Z
Page up	CTRL-R or PGUP
Page down	CTRL-C or PGDN
Last position	CTRL-Q P
Insert and Delete Commands	
Insert mode on/off	CTRL-V or INS
Insert line	CTRL-N
Delete line	CTRL-Y
Delete to end of line	CTRL-Q Y
Delete character left	CTRL-H or BACKSPACE
Delete character	CTRL-G or DEL
Delete word right	CTRL-T

Table 2-1. *Summary of Editor Commands*

Command	Key
Block Commands	
Mark block begin	CTRL-K B
Mark block end	CTRL-K K
Pair matching right	CTRL-Q [
Pair matching left	CTRL-Q]
Mark single word	CTRL-K T
Copy block	CTRL-K C
Move block	CTRL-K V
Delete block	CTRL-K Y
Read block from disk	CTRL-K R
Write block to disk	CTRL-K W
Hide/display block	CTRL-K H
Print block	CTRL-K P
Indent block	CTRL-K I
Unindent block	CTRL-K U

Table 2-1. *Summary of Editor Commands* (continued)

C++ 2nd Edition, or Borland C++, you will see an indexed list of help keywords with the word "complex" highlighted. Press RETURN a second time to see the actual help entry. Instead of displaying help on IDE commands, Topic Help gives a description of the item that was under the cursor when you pressed CTRL-F1. A working example program follows the description of "complex." Press ALT-F3 to close the Help window.

Running a Program in the IDE

You can compile the program by pressing F9. If there are any errors, Borland C++ will stop and locate the errors in the Message window. If you want to compile and immediately run the program, press CTRL-F9. If you like, you can invoke the Run menu (ALT-R) and then select **Run**. Press CTRL-F9 now.

When the Borland C++ IDE runs a program, it returns control to the user after the program is finished. If the program is short, like this one, you won't have a chance to observe the output. However, once you regain control in the IDE, there are two ways to see what is on the user's screen.

To see the entire output screen, press ALT-F5. This shows what the screen would look like if you did not run the program from within the IDE. Press any key to get back to Borland C++. Alternatively, you can open a window that displays the output of the user's screen. This window is called the Output window. Press ALT-W O to open the Output window. Like other windows, you can select, scroll, move, and resize the Output window.

IDE Project Management

The Borland C++ IDE lets you create *projects* to manage programs that require more than one file. Program P2-2 is a slight modification of P2-1. Instead of defining two complex numbers, P2-2 defines one complex number and prompts the user to enter the second one.

Open a new Edit window for P2-2.CPP. Press ALT-F O to invoke the Load a File dialog box. Type **P2-2.CPP** in the Name field and press RETURN when you are finished.

P2-2

```
#include <iostream.h>
#include <complex.h>
#include "p2-3.h"

main()
{
    complex a(3,5);

    complex b;
    input(b);

    cout <<  (a + b) << '\n';
}
```

Two edit windows should now be open. Next open P2-3.CPP in the same way that you just opened P2-2.CPP. Now three edit windows should appear on the screen.

P2-3

```
#include <complex.h>
#include "p2-3.h"

void input(complex& c)
{
    cout << "Input a complex number: ";

    cin >> c;
}
```

Compare the changes in P2-2.CPP to P2-1.CPP. (Move and resize the windows if you have to.) Notice that P2-2 calls a function, **input**, which is defined in the file P2-3.CPP. In order to link P2-2.CPP and P2-3.CPP into one program, you must create a project.

Creating Projects

For each multiple-file program in Borland C++, you must start a new project by creating a *project file*. You may have as many project files as your disk can hold, but only one project may be active. To start a project, invoke the Project menu by pressing ALT-P. At this point Open Project is the only command that is useful on the Project menu. Other items exist on the menu, but the IDE disables them when no project is open. Select **O**pen Project by pressing **O** or RETURN. This command opens the Load Project File dialog box.

Type **P2-2** in the Project field and press RETURN, which activates the Project window shown in Figure 2-7. The new Project window is blank. Press INS to add a file to the project. This opens the Add Item to Project dialog box. Press ALT-F to go to the Files list. Use the DOWN ARROW key to select P2-2.CPP and press RETURN. Select P2-3.CPP and press RETURN. Press ESC to close this dialog box.

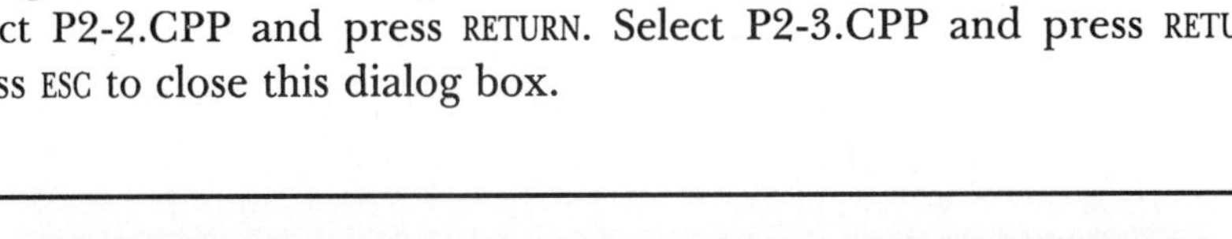

Figure 2-7. *A Project window*

You should see the files P2-2.CPP and P2-3.CPP added to the Project window. Press CTRL-F9 to compile and run the program. Program P2-2 initializes the first complex number to (3,5), which is the same number in Program P2-1. The program then asks you to enter the second complex number. Enter the same complex number as the second one in P2-1. Type **9 4** and press RETURN. What happened? Look at the Output window. The program should have added the same two complex numbers as P2-1, but the result is different this time. The output is "12, 5" instead of the expected "12, 9."

Debugging in the IDE

To see what happened in the program, run the program again. But this time, you will strategically stop the program and examine its operation. Go to the Edit window P2-2.CPP. Do this by pressing the ALT key and simultaneously pressing the number appearing in the upper-right corner of the edit window containing P2-2.CPP. Alternately, you can press F6 to rotate through each of the opened windows in turn until the window containing P2-2.CPP is active. Move the cursor down to the line **input(b);** and press CTRL-F8 to set a breakpoint.

Breakpoint lines are highlighted in red (on color monitors) and will stop a program and return control to the IDE. Breakpoints can also be set from the Debug menu. Press CTRL-F9 to run the program. The program runs briefly and then stops at the breakpoint. Inspect the first complex number, **a**. Move the cursor to the line **complex a(3,5);** under **a** and press ALT-F4.

The Inspect window opens, showing the internals of the complex number **a** (see Figure 2-8). There are two data items, one called **re** and one called **im**, corresponding to the real and imaginary parts of the complex number. (If both **re** and **im** are not visible, press the DOWN ARROW until they are.) The values of these two items are shown to be 3.0 and 5.0. This is what is expected, so the program seems to have run fine up to this point.

You can inspect almost any type of item in your program. For example, you can inspect the function **input**. Move the cursor to the line **input(b);** under the word **input** and press ALT-F4. Inspecting a function

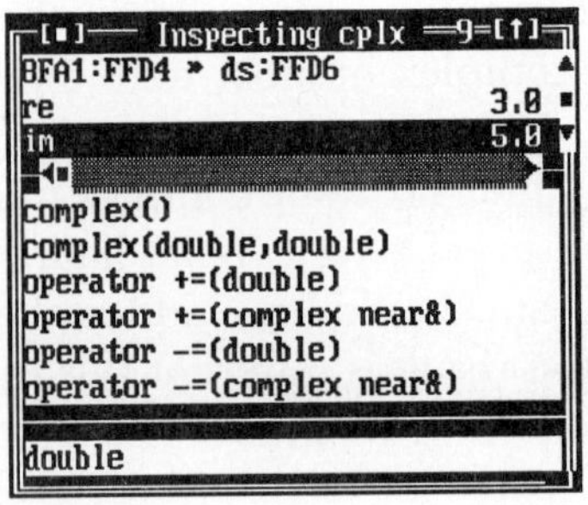

Figure 2-8. *An Inspect window*

will give you the physical address of the function, and the argument types of the function. On the bottom of the Inspect window, there is an indication of the type of function you are inspecting.

From the function Inspect window, press RETURN to find the function **input**. The Borland C++ IDE will activate the P2-3.CPP window and position the cursor on the start of the definition of **input**. The line **cin > > c;** is the statement where the input is taken. Move the cursor to the }at the end of the function and then press CTRL-F8 to set another breakpoint. Press ALT-D to invoke the Debug menu and then press **B** to open the Breakpoints dialog box shown in Figure 2-9.

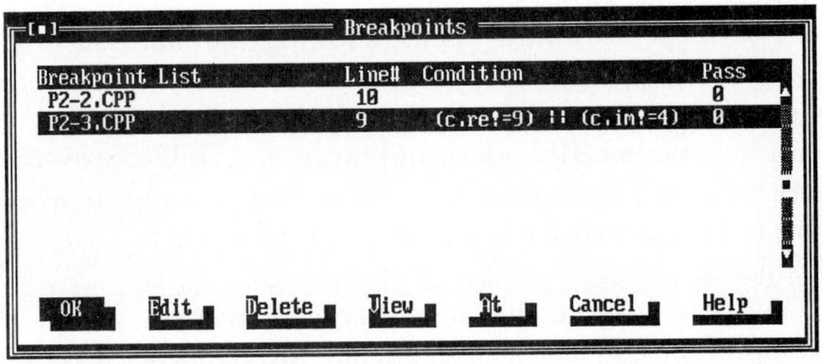

Figure 2-9. *The Breakpoints dialog box*

The dialog box shows two breakpoints set—one in the file P2-2.CPP and the one you just set in P2-3.CPP. You can tell a breakpoint to stop the program only if a certain condition is true. Most C++ expressions are valid breakpoint conditions. Select the P2-3.CPP breakpoint with the cursor keys and press ALT-E to edit it. This brings up the Breakpoint Modify/New dialog box. You know that the input to this function should result in a value of 9 for the real part and 4 for the imaginary part.

In the Condition field, type **(c.re!=9) || (c.im!=4)**. This condition tells the IDE to stop the program at this breakpoint only if the real part of the imaginary number does not equal 9 or the imaginary part does not equal 4. Press RETURN twice to get out of the Breakpoint dialog box; then press CTRL-F9 to continue running the program. When the program asks you for the complex number, type the same input as before: Type **9 4** and press RETURN. The program should stop running and bring up a window with the message "Conditional breakpoint (c.re!=9) || (c.im!=4)". Press RETURN and the IDE will locate the breakpoint that was set in the window P2-3.CPP.

Since the break condition could have been either c.re!=9 or c.im!=4, or both, you must do a little more work to pin down the problem. You can do this by inspecting **c**. Move the cursor to the line **cin >>c;** under **c** and press ALT-F4. The Inspect window shows that the real part of **c** is correct: 9.0. However, the imaginary part appears to have been entered incorrectly because the value of **im** is now 0.0. You can use the Borland C++ IDE to temporarily adjust the data to test the theory that the wrong input is the entire problem.

Press ALT-F3 to close the Inspect window. With the cursor still on **c**, press CTRL-F4 to invoke the Evaluate and Modify dialog box. The Expression field displays **c** as the default expression to evaluate. Press END and then type **.im** to complete the expression "c.im" in the Expression field. Now press RETURN to perform the evaluation.

The Evaluate dialog box is better for inspecting simple expressions than the Inspect window. As the Inspect window told you, the value of **c.im** is now 0.0. Press TAB twice (or ALT-N) to get to the New Value field. Then type **4** and press RETURN. You have just changed the value of **c.im** from 0 to 4 (see Figure 2-10). Press ESC to close the Evaluate dialog box. Continue running the program by pressing CTRL-F9. The program should finish running, this time displaying the correct result (12,9). Press ALT-F5 to view the output screen and verify the result. Then press any key to return to the IDE.

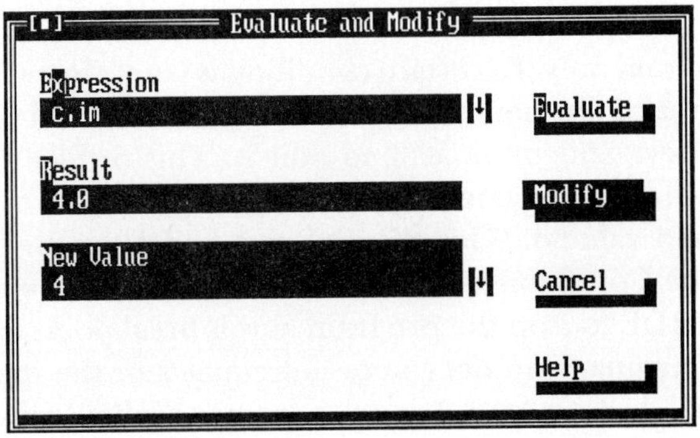

Figure 2-10. *The Evaluate and Modify dialog box*

What was the problem? You should have been suspicious of the format in which the complex number was entered. Run the program using the input format "(re,im)". Open the Breakpoint dialog box by pressing ALT-D and then press **B**. Press ALT-D twice to delete both breakpoints, and RETURN to close the Breakpoint dialog box. Now run the program, but this time type **(9,4)** for the input. You should get the correct answer (12,9).

When you are finished with this chapter, press ALT-X or choose ALT-F Q to quit the Borland C++ development environment.

This chapter provided a quick tour of some of the most common features in the Borland C++ IDE, purposely skimming over some topics and not covering others. To use the more advanced IDE features, you will need to learn a little bit more about the C++ language. Hopefully, most of the IDE's user interface features have been intuitive and easy to learn. If you feel like exploring the IDE before going on with the rest of this book, do it. You can use the online help as a guide through each menu, window, and dialog box.

3 C++ for C Programmers

This chapter is intended to get experienced C programmers started quickly with Borland C++. It is a brisk overview of C++. The importance of understanding what C++ is before plunging into the compiler cannot be overemphasized. C++ is not only a new language but it also offers a new philosophy in programming. Understanding how to use this new philosophy is the key to successful C++ programming.

This chapter is meant to be read rather than followed in a tutorial fashion. Unlike the rest of the book, no complete programming examples are presented. The code fragments and data structures presented here are designed to clarify programming concepts and demonstrate C++ language features.

You do not need to invoke the Borland C++ IDE to follow this chapter. However, you may want to type in example code fragments and write example programs to test your understanding as you read. For this reason, the installation program described in Chapter 1 creates the directory \DT\CH3 in which you may create, test, and save experimental programs of your own design.

In this chapter, some new concepts are introduced without being fully explained. If you know C well, this should not be a problem. These C++ concepts extend rather than conflict with C. If you get lost, don't worry—you will not be left behind in the following chapters. You can use this chapter later to refer to if you have questions about C++ features.

Since C++ is based on C, it is most easily learned by C programmers. If you already know C, you will not have to relearn much of the notation and grammar normally needed to acquire facility with a new language. C's operators, control statements, and data types are retained by C++. C++ was carefully designed not to lose the efficiency, portability, and expressiveness of C.

On the other hand, well-designed C++ programs are not structured like traditional C programs. Programming in C++ requires a new design process. C++ places a much higher emphasis on structure than does C. Nearly all of C++'s enhancements were created to meet this end. Consequently, you can base your learning of C++ on knowledge of C, but you will have to rethink the way you design and code.

Importance of Structure and Style

Structure becomes increasingly important as programming projects get bigger. In order to take advantage of C++, programs must be structured correctly. The emphasis on structure will require more initial design and thought. C++ is very well suited for large programming teams. C++ makes it easy to build and reuse libraries of code. These libraries can be easily shared by other C++ programmers. Libraries allow C++ programmers to design programs at a more abstract level than is possible with standard C libraries. To use C++ libraries it is not necessary to understand or have the source code.

C++'s emphasis on structure, however, does not take away from an individual programmer's creativity. Surprisingly, program structure lends itself easily to experimentation and innovation. A well-designed C++ program is easy to debug, modify, and enhance. C++ programs tend to have *fewer lines of code* than corresponding C programs and are developed in *less time.*

Programming in C++ style is not only good for the sake of style but will also improve your productivity. In C, it is often easiest to write quick-and-dirty code without concern for future maintenance or reusability. In C++, you will discover that good style not only helps other programmers who must read your code but it also helps you to get the job done faster. C++ improves on C in three major areas:

- User-defined data types
- Object-oriented programming
- Language extensions

User-Defined Types

Like C, C++ is equipped with only a few basic *data types*—**char**, **int**, **float**, and **double**. Data types define units of storage for data. These basic types can store a wide variety of data: Integers can represent the number of *at bats, hits,* and *home runs* a baseball player has. The player's *batting average* can be represented as a floating-point number.

```
int at_bats;
int hits;
int home_runs;
float avg;
```

C++ inherits C's **struct** type, which combines basic data types into an *aggregate* data type. To represent a baseball player as a whole, you can combine the statistics into a structure.

```
struct batter
{
    int  at_bats;
    int  hits;
    int  home_runs;
    float avg;
};
```

Each statistic is a *member* of the structure **batter**.

Suppose you are writing a baseball simulation program. You want your simulation to play the game and automatically record each player's at bats, hits, home runs, and batting average. You can use the **batter** structure to write the program.

```
struct batter
{
    int  at_bats;
    int  hits;
    int  home_runs;
    float avg;
};

int bat_player(batter b, pitcher op)
{
  int bases;
  bases=at_bat(b, op);

  /* update player stats */
  b.at_bats++;
  if (bases >=1) b.hits++;
  if (bases==4) b.home_runs++;
  b.avg =(float)b.hits/b.at_bats;

  /* update game */
  switch (bases)
  {
      .
      .
      .
  }

  return bases;
}
```

The definition of the **at_bat** function and the **pitcher** structure is not shown. The function **at_bat** matches the opposing pitcher, **op**, against a batter, **b**. The function returns 1 for a single, 2 for a double, 3 for a triple, 4 for a home run, or 0 for an out. After each **at_bat**, the function updates the individual player's statistics. Fortunately, baseball is a very simple game. The only calculation that needs to be made by **bat_player** is the batting average.

```
b.avg = (float)b.hits/b.at_bats;
```

The **float** type cast on **b.hits** forces floating-point division of two integer variables. After the statistics are calculated, the program updates the game situation.

Data Hiding

In the baseball example, all the statistics are accessible through the **batter** structure. There are situations where you would want to restrict access to the structure. Or, you may want to read, but write-protect, certain structure members.

For example, a function that prints the statistics from **batter** needs to get the statistics, but should not need to change any of the statistics. If the function cannot change any of the variables, then the data in **batter** is safe from unwanted modification. To do this, a way to hide the data is needed.

In C++ terminology, a *class* is a data type that contains data and functions. An *object* is simply a user-defined class variable. The C++ **class** type supports data hiding. Classes are like structures in that they group several data types into one aggregate data type. Unlike a C **struct**, however, a class can have *private* and *public* members. The public members of a class are treated like members of C structures. On the other hand, private members cannot be accessed from outside the scope of the class. (To be fair, C++ **structs** can also have private members, but public is the default in a **struct** and private is the default in a **class**.)

Let's look at how you can declare **batter** as a class.

```
class batter
{
private:
  int  at_bats;
  int  hits;
  int  home_runs;
  float avg;
public:
  int get_at_bats()    { return at_bats; }
  int get_hits()       { return hits; }
  int get_home_runs() { return home_runs; }
  int get_avg()        { return avg; }
  int hit(int bases)   {
                          at_bats++;
                          if (bases >=1) hits++;
                          if (bases==4) home_runs++;
                          avg = (float)hits/at_bats;
                          return bases;
                        }
};
```

The body of the **batter** class definition is divided into a private and a public section. The variables *avg, at_bats, hits,* and *home_runs* are private members of **batter**. These variables cannot be directly accessed by code outside of the class.

The member functions **get_avg**, **get_at_bats**, **get_hits**, and **get_home_runs** are public, meaning that there are no restrictions on accessing them. These functions have access to all the private variables in the **batter** class. The **get** functions simply return the value of individual statistics. There is no way to directly assign a value to any private variable, but you can get the value of a private variable through the public **get** functions. The private variables can be updated only through the **hit** function.

NOTE To reference members of the same class, member functions do not need to specify the class name. That is, for **get_avg** to access **avg**, the function does not need to say **batter.avg**. The class name is implied.

Data hiding has a couple of obvious advantages:

- It is easier to localize bugs because code can only change data through a class's public members. Thus, it is not necessary to search the entire program for the bug.
- Anyone trying to use the class will only have to examine the public section. The public section acts like an interface to the outside world. Learn how to use the interface, and you will know how to use the class.

The **hit** member function allows the **bat_player** function to be simplified, as follows:

```
int bat_player(batter b, pitcher op)
{
  int bases;

  bases=at_bat(b, op);

  /* update player stats */
  b.hit(bases);

  /* update game */
  switch (bases)
  {
      .
      .
      .
```

The syntax for calling a member function looks similar to accessing a data member. A period (member access operator) separates the class from the function call:

```
b.hit(bases);
```

The **bat_player** function simply has to call **b.hit** and the statistics are updated by the **batter** class. Now **bat_player** is freed from managing the players' statistics. The member function **hit** updates the statistics—the **bat_player** function concentrates on the game.

Initialization and Cleanup

Before using the **batter** object, you should initialize hits, at bats, home runs, and average to 0. A C++ *constructor* provides a way to automatically initialize data. A constructor is an optional member function of a class. Each time a new object is defined, its class constructor is automatically invoked.

```
class batter
{
private:
  int  at_bats;
  int  hits;
  int  home_runs;
  float avg;
public:
  /* The following function is a constructor */
  batter() { avg=0; at_bats=0; runs=0; home_runs=0; }
  int get_at_bats()   { return at_bats; }
  int get_hits()      { return hits; }
  int get_home_runs() { return home_runs; }
  int get_avg()       { return avg; }
  int hit(int bases) {
                        at_bats++;
                        if (bases >=1) hits++;
                        if (bases==4) home_runs++;
                        avg = (float)hits/at_bats;
                        return bases;
                     }
};
```

Constructor functions are easily identified because they have the same names as their classes. The constructor **batter** sets all the private variables of the class to 0. Since the constructor is called for each new **batter** object, new objects are guaranteed to be properly initialized.

Just as constructors ensure proper initialization, *destructors* ensure proper cleanup. A destructor function is called when an object is no longer active. For example, if a constructor allocates memory for an object, you can use a destructor to free that memory. You will learn more about destructors in Chapter 8 when you build a string class which automatically manages memory allocation and release.

Object-Oriented Programming

Object-oriented programming is simply an extension of user-defined types that allows new data types to inherit certain features of previously defined data types.

Limitations of User-Defined Types

Let's expand on the baseball example. We want the program to record pitching and batting statistics. First, you might think of developing a new class to keep track of statistics for pitchers, as follows:

```
class pitcher
{
private:
  /* pitching stats */
  float innings;
  int  hits_against;
  int  home_runs_against;
  int  scored_against;
  float era;

  /* batting stats */
  int  at_bats;
  int  hits;
  int  home_runs;
  float avg;
```

```
public:
  pitcher() { innings=0; hits_against=0;    /* constructor */
              home_runs_against=0;
              scored_against=0; era=0;
              at_bats=0; hits=0;
              home_runs=0; avg=0;
            }
  float get_innings()          { return innings; }
  int get_runs_against()       { return runs_against; }
  int get_home_runs_against() { return home_runs_against; }
  int get_scored_against()     { return scored_against; }
  float get_era()              { return era; }
  int pitch(int bases, int scored)
                     {
                        if (bases==4) home_runs_against++;
                        if (bases>=1) hits_against++;
                        else innings += 1.0/3.0;
                        scored_against += scored;
                        era = scored_against/innings;
                     }

  int get_at_bats()   { return at_bats; }
  int get_runs()      { return runs; }
  int get_home_hits() { return home_hits; }
  int get_avg()       { return avg; }
  int hit(int bases) {
                         at_bats++;
                         if (bases>=1) hits++;
                         if (bases==4) home_runs++;
                         avg = (float)hits/(float)at_bats;
                         return bases;
                     }

};
```

Since pitchers also bat, the **pitcher** class maintains pitching and batting statistics. Each call to **pitch** updates the *innings* variable by one-third of an inning if the batter is out. The pitcher's **era** (earned run average) is defined as the number of runs scored divided by the number of innings pitched.

To add the pitcher to the lineup, you need to add a new function that lets the pitcher bat.

```
int bat_player(batter b, pitcher op)
{
  int bases;
```

```
  bases=at_bat(b, op);

  /* update game */
  switch (bases)
  {
      .
      .
      .
  }

int bat_pitcher(pitcher p, pitcher op)
{
  int bases;

  bases=pitcher_at_bat(op, p);

  /* update game */
  switch (bases)
  {
      .
      .
      .
  }
```

There are a couple of problems with this solution:

- The **pitcher** class duplicates code that was written for **batter**—all the batting functions in the **pitcher** class were copied from the **batter** class.
- The code had to be modified to include the **pitcher** class. The function **pitcher_at_bat** was added to the code as a special case to allow pitchers to bat.

Inheritance

How does the pitcher relate to the other members of the team? The **pitcher** class is nothing more than a special case of the **batter** class. A **pitcher** has all the attributes of a **batter**, plus pitching statistics and pitching functions.

C++'s solution to the limits of user-defined types is *inheritance*. To inherit an object, a new class is derived from a *base* class. For example, you can build up on the **batter** class, and use it as a base class for new classes. The *derived* class retains membership in the base class. The inheritance solution makes old code more reusable.

```
class batter
{
private:
  int  at_bats;
  int  hits;
  int  home_runs;
  float avg;
public:
  batter() { /* constructor */
             at_bats=0;   runs=0;
             home_runs=0;   avg=0;
           }
  int get_at_bats()    { return at_bats; }
  int get_hits()       { return hits; }
  int get_home_runs()  { return home_runs; }
  int get_avg()        { return avg; }
  int hit(int bases) {
                        at_bats++;
                        if (bases >=1) hits++;
                        if (bases==4) home_runs++;
                        avg = (float)hits/at_bats;
                        return bases;
                     }
};

class pitcher : public batter        /* inherit from batter */
{
private:
  float innings;
  int  hits_against;
  int  home_runs_against;
  int  scored_against;
  float era;

public:
  pitcher() { /* constructor */
             innings=0; hits_against;
             home_runs_against=0;
             scored_against=0; era=0;
           }
  float get_innings()          { return innings; }
  int get_runs_against()       { return runs_against; }
  int get_home_runs_against()  { return home_runs_against; }
  int get_scored_against()     { return scored_against; }
```

```
    float get_era()             { return era; }
    int pitch(int bases, int scored)
                                {
                                  if (bases==4) home_runs_against++;
                                  if (bases>=1) hits_against++;
                                  else innings += 1.0/3.0;
                                  scored_against += scored;
                                  era = scored_against/innings;
                                }
};
```

Notice the reference to the **public batter** class after the colon in the first line of the **pitcher** class definition. This says that the **pitcher** class inherits the features of the base class **batter**. The use of the **public** keyword here is similar to its use in the body of the class definition. For now, you only need to know that it makes all the public members of **batter** also public members of **pitcher**.

Since the new **pitcher** class is not a unique class, but is actually a special case of the base **batter** class, the **bat_pitcher** function is no longer needed. You can use the **bat_player** function to bring to bat any type of player derived from **batter**.

Likewise, other players on the baseball team can also be built from the **batter** class.

```
class catcher : public batter
{
private:
  int passed_balls;
  int put_out_stealing;
      .
      .
      .
};

class first_baseman : public batter
{
private:
  int assists;
      .
      .
      .
};

struct baseball_team
{
```

```
  pitcher p1;
  catcher p2;
      .
      .
      .
};
```

Each object in **baseball_team** is different but related. All the players have common members from class **batter**—for example, **at_bats**, **hits**, and **home_runs**. In addition, each has its own unique members; for example, the **catcher** class has **passed_balls** and **put_out_stealing**. Since each player is built around the **batter** class, you can write one routine that prints any player's batting statistics.

```
void print_stat(batter* b)
{
    printf("%d %d %d %f",
           b->get_at_bats(), b->get_hits(),
           b->get_home_runs(), b->get_avg());
}
```

The function **print_stat** prints the at bats, hits, and home runs from any object derived from the **batter** class. Each player has different characteristics, but their common batting characteristics are accessed through the base class. When different objects are accessed the same way, the object is said to be accessed through the same *interface*.

Virtual Functions

Suppose you want to calculate each player's salary bonus. The bonus will depend on each player's statistics. Since the bonus is common to all the players, it belongs in the base class.

```
class batter
{
private:
  int  at_bats;
  int  hits;
  int  home_runs;
  float avg;
public:
```

```
  batter() { /* constructor */
             at_bats=0; runs=0;
             home_runs=0; avg=0;
           }
  int get_at_bats()    { return at_bats; }
  int get_hits()       { return hits; }
  int get_home_runs()  { return home_runs; }
  int get_avg()        { return avg; }
  int hit(int bases) {
                        at_bats++;
                        if (bases >=1) hits++;
                        if (bases==4) home_runs++;
                        avg = (float)hits/at_bats;
                        return bases;
                     }
  float calc_bonus() { return 10000.0*avg; }
};
```

This class is acceptable if every player gets the same type of bonus—$10,000 times the player's batting average. But each player's contract is different. The bonus for the catcher might depend on the batting average and home runs. The first baseman's bonus might depend entirely upon the number of home runs hit. The pitcher's bonus will probably not depend on batting average, but on his earned run average.

Like the **print_stat** function, there should be a consistent interface to get at the bonuses. To calculate the pitcher's bonus, you have to use his earned run average. Since era is not in the base class, you cannot really define the **calc_bonus** in the base class. The pitcher's **calc_bonus** function should be defined in the **pitcher** class.

You are left with a dilemma. You want to access different **calc_bonus** functions through the same interface. C++ answers this problem with *virtual* functions. In C++, a base class can define certain functions to be virtual. A virtual function in the base class can be replaced by a similar function in the derived class.

```
class batter
{
private:
  int  at_bats;
  int  hits;
  int  home_runs;
  float avg;
public:
  batter() { /* constructor */
            at_bats=0; runs=0;
```

```
            home_runs=0; avg=0;
          }
   int get_at_bats()    { return at_bats; }
   int get_hits()       { return hits; }
   int get_home_runs()  { return home_runs; }
   int get_avg()        { return avg; }
   int hit(int bases) {
                           at_bats++;
                           if (bases >=1) hits++;
                           if (bases==4) home_runs++;
                           avg = (float)hits/at_bats;
                           return bases;
                        }
   /* virtual function declaration */
   virtual float calc_bonus() { return 10000.0; }
};

class pitcher : public batter
{
private:
  float innings;
  int  hits_against;
  int  home_runs_against;
  int  scored_against;
  float era;

public:
  pitcher() { era=0; innings=0; runs_against=0;
              home_runs_against=0; at_bats=0; runs=0;
              home_runs=0;
            }
  float get_innings()    { return innings; }
  int get_runs_against() { return runs_against; }
  int get_home_runs_against() { return home_runs_against; }
  int get_scored_against() { return scored_against; }
  float get_era() { return era; }
  int pitch(int bases, int scored)
                        {
                          if (bases==4) home_runs_against++;
                          if (bases>=1) hits_against++;
                          else innings += 1.0/3.0;
                          scored_against += scored;
                          era = scored_against/innings;
                        }
  float calc_bonus { return (1/era)*70000.0; }
};
```

If an object is declared as a pitcher or as a catcher,

```
main()
{
     .
     .
     .
     pitcher p1;
     catcher p2;
     .
     .
     .
}
```

then

```
p1.calc_bonus();
```

will call the version of **calc_bonus** defined in the **pitcher** class and,

```
p2.calc_bonus();
```

will refer to the version of **calc_bonus** defined in the **catcher** class.

Often you want to store all members of a team in an aggregate type like an array to make it easier to keep track of everyone and to shorten the code required to process all team members.

```
batter* team[max_team];
.
.
.
team[0] = &p1;      /* pitcher */
team[1] = &p2;      /* catcher */
.
.
.
```

The problem is, a statement like,

```
for (i=0; i<max_team; i++)
     team[i]->calc_bonus();
```

will call the version of **calc_bonus** defined in batter for every member of the team if **calc_bonus** is not defined as virtual in the base class batter. This happens even though the member functions implemented for each type of player indicate different ways to perform **calc_bonus**. The type of **team[i]** is a pointer to a batter so the compiler assumes the object pointed to is a batter even though it might be a pitcher or a catcher. If you declare **calc_bonus** as virtual in the **batter** base class however, the program will look for type information retained automatically inside each player object when the program is run to determine which version of **calc_bonus** should be called.

With virtual functions, each type of player can get special treatment. The bonus of the pitcher is the inverse of his era times $70,000. If a new class does not define its own **calc_bonus** function, the **calc_bonus** from the base class is used as the default.

Other C++ Language Extensions

In addition to objects, there are a number of other significant C++ enhancements. Many of these enhancements can stand on their own without objects. You might recognize some of these because they have been adopted by ANSI C. In turn, C++ has adopted some ANSI C innovations.

Input/Output

The C standard input/output functions, **printf** and **scanf**, have always been a thorn in the side of C programmers. The functions **printf** and **scanf** handle the formatting of built-in data types such as:

chars	ints
strings	unsigned ints
pointers	long ints
floats	hexadecimal ints
doubles	octal ints
long doubles	

Since **printf** and **scanf** must anticipate being able to format all the built-in C data types, these functions are big. Even if you just want to print "hello, world", your program probably contains unused code to format a hexadecimal long int.

Because of the complexity of **printf** and **scanf**, they are hard to use and prone to mistakes. Since these functions don't check parameters, it is common to mismatch the parameters with the format specifiers.

This program fragment passes the *value* of **x** to **scanf**:

```
int x;
scanf("%d", x);
```

What the programmer really wants to do is to pass the *address* of **x** to **scanf**:

```
int x;
scanf("%d", &x);
```

Mistakes like this can be fatal and hard to find.

Instead of expanding upon the standard C input/output facilities, C++ takes an object-oriented approach to input/output. The C++ standard input/output solution is much easier to use than its C predecessor. C++ input/output was designed to allow the programmer to extend it to handle user-defined types; that is, C++ input/output handles objects. A discussion of C++ input/output begins in Chapter 4.

Object Allocation

Standard C memory allocation suffers from the same ailments as C input/output. There are no standard memory allocation operators. The library functions **malloc** and **free** are the standard C library functions used to allocate and free memory.

To allocate a two-dimensional array in C, you typically do this:

```
double (*matrix)[1000];
matrix = malloc(sizeof(*array) * size);
```

This is efficient, but not fully dynamic. The program must be recompiled to change the size of the array because one of the dimensions, **1000**, must be hard-coded.

Another way to handle two-dimensional arrays in C is the double indirection technique:

```
double **matrix;
   .
   .
   .
matrix = malloc(xsize*sizeof(*matrix));
for (i=0;i<xsize;i++)
    *(matrix[i])=malloc(ysize*sizeof(**matrix));
```

This array can be dynamically resized. However, there is an overhead of **xsize*sizeof(*matrix)** bytes. This overhead can be considerable if **xsize** is large. In addition, the code is difficult to understand.

C++ memory allocation is much more flexible. It must be extendable to new classes that the user writes. C++ provides two new operators, **new** and **delete**, to manage memory for objects. These operators also perform the task of automatically calling constructors and destructors. C++ calls these operators *object allocation* operators.

Argument Checking

The lack of function argument checking in some C compilers makes little errors into big ones. If you have used an ANSI C compiler, you will recognize that C++ function definitions use the same syntax as ANSI C function definitions. In fact, ANSI C borrowed this syntax from C++. This new syntax allows the compiler to perform type checking on function parameters.

Consider a C function, **strncmp**, that compares two strings up to a certain length:

```
strncmp(s1, s2, n)
char *s1;
char *s2;
unsigned n;
{
  int i;

  for (i=1; *s1 == *s2; s1++, s2++, i++)
       if (*s1 == '\0'  ||  i >= n)
```

```
            return 0;
    return (*s1 - *s2);
}

main()
{
    int result
    .
    .
    .
    result = strncmp(10, string1, string2);
    .
    .
    .
}
```

In the call to **strncmp** in **main**, the programmer switched the order of the arguments and put the length of the string as the first argument instead of the last. The C compiler would not catch this error.

C++ function definitions let the compiler know what types of arguments are passed to functions. For example:

```
strncmp(char* s1, char* s2, unsigned n)
{
    int i;

    for (i=1; *s1 == *s2; s1++, s2++, i++)
          if (*s1 == '\0'  ||  i >= n)
            return 0;
    return (*s1 - *s2);
}

main()
{
    int result;
        .
        .
        .
    result = strncmp(10, string1, string2); /* compile-time error */
        .
        .
        .
}
```

Using C++'s function definition style, mismatched parameter errors will be caught by the compiler.

Constants

Many C programs rely heavily on the preprocessor. Much preprocessor use is to make up for shortcomings of the C language.

The preprocessor **#define** statement is often used to declare constants. For example:

```
double circumference(double radius)
{
  #define PI 3.14159
  return 2*PI*radius;
}
```

Although the placement of **#define** statement might suggest otherwise, preprocessor constants do not have the scope of C variables. In the example, **PI** is not local to the function **circumference**.

C++ has a **const** type modifier that replaces this use of the preprocessor.

```
double circumference(double radius)
{
  const double pi=3.14159;
  return 2*pi*radius;
}
```

In the revised function, **pi** is a local constant. It is treated like an identifier and does not have the problems of preprocessor constants. Also, C++ constants do not take up memory at run time, while variables do.

Inline Functions

Another frequent use of the C preprocessor is the definition of macros. Macros serve a very important purpose in C. They provide the notational convenience of functions for frequently used constructs, without the speed overhead of functions.

```
#define SQR(x) ((x)*(x))
    .
    .
    .
double a, b;
a = 45;
b = SQR(a) * SQR(a)
```

Macros, however, are not functions. Careless use of macros can cause erroneous results. If the SQR macro is called this way,

```
c = SQR(++a); /* the programmer sees this */
```

the preprocessor expands the macro to increment *a* twice.

```
c = ((++a)*(++a)); /* the compiler sees this */
```

The variable **a** is incremented twice before being squared. Constructs like this can cause bugs that are difficult to track down.

Substituting real functions for macros, like SQR, would solve the problem. However, for time-critical code this is not a good solution since function calls incur run-time overhead that might slow down the program too much. C++ solves this problem with *inline* functions.

```
inline double sqr(double x) { return x*x; }
```

Inline functions are like other functions in that they have scope, type checking, and so forth. However, they are like macros because when a call is made to an inline function, C++ replaces the function call with the code from the body of the inline function. Thus inline functions save the overhead of a function call.

C++ Incompatibilities

C++ was derived from the original C language definition, before the current ANSI C standard. While C++ tried to be compatible with C implementations, the C language has changed somewhat. In the future,

C++ will be updated to be closer to ANSI C.

C++ is nearly a superset of C. Many C programs can be compiled without modification using C++. However, certain C++ extensions may make existing C code incompatible. If you are converting a C program to C++, here are a few things to watch for.

New Keywords

Here is a list of keywords in C++ that are not in standard K&R C:

asm*	catch	class	const*	delete
enum*	friend	inline	new	operator
overload	private	protected	public	signed*
template	this	virtual	void*	volatile*

(*available in ANSI C)

It is not permissible to use these keywords for variables or function names. New keywords should not be a problem, unless your existing code has identifiers with the same names as these keywords.

Empty Argument List

In C, the function declaration

```
foo();
```

specifies that **foo** can take *any number* of arguments. In C++, this states that **foo** can take *no* arguments.

However, in ANSI C, a function that takes no argument is declared as taking a **void**.

```
foo(void);
```

This syntax can also be used in C++.

Using C functions

You may be surprised that the C program,

```
main()
{
    puts("hello, world");
}
```

is not a C++ program. Why? C++ requires that you precede each function call with a function declaration. This allows C++ to perform argument checking, which was discussed earlier in this chapter.

If you know the standard C library, you might be tempted to fix the program by adding your own declaration.

```
int puts(const char* s);
main()
{
    puts("hello, world");
}
```

This doesn't correct the problem because C++ separates C functions from C++ functions. You must declare **puts** as a C function by doing the following:

```
extern "C" int puts(const char* s);
main()
{
    puts("hello, world");
}
```

A better way to declare **puts** is to add the line,

```
#include <stdio.h>
```

to the top of the program. A declaration for **puts** is in the standard header file STDIO.H.

const

In C++, constants have *internal linkage*. This is best demonstrated with an example. The file MYDEFS defines a number of constants.

```
// mydefs.cpp
const int model_number = 3;
    .
    .
    .
```

These constants are accessed in another file, MYPROG.

```
// myprog.cpp
extern const model_number;

if (model_number > 5)
    .
    .
    .
```

The reference to **model_number** in MYPROG will not be found because MYDEFS does not export its definition. To fix this, tell MYDEFS to export **model_number** as follows:

```
// mydefs.cpp
extern const int model_number;
const int model_number = 3;
```

Another technique of exporting constants is to put them in a header file. The header file could then be included by any file that needs the constants.

enum

In C, an integer may be assigned to an **enum** variable.

```
enum color {black, white};

color c = 100;
```

Obviously, 100 is not defined as a color, so C++ protects the programmer from mistakes like this.

In C++, an explicit class qualification is required to access an **enum** declared within a **struct** or **class**. For example,

```
struct Windows
{
    enum Operation {show, hide, clear, scroll};
    void perform(Operation op);
    .
    .
    .
};

struct Document
{
    enum DocumentType {scroll, pamphlet, report, book};
    void setDocument(DocumentType type);
    .
    .
    .
};
```

```
main()
{
    Windows w;
    w.perform(Window::scroll);

    Document doc;
    doc.setDocument(Document::scroll);
    .
    .
    .
}
```

In the previous example, **scroll** is an enumeration of both **Operation** and **DocumentType**. To access **scroll**, you have to precede it with either **Window::** or **Document::**, depending on which enumeration of **scroll** you want to use.

C does not allow the duplication of a name like this. In C++, each instance of **scroll** is considered to be part of the structure in which it is defined. Therefore, the two definitions of **scroll** are unique.

We will encounter more C/C++ incompatibilites in the chapters that follow.

Summary

For many C programmers, C++ may be used simply as "a better C." The language has many features like **inline**, **const**, **new**, and **delete** that help you write better C code. But if you approach C++ this way, you are not taking full advantage of C++ or object-oriented programming.

A *user-defined type* is a **class** that encapsulates functions and data into one entity. A class has an interface, which is declared in the **public** section of the class. A **private** section insulates class members from external abuse. C++'s *object-oriented programming* features allow new classes to be built from the old ones so that old code does not have to be rewritten once the problem expands beyond the design of the original class.

By the end of this book, you will see how an object-oriented design simplifies programming by letting you concentrate on the problem at hand and not the details, and by helping you reuse more code than traditional C programming designs allow.

Before we jump too far ahead, the next chapter will get you some hands-on experience with the Borland C++ programming environment and the C++ I/O system.

4 Input/Output of Basic Data Types

This chapter covers the basic C++ types, type modifiers, variable declarations, and constants. You will find that C++ has a lot in common with C. If your C programming is a little rusty, this is a good chance to review because you will need your C background for object-oriented programming.

If you are a seasoned programmer, you may find the pace slow. This chapter works its way through the review process by introducing the Borland C++ programming environment. The debugger "opens up" programs from the inside out. The Borland C++ integrated debugger is a tool designed to help programmers fix bugs. However, it also helps programmers learn the language.

First, you will learn how to do simple input and output in C++. After all, most programs need to communicate to be useful.

Input and Output

In C, input and output are performed by using functions, but in C++, input and output can be performed by using operators. Input is done with the *get from* >> operator and output is done with the *put to* << operator. You may recognize these to be the C bitshift operators but in C++, operators often have many meanings.

Printing Strings

Start Borland C++ and load Program P4-1. From the DOS command prompt, type **tc p4-1** (or **bc p4-1**) and press RETURN. This invokes the Borland C++ environment and loads Program P4-1 into the editor. The first program looks like this:

P4-1

```
// Our first C++ program
#include <iostream.h>
main()
{
    cout << "Let's get started!\n";
}
```

Let's examine the program before running it. The first line contains a C++ comment. Comments can be placed on a single line. Two slashes (//) start a single-line C++ comment. Anything after that on the line is ignored by the compiler. If you prefer the C commenting style of enclosing your comment between two asterisks, /* . . . */, it is also available in C++.

The second line is a compiler directive that includes IOSTREAM.H. This file contains definitions needed by C++ to perform input/output. The C header, STDIO.H, can also be used in C++. IOSTREAM.H, however, replaces C's standard input/output routines. IOSTREAM.H predefines several objects for input/output. They are as follows:

cout	standard output
cerr	unbuffered standard error
cin	standard input
clog	buffered standard error

The objects that we are concerned with right now are **cout** and **cin**. These two mirror and replace C's **stdout** and **stdin** files, respectively. The identifiers **cout** and **cin** are instances of input and output classes declared in IOSTREAM.H. Remember from Chapter 3 that an object is simply a class variable.

Finally, the statement **cout << "Let's get started!\n";** uses the put to operator to output a string to the screen. When you are ready to compile, do the following:

1. Select the Make command from the main menu. To do this, select **C**ompiler/**M**ake, or simply press F9.

2. When the program is through compiling, run it by selecting **R**un/**R**un.

What do you see? Unless you were really paying attention, you probably missed the output. That's because Borland C++ writes the program to a separate output screen and then flips back to the editor. To see the output screen, you have to press the output key combination, ALT-F5. When you press ALT-F5, the output screen will display

```
Let's get started!
```

To return to the Borland C++ editor from the output screen, press any key. From now on, it's up to you to press ALT-F5 when you want to see the screen.

The backslash (\) character starts a C++ character *escape sequence.* Escape sequences are special codes to represent characters typically not on the keyboard. C++'s escape sequences are identical to C's. Most escape sequences perform an action. Notice that the **\n** at the end of "**Let's get started!**" prints a NEWLINE. Some C++ escape sequences are listed in Table 4-1.

When Borland C++ finds an error in your program, it displays the error in the Message window. To see how this works, add the line **cout <<"Look, I'm programming!\n"** immediately after the first **cout** statement in Program P4-1. After you have added the line, your program should look like this:

```
// Our first C++ program
#include <iostream.h>
main()
{
    cout << "Let's get started!\n";
    cout << "Look, I'm programming!\n"
}
```

As in C, each C++ statement normally ends with a semicolon. We purposely left off the semicolon at the end of the second **cout** statement to see how Borland C++ will react.

The CTRL-F9 key combination is a Borland C++ shortcut that automatically compiles, links, and runs a program. Press CTRL-F9 to try to run the program. With the error in the program, Borland C++ will not finish compiling. It stops and displays a Status window (see Figure 4-1), indicating that there was one error. To see the error, press any key. This brings you to the Message window (Figure 4-2) with the error message highlighted.

The compiler is telling you that it expected a semicolon in line 7 but didn't find one. This is an easy bug to fix. You know that the statement in the preceding line is missing a semicolon.

1. Press RETURN and the IDE will bring the cursor to where it found the error.

2. Move the cursor to line 6 (the line you just added).

3. Press END to go to the end of the line.

4. Fix the program by typing a semicolon.

5. Press CTRL-F9 to go again. Borland C++ should now compile, link, and run your program.

Escape Sequence	Meaning	Action
\a	alert	Beep the speaker
\b	backspace	Move back one space
\f	form feed	Move to the next logical page
\n	newline	Move to the beginning of the next line
\r	carriage return	Move to the beginning of the current line
\t	horizontal tab	Move to the next horizontal tab stop
\v	vertical tab	Move to the next vertical tab stop

Table 4-1. *C++ Escape Sequences*

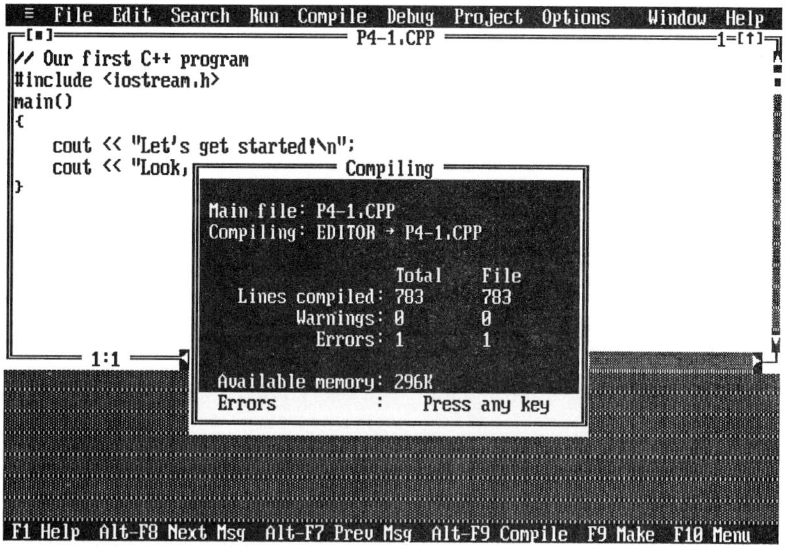

Figure 4-1. *Status window*

6. Again, to see the output, you must press ALT-F5.

The screen will now show

```
Let's get started!
Look, I'm programming!
```

Now you're getting somewhere.

Stringing Output

You can shorten the last program by appending the second message to the first **cout** statement, this way:

```
cout << "Let's get started!\n" << "Look, I'm programming";
```

You can also insert strings and numbers in the middle of your output.

```
cout << 44 << "+" << 9.6 << "=" << 44+9.6;
```

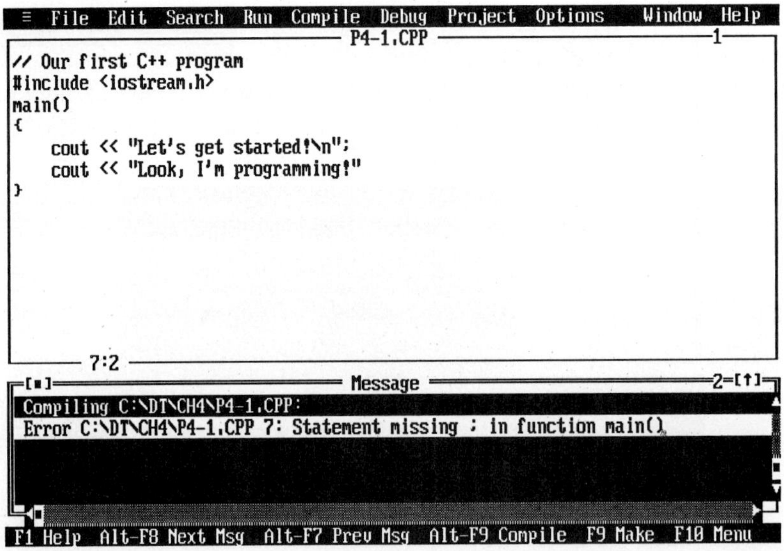

Figure 4-2. *Message window*

Getting Input

C++'s >> (get from) operator gets keys from the keyboard just as << writes characters to the screen. To see an example of C++ input, load Program P4-2 by pressing F3. The Load File window appears. Type **p4-2** and press RETURN.

Program P4-2 looks like this:

P4-2

```
#include <iostream.h>
main()
{
    char line[80];

    cout << "What's your sign?";
    cin >> line;
    cout << "I knew you were a " << line <<"!"
         << " We're completely compatible!\n";
}
```

The declaration **char line[80];** allocates a buffer of 80 characters to hold the input.

The first statement that asks you for your sign is something you've seen before. The second statement reads a line of input from the keyboard by using the >> operator. The object on the left of the >> operator, **cin,** is the standard input device: the keyboard. The input is stored in the **line** buffer. The last statement prints the computer's response.

Type CTRL-F9 to run the program. Borland C++ flips to the output screen and asks

```
What's your sign?
```

Type **Scorpio** and press RETURN.

Again, when the program is finished, Borland C++ immediately goes back to the editor screen. Press ALT-F5 to see the output, which should look like this:

```
What's your sign?  Scorpio
I knew you were a Scorpio! We're completely compatible.
```

Basic Data Types

The basic data types in C++ are the same as those in C. Data types vary from compiler to compiler, so it's a good idea to be familiar with the sizes and ranges of the data types on the compiler you are working with. However, if you intend to write code that will be moved to other compilers, write it so that it's not specific to the compiler.

In Borland C++, the basic data types are as follows:

char	1 byte (range −128 to 127) used to represent a character on the screen, a keystroke, and so forth.
int	2 bytes (range −32768 to 32767) used to represent numbers.
float	4 bytes (range 3.4e−38 to 3.4e+38) represents bigger numbers than **int**, and numbers with fractional parts that cannot be expressed in an integer.

double 8 bytes (range 1.7e−308 to 1.7e+308): same as **float**, only bigger.

Variable Declarations

C++ variables can be declared just as C variables are. Variable names are a sequence of letters, numbers, and underscores (_), but variable names cannot start with a number. In Borland C++, the first 32 characters of variable names are significant. C++ has a number of keywords that do not appear in C. Since keywords may not be used for variable names, it is important that you know what the new C++ keywords are—even if you don't yet know what they do. A complete list of C++ keywords appears in Chapter 3.

Clear the desktop before continuing. Press ALT-SPACEBAR followed by **C**. Answer No when asked if you want to save P4-1.CPP.

NOTE If you don't want to type the full name of the file each time you load a new program, you can pick from the available C++ programs in the current directory. Press F3. For the filename, type * and press RETURN. The file list will show all files in the current directory that end with the .CPP extension. You can then use arrow keys to move the highlight bar to the file you wish to load and press RETURN. Load Program P4-3 this way.

Program P4-3 should look like this:

P4-3
```
#include <iostream.h>
main()
{
        int i;
        i = 1;
        cout << i << "\n";

        float pi=3.14159;
        cout << 3.14159 << "\n";
}
```

Instead of running this program, you are going to *single-step* through it. This allows you to examine what is going on inside the program while it is running. Borland C++ can step through a program one line at a time with the F8 Step key.

Start the trace by pressing F8. As the program starts, a trace highlight bar appears on the function **main**, as shown in Figure 4-3. Press F8 again to move the highlight bar to the line **i = 1;**.

The first statement inside **main** declares the variable **i**. In order to keep track of **i** throughout the program, you can put the variable in the Watch window. Press CTRL-F7 to open the Add Watch dialog box. In the box, type **i**. Your screen should look like Figure 4-4. Now press RETURN. A new Watch window displays the variable **i** and its value after it. At this point, **i** contains garbage since nothing has been assigned to it. Press F8 again.

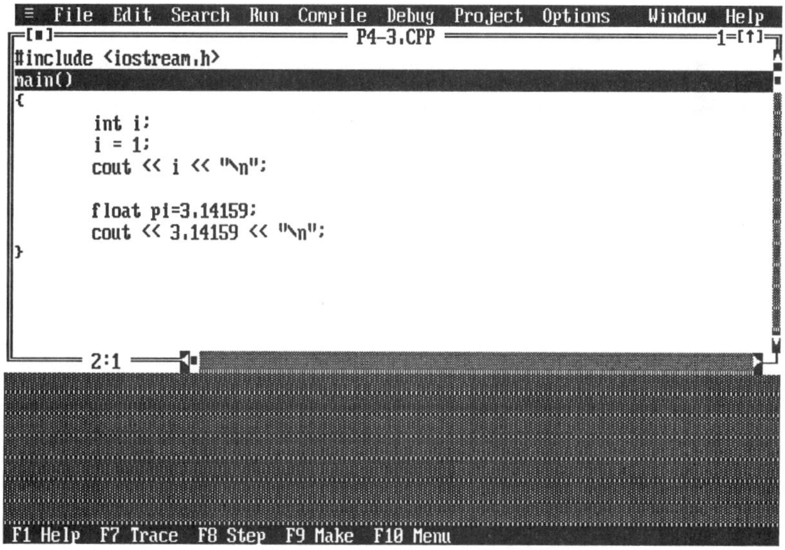

Figure 4-3. *Tracing execution*

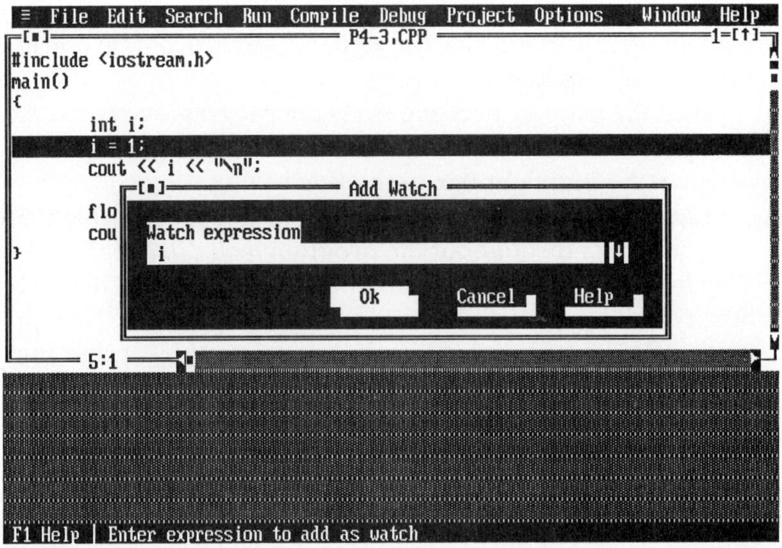

Figure 4-4. *Watch box*

After the assignment statement, the Watch window shows that **i** is equal to 1. The Watch window is consistently updated as variables in the program change. Press F8 and the next statement will print "1" to the screen.

The next statement declares a floating-point number, **pi**. You could put this declaration at the top of **main**, but unlike C, C++ does not require that all the declarations be made before any executable statements. In C++, try to declare variables just before you use them. This makes it easy to see what each variable is used for.

In this statement, **pi** is declared and initialized to 3.14159. In most cases, variables should not be declared without initialization. Initializing variables prevents them from having unknown values. Since C++ allows you to declare variables anywhere inside a function, it is easy to forget to assign an initial value to a variable.

Use CTRL-F7 to add **pi** to the Watch window. Press F8 to execute the statement. As expected, the value of **pi** is 3.14159, as Figure 4-5 shows. Press F8 again to execute the final statement, which prints the value of **pi** to the screen.

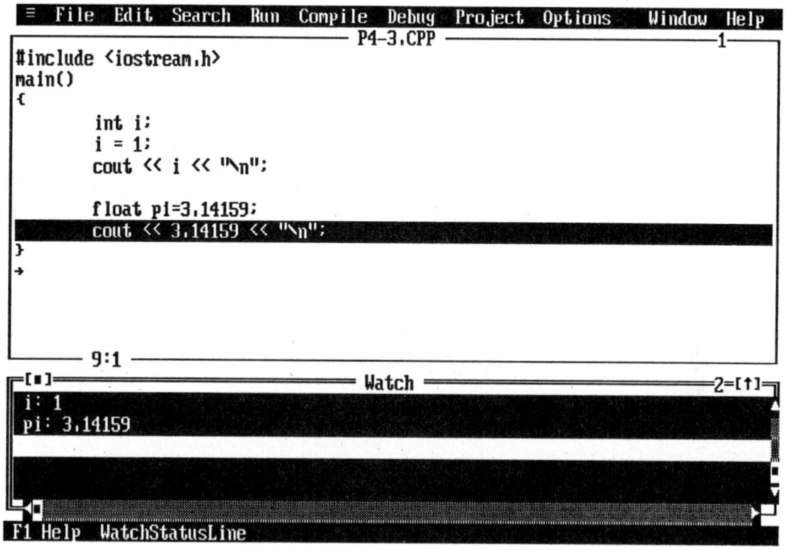

Figure 4-5. *Watch window*

Constants

C++ constants are no different from C constants. *Integer constants* such as 0, −5, and 96 are numbers without a fractional part. C++ can also use a hexadecimal notation for constants. The constant 0x1A is the hexadecimal equivalent to 26. *Floating-point constants* are numbers such as .707, −0.44, and 33.3333. If you prefer, you can use scientific notation for floating-point constants. For example, 1.3e4 is identical to 13000.0 and 1.3×10^4. A character enclosed in single quotation marks, such as 'a', is a *character constant.* Character constants that are not on the keyboard can be specified by using an escape sequence. The general form of a constant escape sequence is **\xhh**, where *hh* is the hexadecimal ASCII value of the constant. For example, the constant **\xE0** is the IBM PC Greek alpha character.

You can give a name to a constant just as you give a name to a variable; for example,

```
const float pi = 3.14159;
```

A constant definition looks like a variable initialization with the **const** keyword in front of it. Like variables, a **const** identifier has a type associated with it. Unlike variables, the value of a **const** identifier cannot change throughout its life and must be initialized in the declaration.

Formatted Output

C++ provides alternatives to C's **printf** for formatted output. C++ has a number of type-specific controls that change the format state of streams.

Load Program P4-4 into the editor and run the program by pressing CTRL-F9.

P4-4

```
#include <iostream.h>
main()
{
    int i = 0;

    cout << "Enter a number: ";

    cin  >> i;

    cout << "The number " << i << " in hexadecimal is "
         << hex << i << ".\n";
}
```

The program will prompt you to enter a number. Type **97** and press RETURN. P4-4 converts the number you've just typed into its hexadecimal equivalent.

```
Enter a number: 97
The number 97 in hexadecimal is 61.
```

In P4-4, the identifier **hex** is called a *manipulator* because it acts like a filter that manipulates the output that passes through it. IOSTREAM also provides the manipulators **dec** and **oct** to change the numeric base to decimal and octal, respectively.

C programmers are used to seeing "**0x**" precede hexadecimal numbers that are printed with **printf**. IOSTREAM can perform this type formatting with the **setf** function. Add the line

```
cout.setf(ios::showbase);
```

to the line before the second **cout** statement in P4-4. Press CTRL-F9 to compile and run this program again. Type in **97** at the program's prompt, and then press RETURN. The output screen shows

```
Enter a number: 97
The number 97 in hexadecimal is 0x61.
```

The line that you just added looks a little strange, but this syntax was introduced in Chapter 3. We know **cout** is an object, therefore **setf** is a member function of **cout**. (IOSTREAM declares **cout** as an object of the class **ostream** and **cin** as an object of the class **istream**. Both **ostream** and **istream** have a base class called **ios**.) The argument to **cout.setf** is a formatting flag, that tells **cout** to display a number's base. The meaning of **ios::showbase** is that **showbase** is an enumeration declared within the class **ios**.

Multiple flags can be combined using the bitwise OR operator like this:

```
cout.setf(ios::showbase|ios::right);
```

Table 4-2 lists some useful formatting flags.

In addition to **setf**, streams have a number of other member functions to control formatting (Table 4-3). Program P4-5 uses some of these formatting controls to print a floating point number, right justified, in fixed point format, with a precision of 2 and a field width of 20. Load and run P4-5 now.

Flag	Meaning
ios::skipws	Skip whitespace (for input)
ios::left	Left-justify (for output)
ios::right	Right-justify (for output)
ios::internal	Padding after sign or base indicator
ios::dec	Decimal base
ios::oct	Octal base
ios::hex	Hexadecimal base
ios::showbase	Show numeric base indicator
ios::showpoint	Force decimal point (for floating point)
ios::uppercase	Uppercase hexadecimal output
ios::showpos	Add + to positive integers
ios::scientific	Use scientific notation (for floating point)
ios::fixed	Use fixed-point notation (for floating point)

Table 4-2. *Stream Formatting Flags*

P4-5

```
#include <iostream.h>
main()
{
    cout.setf(ios::right|ios::showpoint|ios::fixed);
    cout.precision(2);
    cout.width(20);
    cout << 500000.0 << "\n";
}
```

Function Name	Purpose
setf	Set a formatting flag
unsetf	Undo a flag set by setf
width	Read/set the field width
fill	Read/set the padding character
precision	Read/set digits of precision (for floating point)

Table 4-3. *Functions to Control Formatting*

Some stream controls are duplicated as manipulators in IOMANIP.H. You can use these if you prefer. Program P4-6 is a modification of P4-5 that uses manipulators. Load and run P4-6 now.

P4-6

```
#include <iostream.h>
#include <iomanip.h>
main()
{
     cout << setiosflags(ios::right|ios::showpoint|ios::fixed)
          << setw(20)
          << setprecision(2)
          << 500000.0
          << "\n";
}
```

The output for P4-6 should be the same as the output for P4-5.

Table 4-4 compares the manipulators in IOMANIP.H to the definitions in IOSTREAM.H. If you use these manipulators, you must remember to include the file IOMANIP.H as well as IOSTREAM.H in your program.

Type Modifiers

A number of C++ built-in types are simply derived from the basic types **char, int, float,** and **double.** Let's focus on the different types of integers.

IOSTREAM.H	IOMANIP.H
setiosflags(. . .)	setf(. . .)
resetiosflags(. . .)	unsetf(. . .)
setbase(10)	setf(ios::dec)
setbase(8)	setf(ios::oct)
setbase(16)	setf(ios::hex)
setfill	fill
setprecision	precision
setw	width

Table 4-4. *Manipulators Declared in IOMANIP.H*

Some types can be derived from integers with the keyword modifiers **short, unsigned,** and **long**. The sizes and ranges of these types in Borland C++ are listed in Table 4-5.

Normally, the range of values that can be held by an integer is from −32768 to 32767. Sometimes you don't need negative values. A variable can be declared as an **unsigned int**, which can contain values ranging from 0 to 65535. The **unsigned** keyword is a *type modifier* to the **int** type.

To get an even bigger number, a variable can be declared as a **long int**. A long integer can contain values from −2147483648 to 2147483647. If the long integer does not need to contain negative numbers, it can be declared as an **unsigned long int**, in which case its legal range of values is from 0 to 4294967295.

You can also declare a **short int**. In Borland C++, a short integer is defined as identical to an integer. In other implementations of C++, a short integer's size is simply defined as being no bigger than a regular integer. This means that a **short int** can be smaller or equal to the size of an **int**.

C++ also has a **signed** type modifier, but since integers are by default signed, it is unnecessary to use the **signed** modifier on **int**. The size of the integers stays the same whether the type is signed or unsigned. Program 4-7 shows declarations for a couple of integer types. Load this program now.

P4-7

```
#include <iostream.h>
main()
{
    int i = 65535U;
    cout << "i = " << i << "\n";

    long int l = 4294967295L;
    cout << "l = " << l << "\n";

    cout << "i = " << unsigned(i) << "\n";

    cout << "l = " << ( (unsigned long) l ) << "\n";
}
```

Unsigned integer constants have a "U" after them to distinguish from signed integer constants. Similarly, long integer constants use an "L." The letters can be in upper- or lowercase. For unsigned long integer constants, use "UL" or "LU."

Type	Size	Minimum Value	Maximum Value
short int	2 bytes	−32768	32767
unsigned short int	2 bytes	0	65535
int	2 bytes	−32768	32767
unsigned int	2 bytes	0	65535
long int	4 bytes	−2147483648	2147483647
unsigned long int	4 bytes	0	4294967295

Table 4-5. *C++ Derived Integer Types*

Let's analyze each output statement in P4-7. Move the cursor to the line **long int l = 49294967295L**, and then press F4. The F4 key is the Go to cursor hot key. Borland C++ will compile the program (if it hasn't been compiled), and then execute the program until it gets to the line where the cursor is. In this case, the last statement that the IDE should execute is the first **cout** statement. The output screen should look like this:

```
i = -1;
```

The first **cout** statement prints the value of the integer **i**. The variable **i** is declared as a normal integer, but is initialized to 65535U—an unsigned integer. The problem with the first output statement is not in that statement at all. Rather, the problem was caused by initializing **i** to a value greater than it can hold—65535 is one more than two times the maximum value of the largest integer, 32767. The unsigned value 65535 overflowed to −1 when assigned to a signed integer.

Execute the next statements by moving the cursor to the line, **cout << "i = " << unsigned(i) << "\n";**, in the program, and then press F4. The output screen should now look like this:

```
i = -1;
l = -1;
```

Again, l is overflowed because 4294967295 is larger than the maximum value it can hold—2147483647. Press CTRL-F9 to run the rest of the program. When the program is finished, the output screen should look like this:

```
i = -1;
l = -1;
i = 65535;
l = 4294967295;
```

The construct (**unsigned long**) l should be familiar to C programmers. It is a type cast that converts l from its declared type to an unsigned long integer. This type cast corrects the problem in the first output statement. In the line before this, the construct **unsigned(i)** is a C++ function-style type cast. Function-style casts can be used with simple type names like **unsigned**, but not with more complicated ones like **unsigned long**.

Before continuing, clear all windows from the desktop by pressing ALT-SPACEBAR **C**. Answer no when asked if you want to save any modified files.

Summary

The C++ input/output system in IOSTREAM.H replaces the STDIO.H set of functions in C. You have seen that C++'s input/output is more flexible than C's. In Chapter 6, you will really exploit the power of the C++ input/output system when you learn how to expand it.

C++ data types offer few surprises to C programmers. It is important to know the size and ranges of data types, but don't write code that depends on these ranges.

You should be more confident with the Borland C++ integrated environment now. The debugging keys that you have been using are CTRL-F9 to run, F8 to step, F4 to go to a line, and CTRL-F7 to add a watch expression.

5 C++ and Procedural Programming

Although it is possible to write programs that are totally enclosed within **main**, programs are far more manageable if they are broken up into smaller functions. A function combines a set of statements that do a specific job. For example, you can write a function named **read_filename** that gets a filename from the keyboard. The function calls DOS to read keys from the keyboard and then translates those keys into an acceptable string for a filename. There are two obvious advantages of using **read_filename**. First, once you have written the function, you do not have to worry about *how* to read a filename. To read a filename, you simply call **read_filename**. Second, you do not have to duplicate code that you have already written, so the size of your program is reduced by using functions. This philosophy of breaking a program into functions is called procedural programming.

Procedural programming should be familiar to you because it is used in C. Even though C++ is an object-oriented language and C is a procedural language, procedural programming is still very important in

C++ . Object-oriented programming will be discussed in the next chapter. Meanwhile, this chapter will look at some C++ features intended to make procedural programming easier.

Using Standard Library Functions

Borland C++ provides a set of standard library functions that have proven to be useful in procedural programming and will save you time during coding.

All these functions are documented in the on-line help facility. If you are unfamiliar with these functions, or you can't remember the name of a specific function, you can browse the on-line help index. Pressing SHIFT-F1 will display the index of all help topics, including keywords, predefined constants, header files, macros, and functions. Use the PGUP, PGDN, and arrow keys to navigate through the index. When you see a topic of interest move the cursor to that entry and press RETURN. Once you have entered the on-line help system you can exit by pressing ESC.

To call up help for a specific function you can place the cursor over the name of the function and press CTRL-F1. For example, inside the Borland C++ editor type the letters **strcat**. With the cursor on the last **t**, press CTRL-F1. The help entry for **strcat** will appear. The information in the help window is similar to that shown in Table 5-1. Entries like this

strcat

Function	Appends one string to another
Syntax	char *strcat(char *dest, const char *src);
Prototype in	string.h
Remarks	Appends a copy of *src* to the end of *dest*; the length of the resulting string is **strlen**(*dest*) + **strlen**(*src*)
Return value	A pointer to the concatenated strings
Portability	Available on UNIX systems and compatible with ANSI C; defined in Kernighan and Ritchie

Table 5-1. *A Typical Function Entry Description*

are found in most C compiler manuals. The meaning of each section of the entry is described in the following sections.

In addition to the sections shown in Table 5-1, the on-line help entries provide example programs. You can compile and run these programs by pasting them directly into a source file using the editor copy and paste commands.

Syntax

The Syntax section contains the function declaration, which is also called the *function prototype*.

In C, a function does not need to be declared before it is called. In addition, old C-style function declarations do not include arguments. Without parameterized function declarations, C is unable to type check function arguments. In C++, all functions must be declared before they are called. A C++ function prototype is a function declaration that specifies the formal arguments of the function. C++ ensures that the *actual arguments* in a function call are consistent with the *formal arguments* in the function prototype.

A function prototype is defined with a *return type* and a *function declarator,* which are as follows:

- Return type: The type **char *** precedes the function name. A call to **strcat** evaluates to a character pointer.
- Function declarator: The declarator part of the **strcat** prototype is

strcat(char *dest, const char *src)

This is simply the function name, followed by a formal argument list. The two arguments in **strcat** defined inside the parentheses and separated by a comma are both character pointers. The **const** keyword in the second argument indicates that **strcat** will not modify this argument. You will find more information about **const** later in this chapter.

If an argument does not match the function prototype, Borland C++ will automatically use its standard type-conversion rules to try to resolve the mismatch. If Borland C++ cannot find a way to convert the argument, it will issue an error message during the compile process.

```
double fn(double d, int i, char *cp);
main()
{
    long int l = 45;
    float f = 3.14;
    float g = 10.2;
    double answer;

    answer = fn(l,f,g);
}
```

In this example, **l** is converted from a **long int** type to a **double** type before being passed to **fn**. The second argument, **f**, is truncated from 3.14 to 3 when it is converted from a **float** to an **int**. However, Borland C++ will report a "type mismatch" error for the last argument, **g**, because it cannot convert a **float** to a pointer.

Prototype In

The "Prototype in" section of the library function guide lists the standard header file that contains this function's prototype. In this case, STRING.H is the header file that must be included for **strcat**. STRING.H also includes prototypes for other related string functions.

By including STRING.H at the top of the program, there is no need to add your own function declaration for **strcat**.

```
#include <string.h> // declare string functions
#include <dir.h>
#include <iostream.h>
main()
{
    char name[MAXFILE+MAXEXT];
    strcpy(name, "GRAPHS");   // Copy string to name
    strcat(name, ".DAT");     // Append string to name

    cout << name;
}
```

Header files include other useful definitions. **MAXFILE** is the maximum length of an MS-DOS filename string. **MAXPATH** is the maximum length of an MS-DOS file extension string (including the leading period). Both of these constants are defined in DIR.H. As you have already seen, IOSTREAM.H contains definitions necessary to access the standard C++ I/O system.

Portability

The "Portability" section informs the programmer of the function's compatibility with other compilers. The function **strcat** is available for almost every C and C++ compiler, including ANSI C and UNIX C compilers.

The Borland C++ standard library also includes functions that are compatible with many MS-DOS C compilers. Some functions are also compatible with functions and procedures available in Turbo Pascal.

The C++ Function Definition

A C++ function definition is a function prototype (return type and declarator) followed by a function body. The declarator can include default arguments and unnamed arguments. Program P5-1 shows both a function prototype and a function definition for a function called **delPath**. Load Program P5-1 into the editor.

Program P5-1 defines the function **delPath**, which uses the standard library function **fnsplit** to split a filename into four components: drive, directory, name, and extension. Next, **delPath** copies the filename without the drive and directory information back into the original string.

P5-1

```
#include <string.h>
#include <dir.h>
#include <iostream.h>

char *delPath(char *pathname);

main()
{
    char *path = "C:\\DT\\TC.EXE";
    cout << "The filename of " << path;
    cout << " is " <<  delPath(path) << "\n";
}
```

```
char *delPath(char *pathname)
{
     if (*pathname)
    {
          char drive[MAXDRIVE];
          char dir[MAXDIR];
          char name[MAXFILE];
          char ext[MAXEXT];

          fnsplit(pathname, drive, dir, name, ext);

          strcpy(pathname, name);
          strcat(pathname, ext);

          return pathname;
    }
     else
          return NULL;
}
```

Press CTRL-F9 to run the program. The program should output "The filename of C:\DT\TC.EXE is TC.EXE."

REMEMBER The \ character in a string starts an escape sequence. In order to define an actual \ for the DOS path, you must use two \'s. Thus, C:\DT\TC.EXE is written as **C:\\DT\\TC.EXE**.

Let's make some modifications to Program P5-1 to test the function definition mechanism. Near the top of the program, a prototype for **delPath** is given. What will happen if the prototype does not exactly match the definition?

1. Use the editor to change **char *pathname** in the prototype to **char *name**.

2. Press F9 to compile Program P5-1.

The program should compile without an error. C++ does not require you to use the same argument names in prototypes as you use in the function definition. In fact, you can leave out the argument names in the prototype altogether. However, it is recommended that you do not do this because Borland C++ tends to give more descriptive error messages when argument names are used.

***Semantics:** When is a declaration not a definition?*

The difference between a declaration and a definition is important. A *declaration* announces the properties of a variable or a function. The main reason for declaring variables and functions is for type checking. If you declare a variable or function and then later make reference to it with data objects that do not match the types in the declaration, the compiler will complain. The purpose of the complaint is to catch type errors at compile time rather than waiting until the program is run, when the results can be more disastrous.

A *definition,* on the other hand, actually sets aside storage space (in the case of a variable) or indicates the sequence of statements to be carried out (in the case of a function). A function prototype, or declaration, is a return type followed by a function declarator followed by a semicolon. A function definition is a return type followed by a function declarator followed by a function body enclosed in matching braces, { }. A function definition can also serve as a declaration for all source code following the definition. The only time a function declaration is actually required is when a reference is made to a function before the function definition is specified.

A variable declaration with an **extern** specifier is not a definition, unless it has an initializer. The function prototype is a function declaration, but it is not a definition.

Let's see what happens when the prototype's argument type does not match the function call's argument type.

1. Change **char *name** in the prototype to **int name**.
2. Press F9 to compile.

You should see that Borland C++ aborts compiling the program and gives a description of the error: "Type mismatch in parameter 'name' in call to 'delPath' in function main."

What will happen if you leave out the function prototype?

1. Delete the line containing the function prototype. Pressing CTRL-Y deletes a line in the Borland C++ editor.

2. Press F9 to compile.

Again, Borland C++ responds with a descriptive error message: "Function 'delPath' should have a prototype in function main."

You can avoid declaring a function prototype for each function that you write. To do this you must move the function definition above all functions that call it. In Program P5-1 you do not need a prototype if you move the definition of **delPath** above the **main** function.

1. Place the cursor on the beginning of the **delPath** definition and press CTRL-K B. This marks the beginning of the block that you are going to move.

2. Place the cursor after the last line of the function definition and press CTRL-K K. Borland C++ will highlight the block you just defined.

3. Move the cursor above the beginning of **main** and press CTRL-K V. The entire function definition of **delPath** should now precede **main**.

4. Press F9 to compile, and you will see the screen in Figure 5-1.

If everything went right, the program should compile without errors.

Declaring Function Variables

C++ allows more freedom in declaring variables than does C. In particular, C forces all function variables to be declared at the beginning of a block (a block is enclosed in braces: { }), usually at the top of the function body. The C++ philosophy is that variables should be declared just before the statements that use them.

```
int i;                // Declare i.
cin >> i;

for (int j=0; j<i; j++) // Declare j and perform loop.
{
    double k = sin(j);  // Declare k and initialize.

    cout << j << "\t" << k << "\t" << 2*k/j << "\n"
}
```

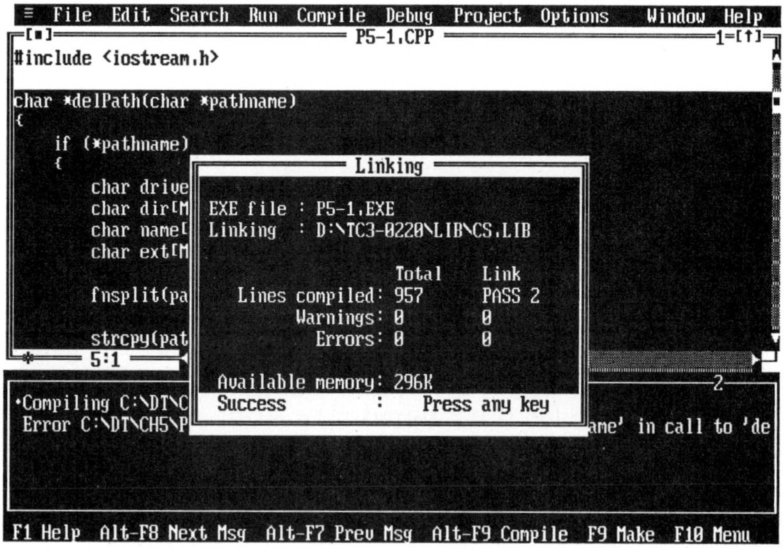

Figure 5-1. *P5-1 compiled without errors*

The rationalization for the new style is that declaring variables near where they are used minimizes the need for the programmer to jump from the declaration section to the statements in a function when reading a program. It is also more natural for most people to think of declaring a variable just before they use it.

Program P5-2 is a "file finder" program. It searches the current directory, and then the directories listed in the MS-DOS environment variable PATH, for a particular file. These are the directories that MS-DOS looks for when you try to execute a file. Clear the desktop and load Program P5-2.

P5-2

```
#include <iostream.h>
#include <dir.h>
main()
{
    cout << "Find file: ";

    char filename[MAXPATH];
    cin >> filename;
```

```
    char *pathname = searchpath(filename);
    cout << "The full path is:  "
         << (pathname ? pathname : "FILE NOT FOUND");
    cout << "\n";
}
/*
    The string returned by search path is set
    in a static buffer area. The buffer is
    over-written on each call to search path.
*/
```

Compile and run the program (CTRL-F9). The first statement in Program P5-2 prompts the user for a filename. Next, the **filename** array is declared and input is taken from the keyboard. The standard library function **searchpath** returns either the full path of the **filename** or 0 (NULL) if the file is not found. The string returned by **searchpath** is assigned to **pathname**. The last statement prints either the file's full pathname or FILE NOT FOUND. Try entering the name, **TC.EXE** (or **BC.EXE** if you are using Borland C++).

Unnamed Arguments

If you are writing a function with a predefined argument list but do not have any use for one or more of the arguments, C++ allows you to leave out the argument name in the function definitions.

```
void errorHandler(char *fileName, int lineNo,
                  char *errorMsg, int exitcode)
{
     cerr << fileName << ": " << errorMsg << "\n";
}

errorHandler("TEST.CPP", 0, "System Error!", 0);
```

This function prints out an error message, but it has no use for the second and last arguments. The function works correctly, but Borland C++ will issue the warnings for arguments that are not used in function definitions. To silence the warnings, simply leave out the formal argument names in the function definition.

```
void errorHandler(char *fileName, int, char *errorMsg, int)
{
     cerr << fileName << ": " << errorMsg << "\n";
}
```

Default Arguments

Default arguments are arguments substituted by the compiler if no argument is given in the function call. A default argument is specified in the function declaration like this:

```
void errorHandler(char *errorMsg = "System Error!");
  .
  .
  .
errorHandler("Stack Overflow!");
errorHandler();
```

The function **errorHandler** prints an error message and aborts the program. The first call prints the message "Stack Overflow!", which is the argument passed to the function. The second call is made without an argument, so the message is the default "System Error!".

You can have multiple default arguments in a function declaration. However, all the default arguments must be specified at the end of the argument list.

In Program P5-3, the function **errorHandler** takes two to four arguments. The first two arguments must be specified. Note that the default arguments are specified in the function prototype and not in the function definition.

P5-3

```
#include <iostream.h>
#include <stdlib.h>

void errorHandler(char *funcName, int lineNo,
                  char *errorMsg="System Error!\n",
                  int exitcode=1);
main()
{
     errorHandler(__FILE__,__LINE__);
}

void errorHandler(char *fileName, int lineNo,
                  char *errorMsg, int exitcode)
{
     cerr << errorMsg << "\n";
     cerr << fileName << " line # " << lineNo << "\n";

     exit(exitcode);
}
```

Load and run Program P5-3. The error handler prints the filename and line number of the calling statement.

The const Type Specifier

The C++ **const** keyword is used to specify a type that cannot have its value changed. It can be used to declare symbolic constants. Since a **const** specifier guarantees that a value cannot change, the compiler can perform more optimization with constants than it can with variables. Programs almost never pay any penalty for using symbolic constants in place of literal constants. Judicious use of symbolic constants will make your programs more readable.

```
#include <iostream.h>
const double pi = 3.14159;
const double degrees_per_radian = 360/(2*pi);
main()
{
 cout << 1 << " radians = " << 1 * degrees_per_radian << " degrees\n";
 cout << pi << " radians = " << pi * degrees_per_radian << " degrees\n";
}
```

Compare the program with one that does not use symbolic constants:

```
#include <iostream.h>
main()
{
 cout << 1 << " radians = " << 1 * 57.29583 << " degrees\n";
 cout << pi << " radians = " << pi * 57.29283 << " degrees\n";
}
```

In the program that uses literal constants, one of the constants specifies the wrong value, but it is difficult to see the error. To make the correction, the programmer must recalculate 360/(2*pi) to see which constant is erroneous.

Each **const** definition must include an initializer. Once a constant has been defined, it cannot be changed.

```
const int enter;    // Illegal - no initializer.

const int esc = 27;
esc = 28;             // Illegal - cannot change a constant.
```

Constants and Pointers

Constants are very useful when they are applied to pointers. The syntax for constant pointers can be confusing. Don't confuse a *constant pointer* with a *pointer to a constant.* You can distinguish the two types by where the **const** keyword is placed in the declaration. To declare a constant pointer, the **const** specifier comes after the * in the declaration.

```
int j, k;
int * const cp = &j; // Constant pointer.
*cp = 45             // OK: j = 45.
cp = &k;             // Illegal: cp is constant.
```

You can assign values to what **cp** is referencing, but you cannot change the value of **cp**.

To declare a pointer to a constant, the **const** specifier is placed before the *.

```
const char *pc = "DiskTutor"; // Pointer to a constant.
*pc = '\0';                   // Illegal : *pc is constant.
pc = "DiskTutor Version 3";   // OK : pc is not constant.
```

You cannot change the value to which a pointer to a constant refers. A pointer to a constant may not be assigned to a pointer to a non-constant.

```
char *p;
p = pc;      // If C++ allowed this...
*p = '\0';   //   the const requirement would be broken
```

Similarly, a pointer to a constant cannot be passed to a function with a pointer to a non-constant argument.

```
char *strcpy(char *dest, const char *src); // Prototype
strcpy(pc, "Version 3"); // Illegal
```

The first argument type (**char ***) in **strcpy** allows modification to **dest** (which is a **char ***), but **pc** (which is a **const char ***) points to an object that cannot be changed, so the function call is rejected by the compiler.

Constants and Internal Linkage

Before understanding the distinction between constants in C++ and constants in C, the concept of scope must be clarified.

Scope, or *linkage,* refers to the visibility of variables and other identifiers such as the symbolic names of constants and functions. A local variable declared inside a function cannot be accessed outside the function. A variable declared outside a function and inside a file can be used by any function that follows the definition of the variable within the file. Such a variable has *file scope.* If the variable name is preceded by the keyword **extern,** the variable has *global,* or *external scope* and can be used by functions defined outside of the file with the variable definition.

Sometimes the terms external (global) linkage and internal (local) linkage are used to describe scope. Usually these two terms are used in relation to the concept of a file or module. If an identifier has external linkage, it is visible outside the file or module that defines it. If an identifier has internal linkage, it is local and can only be used inside the module that defines it.

C++ supports four scopes for identifiers: global, file, class, and block. A global identifier is accessible at all levels and across all source files used to build a program. An identifier of file scope is available only inside the file in which it is defined. An identifier that is a member of a class is accessible only through an object that is an instance of that class. Class scope is flexible in that object instances cannot access private members of the class except indirectly by public or protected member functions.

Identifiers that have *block scope* are visible only inside the beginning and ending curly braces defining the block. The braces at the beginning and end of a function definition constitute such a block. Most frequently, block scope refers to variables defined inside a function. But block scope can be smaller than the scope of a function if the curly braces are nested inside a function definition, such as in compound statements controlled by the **while**, **for**, **if**, and **else** expressions.

All functions that are not members of a class are said to have external linkage. Such functions can be called from any other function even if the calling function is defined in a file other than the function being called. Such is the case with calls to the standard Borland C++ library functions, which have global scope. Preceding a function with the keyword **static** changes its scope from external to internal. Only functions defined in the same file with a **static** function can call that **static** function.

C supports all scopes supported by C++ with the exception of class; however, there are some subtle differences in the linkage of constants. Unlike ANSI C constants, C++ constants default to internal linkage. In ANSI C, a **const** that is not local to a function has external scope. In C++, these constants have file scope. This means that a C++ constant defined in one source file cannot be accessed by other source files linked together into a single program.

A C++ **const** definition is very much like a preprocessor macro definition. Since preprocessor definitions have a scope that extends from the **#define** statement to the end of the source file, header files are used to extend them to multiple files. In the same way, a **const** can be put into a header file to extend its scope across files. To get a sense of how this works, load Program P5-4 now.

P5-4

```
#include <iostream.h>

const int i = 1;
#define j 2

main()
{
    cout << "i==> " << i << "\n";
    cout << "j==> " << j << "\n";
}
```

Use the F8 key to step through the program until the highlight bar rests on the first **cout** statement, which prints the value of **i**. Now look at the value of **i** in the Evaluate and Modify dialog box (**D**ebug/**E**valuate). Enter **i** in the expression field and you will see "1" appear in the result field. However, if you try to enter **j** in the expression field, the result field displays

```
Undefined symbol 'j'
```

A constant, whose linkage by default is local to the file that defines it, is similar to a symbolic constant created with the **#define** preprocessor directive:

```
#define j 2
```

However, when the compiler encounters the identifier **j** throughout the rest of the source file, it is replaced with the constant **2**. Once the file is compiled, no record of the existence of a symbol called **j** remains. Neither the linker nor the debugger knows about **j**, so you cannot look at it with the Evaluate and Modify dialog box.

Using **const** is similar to using **#define**, but it has the advantage of assigning a type to the identifier so that the compiler can ensure that it is used properly throughout the rest of the file.

If the keyword **extern** precedes **const**, the linkage of the constant is external or global. This means that information about the constant is available to other modules as well as to the linker and debugger. An **extern const** is like a variable, except that its value cannot be changed.

Modify program P5-4 to make **j** an external constant. Move the cursor to the beginning of the line that declares

```
#define j 2
```

Change the line to read

```
extern const int j = 2;
```

Now, recompile the program (F9) and step through the program with F8 until the highlight bar rests on the first **cout** statement. Now enter **j** in the expression field of the Evaluate and Modify dialog box. The result field displays "2."

Remember that initializing an external constant or variable changes it from a declaration to a definition. You can have as many declarations of a global symbol as you want as long as the type information in the declarations does not conflict. However, you can have only one definition of a global symbol in all the source modules that make up a program. What's the difference? The statement,

```
extern const j = 2;
```

is a definition because it initializes **j**. It actually sets aside storage for **j** and assigns **j** a value. On the other hand, the statement,

```
extern const j;
```

is only a declaration. Its purpose is to let the rest of a source file know that somewhere an identifier, **j**, is defined and that it is an integer. This makes it legal for the rest of the source file to refer to **j**.

Since only one definition of a global symbol is allowed in all source files, you should never initialize external constants in header files, because header files are likely to be included by more than one source file.

Constants as Function Arguments

The file finder program, P5-2, does not accept wildcards. The standard library function **searchpath** will return an error if a wildcard is given as its argument. One way to remedy this is to write our own function to search directories. Load Program P5-5 into Borland C++.

P5-5

```
/*
        File finder program with wildcards.
*/
#include <string.h>
#include <stdlib.h>
#include <dir.h>
#include <iostream.h>

/*
  getNextPath: Returns the next pathname from a DOS PATH
      formatted string (each path in the DOS PATH variable
      must be separated by a semicolon).

      The input, envpath, is a pointer to a string. The path
      returned is a pointer to a static area, which is overwritten
      on the next call.  This path is deleted from the input
      string.  If no path is found NULL is returned.
*/
```

```
char *getNextPath(char **envpath)
{
   char *oldptr = *envpath;

   if (**envpath=='\0')
      return NULL;

   // Declare and reset the buffer to all 0's.
   static char foundpath[MAXPATH];
   strnset(foundpath, 0, sizeof(foundpath));

   // Scan envpath until a ';' or end of string.
   while (**envpath != ';' && **envpath != '\0')
      (*envpath)++;

   strncpy(foundpath, oldptr, (int)(*envpath - oldptr));

   if (**envpath != '\0') // Point to the character after ';'
      (*envpath)++;

   return foundpath;

}

/*
  Look for filename in the DOS PATH and return that path.  If the
  file is not found, return NULL.

  Wildcards are accepted.

  The filename may not contain a drive or directory.
*/
char *findfile(char *path, const char *drive, const char *dir,
          const char *name, const char *ext)

{
     if (*drive || *dir)
          return NULL;

     const int findfirstOK = 0;
     ffblk fileblock;
     int attrib = 0;

     // Look in current directory first.
     fnmerge(path, "", "", name, ext);
     if (findfirst(path, &fileblock, attrib) == findfirstOK)
     {
        char curDir[MAXDRIVE+MAXDIR];
        char curDrive[MAXDRIVE];

        curDrive[0] = getdisk() + 'A';
        curDrive[1] = ':';
```

```
        curDrive[2] = '\0';

        getcurdir(0, curDir);

        fnmerge(path, curDrive, curDir, name, ext);

        return strupr(path);
    }

    char *envpath = getenv("PATH");

    // Copy the environment string to a safe place.
    char *envbuf = strdup(envpath);

    char *nextpath;

    // Look in DOS PATH.
    while ((nextpath=getNextPath(&envbuf)) != NULL)
    {
        char envDrive[MAXDRIVE];
        char envDir[MAXDIR];
        char envName[MAXFILE];
        char envExt[MAXEXT];

        fnsplit(nextpath, envDrive, envDir, envName, envExt);

        /* If you call fnsplit on a directory name, it will
           put the last subdirectory in the name argument.
           So we must append the name to the dir.
        */
        strcat(envDir, envName);

        fnmerge(path, envDrive, envDir, name, ext);

          if (findfirst(path, &fileblock, attrib) == findfirstOK)
          {
               return strupr(path);
          }

    }

    return NULL;
}

/*
  deepSearchpath: Construct the full pathname for a file.
    deepSearchpath returns a pointer to a static area which is
    overwritten after the next call. If the file is not found
    NULL is returned.
```

```
     Drive and directory names are not accepted.

     If flag is not 0, wildcards will be accepted.
*/
char *deepSearchpath(const char *pathname, int flag)
{
     int fn_flags;
     char drive[MAXDRIVE];
     char dir[MAXDIR];
     char name[MAXFILE];
     char ext[MAXEXT];

     if (*pathname)
          fn_flags = fnsplit(pathname, drive, dir, name, ext);
     else
          return NULL;

     if (fn_flags & (DRIVE|DIRECTORY))
          return NULL;

     if ((fn_flags & WILDCARDS) && flag==0)
          return NULL;

     static char fullPathName[MAXPATH];
     return findfile(fullPathName, drive, dir, name, ext);
}

main()
{
     cout << "Find file: ";

     char filename[MAXPATH];
     cin >> filename;

     char *pathname = deepSearchpath(filename, WILDCARDS);

     cout << "The full path is:  "
          << (pathname ? pathname : "FILE NOT FOUND");
}
```

The function **deepSearchpath** is similar to **searchpath**, but if it finds a wildcard argument, the first matching file will be found.

1. Press CTRL-F9 to run the program.

2. For the filename, type ***.cpp** and press RETURN.

The program will look in the current directory for any file matching ***.cpp**. If no files are found, **deepSearchpath** will look in the DOS PATH for such a file. The output should be something like this:

```
The full path is:  C:\DT\CH5\*.CPP.
```

The first argument to function **deepSearchpath** is a **const char** *. The **const** specifier ensures that the contents of **pathname** are not changed by **deepSearchpath.** It is an error for **deepSearchpath** to try to change the string referenced by **pathname.**

```
char *deepSearchpath(const char *pathname, int flag)
{
    *pathname = '\0';                   // Error.
    pathname = "new string";            // OK.
    strcpy(pathname, "new string");     // Error.
// ...
}
```

References

A *reference* in C++ is a way to assign another name or alias to a variable. For example:

```
int i;
int &r = i; // r is an alias for i.
r = 100;    // i=100;
```

The syntax for references can be compared to the syntax for pointers. A similar piece of code using pointers would look like this:

```
int i;
int *p = &i;
*p = 100;   // i=100;
```

Instead of the * in the declaration of pointer **p**, you use **&** to declare a reference **r**. To dereference **p**, or get the value of what **p** is pointing to, you use the * notation again. But for the reference, you use **r** by itself. You can think of a reference as a pointer that is always dereferenced.

A reference cannot be changed once it has been declared. In the previous code, the declaration of **r** initializes **r** to refer to **i**. Although it looks like you are changing **r** in the statement,

```
r = 100;
```

you are actually changing **i**. From this, it is clear that the declaration for a reference variable must also initialize it. It is illegal to declare a reference like this:

```
int &r; // Illegal - no initializer.
```

A reference can assign an alias to a constant. For example:

```
double &constRef = 3.14159;
constRef = 0; // The temporary variable gets the value 0.
```

The constant reference causes Borland C++ to create a temporary hidden variable with the value 3.14159. The alias **constRef** is then applied to the hidden variable. The following code has the same effect:

```
double temp = 3.14159;
double &constRef = temp;
constRef = 0; // temp gets the value 0.
```

Reference Arguments

Consider the following code fragment:

```
struct BigStruct
{
    char array[100];
    // ... more data
};

void printBigStruct(BigStruct bs, int n)
{
    for (int i=0; i<n; i++)
        cout << bs.array[i];
}

main()
{
    BigStruct x;
```

```
    printBigStruct(x,100);
}
```

BigStruct x is passed by value to **printBigStruct**. A local variable, **bs**, is created by making a copy of the data in **x**. Passing arguments by value is acceptable for small arguments, but in this case, the overhead needed to copy the entire structure is high. The traditional C solution is to use pointers to structures for function arguments.

```
void printBigStructP(const BigStruct *bsp, int n)
{
    for (int i=0; i<n; i++)
         cout << bsp->array[i];
}

main()
{
    BigStruct x;

    printBigStructP(&x, 100);
}
```

This changes the syntax of the original program. In particular, you can no longer pass **x** to the function to print it; you have to pass the address of **x**. The interface to the function is complicated by the need for efficiency. A reference to a structure is a good alternative to the structure pointer in **printBigStructP**.

```
struct BigStruct
{
    char array[100];
    // ... more data
};

void printBigStructR(BigStruct &bsr, int n)
{
    for (int i=0; i<n; i++)
         cout << bsr.array[i];
}

main()
{
    BigStruct x;
```

```
    printBigStructR(x,100);
}
```

From the caller's point of view, the function **printBigStructR** is used just like **printBigStruct**. The argument **bsr** is actually an alias to the structure **x**. No copying was needed to create **bsr**.

A problem with using references as function arguments is that the original variable can be modified without the caller knowing about it.

```
void printBigStructR(BigStruct &bsr, int n)
{
    for (int i=0; i<n; i++)
         cout << (bsr.array[i] += 5 );
}

main()
{
    BigStruct x;

    printBigStructR(x, 100);

    printBigStructR(x, 100);
}
```

If you were only looking at the statements in **main**, it would appear that the two function calls should produce identical results. But actually, the first call to **printBigStructR** has modified the contents of **x** by adding 5 to each element of **array**. This is not obvious from the caller's perspective; thus, tracing down the change can be difficult. Be careful to avoid side effects that might modify reference arguments.

Temporary Variables and Reference Arguments

If a function with reference arguments is called, but the function call arguments do not match the function definition, C++ will perform a type conversion. The only problem with most type conversions is loss of precision. But for reference arguments, the fact that a reference is an alias for a variable presents another problem. In such a case, C++ performs type conversions by creating temporary variables.

```
void inc(int &i)
{
    i++;
}

int j = 0;
inc(j);

double d = 0;
inc(d);  // Temporary variable used - d not changed.

inc(0);  // Temporary variable used - call has no effect.
```

The function **inc** adds 1 to an integer reference passed to it. This will work as expected as long as you call **inc** with an **int** variable. In this example, Borland C++ has to create a temporary hidden **int** variable for the **double** argument **d**. A conversion from **double** to **int** is made and the converted value is assigned to the temporary variable. The actual argument passed to **inc** is a reference to the temporary variable, not **d**! When the function returns to the caller, the temporary variable has been incremented but is immediately deleted without updating **d**. As a result, the function call has no effect on **d**. For the constant 0, a temporary variable is also created and the call to **inc** has no effect.

In cases where a temporary variable is created for a reference argument, Borland C++ will generate a "Temporary used for variable" warning to make the programmer aware of potential problems.

Functions Returning References

In addition to passing reference arguments, C++ also allows functions that return references.

```
struct S
{
    char array[100];
};

char &base(S &str)
{
```

```
    return str.array[0];
}

main()
{
    S string;

    base(string) = '\0';
}
```

The function **base** returns a reference to the first element of the member **array** in **S**. In **main**, it appears that **'\0'** is assigned to the function **base**. What is actually happening is that **'\0'** is assigned to the reference returned by **base**. Thus, this assignment has the same effect as

string.array[0] = '\0';

There does not appear to be a lot of obvious uses for functions returning reference types yet. But when you learn about operator functions, you will see why this syntax is essential.

Function Overloading

C++ allows two or more functions to share identical names. When this happens, those functions are *overloaded*. For example:

```
int compare(const char *s1, const char *s2)
{
    return strcmp(s1, s2);
}

int compare(int i1, int i2)
{
    return i1 - i2;
}
```

The functions differ in argument types and in the function body, but both perform the operation of comparing two arguments. From the caller's viewpoint, the **compare** function does for strings the same thing it does for integers—each function returns a positive number if the first argument is greater than the second, 0 if both arguments are equal, and a negative number if the second argument is greater than the first.

Without the overload feature, the programmer would be forced to define these functions using differing names.

```
int string_compare(const char *s1, const char *s2)
{
    return strcmp(s1, s2);
}

int int_compare(int i1, int i2)
{

    return i1 - i2;
}
```

This approach has been used by C programmers for years. But it is inconvenient for the programmer to have to make up and remember multiple names for a single operation.

Argument Type Matching

A function is overloaded when another function has an identical name, but a different argument list. The argument list can differ in the type or number of arguments.

```
int max(int i1, int i2);
double max(double d1, double d2);
int max(int i1, int i2, int i3);
int max(double d1, int d2);
int max(double d1, int d2, int d3);
int max(int list[], int size);
```

Each function **max** has a unique argument list. You cannot overload two functions by giving them the same arguments but different return types.

```
int max(int i1, int i2);
unsigned int max(int i1, int i2);  // Error.
```

C++ can distinguish overloaded functions only by their argument lists, not by the return types. Thus, this listing will not compile.

If a function call does not match any overloaded function, C++ will promote all **char** types to **int** and all **float** types to **double**. If the promotions still do not provide an exact match, C++ will convert any numeric type to match any other numeric type in the argument list and any pointer type to match a **void** pointer in the argument list. If conversions are necessary, the call might lead to ambiguity.

```
int max(int i1, int i2);
double max(double d1, double d2);

float f1, f2;
cout << max(f1, f2); // No exact match, but float converted to double

long int l1, l2;
cout << max(l1, l2); // Error : Convert long to int or double?
```

A Directory Tree Program

Program P5-6 recursively prints each subdirectory of the current directory. You could modify this program to look for directory information under one directory. Some applications include printing, modifying, or deleting all the files, and checking the sum of total disk usage in the current directory and its subdirectories. Clear the desktop and load Program P5-6 now.

P5-6

```
#include <dir.h>
#include <dos.h>
#include <string.h>
#include <iostream.h>

void dirTree(char *curDir)
{
     // Print current directory.
     cout << curDir << "\n";

     // Find all subdirectories and put them in an array.
     char curPath[MAXPATH];
     strcpy(curPath, curDir);
     strcat(curPath, "*.");
```

```
    char dirList[30][MAXDIR+1];
    ffblk fileblock;
    int maxList;
    int done = findfirst(curPath, &fileblock, FA_DIREC);
    for (maxList=0; !done;)
    {
         if (fileblock.ff_attrib & FA_DIREC)
              if (*(fileblock.ff_name) != '.')
              {
                     strcpy(dirList[maxList], curDir);
                     strcat(dirList[maxList], fileblock.ff_name);
                     strcat(dirList[maxList], "\\");
                     maxList++;
              }

         done = findnext(&fileblock);
    }

    // Process each subdirectory.
    for (int i=0; i<maxList; i++)
         dirTree(dirList[i]);
}

main()
{
    char curDir[MAXDIR];
    getcwd(curDir, MAXDIR);

    // The directory name must end with a backslash ('\').
    if (curDir[strlen(curDir)-1] != '\\')
         strcat(curDir, "\\");

    dirTree(curDir);
}
```

The basic algorithm of **dirTree** is rather simple:

dirTree(directory)
    Print directory
    Find all the subdirectories
    For each subdirectory call dirTree(subdirectory)

To see anything interesting you need to create subdirectories before running Program P5-6. Shell out to DOS (ALT-F D) and create three directories with MKDIR. Type **exit** to reenter the Borland C++ IDE and run Program P5-6.

Alternatively, replace

```
dirTree(curDir)
```

with

```
dirTree("\\")
```

which prints all subdirectories below the root directory. Clear the desktop before continuing.

Program P5-7 augments the **dirTree** function by printing the directory information of each file in each subdirectory. This is done by adding a new function: **printFileBlock**. The main change to **dirTree** is inserting a call to **printFileBlock** after each file is found. Load Program P5-7.

P5-7

```
#include <dir.h>
#include <dos.h>
#include <string.h>
#include <stdio.h>

void printFileBlock(ffblk &ffblk)
{
     // The format of the DOS File Control Block date and time information
     struct fcb_date
     {
          unsigned fd_day : 5;
          unsigned fd_month : 4;
          unsigned fd_year : 7; // Relative to 1980
     } *fd = (fcb_date *) &(ffblk.ff_fdate);

     struct fcb_time
     {
         unsigned ft_sec : 5;
         unsigned ft_min : 6;
         unsigned ft_hour : 5;
     } *ft = (fcb_time *) &(ffblk.ff_ftime);

     printf("  %-13s  %10ld" , ffblk.ff_name, ffblk.ff_fsize)
     printf("  %02u-%02u-%02u", fd->fd_month, fd->fd_day, fd->fd_year+80)
     printf("  %02u:%02u:%02u", ft->ft_hour, ft->ft_min, ft->ft_sec)
     printf("\n");

}

void dirTree(char *curDir)
{
     // Print current directory.
     printf("%s\n", curDir);

     // Find all subdirectories and put them in an array.
     char curPath[MAXPATH+1];
     strcpy(curPath, curDir);
     strcat(curPath, "*.*");

     char dirList[30][MAXDIR+1];
```

```
    ffblk fileblock;
    int maxList;
    int done = findfirst(curPath, &fileblock, 0xFF);
    for (maxList=0; !done;)
    {
         if (fileblock.ff_attrib & FA_DIREC)
         {
              if (*(fileblock.ff_name) != '.')
              {
                   strcpy(dirList[maxList], curDir);
                   strcat(dirList[maxList], fileblock.ff_name);
                   strcat(dirList[maxList], "\\");
                   maxList++;
              }
         }
        else
             printFileBlock(fileblock);

        done = findnext(&fileblock);
    }
    maxList--;

    // Process each subdirectory.
    for (int i=0; i<=maxList; i++)
         dirTree(dirList[i]);
}

main()
{
    char curDir[MAXDIR+1];
    getcwd(curDir, MAXDIR);

    // The directory name must end with a backslash ('\').
    if (curDir[strlen(curDir)-1] != '\\')
         strcat(curDir, "\\");

    dirTree(curDir);
}
```

The function **dirTree** passes a structure **ffblk** by reference to **printFileBlock**. An actual structure was not passed for reasons of efficiency. The structure type **ffblk** holds the MS-DOS File Control Block information and is defined in the file DIR.H:

```
struct ffblk {
   char     ff_reserved[21];
```

```
    char     ff_attrib;
    unsigned ff_ftime;
    unsigned ff_fdate;
    long     ff_fsize;
    char     ff_name[13];
};
```

Bitfields are used in **printFileBlock** to access the individual fields of the file block.

The information for this structure is filled in by the **findfirst** and **findnext** functions and **printFileBlock** accesses each member of the structure to print the directory information.

Run Program P5-7. Now, in addition to directories, you will see all the files in the current directory and its subdirectories. Each line now prints the file size, date, and time.

This chapter has introduced language features of C++ that support procedural programming. These features improve error checking and add flexibility to the features already provided by ANSI C. Features discussed include function prototypes, which enforce stronger type checking, default arguments, symbolic constants and their scope differences for C++ and C, constant pointers, references, and the use of constants and references in function arguments. Function overloading was presented as a way to allow many different function definitions with a common function name. The appropriate function is selected by matching the type and number of arguments in the caller against the arguments in the definitions.

The final two example programs show how a larger program can be broken up into a procedure-oriented structure. These examples also demonstrate how using predefined library functions minimizes the work required to get small programs up and running.

On-line help can be used to browse functions by an alphabetized index of names or by finding the function directly inside a program text file, placing the editor's cursor on the function, and pressing CTRL-F1.

Before moving on, use the on-line help to look up some of the functions, structures, and constants found in programs P5-6 and P5-7. For instance, look up **strcpy**, **findfirst**, **findnext**, **getcwd**, **ffblk**, and **MAXDIR**. When you're finished, clear the desktop.

Object-Oriented Programming: Structuring with Objects and Classes

Part Two

6 Object-Oriented Programming

The goal of this chapter is to present the basic methodology and conceptual framework for working with objects. Most books teach C++ through the presentation of new language features. This approach is useful, but it does not explain why object-oriented programming can make programming easier. This chapter first focuses on the major issues of building object-oriented systems and then shows how new language features in C++ help support object-oriented programming techniques.

Building Object-Oriented Programs

The main focus of this chapter is methodology rather than language features. Language features will be introduced only as needed and will be glossed over in order to present the concept of object-oriented programming as an integrated whole rather than going into the issues of semantics and syntax.

The general approach for building object-oriented programs is to create classes, then instances of classes, and then to specify the exchange of messages between object instances.

1. Create classes
2. Create instances of classes (objects)
3. Specify messages to be exchanged by objects

Classes, Objects, Methods, and Messages

Some of this terminology is new. The main terms that will be defined at this point are class, object, method, and message. All of these terms come from the Smalltalk programming language. A *class* is a structure that can have functions as members as well as data elements. In Smalltalk, these member functions are called *methods.* One thing that trips people up is distinguishing between classes and objects. It might help to remember that object is not a new word. C has traditionally referred to the storage space set aside for a data item as an *object.* Thus, in the definition

```
int i;
```

the variable **i** is an object. The keyword **int** is a type specifier. It specifies the internal representation of variables of type **integer**—two bytes of storage in the case of Borland C++. You can think of **int** as a template. While a data type specifier such as **int** is a template for a variable, a class is a template for an object. An object is frequently referred to as an instance of a class. This is because the declaration of a class, just like the declaration of a type, does not set aside storage. Only instances of classes, or objects, actually have storage set aside for them. Consider the following class declaration:

```
class Point
{
    int x, y;
public:
```

```
    void print();
};
```

This declares a new data type, **Point**, which can be used like a built-in data type such as **int**, **char**, or **float**. **Point** is a class. No storage is set aside by the declaration of the class **Point**. An object can be created from class **Point** as follows:

```
Point p1;
```

This definition sets aside enough storage space for the object **p1**. Objects are variables. Classes are data types. The other term to define is message. A *message* is equivalent to a call to one of an object's member functions. Recall that Smalltalk refers to its member functions as methods. In order to initiate a computational process in Smalltalk, a message is sent to an object. This terminology tries to reinforce the concept of structuring that is based on data (objects) rather than on actions (functions). That is why the third step in programming an object-oriented system is to specify messages to be exchanged among the objects.

If you want to see the contents of object **p1**, you can send the print message to the object:

```
p1.print();
```

In Smalltalk terminology you would say the object, **p1**, is sent the message **print**. The object then looks for a method (member function) that matches the message and invokes the method (calls the function). C++ tends not to rely on this message-passing terminology, but it is important to understand its origin and its conceptual implications.

To rephrase the terminology in step 3 for building object-oriented programs, the process of specifying sequences of calls to member functions does not quite make the shift in thinking away from actions and toward objects.

Again, to summarize the process of creating object-oriented programs: first, create classes that model the world of the problem; next, create objects, or instances of those classes; then, arrange for a sequence of messages to be passed back and forth among the objects.

Designing Text-Based Windows and Menus

In order to make the discussion of methodology concrete, classes and objects will be used as the basis for building a text-based windowing system. Object-oriented design does not strictly adhere to the top-down approach advocated for procedural languages. Design is often bottom-up; that is, lower-level objects may be defined before higher-level objects that use them. You will usually break a system down into a set of objects that are abstractions of their counterparts in the real world. For instance, windows are rectangles that are surrounded by a frame border. These windows usually give you a view into some portion of a text buffer. A text buffer in a word processor contains a document, which is composed of characters, words, and paragraphs. A rectangle can be defined by two points: an origin and an opposing corner.

Thinking in Terms of Objects

Objects that might become components of a window system are rectangle, point, window, document, paragraph, line, word, or character. Once you have defined the basic object components of a system, you can take each object and think about the things you might want to do with it—**Paragraph::reformat**, **Point::move**, **Window::open**, and so forth. You can see how a system breaks down quite naturally into manageable units with this approach. Let's start with the notion of a point. Load Program P6-1 now.

NOTE It is very important that you log into the right directory before loading and compiling example programs. If you do not do this, the wrong versions of header files (*.H) will be loaded. The compiler will report errors such as

```
'print' is not a member of the 'point' class in function 'rectangle'
```

This error will occur in this chapter if you do not log to \DT\CH6 before starting up TC or BC and then attempting to compile Program P6-4. Not logging to \DT\CH6 causes the header file \DT\INCLUDE\POINT.H to be used with Program P6-4 when the program actually needs to include the file \DT\CH6\POINT.H. Similar problems can occur in other chapters as well.

You must log to the appropriate directory each time you start a chapter. Do this *before* you invoke the Borland C++ programming environment. Before starting this chapter, for example, execute the following command at the DOS prompt:

```
cd \dt\ch6
```

This assumes you are already logged onto the hard disk drive where the DiskTutor example programs were installed. Once you have logged to the appropriate subdirectory for the current chapter, you can invoke Turbo C++ with the following command:

```
tc
```

Or invoke Borland C++ with

```
bc
```

from the DOS prompt. Once you are logged to the appropriate directory, you are ready to follow the example programs for the current chapter.

P6-1

```
#include <conio.h>

class Point
{
    int x, y;
public:
    Point(int u, int v) { x=u; y=v; }
    void print() { cprintf("x->%5d  y->%5d\r\n", x, y); }
};

main()
{
    Point p1(3,10);
    p1.print();
}
```

Program P6-1 illustrates the most simple use of a class. The class **Point** consists of two data items and two methods. One of these methods is a constructor. Remember that a member function with the same name as the class is a constructor. A constructor is invoked automatically when an object of a class is defined. Consequently, the definition

```
Point p1(3,10);
```

automatically creates an object, **p1**, and calls the constructor with the arguments **3** and **10**. In this case, the constructor initializes the coordinates **x** and **y** inside object **p1**.

Object **p1** has one other method: **print**. The purpose of the **print** member function is to see the contents of **Point** objects. Since **x** and **y** are private members of an object of class **Point**, the only way you can access them is through member functions. The statement

```
p1.print();
```

calls the member function **print** for the object **p1** and produces the output you see when you run the program. Run the program now by pressing CTRL-F9. You should see the following output:

```
x->    3 y->   10
```

The purpose of the **print** method inside the class **Point** is mainly diagnostic. It provides a useful way to see if a point object actually contains the values it should. In order for points to be of more general utility, they need other operations. For instance, it would be useful to add or subtract one point from another. Program P6-2 adds two new methods for carrying out these operations.

P6-2

```
#include <conio.h>

class Point
{
    int x, y;
public:
    Point(int u, int v) { x=u; y=v; }
    void print() { cprintf("x->%5d  y->%5d\r\n", x, y); }
    Point operator +(Point p)
```

```
        { return Point(x+p.x, y+p.y); }
    Point operator -(Point p)
        { return Point(x-p.x, y-p.y); }
};

main()
{
    Point p1(3,10), p2(20,15);
    p2.print();
    p1.print();

    cout << "---sum------------\n";
    Point p3 = p1 + p2;
    p3.print();
}
```

The member functions for adding and subtracting points are specified as operators. Doing this lets you use syntax like **p1 + p2** instead of saying **p1.add(p2)**.

Operator member functions and operator overloading are covered in the following section. When you want to find the difference between or sum of two points, you can simply apply the + and – operators to the objects. You do not need to know how a point is represented. It could be in Cartesian or polar coordinates for all you care. You can leave the details up to the class implementation.

Distinguishing Class Implementation from Class Use

There is a distinction between implementing a class and using it. Right now, you are implementing a class that will later be used to draw borders around rectangles and to draw and resize windows. In order to meet those objectives, the class needs a little more functionality.

Program P6-2 takes a small step in adding functionality to the **Point** class. Two operators, + and –, are added to the **Point** class.

Load this program now and look at the declaration for the + and – operator methods. Notice that they are preceded by the keyword **operator**. Preceding a member function with this keyword allows you to redefine the meaning of C++'s built-in operators: +, –, *, /, +=, <, >, and so forth. What this means in the case of the **Point** class is that when the + operator is applied to two data objects, both of type **Point**, the member function associated with + inside the **Point** class will be executed. The value returned by such an expression is a point. Thus, you can assign the return value to another point or you can add a series of terms in sequence.

```
p = p1 + p2 + p3 + p4;
```

This works as long as each object in the expression is of type **Point**. Note that a point can be assigned a value at the place where it is declared. For example, look at the statement where **p3** is declared:

```
Point p3 = p1 + p2;
```

The object **p3** is created and assigned a value, which is the result of an addition operation for class **Point**. Later, **p3** is assigned the difference between **p2** and **p1**.

```
p3 = p2 - p1;
```

In this case no new object is created; the old object is simply assigned a new value. One of the great advantages of C++ is the ability to treat data declarations like statements. This allows you to declare variables and objects at the point where they will be used, making it much easier to keep track of stray variables. Run the program now. You will see the following output:

```
x->   20  y->   15
x->    3  y->   10
---sum-----------
x->   23  y->   25
---difference-----
x->   17  y->    5
```

The resulting output verifies that the addition and subtraction operators are working correctly.

Improving the Point Class

To start using the **Point** class for some practical applications, you need a few more operators. One operation that would be useful would print a character at the screen position described by a point. For this you can add a **putch** method.

```
void putch(char c) { gotoxy(x, y); ::putch(c); }
```

You will probably want to move points around on the screen. For this you can use the += operator to move a point by an offset defined by another point.

```
Point operator +=(Point p)
    { return Point(x+=p.x, y+=p.y); }
```

Finally, you will need comparison operators (such as ==, <=, and so on) to see when a point is equal to, less than, or greater than another point.

```
int operator <=(Point p)
    { return x<=p.x && y<=p.y; }
int operator ==(Point p)
    { return x==p.x && y==p.y; }
```

The next program adds the <= and += operators. These operators behave exactly like the built-in operators, except that they now operate on **Point** objects. The <= operator returns a **1** if its first point is less than or equal to its second point. For a **Point**, <= is defined to mean that if both the **x** and **y** components of the first object are less than or equal to both the **x** and **y** components of the second object, then the first object is less than or equal to the second object. The assignment operator, +=, also gets two points. It changes the first point by adding itself to the second point. For example, if point **p1** had a value of **2,3** and point **p2** had a value of **1,1**, the statement,

```
p1 += p2;
```

would set the value of **p1** to **3,4**.

The main section of Program P6-3 contains only two statements: one to clear the screen, and another to draw a line of x's from the point **3,10** to the point **40,10**.

P6-3

```
#include <conio.h>

class Point
{
    int x, y;
public:
    Point(int u, int v) { x=u; y=v; }
    void print() { cprintf("x->%5d  y->%5d\r\n", x, y); }
    Point operator +(Point p)
        { return Point(x+p.x, y+p.y); }
    Point operator -(Point p)
        { return Point(x-p.x, y-p.y); }
    void putch(char c) { gotoxy(x, y); ::putch(c); }
    int operator <=(Point p)
        { return x<=p.x && y<=p.y; }
    int operator ==(Point p)
        { return x==p.x && y==p.y; }
    Point operator +=(Point p)
        { return Point(x+=p.x, y+=p.y); }
};

main()
{
    clrscr();
    for (Point p1(3,10); p1 <= Point(40,10); p1 += Point(1,0))
    {
        p1.putch('x');
    }
}
```

This is a good illustration of the notion that in object-oriented programming, most of the work goes into designing classes rather than specifying actions. All the effort has gone into defining the **Point** class and now all of the work for the program is carried out by a single **for** statement. Remember that in general, the process of programming with objects is, first, to create classes; then, to create instances of classes (objects); and then, to specify messages to be exchanged by objects. The first step, creating classes, is what the definition of class **Point** is all about. One permanent object is created by this program, point **p1**, which is declared inside the **for** loop. Another temporary object is created each time the test condition is evaluated at the top of the **for** loop. The expression

```
pl <= Point(40,10)
```

creates a temporary point using the constructor inside of class **Point**. Each time the comparison is tested, a temporary object is created, and as long as that object's value is greater than **pl**, the test returns true and the statement inside the **for** loop is executed again.

A second temporary **Point** object is created and added to **pl** in the update expression of the **for** statement. After each execution of the method inside the **for** loop, the loop modifier expression is evaluated.

```
pl += Point(1,0)
```

Thus, on each pass through the loop, the x value of **pl** is incremented by 1 and its y value is unchanged.

Building Methods with Turbo C++ I/O Functions

In addition to the **< =** and **+ =** operators, Program P6-3 includes a new method for class **Point**. This method is called **putch** and takes a single character as an argument. In order to do the cursor addressing and screen output, this program relies on three functions whose prototypes are defined in the CONIO.H header file. These functions are **gotoxy**, **putch**, and **clrscr**. Note, however, that the **putch** declared in this header file is different from the **putch** declared inside of class **Point**. You can always tell which function is being referred to by the context or scope. In the statement inside the **for** loop

```
pl.putch('x');
```

you know that you are invoking the **putch** defined in class **Point**. If you were invoking the global **putch** function, you would not precede the function name with an object followed by a period. There is one place, however, where this causes a problem. Inside the definition of class **Point**, how do you know if **putch** refers to the **putch** method or the **putch** global function?

Scope Resolution Operator

To avoid this sort of confusion, C++ introduces the operator **::**, known as the *scope resolution operator*. Any function or variable that is preceded by this operator, in effect, is told to use a definition that is outside the scope of the current class. There can be several levels of scope, as explained in the section on linkage in Chapter 5. For now, it is enough to know that the second **putch** in the method definition inside of class **Point**

```
void putch(char c) { gotoxy(x, y); ::putch(c); }
```

refers to the global Borland C++ function whose prototype appears in the CONIO.H header file. The first **putch** simply names a method inside class **Point**. If the second **putch** were not preceded by **::**, the **putch** method would recursively call itself over and over in an endless loop. Run Program P6-3 now and you will see that a line is drawn with x's from point **3,10** to point **40,10**. See if you can modify the program to draw a box on the screen. There is a hint: Even if the y value of point one is less than the y value of point two, the test in this program's **for** loop will fail, provided that the x value of **p1** is greater than the x value of **p2**. See if you can get the answer before moving on to the next program.

Building a Rectangle Class

To move forward toward the goal of creating a text-based window and menu system, you need to be able to draw rectangles to define windows.

Program P6-4 starts by building a rectangle class. As was said in the problem definition, a rectangle can be defined by two points: an origin and an opposing corner. Load Program P6-4 and study the definition of the **Rectangle** class.

P6-4

```
#include "point.h"

class Rectangle
{
protected:
    Point  origin, corner;
public:
    Rectangle(Point p, Point q)
        : origin(p), corner(q) { }    // ctor initializer
    void print() { origin.print(); corner.print(); }
    void draw();
};

enum Frame
{
    TopLeft=218,    Top=196,    TopRight=191,
    Left=179,                   Right=179,
    BottomLeft=192, Bottom=196, BottomRight=217
};

void Rectangle::draw()
{
    Point p = origin;

    // top
    p.putch(TopLeft);
    for (p += Point(1,0); p<corner; p+=Point(1,0))
        p.putch(Top);
    p.putch(TopRight);

    // right
    for (p+=Point(0,1); p<(corner+Point(1,0)); p+=Point(0,1))
        p.putch(Right);

    // bottom
    p.putch(BottomRight);
    for (p+=Point(-1,0); p>origin; p+=Point(-1,0))
        p.putch(Bottom);
    p.putch(BottomLeft);

    // left
    for (p+=Point(0,-1); p>(origin-Point(1,0)); p+=Point(0,-1))
        p.putch(Left);
}
```

```
main()
{
    clrscr();
    Rectangle r1(Point(5,2), Point(40,12));
    r1.draw();
    gotoxy(1,15);
    r1.print();
}
```

This program defines a class, **Rectangle**, with two data members and three public member functions, one of them a constructor. Since there is only one constructor in this class, a rectangle must be declared with two point arguments.

```
Rectangle(Point p, Point q)
    : origin(p), corner(q) { }    // ctor initializer
```

The second line of this constructor shows an alternate form of initializing member data elements. When a constructor argument list is followed by a **:**, the expressions between the **:** and the function body indicate initializations that should take place before the code in the function body is executed. This form of initialization is called a *constructor initializer*. The **Rectangle** class also provides a method for printing out the values of its two data members. It is always handy for a class to provide such a method in order to inspect the contents of objects and help in debugging. The last method is called **draw**. Only the prototype declaration for **draw** is included inside class **Rectangle**. The actual definition for the method appears outside the class and begins with the line

```
void Rectangle::draw()
```

This syntax indicates a function with no return value. The function's name is **draw** and it is a member of the class **Rectangle**. The general notation for defining methods outside of a class declaration is

ReturnType ClassName::MethodName( ) { }

The **draw** method actually draws a frame on a screen. It uses a single point, which is set equal to the origin. The point traces along the top, down the right, back leftward across the bottom, and then upward along the left side of the rectangle, printing the appropriate characters as it goes. There are eight different characters used to draw the frame. They are defined in the enumerated type declaration, **Frame**.

```
enum Frame
{
    TopLeft=218,    Top=196,    TopRight=191,
    Left=179,                   Right=179,
    BottomLeft=192, Bottom=196, BottomRight=217
}
```

The enumerated type declaration gives symbolic names like **TopLeft** and **BottomRight** for the IBM graphics characters used to draw the rectangle. Drawing each of the four lines of the frame is handled by **for** loops similar to the one introduced in Program P6-3. Instead of using the **Point::putch** method to put x's on the screen, you use the method to put the characters represented by **Top**, **Left**, **Right**, and **Bottom**. The only additional things to be handled are the corners, so the technique for drawing the top and bottom lines is modified. To draw the top line, print the **TopLeft** character followed by a line composed of the **Top** character followed by the **TopRight** character. The bottom line is drawn from right to left using the **BottomRight**, **Bottom**, and **BottomLeft** characters.

Run the program now and you will see that a frame is drawn around a rectangle whose origin is at point **5,2** and whose opposing corner is at point **40,12**. The definition for the **Point** class used by **Rectangle** has been expanded to include a full set of operators. Notice that **Rectangle::draw** uses two point operators not previously defined, < and >. The declaration for the **Point** class is now in a separate header file called POINT.H. Now, anytime you want to make use of the **Point** class you can include the code with the following directive at the top of your program:

```
#include "point.h"
```

Again, notice that most of the work for this program went into defining the **Rectangle** class. Using the class is easy. Simply declare a **Rectangle** object, **r1**, with two initial point values, and then invoke the **draw** method for the object with the statement

```
r1.draw();
```

Finally, call the **print** method for **r1** just to make sure that it contains the proper point values.

Designing Classes to be Reused

The beauty of going to all the trouble to define classes like **Point** and **Rectangle** is that the classes can be used over and over again to draw rectangle frames and print characters at point positions on the screen. In fact, that is exactly what happens in Program P6-5. Load Program P6-5 now.

P6-5

```
#include "point.h"

class Rectangle
{
protected:
    Point  origin, corner;
public:
    Rectangle(Point p, Point q)
        : origin(p), corner(q) { }    // ctor initializer
    void print() { origin.print(); corner.print(); }
    void draw();
};

enum Frame
{
    TopLeft=218,    Top=196,    TopRight=191,
    Left=179,                   Right=179,
    BottomLeft=192, Bottom=196, BottomRight=217
};

void Rectangle::draw()
{
    Point p = origin;

    // top
    p.putch(TopLeft);
    for (p+=Point(1,0); p<corner; p+=Point(1,0))
        p.putch(Top);
    p.putch(TopRight);

    // right
    for (p+=Point(0,1); p<(corner+Point(1,0)); p+=Point(0,1))
        p.putch(Right);

    // bottom
    p.putch(BottomRight);
```

```
    for (p+=Point(-1,0); p>origin; p+=Point(-1,0))
        p.putch(Bottom);
    p.putch(BottomLeft);

    // left
    for (p+=Point(0,-1); p>(origin-Point(1,0)); p+=Point(0,-1))
        p.putch(Left);
}

class Window : public Rectangle
{
public:
    Window(Point p, Point q)  : Rectangle(p, q) { }
};

main()
{
    clrscr();
    Rectangle r1(Point(5,2), Point(40,12));
    r1.draw();
    gotoxy(1,15);
    r1.print();
    Window w1(Point(6,3), Point(41,13));
    w1.draw();
    gotoxy(1,18);
    w1.print();
}
```

This program makes a single modification to the **Rectangle** class. Notice the word **protected** that precedes the data elements **origin** and **corner**. By default, class elements are **private**; that is, they are accessible only to other members of the class. It is as though the keyword **private** appeared right after the opening brace of the class declaration.

```
class Rectangle
{
private:
   //...
public:
   //...
};
```

Building a Window Class

All member elements declared between the keywords **private** and **public** are accessible only to other members of the class. Any members that are to be accessed from outside the class must be declared after the **public** keyword. The keyword **protected** is similar to the keyword **private** and is introduced mainly to deal with the concept of derived classes. Any classes derived from class **Rectangle** will have access to the protected members of class **Rectangle**, but not to the private members of class **Rectangle**. Program P6-5 creates a new class, **Window**, which is derived from class **Rectangle**. One of **Window**'s methods needs to access the origin and corner variables of a **Rectangle** object. These variables are therefore declared **protected** in the class declaration for **Rectangle**. All members following the word **protected** are considered **private** inside classes derived from the **Rectangle** class.

Derived Classes

Normally, you would derive one class from another if the original class had most of the operations required to solve your problem, but needed to be specialized for a particular application. This would be the case if you bought an object library from a third party. You would probably be provided with the interface specification, but not the source code for the library. The interface specification would be a header file with a declaration for all public classes and methods in the library. Program P6-5 derives a new class, **Window**, from the existing **Rectangle** class. The class from which a new class is derived is called the base class. The declaration for the **Window** class is similar to other class declarations you have seen—namely, **Point** and **Rectangle**. The difference is that the declaration is modified by an inheritance specification.

```
class Window : public Rectangle
```

The colon after the declaration of class **Window** indicates that the class is inherited from another class, in this case **Rectangle**. Normally, when a derived class inherits methods from a base class, public members of the base class become private members of the derived class. Also, private members of the base class are not accessible to the derived class. These restrictions can be avoided by preceding the name of the base class with the keyword **public**. If **public** precedes the name of the base class, as in the previous declaration, then public members of the base class become public members of the derived class, and protected members of the base class become private members of the derived class. This is probably the method of inheritance you will use most often.

The new **Window** class in Program P6-5 adds no new methods to the **Rectangle** class from which it is derived. The purpose of the program is to show that a derived class behaves exactly like its base class. Run the program now.

Two rectangles are drawn on the screen, but if you examine the code in **main**, you will see that one rectangle is declared as a **Rectangle**, and the other is declared as a **Window**. All the methods available to **Rectangle** are available to **Window**. This means that a **Window** object can call a **print** method or a **draw** method without needing to define either one.

Note that the code used to invoke the **draw** method for a **Window** object is identical to the code to invoke the **draw** method for a **Rectangle** object. Only the object declarations are different. The next step is to add methods to **Window** objects to distinguish them from **Rectangles**.

You may have noticed that a constructor was specified for the **Window** class. Unlike other class members, constructors are not inherited by derived classes. Even if the constructor for the new class performs exactly the same function as the constructor for its base class, it must still be defined. For now, **Window**'s constructor duplicates the constructor of **Rectangle** and uses a constructor initializer to call **Rectangle**'s constructor. Eventually **Window**'s constructor will be modified to perform more elaborate initializations than are required for a **Rectangle**.

Adding Methods to Derived Classes

Program P6-6 extends the functionality of the **Window** class. Three new methods are added to the **Window** class in preparation for handling text output. When you are designing a class, you need to think about what actions will be carried out on an object created from the class. Think about what you would want to do with a window. Besides defining a window, which is handled by the constructor, you would want to open it, select it (in the case where you have more than one window open on the screen), and send text to be output in the window. It is also useful to have a print method that prints the values of the window's coordinates for debugging purposes. Thus, Program P6-6 adds three methods: **open**, **select**, and **print**. In addition, a < < **friend** operator is defined for the **Window** class in order to send text strings to the window to be printed.

P6-6

```
#include <conio.h>
#include "point.h"

class Rectangle
{
protected:
    Point  origin, corner;
public:
    Rectangle(Point p, Point q)
        : origin(p), corner(q) { }    // ctor initializer
    void print() { origin.print(); corner.print(); }
    void draw();
};

enum Frame
{
    TopLeft=218,     Top=196,     TopRight=191,
    Left=179,                     Right=179,
    BottomLeft=192, Bottom=196, BottomRight=217
};

void Rectangle::draw()
{
    Point p = origin;

    // top
    p.putch(TopLeft);
    for (p+= Point(1,0); p<corner; p+=Point(1,0))
        p.putch(Top);
    p.putch(TopRight);

    // right
    for (p+=Point(0,1); p<(corner+Point(1,0)); p+=Point(0,1))
        p.putch(Right);

    // bottom
    p.putch(BottomRight);
    for (p+=Point(-1,0); p>origin; p+=Point(-1,0))
        p.putch(Bottom);
    p.putch(BottomLeft);

    // left
    for (p+=Point(0,-1); p>(origin-Point(1,0)); p+=Point(0,-1))
        p.putch(Left);
}
```

```
void fullScreen()
{
    window(1,1,80,25);
}

class Window : public Rectangle
{
public:
    Window(Point p, Point q)  : Rectangle(p, q) { }
    void select()
    {
        window(origin.getx()+1, origin.gety()+1,
               corner.getx()-1, corner.gety()-1);
    }
    void open ()
    {
        select();
        clrscr();
        fullScreen(); draw();
        select();
    }
    void close ();
    void print ()
    {
        cprintf("%5d %5d %5d %5d ",
                origin.getx(), origin.gety(),
                corner.getx(), corner.gety());
    }
    friend Window& operator <<(Window& w, char *s);
};

Window& operator <<(Window& w, char *s)
{
    cputs(s); return w;
}

main()
{
  clrscr();
  Rectangle rl(Point(5,2), Point(40,12));
  rl.draw();
  gotoxy(1,15);
  rl.print();

  Window wl(Point(6,3), Point(41,13));
  wl.open();
  fullScreen();
  gotoxy(1,18);
  wl.print();
  wl.select();
  for (int i=0; i<100; i++)
    wl << "--Testing--";
```

```
  wl << " Here is" << " the last line\n";
  fullScreen();
  gotoxy(1,24);
}
```

Program P6-6 makes use of Borland C++'s built-in **window** function. This function is defined in the CONIO.H header file. It takes four arguments, corresponding to the left, top, right, and bottom coordinates for defining a window. After a call to this **window** function, text output is restricted to the area defined by these coordinates. Two methods had to be added to the **Point** class in order to interface with this built-in function. You need to be able to extract the **x** and **y** values of a point in order to pass the proper arguments to the built-in **window** function.

Mixing C and C++

It might seem odd to go to the trouble of defining a **Point** object and then having to pull out individual components in order to call functions like **window**. But this is typical of the real-world problems you will encounter when you are using C++. The **window** function was written before the **Point** class was designed. Things would be smoother if **window** accepted two **Point** variables rather than four integer variables. There are ways to do this. One way is to build a class around the console I/O functions already available in Turbo C++. In a way, that is what you are doing with the **Window** class. Another way is to overload the **window** function so that it can accept either **Points** or integers as arguments. For quick solutions it is often most convenient to provide class methods that break up complex structures into the more basic elements required by older code with which the class must interface.

Overloading << for Window Objects

The << operator takes two arguments. The first is a window and the second is a string. The string is output to the screen using Borland C++'s built-in **cputs** function, whose prototype is defined in CONIO.H. The << operator returns a reference to a window object, making it possible to send a series of strings to a window with a sequence of << operators, as illustrated here,

```
wl << sl << s2 << s3;
```

where **wl** is a window and **sl**, **s2,** and **s3** are strings. This statement prints three strings inside window **wl**.

Run Program P6-6 now. First, a rectangle is drawn and its coordinates are printed. Then, a window is opened. Its coordinates are printed and a test string is sent to the window 100 times, causing it to scroll. Finally, to test that the << operator will handle multiple strings in a single expression, the line

```
wl <<  " Here is" << " the last line\n";
```

is executed to print the last line in the window. This behaves exactly like output to the standard C++ output device, **cout**, using notation such as

```
cout << "Hello, " << "world\n";
```

Window-Relative Cursor Positioning

Once you have opened a window, all cursor positioning with the **gotoxy** function is relative to the active window. If you want to make cursor positioning relative to the entire screen, you must make a call to the **fullScreen** function, which is defined in the program as

```
void fullScreen()
{
    window(1,1,80,25);
}
```

A List Class for Menu Choices

Now that you can print text to windows, you might get ambitious and try to develop your own little program environment controlled by pop-up menus. Building on the **Window** class will make implementing pop-up menus easy. Think of a menu as an object and think about what you want to do to a menu. A menu is a list of choices. Normally, you will add choices to the list, display the list of choices, and get a choice selection from the user. Before you can attack the menu itself, you really need a list object to build the list of choices and to move through the list, always keeping track of the currently highlighted choice, as shown in Program P6-7.

P6-7

```
#include <string.h>
#include "window.h"

class Choice
{
public:
    char *str;
    Choice *next;
    Choice *prev;
    Choice(char *s)
        { str=new char[strlen(s)+1]; strcpy(str,s); }
    ~Choice() { delete str; }
    void print() { cputs(str); }
};

class List
{
    Choice *h;
public:
    List() { h=0; }
    void add(char *s);
    void print();
    Choice* first()  { return h; }
};

void List::add(char *s)
{
    Choice *temp = new Choice(s);
    if (h)                          // List not empty
    {
        temp->next      = h;
        temp->prev      = h->prev;
        h->prev->next   = temp;
        h->prev         = temp;
```

```
    }
    else
    {
        temp->prev      = temp;
        temp->next      = temp;
        h               = temp;
    }
}

void List::print()
{
    if (h==0) return;
    h->print();
    cputs("\r\n");
    for (Choice *i = h->next; i != h; i = i->next)
    {
        i->print();
        cputs("\r\n");
    }
}

main()
{
    clrscr();
    Window w1(Point(5,2), Point(40,12));
    w1.open();
    for (int i=0; i<100; i++)
        w1 << "--Window 1--";
    getch();

    highlightOn();
    Window w2(Point(6,3), Point(41,13));
    w2.open();
    for (i=0; i<100; i++)
        w2 << "--Window 2--";
    highlightOff();
    getch();

    fullScreen();
    gotoxy(1,15);
    List l;
    l.add("Compile");
    l.add("Link");
    l.add("Run");
    l.print();
    gotoxy(1,24);
}
```

Program P6-7 implements a list class. Three methods are available to this list class: **add**, **print**, and **first**. The **add** method adds a string onto the list of choices and maintains connections between the new item, the previous element on the list, and the top or head of the list. The **print** method prints out the entire list, one choice per line; and the **first** method returns a pointer to the first element in the list.

The concept of a list automatically implies two types of objects. One is the list itself, which is a series of nodes pointing to some object; the other is the element pointed to by each list node. The class **Choice** represents the objects that will be pointed to by list nodes. All members of the **Choice** class are **public**. **Choice** contains three data members and three methods. The first data member is a pointer to a string. No space is automatically set aside for this string, but when an object of class **Choice** is created, the constructor for the class calls C++'s **new** operator and sets aside enough storage space to contain the string that is passed as an argument to the constructor. The string pointer, which is a member of the **Choice** object, is then set to point to the new string. The second method in **Choice** is a *destructor*. You can tell this because it has the same name as the class, but is preceded by a ~. The destructor method is executed automatically when the object variable goes out of scope. In order to maintain linkages between previous and successive choices in the menu list, the **Choice** class has two data members, **prev** and **next**. Both are pointers to a **Choice** object. This structure is called a *doubly linked list*. You can set up a list structure so that the pointers are declared in either the elements themselves or in the list nodes. Program P6-7 maintains the pointers in the elements to make the implementation easier to follow.

The **List** class has only one data member. This member is a pointer to a **Choice** object and will always point to the head of the menu list—that is, the first choice in the menu. Further, the structure defined for this particular list is set up so that the **prev** pointer of the first element in the list points to the last element in the list. The next pointer of the last element in the list points to the first element in the list. Thus, the basic structure of a list composed of three elements appears as shown in Figure 6-1.

The wraparound pointers at the beginning and end of the list make sure that when you move a selection past the last menu choice, you will wind up at the first menu choice and vice versa. These pointers are updated and maintained automatically by the **List::add** method each time you add a new choice to the list.

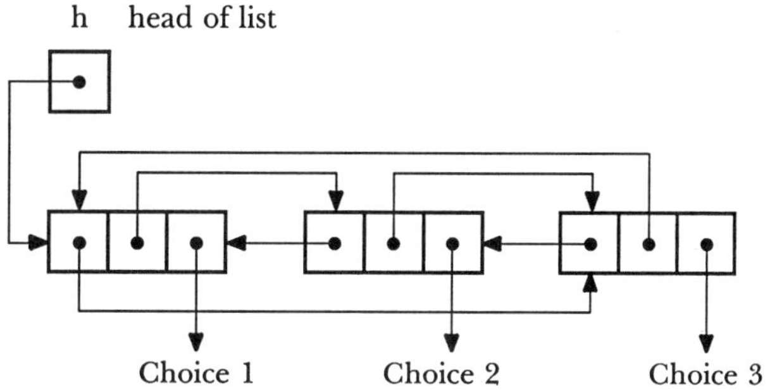

Figure 6-1. *List of three menu choices*

Utility Functions: Highlighting Text and Reading Arrow-Key Input

Several utility functions are required for menus: turning on and off highlighting for printed text and reading input from the keyboard for cursor-control keys—specifically, the UP ARROW and the DOWN ARROW keys on the cursor keypad in the case of menus. These are all included in UTIL.H. UTIL.H in turn is included in WINDOW.H. The declarations for all rectangle and window functions previously defined in this chapter are now included in WINDOW.H. It is now necessary for you to link to WINDOW.CPP. Open a project (ALT-P O). Enter the project name, P6-7 and press RETURN. Press INS and add the files P6-7.CPP and WINDOW.CPP to the project. Press ESC.

You can see when you examine the code for **main** that most of the work is done by the objects themselves. Run Program P6-7 now. You will see one window open and a text string printed to that window 100 times, causing the window to scroll. The program then waits for you to press a key.

The **highlightOn** utility function causes all output to the screen to be in inverse video until the **highlightOff** function is called. As soon as you press a key, highlighting is turned on, window **w2** is defined and opened, and 100 test strings are printed to this window—all output in inverse video.

Building a List

The program now waits for you to press another key. When you do so, output is set to full screen, the cursor is positioned to column 1, line 15, and List l is declared. At this point, only a pointer to the head of the list exists. After the line

```
l.add("Compile");
```

is executed, you have a list of one element. Next, two more choices are added to the list. The **print** method for the list class is invoked, and you can see the contents of the list on the screen. The cursor is repositioned to the bottom of the screen, and the program terminates. You can now see that if you combine the functionality of windows and the list class for menu choices, you are well on your way to implementing a small pop-up menu system.

A Menu Class

Finally, the **Menu** class is defined. The declaration for **Menu** class is found in the header file, MENU.H. Load that file now and look at the declaration for **Menu**.

```
class Menu
{
    List ll;
    int nentries;
    int width;
    Point org;
    Choice *ip;
    int current;
public:
    Menu(Point p) { org=p; nentries=width=current=0; }
    void add(char *s);
    void print();
    int getChoice();
};
```

A **Menu** object contains a **List** object as a **private** member. Other private members of the **Menu** class keep track of the number of entries; the width of the longest string in the list of choices; a point corresponding to the upper-left corner of the menu; a pointer to a **Choice** element, which is the currently highlighted menu selection; and **current**, which corresponds to the number of the currently highlighted menu selection. The value of **current** is returned by a menu object when the RETURN key is pressed. None of these data elements is available outside of the class.

Menu's Public Interface

There are only four public members of **Menu**. One of them is the constructor. The constructor is passed the value of a point when a menu object is declared. That point is assigned to the private data member that keeps track of the menu's origin. The constructor also sets the number of entries, the menu width, and the current choice to 0. The first choice in the menu is considered element 0. Besides declaring a menu object, the public methods in **Menu** let you add a character string as a menu choice, print a menu list, and get a menu choice selection from user input. The actual definitions for these three methods are found in MENU.CPP. The methods for **List::add** and **List::print** are also found in this file. This means that Program P6-8 (shown later) is composed of three source modules: P6-8.CPP, WINDOW.CPP, and MENU.CPP. Create a new project with these names in the project list in order to compile this program.

Adding Menu Choices Open the file MENU.CPP to look at the three new methods for **Menu**. **Menu::add** is straightforward:

```
void Menu::add(char *s)
{
    ll.add(s);
    width = max(width, strlen(s));
    nentries++;
}
```

This method adds a string to the list, **ll**, declared as a private member of the **Menu** class. It then checks to see if this is the widest string added so far. If so, it sets the width equal to the length of this string. The number of menu entries is then incremented.

Printing Menu Choices **Menu::print** prints each choice in a menu list. The currently selected choice is printed in inverse video.

```
void Menu::print()
{
    Choice *ip = ll.first();
    for (int i=0; i<nentries; i++, ip=ip->next)
    {
        gotoxy(1, i+1);
        if (i==current)
            highlightOn();
        ip->print();
        highlightOff();
    }
}
```

The method starts off by declaring a pointer to a choice, **ip**, and setting that variable to point to the first element of the list. The method then loops for each element of the list and uses the next pointer of each element to walk down the list until each element has been printed. Each element is printed by invoking the **print** method from the **Choice** class with the statement

```
ip->print();
```

Before each element is printed, the method tests to see if the element it is about to print is the currently selected **Menu** choice. If so, it turns highlighting on. After each element is printed, highlighting is always turned off.

Getting Menu Input The last thing that you need to complete the **Menu** system is a method for getting input from the user. This is all handled by **Menu::getChoice**.

```
int Menu::getChoice()
{
    Window w(org, org+Point(width+2,nentries+1));
    w.open();
    print();
```

```
    while(1)
    {
        switch(getkey())
        {
            case ESC : return -1;
            case CR  : return current;
            case DNARROW :
                if (++current>=nentries)
                    current=0;
                print();
                break;
            case UPARROW :
                if (--current<0)
                    current = nentries-1;
                print();
                break;
        }
    }
}
```

This method declares a temporary window, which is calculated from the origin specified in the constructor, the width of the widest **Menu** string, and the number of entries in the **Menu**. The window is opened, the **Menu** is printed, and program execution enters a **while** loop that is exited only if the ESC or RETURN key is pressed. If the ESC key is pressed, the value **-1** is returned. If RETURN is pressed, the value of the currently highlighted choice is returned. The first entry is choice 0. This is all accomplished within a **switch** statement. The **switch** statement calls the **getkey** utility function defined in UTIL.H. Both this function and the symbolic names for special IBM PC keys are defined in this header file. The only symbolic names of concern here are ESC, RETURN , DOWN ARROW, and UP ARROW.

Most of the processing in **Menu::getChoice** is done when one of the two arrow keys is pressed. The actions carried out for both keys are almost identical. If the DOWN ARROW key is pressed, the value of the variable **current**, which keeps track of the currently selected choice, is incremented. The resulting value is tested to see if it is greater than or equal to the number of entries in the menu list. If it is, **current** is set to the first element of the list. This is what happens if the currently highlighted choice is the last one in the menu and you press the DOWN ARROW key. If the UP ARROW key is pressed, **current** is decremented and the resulting value is tested to see if it is less than 0. This is what happens if you press the UP ARROW key when the first element of the list is highlighted. If this is the case, the current selection wraps around to the end of the list by setting **current** equal to **nentries - 1**. The menu list is then printed.

Now the **main** function for Program P6-8 can be defined. Load and run the program now.

P6-8

```
#include <conio.h>
#include "window.h"
#include "menu.h"

main()
{

    clrscr();
    Window w1(Point(4,2), Point(40,10));
    w1.open();
    w1.test("---Window 1---");
    getch();

    Window w2(Point(6,4), Point(42,12));
    highlightOn();
    w2.open();
    w2.test("---Testing Window 2---");
    highlightOff();
    getch();

    Window w3(Point(8,6), Point(44,14));
    Window w4(Point(44,8), Point(78,16));
    w3.open();
    w3 << "Window 3";
    highlightOn();
    w4.open();
    w4 << "Window 4";
    highlightOff();

    fullScreen();
    //-----build menu
    Menu m1(Point(40,15));
    m1.add("Test Window 1");
    m1.add("Test Window 2");
    m1.add("Test Window 3");
    m1.add("Test Window 4");
    m1.add("Quit");
    int done = 0;
    while(!done)
    {
        switch(m1.getChoice())
        {
            case 0 : w1.test("---Window 1 Selected---"); break;
            case 1 : highlightOn();
```

```
                    w2.test("---Window 2 Selected---");
                    highlightOff();
                    break;
          case 2 : w3.test("---Window 3 Selected---"); break;
          case 3 : highlightOn();
                     w4.test("---Window 4 Selected---");
                     highlightOff();
                     break;
          case -1:
          case 4 : done = 1; break;
      }
   }
   fullScreen();
   gotoxy(1,24);
}
```

The program declares and opens four windows: **w1**, **w2**, **w3**, and **w4**. The first two windows pause for a keypress after printing out 100 test strings. One of the methods that was added to the **Window** class is called **test**. This method takes one string as an argument and prints the screen 100 times in the object **Window**. Thus, the code

```
w1.test("---Window 1---");
```

will print the string "---Window 1---" 100 times inside window **w1**. This automates testing. Windows **w2** and **w4** handle all output in inverse video. That means that highlighting must be turned on before the window is opened and before any text is printed to the window. Highlighting should also be turned off before text is sent to a normal window.

Setting Up a Menu

After the first two windows are open, windows 3 and 4 are opened with simple identifier strings printed inside the windows. Output is then set to full screen so that the menu is positioned relative to the entire screen rather than relative to the active window. Now, the menu is declared with the upper-left corner at point **40,15**. Five menu choices are then added. The entire menu setup is accomplished with the following code:

```
Menu m1(Point(40,15));
m1.add("Test Window 1");
m1.add("Test Window 2");
m1.add("Test Window 3");
m1.add("Test Window 4");
m1.add("Quit");
```

Now, program execution enters a **while** loop controlled by the variable **done**. As long as **done** is set to 0, the loop will be executed over and over. Menu selection is activated by the call

```
m1.getChoice()
```

inside the **switch** statement. The method will return a value between **−1** and **4**. A **−1** is returned if ESC is pressed. Otherwise, a value associated with the currently highlighted choice is returned. The value **4** corresponds to the menu entry "Quit." Selecting "Quit" or pressing ESC sets the loop variable **done** to 1 and program execution terminates. The values **0** through **3** correspond to windows **w1** through **w4**. If any of these choices is selected, the test method for these windows is invoked with the string that uniquely identifies the window. In the case of ESC or "Quit," output is set to full screen and the cursor is positioned at the bottom of the screen before exiting. You must set full-screen output after invoking a menu; otherwise, cursor operations will be relative to the menu window. See Figure 6-2.

Summary

Programming with objects centers more on design of classes than on specification of actions. When building systems, think in terms of the language used to talk about the problem. Object names will emerge: points, lines, rectangles, windows, menus, complex numbers. From object names, build class declarations. First add attributes (member data) for information which objects must remember. Next add methods (member functions) for communicating with objects. Method names and definitions evolve as you think about what you want to do with geometric shapes, menus, and complex numbers: **line.draw**, **menu.getChoice**, c3 = c2 + c1.

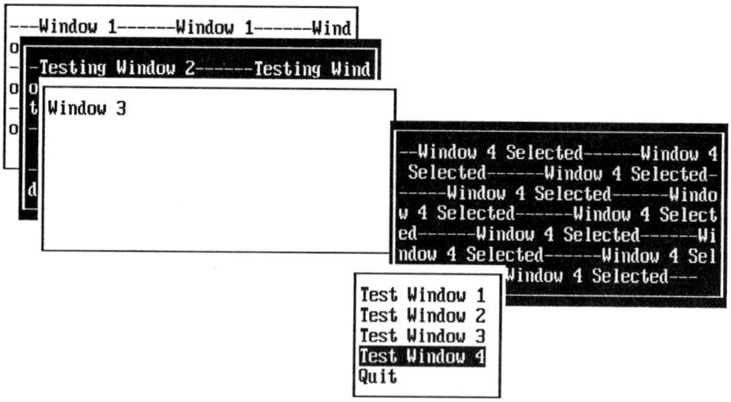

Figure 6-2. *Simple menu and window output*

It pays to familiarize yourself with classes provided by others. It's easier to modify an existing class than to develop one from scratch. Reusing **Point**, **Rectangle**, **Window**, and **Menu** will reinforce the idea of extending third party class libraries for your own designs. Take advantage of the design, development, and testing others have done. Once you have classes, the solution follows naturally. Create objects (instances of classes). Next, arrange messages to be passed among the objects. OOP makes management of complex problems possible, and even enjoyable. Before continuing, close the project and clear the desktop.

7 Lists, Iterators, and Control Abstraction

This chapter discusses lists and control abstraction. *Control abstraction* is the process of developing functions and objects that will determine the order of execution of a given set of code. Conditional execution and repetition are examples of control abstraction. Both the **for** loop and the **while** loop are control abstractions. Most languages offer these simple forms of control abstractions. Loops are useful for processing the elements of an array such as strings, which are arrays of characters. For an array of integers, you might use a **for** loop to find the maximum value.

Control Abstraction

When data structures become more complex, however, additional computations must be made inside a **for** loop in order to process each member of a collection, such as a list. An array is a collection just as a list is a collection. A collection refers to any group of items that are associated with one another. A collection is usually defined by properties. For example, a sorted binary tree is a collection that implies certain ordering. A sorted array of integers is also a collection that ensures an ordering of its components.

The distinguishing property of a list is that each element in the list knows how to find the next element. Lists can be singly linked, in which case you can only move in one direction through the list, or they can be doubly linked, in which case you can move in either direction. Lists can be either *circular* or *terminal.* When you come to the end of a circular list, the last element points back to the first element in the list. This was the case with the menu program in Chapter 6. Terminal lists, on the other hand, have values in the first and last elements of the list, indicating that there are no more elements beyond the terminal. A typical way of handling this is to assign the next pointer to zero for the last element of a list, and to assign the previous pointer to zero for the first element of a list.

This chapter develops a control abstraction called an iterator. An *iterator* is used to walk through each element of a collection. It is associated with the collection class on which it will operate—in this case an instance of the **List** class. Developing an iterator for the **List** class will bring up a number of useful features in C++, including function overloading, operator overloading, multiple constructors, and default arguments for functions.

Iterators must have intimate knowledge about the structure of the lists on which they operate. The **List** class for this chapter will be a doubly linked list with terminals at either end. This means that it is not circular like the **List** class of the previous chapter. The iterator has to know how the elements of a list are linked to one another, and it must know what condition to look for when it arrives at the end of the list. The elements of the **List** class in this chapter will be **Choice** objects similar to those developed in the last chapter. Iterators do not need to know how the **Choice** class is implemented. You know that the **Choice** class contains a private member, which is a string. You used **Choice** in the last chapter to print a menu that was constructed from a list of choices. You used a loop to update a pointer to the current element of the list, which was associated with a highlighted menu choice. Unlike the iterator that you are going to develop in this chapter, you had to explicitly manage the current pointer inside the menu list each time the user pressed a valid key.

Control abstractions such as iterators eliminate the need for this explicit management of object data members, which should probably be private. You use an iterator by declaring it and setting it to the first element of the list. The iterator is an object containing a pointer to a list element as well as a member function, which is an overloaded operator that changes the value of that pointer. Each time the iterator's operator is called, the iterator remembers the **Choice** object that it is currently pointing to and advances to the next **Choice** object in the list. The iterator then returns a pointer to the remembered **Choice** object. This means that each time you call the iterator, it will return the value of a new **Choice** object, which you can then process. The iterator keeps doing this until it walks off the end of the list, in which case it returns a 0. Thus, you can use an iterator for a choice list as follows:

```
Iter itl = lst;      // create iterator
                     // and set to beginning of list
//...

Choice *cl;          // pointer to retrieve next Choice
while ( (cl = ++itl) != 0 )  // while more elements
{
    // process cl
}
```

Since an iterator needs to have knowledge of how a list is constructed, changing the structure of the list will usually force you to build a new iterator. Iterators and the collections they process go hand in hand. But the main advantage of an iterator is that it does not need to know about the implementation of the elements of a collection. This will be shown by changing the structure of the **Choice** object and seeing what impact it has on the iterator itself.

Hiding Implementation Details

Start off by loading Program P7-1. Remember to log to the directory for this chapter (\DT\CH7) before invoking the Borland C++ development environment. Look at the implementation of the **Choice** class. It has been modified slightly since Chapter 6. The **Choice** object in Chapter 6 had all public members. That made it possible to change the value of the string that represented a menu choice. But this is probably not what you would want in a menu class. Object-oriented programming advocates hiding as much detail as possible. Program P7-1 shows how you can hide the implementation details of a **Choice** object from the users of the **Choice** class.

P7-1

```
#include <string.h>
#include <iostream.h>

class Choice
{
private:
    char *str;
public:
    Choice *next;
    Choice *prev;
    Choice(const char *s)
        { str=new char[strlen(s)+1]; strcpy(str, s); }
    ~Choice() { delete str; }
    const char *getStr() { return str; }
};

class List
{
private:
    Choice *tail;
public:
    List () { tail=0; }
    void add(const char *s);
    Choice *getTail() { return tail; }
};

void List::add(const char *s)
{
    Choice *temp = new Choice(s);
    temp->next = tail;
    temp->prev = 0;
    if (tail) tail->prev = temp;
    tail = temp;
}

class Iter
{
private:
    Choice *current;
public:
    Iter(List l) { current = l.getTail(); }
    Choice *operator++();
};
```

```
Choice *Iter::operator++()
{
    if (current)
    {
        Choice *temp = current;
        current = current->prev;
        return temp;
    }
    else
        return 0;
}

main()
{
    // Create a list
    List lst;
    lst.add("one");
    Iter itl = lst;
    lst.add("two");
    lst.add("three");

    // Print the list
    Choice *cl;
    while ( (cl = ++itl) != 0 )
        cout << cl->getStr() << "\n";
}
```

The declaration

```
char *str;
```

appears in the private section of the **Choice** class. This is a choice on the part of the designers, indicating that users of this class do not need to know that **Choice** is implemented as a pointer to a **char**. The only things that users of the class need to know about are specified in the public interface. These include two pointers, **next** and **prev**, which will point to the next and previous elements in a list. A constructor, which gets a string as an argument, is also provided in the public interface to create a **Choice** object. A destructor clears the memory used by an object when it is time to discard it. The **print** function, formerly in the **Choice** class, has been replaced by an access member function, **getStr**, which returns a pointer to a string.

The main things you need to worry about when using a **Choice** object are how to create one, and how to get the information you need from it. The public interface section tells you that you create a **Choice** object from a string and that you can get the value of that string by calling

getStr. If you read the interface carefully, you can tell that the designers do not want you to change the value of the string inside a **Choice** object. You know this because the string is private and the member access function, **getStr**, returns a pointer to a constant. If **const** were not indicated, you could change the value of the string pointed to, and this would corrupt the internal value of **str**. If you were to try to replace the original string with a longer string, you would write to memory beyond that allocated for the original string and very likely cause the system to crash. The **const** declaration foresees this potential bug and prevents it from happening.

A Noncircular List Class

Let's look at the implementation of **List**. The list used for the menu program in Chapter 6 was implemented as a pointer to the head of the list. This **List** class instead keeps a pointer to the tail of the list. This is really a trick. Actually, **tail** points to the head of a list, but when a member is added to the list, it is put onto the front of the list instead of the end. This is the opposite behavior of the **List** class in Chapter 6. Since you are going to be using this **List** class to implement another menu class, you will want to process the members in the same order in which they are added to the list. But **tail** always points to the most recently added member. To get around this you can save a pointer to the first element of the list when it is created and set the iterator to point to that element before it begins processing the list. Thus, the pointer here is called **tail** simply to remind you that it points to the end and not the beginning of the list.

The public interface to **List** tells you that a list is created from a constructor that accepts no arguments. You can add a new element to the list. This element is a string and you can find the last element of the list by calling the member access function, **getTail**.

Adding a Member to the List

Adding an element to a list is straightforward. Look at the **List::add** function. It gets a pointer to a **char** as an argument. The first thing that happens is that a new **Choice** object called **temp** is created from this string. There are two conditions under which you can add an element to a list. In the first case the list is empty, so the value of **tail** is 0, meaning that it points to nothing. Figure 7-1 reflects this condition. The other case is when the list has one or more elements, as shown in Figure 7-2. The four lines of code that follow the creation of the new **Choice** object handle both situations. Notice that when the constructor is called for the **List** class, **tail** is immediately set to 0. This ensures that the structure of a list is always defined. The following four statements handle the addition of a new element, regardless of whether or not the list is empty.

```
temp->next = tail;
temp->prev = 0;
if (tail) tail->prev = temp;
tail = temp;
```

The first statement sets the **next** pointer of the newly created object to point to whatever **tail** is pointing to. If the list is empty, this value will be 0, meaning that there is no **next** object in the list. The second statement sets the previous pointer for the new object to 0. There is never an object that comes before the end of a list. Finally, if **tail** is not equal to 0—that is, if you are adding an element to a non-empty list—the previous field of the member element pointed to by **tail** is set to point to the newly created object. In other words, the element that was formerly the last member of the list is set to point to the newly created object. Finally, the **tail** pointer of the list is set to point to the newly created **Choice** object. From this definition, you know that the next field of the first element in the list always points to 0. You also know that the previous field of the last element of the list always points to 0. Remember, the semantics are a little tricky here, because **tail** really points to the head of the list. But when you actually use this class, the word **tail** will make more sense.

Building an Iterator

The declaration for the iterator class is pretty simple. The name of the class is **Iter**. It has one private member, which is a pointer to a **Choice**

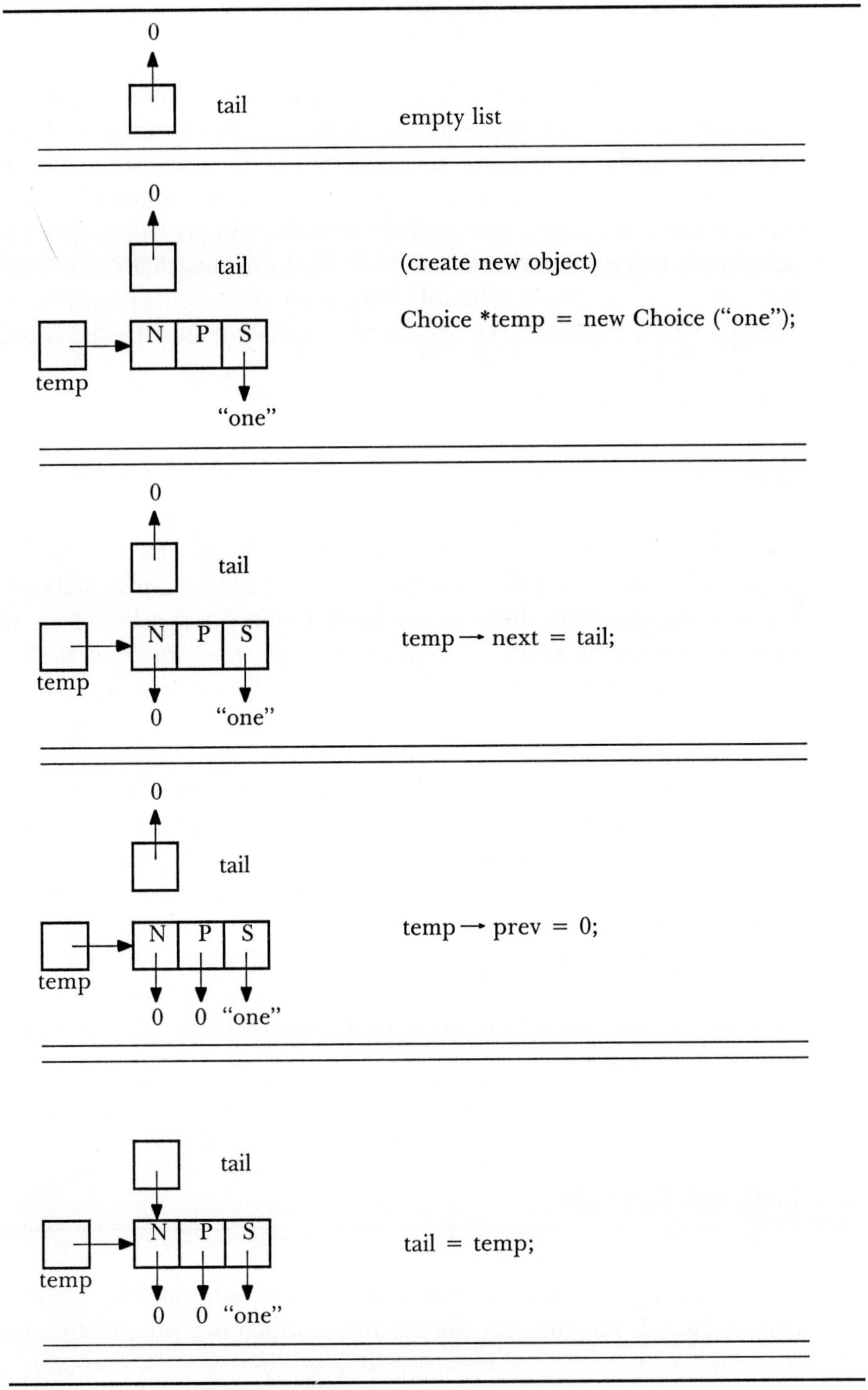

Figure 7-1. *Adding an element to an empty list*

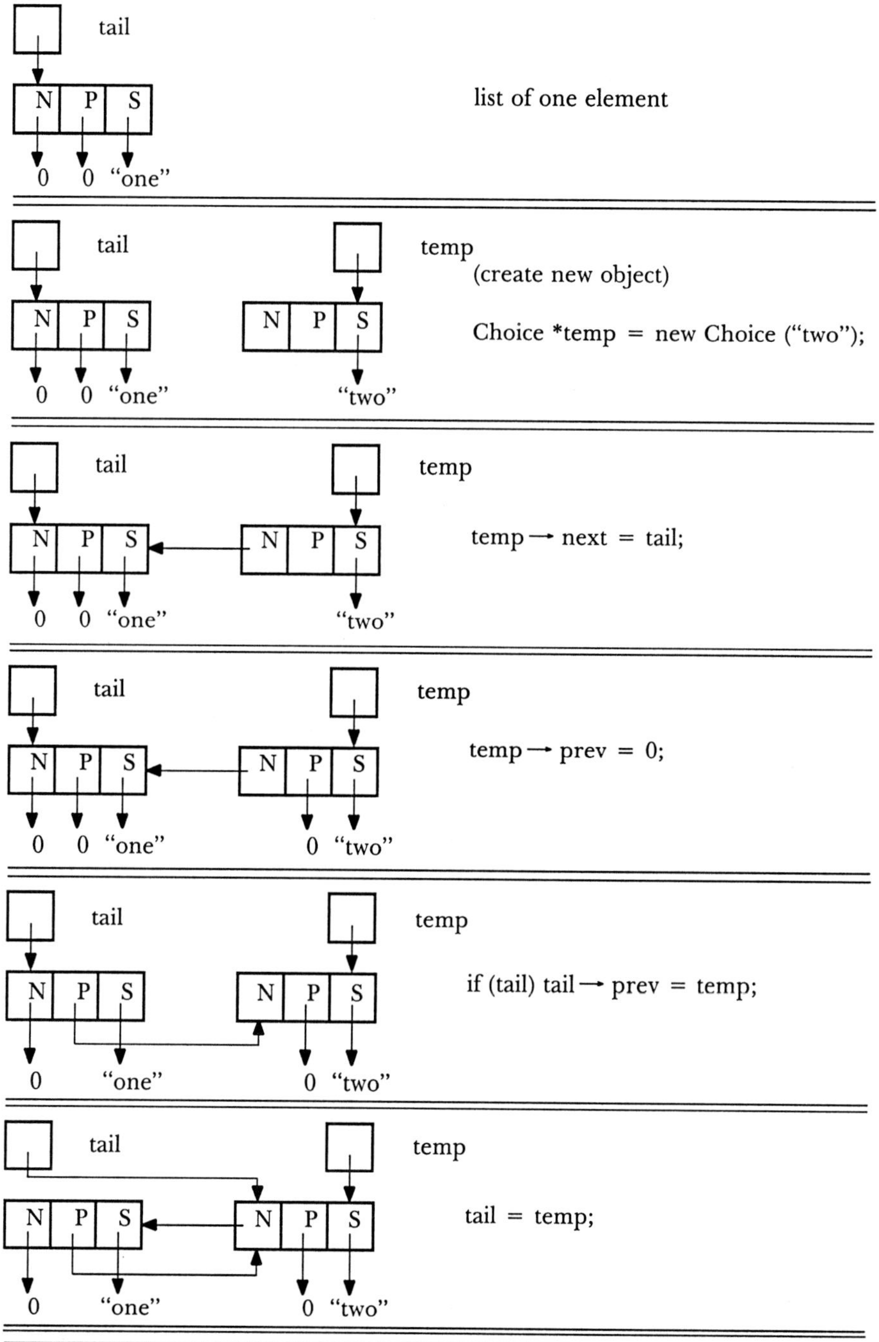

Figure 7-2. *Adding an element to an existing list*

object. This is the value that will be returned and changed each time the iterator is invoked. An iterator object is created through a constructor, which gets a list as an argument. The value of the current **Choice** is set to whatever element happens to be at the tail of the list at the time that the iterator is defined. From the present declaration there is only one thing you can do with an iterator, and that is to apply the ++ operator. The declaration

```
Choice *operator++();
```

specifies that when the ++ operator is applied to an **Iter** object, it will do something different from what it normally does. This is called *operator overloading*. To see exactly what ++ will do to an **Iter** object, look at the definition for **Iter::operator++**.

```
Choice *Iter::operator++()
{
    if (current)
    {
        Choice *temp = current;
        current = current->prev;
        return temp;
    }
    else
        return 0;
}
```

The ++ operator must return a pointer to the current **Choice** object. Yet it must also change the value of **current** so that it moves to point to the next element in the list. In order to carry out both these operations, this function must save the value of **current** in a temporary pointer variable before it changes **current** to point to the next element of the list. Once the pointer is saved, ++ advances **current** and returns the value of the temporary pointer. The implementation of ++ is slightly more complicated, because it needs to test to see if it has walked beyond the end of the list. If this is true, the value of **current** will be 0, the test

```
if (current)
```

will fail, and the ++ member operator will return a value of 0.

Using an Iterator

A **while** loop can use the value returned by the **Iter ++** operator. First, create an **Iter** object and set it to the first element of a list. Then create a **Choice** object. Inside the test of the **while** loop, set **Choice** equal to the value returned by the **++** operator applied to the **Iter** object.

The basic template for the code looks like this:

```
// create a list
// add one element

Iter itl = lst;     // create iterator

// add remaining list elements
//...

// define a choice object to retain
// value returned by iterator
Choice *cl;

// process list
while ( (cl = ++itl) != 0 )
{
   //...
}
```

This is exactly what happens inside the code for **main**.

```
main()
{
    // Create a list
    List lst;
    lst.add("one");
    Iter itl = lst;
    lst.add("two");
    lst.add("three");

    // Print the list
    Choice *cl;
    while ( (cl = ++itl) != 0 )
        cout << cl->getStr() << "\n";
}
```

First, a list, **lst**, is created. Then, one element is added to the list. This is the point at which the **Iter** object, in this case **itl**, must be created if you want to point to the beginning of the list. Remember that the constructor for **Itr** gets a single argument, which is a list. Note that the following two definitions for creating **itl** are equivalent:

```
Iter itl = lst;
Iter itl(lst);
```

The current pointer inside of **itl** is set to point to the tail of **lst**. If you had waited until the entire list was created before defining **itl**, only the last choice in the list would be printed inside the **while** statement.

Now the second and third choices are added to the end of the list. The construction of the list is complete and you are ready to print it. First, a pointer to a **Choice** object must be created to remember the value returned by the iterator, **itl**, on each pass through the loop. As long as this value points to something—that is, it is not equal to 0—the **cout** statement inside the loop is executed. The **Choice** object, **cl**, can get access to the string representing the menu choice through the **Choice** member access function.

```
cl->getStr()
```

This expression returns a string pointer, which **cout** prints to the screen, immediately followed by a NEWLINE for each member of the list.

Run the program now. You should get the following output:

```
one
two
three
```

Refinements and Fine Points

You may want to save each of the modifications you make to Program P7-1 with different names (such as P7-1A, P7-1B, and so forth) in case you want to retain the original program for future reference.

You can modify Program P7-1 to make it more refined. For example

```
!= 0
```

is redundant in the expression

```
while ( (cl = ++itl) != 0 )
```

As long as the expression

```
(cl = ++itl)
```

returns a nonzero value, the loop will continue to execute. Also, you can clarify the relationship between the **Choice** object, **cl**, and the test condition inside the loop by using a **for** statement as follows:

```
for (Choice *cl;  cl = ++itl; )
    cout << cl->getStr() << "\n";
```

If you were to make these changes to the program, you would see that the output has not changed. Note that the preincrement and postincrement distinctions that normally apply to the ++ operator disappear when ++ is applied to objects for which it is overloaded. It will still operate correctly on integers and pointers. There is no difference between the expressions

```
cl = ++itl
```

and

```
cl = itl++
```

In both cases, the value of the current choice is returned and the iterator is advanced to point to the next element of the list.

Overloading List Constructors

Now you are going to make several changes to Program P7-1 to make it a little easier to use. It would be nice if you could add the first element of the list at the same time that the list object is created. In order to do this, you need a second constructor. This constructor will get a string as an argument. The constructor will set the **tail** pointer for the list equal to zero, just like the **List** constructor, which gets no arguments. In addition to this, the second constructor calls the list member function, **add**, with the string pointer as an argument. The definition looks like the following:

```
List (char *s) {tail=0; add(s);}
```

Go ahead and add this new constructor immediately after the existing list constructor. The class declaration for **List** now looks like this:

```
class List
{
private:
    Choice *tail;
public:
    List () { tail=0; }
    List (char *s) {tail=0; add(s);}      // new constructor
    void add(const char *s);
    Choice *getTail() { return tail; }
};
```

Now go down to main and modify the **lst** definition by giving it an argument of **"zero"** so that it looks like this:

```
List lst("zero");
```

The code for **main** should now look like this:

```
main()
{
    // Create a list
    List lst("zero");      // modified List definition
    lst.add("one");
    Iter itl = lst;
    lst.add("two");
    lst.add("three");

    // Print the list
    Choice *cl;
    while ( (cl = ++itl) != 0 )
        cout << cl->getStr() << "\n";
}
```

Once you have made these modifications, save the program as P7-1A.CPP, recompile it, and then run it.

What happened? Even though you added a new element to the list, the output is exactly the same as it was before you modified the program. The reason for this is because the iterator is not initialized until after choice "**one**" is added. Remember that the iterator is initialized to point to the tail of the list. Thus, if you want to point to "**zero**", which is the beginning of the list, you must initialize the iterator immediately after choice "**zero**" is added. To fix this, move the definition for iterator **itl** so that it immediately follows the definition

```
List lst("zero");
```

which both creates a list and adds a first element. Your code should now look like this:

```
main()
{
    // Create a list
    List lst("zero");
    Iter itl = lst;
    lst.add("one");
    lst.add("two");
    lst.add("three");
    //...
}
```

Now recompile and run the program again. You should see the following output:

```
zero
one
two
three
```

That's more like it. The program now runs as it should, but the error that resulted from the first modification brings up an interesting possibility, explored in the next section.

Using Multiple Iterators

What if you want an iterator to start off pointing to the middle of a list? To do this you declare a second iterator as follows:

```
Iter it2 = lst;
```

This statement is inserted immediately after choice "**two**" is added to the list with the statement

```
lst.add("two");
Iter it2 = lst;
```

Now you need to add the following code to print out everything from the second iterator to the end of the list:

```
while ( (cl = ++it2) != 0 )
    cout << cl->getStr() << "\n";
```

To keep the output of the two **while** statements separate, insert the following line of code just before the second **while** statement:

```
cout << "==========\n";
```

This is the same as the previous code, except that iterator **it2** replaces **it1**. The **main** function should now look like this:

```
main()
{
    // Create a list
    List lst("zero");
    Iter it1 = lst;
    lst.add("one");
    lst.add("two");
    Iter it2 = lst;
    lst.add("three");

    // Print the list
    Choice *cl;
    while ( (cl = ++it1) != 0 )
        cout << cl->getStr() << "\n";
```

```
    cout << "==========\n";
    while ( (cl = ++it2) != 0 )
        cout << cl->getStr() << "\n";
}
```

Now save the changes as P7-1B.CPP and run the program. You should get the following output:

```
zero
one
two
three
==========
two
three
```

This new flexibility in initializing lists makes iterators a little more useful. But there is a problem. Once the iterator has moved beyond the last element in a list, it is useless. With the current implementation of the **Iter** class, there is no way to reuse an iterator once its current pointer takes on a value of 0. You can solve this problem by adding an assignment operator to the **Iter** class.

Making Iterators Reusable

The assignment operator for an **Iter** object can be implemented in two lines. Here is one possibility:

```
Iter &operator =(const Iter &iter)
    { current = iter.current; return *this; }
```

Add these two lines to the **Iter** class declaration immediately after the declaration for the overloaded ++ operator:

```
Choice *operator++();
Iter &operator =(const Iter &iter)
    { current = iter.current; return *this; }
```

Now you can use the same iterator to process a list several times or to process different lists. All you need to do is retain a reference to the point in the list where you want to start processing.

You are going to make another modification to the program so that two iterators are created as reference points. The first, **itStart**, is set to point to the beginning of a list immediately after the first element is added. The iterator **itTwo** is initialized immediately after choice "**two**" is added to the list. These two iterators simply provide references to different nodes in the list. Finally, a third iterator, **it**, is used to walk through the list three times. The **it** iterator is declared and initialized with the statement

```
Iter it = itStart;
```

This is an assignment and is not to be confused with a constructor. Remember that a constructor that gets a single argument can be specified in either of these two forms:

```
class c(arg);
class c = arg;
```

These two forms carry out exactly the same action. The alternative syntax is provided simply for convenience. It is also possible to initialize an iterator at the point where it is declared with an assignment operator, which could be confused with the latter form of the constructor. The reason you know that the statement

```
Iter it = itStart;
```

uses the assignment operator rather than the constructor is because **itStart** is an iterator. There is no constructor for the **Iter** class which takes another **Iter** as an argument. If you look back at the constructor for the **Iter** class, you will see the definition

```
Iter(List l) { current = l.getTail(); }
```

which specifies that the constructor expects a **List** as an argument. Since **itStart** does not match this argument prototype, the assignment operator is used instead of the constructor.

Edit the **main** program now so that it looks like this:

```
main()
{
    // Create a list
    List lst("zero");
    Iter itStart = lst;
    lst.add("one");
    lst.add("two");
    Iter itTwo = lst;
    lst.add("three");

    // Print the list
    Choice *cl;
    Iter it = itStart;
    while ( (cl = ++it) != 0 )
        cout << cl->getStr() << "\n";
    cout << "==========\n";
    it = itTwo;
    while ( (cl = ++it) != 0 )
        cout << cl->getStr() << "\n";
    cout << "==========\n";
    it = itStart;
    while ( (cl = ++it) != 0 )
        cout << cl->getStr() << "\n";
}
```

Save the modifications you have made as P7-1C.CPP. Now compile and run the program. Here is what you should see

```
zero
one
two
three
==========
two
three
==========
zero
one
two
three
```

The iterator is set to point to the beginning of the list. It then prints out the list and is reset to point to choice "**two**". The second **while** loop reuses **it** to print the list from "**two**" to the end of the list. Finally, **it** is reset to the beginning of the list and the entire list is printed again.

A Decrementing Iterator

Iterators are a lot more handy when they can be reused. Another thing you can do to make iterators more useable is to provide an operator to decrement them as well as to increment them. This is done by adding another operator member function to the **Iter** class. The following declaration is added as a member of the **Iter** class:

```
Choice *operator--();
```

Add the above declaration to the **Iter** class just after **operator++**. The definition for the **Iter --** operator is as follows:

```
Choice *Iter::operator--()
{
    if (current)
    {
        Choice *temp = current;
        current = current->next;
        return temp;
    }
    else
            return 0;
}
```

It is exactly like the definition for **Iter ++** except that **current** is set to **current->next** instead of **current->prev**. Add this definition just after the definition for **Iter::operator++**.

Now you can declare a single iterator and walk it both forward and backward through the list.

First, delete the definition for **itTwo** inside **main**. Then save the end of the list.

```
Iter itTail = lst;
```

This initializer must occur after the last element of the list has been added if **itTail** is going to point to the right place. Now you can walk backward through the list with the following code:

```
it=itTail;
while ( (cl = --it) != 0 )
    cout << cl->getStr() << "\n";
```

Replace the second and third **while** loops with this code. Save the program as P7-1D.CPP and run. Note that it is necessary to reset **it** to point to the last element of the list. This is because **it** has walked off the end of the list by the time the first **while** loop terminates. When an iterator walks off the end of a list, its current member, which points to a **Choice** item, is set to zero. This is the limitation of a list that uses sentinels to mark its end points rather than wrapping around to point back to the other end of the list.

There are advantages to both circular and terminal lists, but you must know the characteristics of the list you are using and what an iterator will do when it goes beyond the last element of the list. Intuition might tell you that applying -- to **it** after the first **while** loop would immediately back up to the list element immediately preceding the last element in the list. But this is not the case, because once the current member of the iterator is set to 0, it knows nothing about previous and next elements in the list.

One way around this problem would be to maintain pointers to both the head and the tail of the list. Then the ++ and -- operators could check to see whether they have reached the beginning of the list.

Function Overloading for Multiple Constructors

There is another way to specify multiple forms of constructors. This is also a form of function overloading. In the **List** class declaration, change

```
List () { tail=0; }
```

to

```
List(Choice *ch=0) { tail=ch; }
```

The second form uses a default argument. If no argument is supplied, the variable **ch** is set to 0; otherwise, **ch** is set to the value supplied in the argument. Thus, the new form of the constructor will behave exactly like the old form. In addition, the new form allows you to create a new list and to set its head to one of the choices in an existing list. The second form of the constructor behaves as though two constructors were supplied for the **List** class:

```
List () { tail=0; }
List(Choice *ch) { tail=ch; }
```

Note that the second form here supplies no default argument. You can use the constructor as you always have, as follows:

```
List lst;
```

But now you can also use the constructor to create a new list that points into the middle of the existing list. Try this. You can create a new list by giving the list constructor a **Choice** argument, for example, the tail of a given list:

```
List save = lst.getTail();
```

The head of the new list will continue to point to the same list element even after more members are added to the original list. What happens if you add a new **Choice** member to the newly created list after additional elements have been added to the original list?

Add the above statement immediately after choice "**one**" is added to the list. Next, modify **main** to insert the choice "**where will this go?**" in the save list, and use the iterator **it** to print both lists. The entire program should now look like this:

```
#include <string.h>
#include <iostream.h>

class Choice
{
private:
    char *str;
```

```
public:
    Choice *next;
    Choice *prev;
    Choice(const char *s)
        { str=new char[strlen(s)+1]; strcpy(str, s); }
    ~Choice() { delete str; }
    const char *getStr() { return str; }
};

class List
{
private:
    Choice *tail;
public:
    //List () { tail=0; }
    List(Choice *ch=0) { tail=ch; }
    List (char *s) {tail=0; add(s);}
    void add(const char *s);
    Choice *getTail() { return tail; }
};
void List::add(const char *s)
{
    Choice *temp = new Choice(s);
    temp->next = tail;
    temp->prev = 0;
    if (tail) tail->prev = temp;
    tail = temp;
}

class Iter
{
private:
    Choice *current;
public:
    Iter(List l) { current = l.getTail(); }
    Choice *operator++();
    Choice *operator--();
    Iter &operator =(const Iter &iter)
        { current = iter.current; return *this; }
};

Choice *Iter::operator++()
{
    if (current)
    {
        Choice *temp = current;
        current = current->prev;
        return temp;
    }
    else
        return 0;
}
```

```
Choice *Iter::operator--()
{
    if (current)
    {
        Choice *temp = current;
        current = current->next;
        return temp;
    }
    else
        return 0;
}

main()
{
    // Create a list
    List lst("zero");
    Iter itStart = lst;
    lst.add("one");
    List save = lst.getTail();

    lst.add("two");
    lst.add("three");
    save.add("Where will this go?");
    Iter itTail = lst;

    // Print the list
    Choice *cl;
    Iter it = itStart;
    while ( (cl = ++it) != 0 )
        cout << cl->getStr() << "\n";
    cout << "==========\n";
    it=itTail;
    while ( (cl = --it) != 0 )
        cout << cl->getStr() << "\n";
}
```

Save the program as P7-1E.CPP. Now compile and run the program. The output looks like this:

```
zero
one
Where will this go?
==========
three
two
one
zero
```

This is not what you really want. Unfortunately, the original **add** routine made the assumption that elements will only be added onto the end of the list. But it might be useful to add elements to the middle of a list. You can modify **List::add** so that it handles all the possibilities.

Modifying the List Class to Handle Insertions

The next thing to do is to modify the code that maintains lists to make it possible to insert a **Choice** object in the middle of the list so that the list structure is not destroyed.

There are three possible conditions that **List::add** can encounter:

- Add a choice to an empty list
- Add a choice to the tail of a list
- Add a choice to the middle of a list

Looking at a graphic representation of each of the possibilities makes it easy to understand the code that needs to be written to handle each of the possibilities.

Adding a Choice to an Empty List

Before any elements are added to a list, the **List** class constructor sets the tail pointer to 0 so that it points to nothing (see Figure 7-3). Adding a new element to such a list is easy. First, the **Choice** object is created. Since there is no previous element and no next element in the list, both the **prev** and **next** fields of the object are set to 0.

```
if (!tail)
{
    temp->prev = temp->next = 0;
}
```

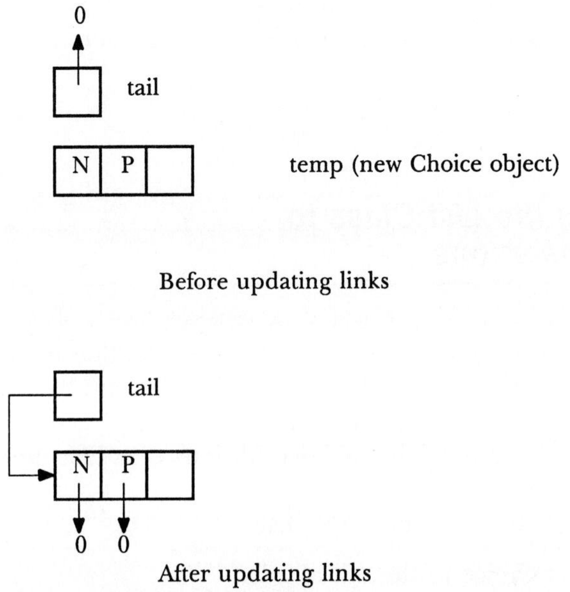

Figure 7-3. *Adding a choice to an empty list*

Adding a Choice to the Tail of a List

Adding a new element to the tail of the list is not too difficult (see Figure 7-4). By definition, no element comes after this element, so **prev** is set to 0. The **next** field is set to point to the element that used to be the last element of the list, and the **prev** field of the former last element is set to the newly created element.

```
else if (!tail->prev)
{
    temp->prev = 0;
    temp->next = tail;
    tail->prev = temp;
}
```

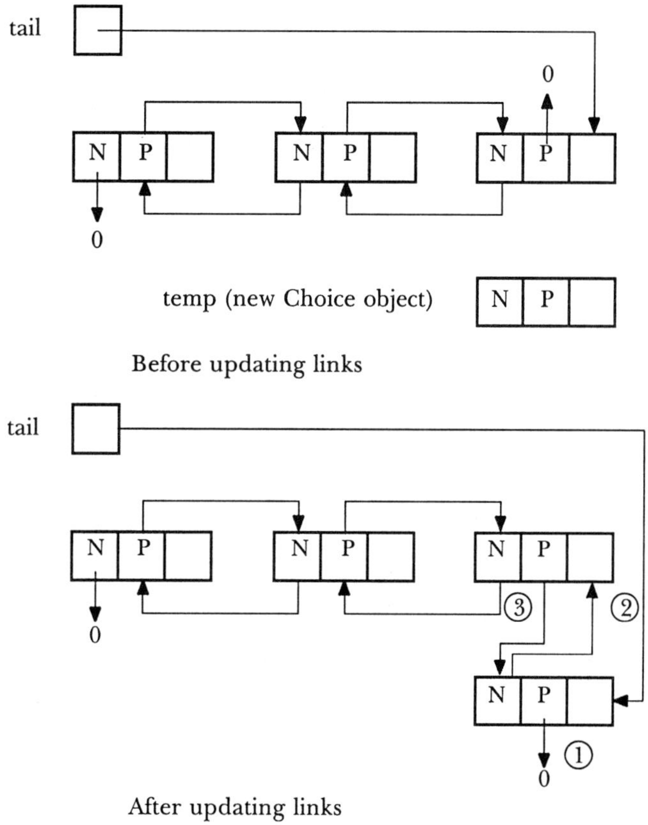

Figure 7-4. *Adding a choice to the tail of a list*

Adding a Choice to the Middle of a List

This is equivalent to list insertion. This is the only case where there will be a previous element after the new element is inserted. The previous field of the new object is set to the previous field of the member pointed to by **tail** (see Figure 7-5). The next field of the new object is set to the member pointed to by **tail**. The **next** field of the previous member is set

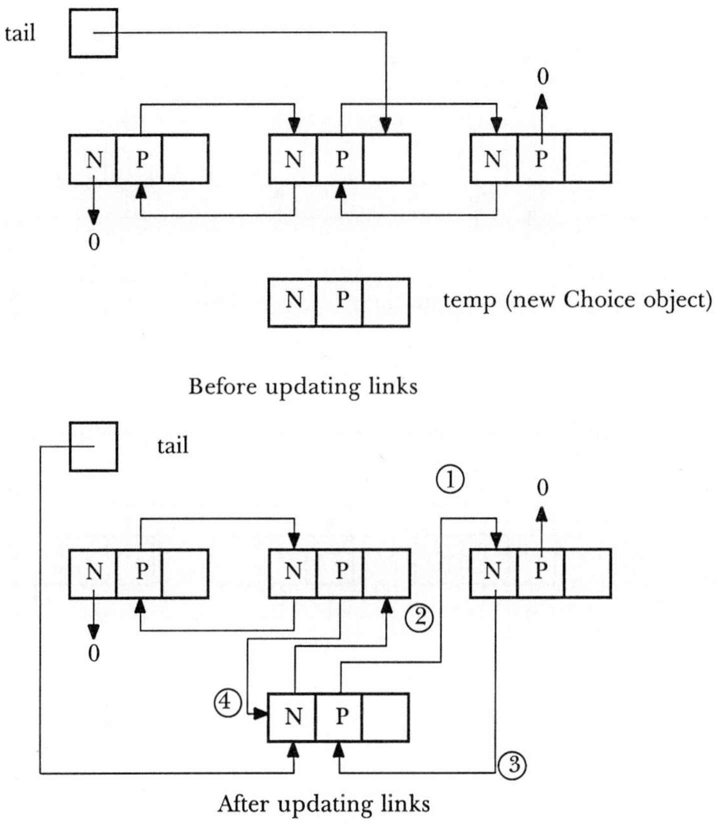

Figure 7-5. *Adding a choice to the middle of a list*

to point to the new object as is the **prev** field of the member pointed to by **tail**.

```
else
{
    temp->prev = tail->prev;
    temp->next = tail;
    tail->prev->next = temp;
    tail->prev = temp;
}
```

Make these changes to the **List::add** function. Just to be sure that everything is operating as it should, insert the following diagnostic output statements, one in each of the respective **if** clauses:

```
cout << "List::add item to empty list\n";
cout << "List::add item to end of list\n";
cout << "List::add item to middle of list\n";
```

The whole member function **List::add** now looks like this:

```
void List::add(const char *s)
{
    Choice *temp = new Choice(s);
    if (!tail)
    {
        cout << "List::add item to empty list\n";
        temp->prev = temp->next = 0;
    }
    else if (!tail->prev)
    {
        cout << "List::add item to end of list\n";
        temp->prev = 0;
        temp->next = tail;
        tail->prev = temp;
    }
    else
    {
        cout << "List::add item to middle of list\n";
        temp->prev = tail->prev;
        temp->next = tail;
        tail->prev->next = temp;
        tail->prev = temp;
    }
    tail = temp;
}
```

Save the program as P7-1F.CPP. Now recompile the program and run it. You will see the following output:

```
List::add item to empty list
List::add item to end of list
List::add item to end of list
List::add item to end of list
List::add item to middle of list
zero
one
Where will this go?
two
three
==========
three
```

```
two
Where will this go?
one
zero
```

The first five output statements verify that each of the three possible list conditions was encountered at least once. Now, when **List::add** is called from a **List** object whose tail points to the middle of a list, the action behaves as an insertion, properly maintaining all links in the list.

Iterator Assignment from Different Object Types

With one small addition to the **Iter** class, you can make it possible to assign an iterator object from a **Choice** pointer as well as from another iterator. This means that if you have a pointer to a **Choice** element in a list, you can assign an iterator to point to that element. This will let you eliminate the need entirely for the **itTail** iterator if all you want to do is print the list backward. All you need to print the list backward is a pointer to the tail, which is always available through the **List** member function, **getTail**:

```
it = lst.getTail();
```

Add the following assignment operator as the last definition in the **Iter** class:

```
Iter &operator=(Choice *ch)
    { current = ch; return *this; }
```

Modify **main** now so that it looks like this:

```
main()
{
    // Create a list
    List lst("zero");
    Iter it = lst;
    lst.add("one");
    lst.add("two");
```

```
    lst.add("three");

    // Print the list
    Choice *cl;
    while ( (cl = ++it) != 0 )
        cout << cl->getStr() << "\n";
    cout << "==========\n";
    it = lst.getTail();
    while ( (cl = --it) != 0 )
        cout << cl->getStr() << "\n";
}
```

Also, go back and delete each of these three **cout** statements inside **List::add**:

```
cout << "List::add item to empty list\n";
cout << "List::add item to end of list\n";
cout << "List::add item to middle of list\n";
```

Save the program as P7-1G.CPP. Now when you run the program you should get the following output:

```
zero
one
two
three
==========
three
two
one
zero
```

Lists with Head and Tail Pointers

You can even add another private member to the **List** class, called **head**, declared as

```
Choice *head;
```

which will point to the head of a list. This way, given a **List** object, you can always find the head or tail of a list. The only thing you need to do is to make sure that when the first element is added to the list, **head** is set to point to that element. You will also need to add a public member function called **List::getHead** that is similar to **List::getTail**. See if you can make these modifications to the **List** class.

All the changes to Program P7-1 up to this point have been incorporated into Program P7-2. That listing is provided here for your convenience and is also on the disk accompanying this book. You can load the program now and run it to verify that you have correctly implemented the changes covered so far.

P7-2

```
#include <string.h>
#include <iostream.h>

class Choice
{
private:
    char *str;
public:
    Choice *next;
    Choice *prev;
    Choice(const char *s)
        { str=new char[strlen(s)+1]; strcpy(str, s); }
    ~Choice() { delete str; }
    const char *getStr() { return str; }
};

class List
{
private:
    Choice *tail;
public:
    List(Choice *ch=0) { tail=ch; }
    List (char *s) {tail=0; add(s);}
    void add(const char *s);
    Choice *getTail() { return tail; }
};

void List::add(const char *s)
{
    Choice *temp = new Choice(s);
    if (!tail)
    {
        temp->prev = temp->next = 0;
    }
    else if (!tail->prev)
    {
```

```
        temp->prev = 0;
        temp->next = tail;
        tail->prev = temp;
    }
    else
    {
        temp->prev = tail->prev;
        temp->next = tail;
        tail->prev->next = temp;
        tail->prev = temp;
    }
    tail = temp;
}

class Iter
{
private:
    Choice *current;
public:
    Iter(List l) { current = l.getTail(); }
    Choice *operator++();
    Choice *operator--();
    Iter &operator =(const Iter &iter)
        { current = iter.current; return *this; }
    Iter &operator =(Choice *ch)
        { current = ch; return *this; }
};

Choice *Iter::operator++()
{
    if (current)
    {
        Choice *temp = current;
        current = current->prev;
        return temp;
    }
    else
        return 0;
}

Choice *Iter::operator--()
{
    if (current)
    {
        Choice *temp = current;
        current = current->next;
        return temp;
    }
    else
        return 0;
}
```

```
main()
{
    // Create a list
    List lst("zero");
    Iter it = lst;
    lst.add("one");

    lst.add("two");
    lst.add("three");

    // Print the list
    Choice *cl;
    while ( (cl = ++it) != 0 )
        cout << cl->getStr() << "\n";
    cout << "==========\n";
    it = lst.getTail();
    while ( (cl = --it) != 0 )
        cout << cl->getStr() << "\n";
}
```

Summary

Control abstraction is an important concept for processing elements of a collection such as a list or an array. This chapter has shown how to build a simple list class and an iterator class, which provides sequential access to the elements of a list. An interator is a user-defined form of control abstraction that adds flexibility to built-in abstractions such as loops and conditional statements. Each unique type of collection needs to provide its own iterator.

In Chapter 8 you'll see how easy it is to modify iterators to handle lists of objects created from a newly developed **String** class. Then the same iterator class is adapted to handle lists of **Choice** objects like those used for menus in Chapter 6. Applicators are another form of control of abstraction which will be introduced in Chapter 9.

8 Strings and Iterators

Dealing with strings in C is, at best, awkward. This is because string processing in C is handled through functions. With user-defined types, C++ will let you build a **String** class that behaves as if it were a built-in type of the language. Once such a class is developed, it is as easy to build a list composed of **String** objects as it is to build a list of standard C strings. To show this, the iterator class (**Iter**) from Chapter 7 will be adapted to operate on a list of the newly created **String** objects. Finally, the **List** class will be updated to initialize and return a pointer to the head as well as the tail of a list.

String Handling in C

One of the primary advantages of a language like C++ is that it allows you to build abstract data types and operations that make it more natural to express solutions to problems. Many people complain about the way in which C deals with strings. Newcomers are puzzled, for instance, by expressions like,

```
char s[100];
strcpy(s, "Now is the time");
```

which copy the string "Now is the time" into the character buffer **s**. People who are used to Pascal wonder why you can't just type

```
s = "Now is the time";
```

to assign the string to **s**.

This is where the low-level nature of C rears its head. C is really a portable assembly language, and not truly a high-level language like Pascal. C programmers need to know the internal structure of strings in order to perform operations on them. In fact, there is no string type in C. There is merely a convention that strings are represented by arrays of **chars** terminated by a null, or 0. All processing of strings is then handled by library functions, rather than by built-in operators like =, = =, +, <, >, and so forth. You can see the declarations for C's standard string functions by looking in the STRING.H header file. The more common operations are **strcpy** for assignment, **strcmp** for string comparison, and **strcat** for string concatenation.

There are many more string-handling functions in both the UNIX and Borland C++ libraries. These functions can easily be implemented in C itself. In fact, you can see definitions for all the string functions just mentioned in Kernighan and Ritchie's *The C Programming Language.* One of the reasons it is so easy to implement a C compiler is that the language itself is small, and most of its functionality is provided by library functions, which are easy to port as well as efficient because of the low-level nature of C. The price paid for this portability and efficiency is the awkward syntax and explicit handling of string operations by the programmer through function calls.

C++'s ability to create user-defined types circumvents these objections. Once an abstract representation of a string is defined, you can easily add operators like =, = =, !=, +, and < < to work on string objects. Once these member operator functions are defined, you can treat strings just as you would in any high-level language that implements a string as a built-in type.

A String Class

A simple **String** class is quite easy to implement. Consider the following class declaration:

```
class String
{
private:
    char *str;        // A traditional string
    int size;         // Size of str buffer
public:
    String(const char *s);
    ~String();
     void print();
};
```

It takes a little more data space to implement a **String** object than a traditional C string. In fact, it would take no more, except that in addition to a pointer to the string, **str**, the **String** class specifies a **size** variable in the private section of the declaration. The public section of **String** specifies a constructor, a destructor, and a member **print** function used to display the string currently represented.

String's constructor expects a single argument, which is a pointer to a traditional C string. You can create a **String** object with a statement such as

```
String s("This is a string");
```

You still need to define what will happen when the compiler encounters this expression. Here is the definition for the constructor:

```
String::String(const char *s)
{
    size = strlen(s);
    str = new char[size + 1];
    strcpy(str, s);
}
```

This is very similar to the definition of the **Choice** class used for menu strings in Chapter 6. The difference is that the **String** class retains the value of the string length. When the constructor is called, the built-in C++ operator **new** is called to allocate enough storage for the string. The other side of this is that when a string goes out of scope or is purposely discarded, the destructor needs to return the allocated storage to the free storage pool. This is done with a **delete** operator in the following destructor definition:

```
String::~String()
{
    delete str;
}
```

The only thing remaining to define before you can use this class is the code for the **print** member function. Since the definition is short, **print** is defined as an inline function in the declaration of **String** itself.

```
class String
{
private:
    char *str;
    int size;
public:
    String(const char *s);
    ~String();
     void print() { cout << str; } // inline definition
};
```

The complete implementation of the first version of **String** is found in Program P8-1. Be sure you are logged to the example program directory for this chapter (\DT\CH8) before invoking Borland C++ and loading Program P8-1. Clear the desktop and load program P8-1 now.

P8-1

```
#include <iostream.h>
#include <string.h>  // required by strlen, and strcpy
class String
{
private:
    char *str;      // A traditional string
    int size;       // Size of str buffer
public:
    String(const char *s);
    ~String();
     void print() { cout << str;}
};

String::String(const char *s)
{
    size = strlen(s);
    str = new char[size + 1];
    strcpy(str, s);
}
```

```
String::~String()
{
    delete str;
}

main()
{
    String s("Strings should be easy to use.\n");
    s.print();
}
```

As you can see by looking at **main**, creating and printing **String** objects is easy. Run the program now and you should get the following output:

```
Strings should be easy to use.
```

At first glance, this does not look like much of an improvement over standard C, which could implement **main** as follows:

```
main()
{
    char *s = "Strings should be easy to use.";
    puts(s);
}
```

But the real power of a **String** object comes from the ability to define any operators you want for the class. For example, it might make more sense to implement the print function as a member operator. If you use < < as the print operator, you can implement it in a way that lets **cout** statements handle strings. The declaration,

```
friend ostream &operator<<(ostream &os, const String &s);
```

indicates that the < < operator function for **String** objects is implemented as a friend function rather than as a member function. Friend functions behave like normal functions outside of class implementations. The difference is that friend functions have access to the private members of the **String** class. Thus, a friend function that is passed a **String** object, **s**, has access to **str**, which is a private member of **String**.

```
cout << s.str;
```

Such a reference is illegal in a function that is not a friend of **String**. The actual definition for < < follows:

```
ostream &operator<<(ostream &os, const String &s)
{
        return os << s.str;
}
```

The reason for declaring < < as a friend instead of making it a member function is that the first argument for < < will be an ostream. Since an ostream is not a **String**, it does not have access to member functions of the **String** class. Remember that the < < operator defined for a **String** object is different from the < < operator defined for an **ostream** object. This is the essence of operator overloading. By defining the member operator < < for **String**, you are saying that **String** objects will behave differently than other objects (such as **ints** and **char** *s) when the < < operator is applied to them. Without defining such an operator, it would be an error to reference a **String** object in a **cout** statement as follows:

```
String s("string");
cout << s;  // error
```

Having < < return a reference to an ostream makes it possible to surround **String** objects with other objects that return ostreams in a **cout** statement.

```
String s("string");
cout << "This is a " << s << "\n";
```

Program P8-2 provides a complete implementation for the friend operator, < < , for the **String** class. Load Program P8-2 now.

P8-2

```
#include <iostream.h>
#include <string.h>  // required by strlen, and strcpy
class String
{
private:
    char *str;        // A traditional string
    int size;         // Size of str buffer
public:
    String(const char *s);
    ~String();
    friend ostream &operator<<(ostream &os, const String &s);
```

```
};

String::String(const char *s)
{
    size = strlen(s);
    str = new char[size + 1];
    strcpy(str, s);
}

String::~String()
{
    delete str;
}

ostream &operator<<(ostream &os, const String &s)
{
    return os << s.str;
}

main()
{
    String s("make efficient use of memory");
    cout << "Strings should also\n"
         << s
         << "\n"
         << "and be reuseable.\n";
}
```

Run the program and verify the following output:

```
Strings should also
make efficient use of memory
and be reusable.
```

Careful study of **main** reveals that the program consists of a single **cout** statement that is similar to the previous listing. Note that using infix notation is a matter of convenience provided by overriding C++'s built-in operators (< <, +, -, and so on). You can also use operator functions in their functional forms. Add the following four lines at the end of **main** in Program P8-2:

```
String s2("\nOverloaded infix operators\n");
String s3("can use infix or functional notation.\n");
operator<<(cout, s2);
cout << s3;
```

After recompiling and running the program, you should get the following output:

```
Strings should also
make efficient use of memory
and be reusable.

Overloaded infix operators
can use infix or functional notation.
```

From the output you can see that the different notations for << produce similar results. There is one difference, however. If the functional notation is used, the function call must be followed by a semicolon to indicate the end of a statement. The functional form of the << operator cannot be cascaded in the same manner as the infix form. This is because the infix statement,

```
cout << s2 << s3;
```

is equivalent to

```
operator<<(operator<<(cout, s2), s3);
```

To verify this, add the following two lines to the end of Program P8-2:

```
cout << "===\n";
operator<<(operator<<(cout, s2), s3);
```

Compile and run the program and note the following output:

```
Strings should also
make efficient use of memory
and be reusable.

Overloaded infix operators
can use infix or functional notation.
===

Overloaded infix operators
can use infix or functional notation.
```

Infix notation helps simplify expression syntax. It was awkward enough printing two cascaded **String** objects using functional notation for the << operator. Three or more **ostream** objects would be a nightmare. This is precisely why the **ostream** class in C++ uses infix notation. Infix notation and operator overloading make it easier to build expressions in a form that closely models the way we think about expressing solutions to problems.

String Class Design Goals

A string should be easy to use. That means it should be easy to create, copy, print, and compare strings. Also, it would be nice to automate the memory management associated with traditional C strings. All of this can be done by adding new constructors and operators to the **String** class. A good starting point would be to define a second constructor for **String** that accepts a **String** object rather than a **char *** as an argument. The declaration and definition for such a constructor follow:

```
class String
{
    //...
    String(const String &s);  // declaration
    //...
};

String::String(const String &s) // definition
{
    size = s.size;
    str = s.str;
}
```

Now it is easy to create a new copy of an existing string. Add the previous code to Program P8-2, and then change **main** to look like this:

```
main()
{
    String s1("string1");
    String s2(s1);
    cout << "s1==> " << s1 << "\n";
    cout << "s2==> " << s2 << "\n";
}
```

Save the program under a temporary name, either TEMP.CPP or P8-2B.CPP, and run the modified program. The output is predictable:

```
s1==> string1
s2==> string1
```

This is fine, but not really useful since there is no way to change a string after it has been defined. There really is not much use in having two copies of the same string.

It would be nice if strings were reusable. At first, this might look like an easy feature to add to the **String** class. However, there is a problem. Once a **String** object has been allocated, the buffer used to hold the string is set to a fixed size. That means that the **String** object can now only contain strings that are the same length, or shorter than the length of the original string.

Although people complain about having to manage character buffers when dealing with strings in C, there is one advantage of the traditional C string-handling functions. The buffers used to contain strings are reusable. The usual technique is to declare some global constant that indicates the maximum size of a string that could be contained in a buffer, as in

```
#define MAXSTR 100
char buf[MAXSTR];
```

and then to write code that signals an error or guards against buffer overflow.

The current implementation of **String** avoids having to estimate a buffer size that will handle all strings likely to be encountered, but it lacks flexibility when reassigning a new string to the buffer. A constructor accepting **String** object as an argument would be a little more useful, however, if it were possible to alter the contents of a **String** object after it was created. This can be done by implementing an assignment operator for the **String** class as follows:

```
String& String::operator=(const char *s)
{
    size = strlen(s);
```

```
    strcpy(str, s);
    return *this;
}
```

Now it is possible to change the value of a string at any point in the program. For example:

```
main()
{
    String s1("string");
    String s2 = "longer string";
    String s3(s1);

    cout << s2 << "\n";
    cout << s3 << "\n";

    s2 = s1;
    cout << s2 << "\n";

    s2 = "STRING 2";
    cout << s2 << "\n";
}
```

See if you can predict the output from this listing. This is an improvement, but there are still problems. You can only assign new values to **String** objects if the buffer of the destination object is large enough to contain the buffer of the source object. For example, if the program in this listing contained the statement,

```
s1 = s2;
```

the results would be unpredictable. The buffer created for **s1** is smaller than the buffer created for **s2**. Thus, copying a long string to a buffer that is too small to contain it will overwrite the area of memory just beyond the destination string's buffer. One way around this problem would be to simply reassign **str** inside **s1** to point to the **str** referenced in **s2**. This has the disadvantage of making the old buffer that **s1.str** formerly pointed to inaccessible. Once you change what **s1.str** points to, there is no way to reclaim the memory allocated for the original **str** buffer. So the next step is to delete the current buffer before assigning **s1.str** to point to the string buffer of the source object.

But what do you do in the case where the source is a **char *** rather than a string? One solution is to delete the old buffer in **s1** and allocate storage for the new string. Then use **strcpy** to make a new copy of the source string. This seems like a good strategy.

Another way to solve this problem is the way it is done in traditional C. Create a buffer large enough to contain the largest possible string expected to be assigned to the object. This can be done by providing another constructor that accepts an integer argument.

```
String::String(const int length)
{
    size = length;
    str = new char[size + 1];
    str[0] = '\0';
}
```

Another possibility is to delete the old **str** buffer and set **str** to point to the string being assigned. This would save on storage space by eliminating duplicated strings, which will occur for every assignment.

This can be dangerous, however. What if the second **String** object or **char *** to which the destination object now points is deleted? An object can be deleted explicitly by the program or implicitly when a variable goes out of scope. If this happens, the string buffer is deleted and **s1**'s **str** pointer is left pointing to an undefined region of memory. A user of **s1** has no way of knowing that it points to garbage. However, there is a way to make this scheme work. Since the deletion of an object always invokes its destructor, you could have the destructor check to see if any other objects refer to the **str** buffer of the object being deleted. If other objects refer to this buffer, the destructor won't delete it. The question then is how the destructor can know if more than one **String** object refers to a buffer it wants to delete.

One way to do this is to create a reference counter, one per **str** buffer, which is incremented every time a new **String** object is assigned to point to the buffer. Adding a reference counter is slightly more complicated than adding an integer variable to the private section of the **String** class. For example:

```
private:
    char *str;
    int size;
    int refs;  // reference counter
```

In this implementation, each time a new **String** object is created, the object gets its own private copy of the reference counter. In an assignment like,

```
s1 = s2;
```

s1's **str** buffer will be deleted, **s1.str** will be set to point to **s2.str**, and the reference counter in **s2** will be incremented before it is assigned to the reference counter in **s1**. But maintaining multiple reference counters for a single buffer can be unwieldy. For instance, what happens if a new reference to the buffer is created?

```
String s3 = s2;
```

The reference counters in **s2** and **s3** will contain the right value, but there is no easy way to update the reference counter in **s1** or any other **String** objects that might refer to the same buffer. Besides, it does not make sense to maintain multiple copies of a reference counter when all copies should have exactly the same value.

There is a fairly easy solution. Instead of each **String** object maintaining a separate reference counter, why not have each object that points to the same **str** buffer also point to the same reference counter for that buffer? This can be done by making **refs** a pointer to an integer.

```
private:
    char *str;
    int size;
    int *refs;  // pointer to reference counter
```

But ***refs** must point at something. Each time a string is created (as opposed to being duplicated through assignment), in addition to creating a buffer for **str** to point to, the constructor or assignment operator will create an integer for ***refs** to point to. Then when an assignment is made, the old buffer pointed to by **str** and the old **int** pointed to by **refs** are deleted, as long as no other reference is made to the **str** buffer. The number of references made to a **String** object, **s**, can be incremented with the expression **(*s.refs)++** as in the following definition:

```
String& String::operator=(const String &s)
{
    (*s.refs)++;
    //...
}
```

This adds 1 to the number of references made to the source object in an assignment statement. Next, the assignment operator function tests to see if it can delete the objects pointed to by **str** and **ref** for the destination object, in this case, **s1**.

```
if (--(*refs) == 0)
{
    delete refs;
    delete str;
}
```

Note that ***refs** here refers to the destination object, whereas ***s.refs** in the previous listing refers to the source object. After the destination object determines whether to delete its buffers, the destination object's private members take on the values of the source object.

```
refs = s.refs;
size = s.size;
str = s.str;
```

Finally, a pointer to the destination object is returned.

```
return *this;
```

Returning a pointer to the destination object makes it possible to cascade multiple assignments of **String** objects.

```
s1 = s2 = s3 = s4;
```

After executing this statement, all objects will refer to the string originally contained in **s4**.

For a complete implementation of the **String** class, you need to handle two more things: creating objects for the first time, and deleting objects when they are to be discarded. When creating an object for the first time, **String** must be sure to create a buffer and an integer for **str** and **refs** to point to. A first-time object is always created when a constructor receiving either a **char *** or an **int** is invoked. An object is also created for the first time as the result of an assignment from a **char ***. In all three of these cases, **new** is invoked twice, once for the **str** buffer and once to create an **int** for **refs** to point to.

When deleting an object, **String** must be sure that no other references are made to **str**'s buffer. If other objects do refer to the buffer, only the counter pointed to by **refs** is changed. **String** member functions that can delete the **str** and **refs** buffers (other than the destructor) are the constructor, which accepts a **String** object as an argument, and the assignment operator, which also accepts a **String** object as an argument. The definitions for all these member functions are shown here:

```
//////////////////////////////////////////////////////
// constructors
//////////////////////////////////////////////////////
String::String(const String &s)
{
    refs = s.refs;
    (*refs)++;
    size = s.size;
    str = s.str;
}

String::String(const char *s)
{
    refs = new int;
    *refs = 1; // refs must be a pointer because
               // two string objects might refer
               // to the same char *. A reference
               // to either should update the SAME
               // reference counter. This would not
               // be possible if each String object
               // maintained a private reference
               // count.
    size = strlen(s);
    str = new char[size + 1];
    strcpy(str, s);
}

String::String(const int length)
{
    size = length;
    str = new char[size + 1];
    str[0] = '\0';
    refs = new int;
```

```
    *refs = 1;
}

//////////////////////////////////////////////////
// destructor
//////////////////////////////////////////////////
String::~String()
{
    if (--(*refs) == 0)
    {
        delete str;
        delete refs;
    }
}

//////////////////////////////////////////////////
// assignment
//////////////////////////////////////////////////
String& String::operator=(const String &s)
{
    (*s.refs)++;
    if (--(*refs) == 0)
    {
        delete refs;
        delete str;
    }
    refs = s.refs;
    size = s.size;
    str = s.str;
    return *this;
}

String& String::operator=(const char *s)
{
    if (--(*refs) == 0)
    {
        delete refs;
        delete str;
    }
    refs = new int;
    *refs = 1;
    size = strlen(s);
    str = new char[size + 1];
    strcpy(str, s);
    return *this;
}
```

With these tools in place, it is easy to build the functionality that will make **String** behave like a built-in type.

The first two friend functions allow comparison for equality and inequality of strings.

```
//////////////////////////////////////////////////
// comparison
//////////////////////////////////////////////////
int operator==(const String &s1, const String &s2)
{
    return strcmp(s1.str, s2.str)==0;
}

int operator!=(const String &s1, const String &s2)
{
    return strcmp(s1.str, s2.str)!=0;
}
```

Now you can say

```
if (s1 == s2)
    statement
```

instead of

```
if (strcmp(s1, s2) == 0)
    statement
```

You can take this a step further and implement a < operator if you plan to implement a function to help sort an array or a list of strings. Although this friend operator is defined for the **String** class, it would be a good exercise to see if you can figure out its definition before looking at the code.

By making the operators ==, !=, and + friends, you allow operator overloading and automatic type casting to take place when the first argument is a **char *** rather than a string. Consider the following:

```
String s("str1");

if ("str1" == s)
    statement
```

If == was a member of **String** rather than a friend, the compiler would not be able to find an overloaded function for the expression inside the **if** statement, since the first argument is a **char** *. The built-in type **char** * is not a class and therefore provides no member operator equivalent to the following:

```
int operator==(const char &s, const String &s2);
```

Consequently, the compiler will complain that it does not know how to resolve the **if** statement. Making the == operator a friend function and declaring both arguments references to strings makes it possible to cast **char** *s as strings when they are arguments to ==. This conversion is possible because of the implicit casting provided by the **String** constructor, which accepts a **char** * as an argument.

```
String::String(const char *s)
{
    //...
}
```

Because == is defined as a friend function, it has global scope, giving the compiler a chance to see if there is a way to cast the **char** * argument to another type, which it can resolve against the prototype for the == operator function. In fact, having == defined as a friend with global scope allows comparison of normal C strings:

```
char *s = "strl";

if ("strl" == s)
    statement
```

This statement is perfectly legal as long as STRCLASS.H is included at the top of the source file and the required linkage is made with STRCLASS.OBJ (the file created by compiling STRCLASS.CPP). STRCLASS.H contains the declaration for class **String**. In this case, both **char** *s in the **if** statement would be cast as **String** objects before calling the overloaded == operator function, producing a result of 1, or true, for this comparison.

Another friend function of the **String** class provides for concatenation of **String** objects.

```
////////////////////////////////////////////////////
// concatenation
////////////////////////////////////////////////////
String& operator+(const String &s1, const String &s2)
{
    String *s3 = new String(strlen(s1.str)+strlen(s2.str)+1);
    strcpy(s3->str, s1.str);
    strcat(s3->str, s2.str);
    return *s3;
}
```

A new buffer is created through the **String** constructor, which accepts a buffer size as an argument. Neither of the original **String** objects is altered. This sets up a natural syntax for expressing concatenation.

```
s3 = s1 + s2;
```

Executing this statement is more complex than it appears. First, the concatenation operator, **+**, creates a new object. A pointer to this object is returned by the following expression:

```
s1 + s2
```

Now the **=** operator takes over. It checks to see that the **str** and **refs** buffers of **s3** are not referred to by other **String** objects. If this is the case, they are deleted; otherwise, ***refs** is decremented. Now the private members of **s1** take on the values of the private members of the object created from the expression in the previous listing. Remember that this expression returns a pointer to a **String** object, so the = operator function acts as though it is getting a **String** object as an argument. Once the assignment to **s3** is made, the temporary string pointer returned by the expression goes out of scope and can no longer be referenced. However, the object created by the expression remains and is pointed to by **s3**'s private member elements.

The final operator in the **String** class is not strictly necessary.

```
operator char*() const { return str; }  // cast String as char*
```

This is another form of an implicit cast operator, called a *conversion operator function.* It is just the opposite of the constructor provided by the **String** class. Where the constructor provides a way to convert **char *s** to **Strings**, the **char*** conversion operator function provides a way to convert **Strings** to **char** *s. In the case of the **String** class, **char*** simply returns **str**. When such an operator is defined, you can pass a string as an argument to any function that expects a **char *** as an argument, including standard library functions. The compiler will automatically convert the string to a **char *** according to the definition provided for operator **char***.

For example, the Borland C++ library function **searchpath** expects to receive a **char *** as an argument and returns a **char ***. If you supply a **String** as an argument or assign the return value to a **String**, the compiler will automatically handle all the conversions for you.

```
// prototype for searchpath
char *searchpath(const char *file);
//...
String s1("strclass.h");
String s2 = searchpath(s1);
//...
```

The entire interface specification for the **String** class now looks like this:

```
#ifndef __STRCLASS__      // This insures that String class
#define __STRCLASS__      // is not defined more than once
                          // in case this header file is
                          // included by more than one
                          // source  file.
#include <iostream.h>
class String
{
private:
    char *str;         // A traditional string
    int size;          // Size of str buffer
    int *refs;         // Number of references to str
public:
    String(const String &s);
    String(const int length=0);
    String(const char *s);
    ~String();
    String &operator=(const String &s);
    String &operator=(const char *s);
    friend int operator==(const String &s1, const String &s2);
    friend int operator!=(const String &s1, const String &s2);
    friend int operator<(const String &s1, const String &s2);
    friend String &operator+(const String &s1, const String &s2);
```

```
    friend ostream &operator<<(ostream &os, const String &s);
    operator char*() const { return str; }

};
#endif
```

The source code for the interface and implementation of **String** can be found in STRCLASS.H and STRCLASS.CPP, respectively. From now on in the book, programs that make use of the **String** class will include the STRCLASS.H file at the beginning of the source file.

```
#include "strclass.h"
```

Such programs must be linked to the object file that is created from STRCLASS.CPP by adding the filename STRCLASS.CPP to the project manager file list for the program being compiled.

The next program shows some of the capabilities of the new **String** class. Clear the desktop and load Program P8-3 now.

P8-3

```
#include <iostream.h>
#include "strclass.h"

main()
{
    String s1 = "str1";
    char p[10] = { "str2" };
    String s2 = p;

    String s3 = s1+s2;
    cout << "s3: " << s3 << "\n";                    // 1

    String s4;
    s4 = s1+s2;
    cout << "s4: " << s4 << "\n";                    // 2

    String s5 = s1+" characterPointer";
    cout << "s5: " << s5 << "\n";                    // 3

    String s6 = "characterPointer "+s1;
    cout << "s6: " << s6 << "\n";                    // 4

    cout << (s1+s2) << "\n";                         // 5
    cout << (s1+" StringConstant") << "\n";          // 6
    cout << ("StringConstant "+s2) << "\n";          // 7

    String *s1p = new String;
    *s1p = "pointer";
    cout << (*s1p+" <=") << "\n";                    // 8
```

```
    String *s2p = new String;
    *s2p = *s1p;
    delete s1p;
    cout << *s2p << "\n";                       // 9

    String *s3p = new String("Hello");
    *s3p = *s3p+*s3p;
    cout << *s3p << "\n";                       // 10
}
```

Create a project, P8-3.PRJ. Add two files to the list: P8-3.CPP and STRCLASS.CPP. Then compile and run the program.

```
s3: str1str2
s4: str1str2
s5: str1 characterPointer
s6: characterPointer str1
str1str2
str1 StringConstant
StringConstant str2
pointer <=
pointer
HelloHello
```

Study the output for the program while referring to the source listing to get an idea of how the new **String** operators work.

This program shows that assignment is possible for **String** objects from source objects of various types. For instance, **s1** is initialized from a string constant, **s2** is initialized from an array of characters, and **s3** is initialized from a **String** object resulting from the concatenation of **s1** and **s2**. The first **cout** statement verifies that all the preceding operations were properly performed. Whereas the **String s3** is created and initialized simultaneously, **s4** is first declared without initialization. It is not initialized until the statement following the declaration.

The first case, **s3**, invokes the constructor receiving a **String** argument. The second case tests the assignment operator. For output, both use the << friend function that receives a **String** argument. The initialization of **s5** shows that a **String** object can be concatenated with a string constant. In the next declaration, the order of concatenation for **s6** is reversed so that the string constant is the first argument to the concatenation operator and the **String** object is the second argument.

The definition of **s5** would be possible even if the + operator were a member function and not a friend. However, in the case of **s6**, + would not work as a member function because the compiler would not know how to apply the + operator to the first argument, which is a string constant.

The fifth **cout** statement shows that two **String** objects can be concatenated, creating a temporary pointer that is used as an argument to the **cout <<** operator. The sixth and seventh **cout** statements show that this concatenation works with a **String** object and a string constant, regardless of the order of arguments.

Next, you can see how to declare a pointer to a string and initialize it to point to an anonymous **String** object created with the new operator. Since no argument is given to this constructor, the **String** object contains an empty string. Even though the buffer for this string is only one byte containing a null, or 0, the object can be assigned a new string by indirect reference through the pointer.

```
String *slp = new String;
*slp = "pointer";
```

This shows some of the real power of automatic memory management. Make sure that you understand the first statement in this listing. It is very common practice in C++ to use pointers to anonymous objects. Because automatic memory management facilitates the creation and destruction of such objects, the programmer is free to worry about other problems. The four statements associated with the ninth **cout** statement in the program show how some of this memory management works. By using indirection (*), an entirely new object is created for **s2p** with the following statement:

```
*s2p = *slp;
```

If the * had not preceded both pointers, then **s2p** would merely be assigned to point to the same object pointed to by **s1p**. In that case, the subsequent delete operation would delete the only copy of the **String** object containing "pointer" as its string constant. The ninth **cout** statement would then be in error because no object would exist to print. However, since

```
*s2p
```

denotes an object, not a pointer to an object, the assignment statement increments the number of references to the "pointer" string. Now when **delete** is called, the number of references is decremented, but the string is not actually deleted. The final **cout** statement shows that an anonymous **String** object can be initialized through the constructor receiving a **char *** or string constant as an argument. You can also see that it is possible to reassign a **String** object with the value of a new string, resulting from concatenating the object with itself.

String Comparison Operators

Program P8-4 verifies that the string comparison operators work properly. Create a project file, P8-4.PRJ, which includes P8-4.CPP and STRCLASS.CPP.

P8-4

```
#include <iostream.h>
#include "strclass.h"

main()
{
    String s1 = "one";
    String s2 = "two";

    cout << "s1 == s2      : "  << (s1 == s2) << "\n";
    cout << "s1 != s2      : "  << (s1 != s2) << "\n";
    cout << "s1 == \"one\"   : " << (s1 == "one") << "\n";
    cout << "\"two\" == s2   : " << ("two" == s2) << "\n";
    cout << "s1 < s2       : "  << (s1 < s2) << "\n";
    cout << "s2 < s1       : "  << (s2 < s1) << "\n";
    cout << "s1 < s1       : "  << (s1 < s1) << "\n";
    cout << "s1 < \"one\"    : " << (s1 < "one") << "\n";
    cout << "s1 < \"onex\"   : " << (s1 < "onex") << "\n";
}
```

Compile and run the program to see the following output:

```
s1 == s2     : 0
s1 != s2     : 1
s1 == "one"  : 1
"two" == s2  : 1
s1 < s2      : 1
s2 < s1      : 0
```

```
sl < sl      : 0
sl < "one"   : 0
sl < "onex"  : 1
```

String **sl** is set to "one" and **s2** gets "two" as its initial value. Each of the statements in the program prints the expression being evaluated followed by a number that indicates the result of evaluating that expression. The number is always 0 or 1. In C++, 0 represents false and 1 represents true. So these expressions can be used inside tests in loops and conditional expressions. It is important to note that the < operator returns true if the second argument is longer than the first, even though all characters in the first string are matched in the second string. This supports standard lexical sorting and will prove useful later in the ordering of lists.

Programs P8-3 and P8-4 show that the initial goals of ease of use and reusability have been met for the **String** class.

Lists and Iterators with Strings

With a small number of changes, it is easy to adapt the **Iterator** and **List** classes developed in Chapter 7 to use strings instead of **char** *s. Program P8-5 takes the last program in Chapter 7 and implements these changes. Close Project P8-4 and clear the desktop. Load Program P8-5 and create a project file, P8-5.PRJ. Add P8-5.CPP and STRCLASS.CPP to the project.

P8-5

```
#include <string.h>
#include <iostream.h>
#include "strclass.h"

class Choice
{
private:
    String str;
public:
    Choice *next;
    Choice *prev;
    Choice(const String &s) : str(s) { }
    ~Choice() { }
    const String &getStr() { return str; }
};
```

```
class List
{
private:
    Choice *tail;
public:
    List(Choice *ch=0) { tail=ch; }
    List (String &s) { tail=0; add(s); }
    void add(const String &s);
    void add(const char *s);
    Choice *getTail() { return tail; }
};

void List::add(const String &s)
{
    Choice *temp = new Choice(s);
    if (!tail)
    {
        temp->prev = temp->next = 0;
    }
    else if (!tail->prev)
    {
        temp->prev = 0;
        temp->next = tail;
        tail->prev = temp;
    }
    else
    {
        temp->prev = tail->prev;
        temp->next = tail;
        tail->prev->next = temp;
        tail->prev = temp;
    }
    tail = temp;
}

void List::add(const char *s) { add(String(s)); }

class Iter
{
private:
    Choice *current;
public:
    Iter(List l) { current = l.getTail(); }
    Choice *operator++();
    Choice *operator--();
    Iter &operator =(const Iter &iter)
        { current = iter.current; return *this; }
    Iter &operator =(Choice *ch)
        { current = ch; return *this; }
};
```

```
Choice *Iter::operator++()
{
    if (current)
    {
        Choice *temp = current;
        current = current->prev;
        return temp;
    }
    else
        return 0;
}

Choice *Iter::operator--()
{
    if (current)
    {
        Choice *temp = current;
        current = current->next;
        return temp;
    }
    else
        return 0;
}

main()
{
    List lst("zero");               // Create a list
    Iter it = lst;
    lst.add("one");
    lst.add("two");
    lst.add("three");

    Choice *cl;                     // Print the list
    while ( (cl = ++it) != 0 )
        cout << cl->getStr() << "\n";
    cout << "==========\n";
    it = lst.getTail();
    while ( (cl = --it) != 0 )
        cout << cl->getStr() << "\n";
}
```

Any program that wants to use the **String** class must include the following line at the top of the program:

```
#include "strclass.h"
```

Now the **Choice** class is modified. The private member, **str**, is changed from a **char *** to **a String**. All subsequent references to **str** must reflect this type change. The affected definitions in the **Choice** class are these:

```
Choice(const String &s) : str(s) { }
~Choice() { }
const String &getStr() { return str; }
```

There are a couple of other changes that you might not expect. Since a **String** object knows how to initialize itself, it is no longer necessary to put initialization code in the body of the constructor definition, which now receives a string reference as an argument. Thus,

```
Choice(const char *s)
    { str=new char[strlen(s)+1]; strcpy(str, s); }
```

is replaced by

```
Choice(const String &s) : str(s) { }
```

The expression following the **:** and preceding the {} is called a *constructor initializer* (sometimes referred to as a *ctor initializer* in technical documentation and grammar specifications). The **str** in this initializer refers to the **str** private member of the **String** class. The argument in the subsequent parentheses must have the same type as **str**. The initializer assigns **str** the value of the argument, **s**. The constructor initializer is called before the code in the body of the **Choice** constructor definition.

Some changes must also be made to the **List** class. The following statements were modified when Program P7-2 was adapted to use **String** objects:

```
class List
{
//...

    List(Choice *ch=0) { tail=ch; }
    List (String &s) { tail=0; add(s); }
    void add(const String &s);
}
//...
void List::add(const String &s)
{
//...
}
```

Compile and run Program P8-5 now. These are the only changes that are required. The **Iter** class uses pointers to **Choice** objects but does not manipulate them directly, so no changes are required for **Iter**.

When you compile and run the program, you should get exactly the same output that you did for Program P7-2.

```
zero
one
two
three
==========
three
two
one
zero
```

Access to a List's Head

Before moving on to more advanced uses of lists and iterators, it is useful to modify the **List** class to maintain a pointer to the head of a list. Four changes are required to make the **List** class in Program P8-5 initialize and give access to a pointer to the head of a list. First, in the private section of the **List** class, add the line,

```
Choice *head;
```

to point to the head of the list. Next, change the first two constructors. Replace

```
public:
    List(Choice *ch=0) { tail=ch; }
    List (String &s) { tail=0; add(s); }
```

with

```
public:
   List(Choice *h=0, Choice *t=0)
       { head=h; tail = t ? t : h; }
   List (const String &s) { tail=0; add(s); head=tail; }
```

The first constructor gets two arguments; both are pointers to a **Choice** object. Both of these arguments have a default value of 0. This means that when this constructor is called, it can be supplied with zero, one, or two arguments. If two arguments are given, **head** and **tail** are assigned these respective **Choice** pointers. If only one argument is given, **head** and **tail** will both be assigned the value of that argument. If no arguments are given, both **head** and **tail** are assigned 0, meaning that they point to nothing. Such a list would be completely empty. With all these options, you can use the same constructor to create a new empty list, or a list that points to a subset of an existing list, or a list that points to the head and tail of an existing list.

The expression,

```
{ head=h; tail = t ? t : h; }
```

is not as complicated as it looks. Remember that **h** and **t** have default values of 0 if they are not supplied; **head** is always set to **h**, even if **h** is 0. Before **tail** is assigned a value, the subsequent expression tests to see whether **t** is 0. If it is not, then **tail** is assigned the value of **t**. Otherwise, it is assigned the value of **h**. If no arguments are supplied, both **head** and **tail** are set to 0. If one argument is supplied, **head** and **tail** are set to the same value. If two arguments are supplied, **head** and **tail** are set to the respective values of those arguments.

Now you need a way to get the head of a list. Add the following method immediately after the **getTail** method:

```
Choice *getHead() { return head; }
```

The only situation not handled is the case of adding a new element to an empty list; **head** must be set to point to a new element only if **head**'s current value is 0. This code is inserted at the end of **List::add** just before the final }, which terminates the definition.

```
if (!head)            // Only true when adding first
    head = tail;      // element to an empty list.
```

For convenience, add two lines as the first public definitions in the **Iter** class.

```
Iter() { current=0; }
Iter(Choice *c) { current = c; }
```

Program P8-6 reflects all the changes discussed. If you have been implementing these changes all along, save your program now under a unique name, like P8-5B.CPP, or simply load Program P8-6. Make sure **main** looks like Program P8-6 and your project contains either P8-5B or P8-6 in addition to STRCLASS.CPP.

P8-6

```
#include <string.h>
#include <iostream.h>
#include "strclass.h"

class Choice
{
private:
    String str;
public:
    Choice *next;
    Choice *prev;
    Choice(const String &s) : str(s) { }
    ~Choice() { }
    const String &getStr() { return str; }
};

class List
{
private:
    Choice *tail;
    Choice *head;
public:
    List(Choice *h=0, Choice *t=0)
        { head=h; tail = t ? t : h; }
    List (const String &s) { tail=0; add(s); head=tail; }
    void add(const String &s);
    void add(const char *s);
    Choice *getTail() { return tail; }
    Choice *getHead() { return head; }
};

void List::add(const String &s)
{
    Choice *temp = new Choice(s);
    if (!tail)
    {
        temp->prev = temp->next = 0;
    }
    else if (!tail->prev)
    {
```

```
        temp->prev = 0;
        temp->next = tail;
        tail->prev = temp;
    }
    else
    {
        temp->prev = tail->prev;
        temp->next = tail;
        tail->prev->next = temp;
        tail->prev = temp;
    }
    tail = temp;
    if (!head)          // Only true when adding first
        head = tail;    // element to an empty list.
}

void List::add(const char *s) { add(String(s)); }

class Iter
{
private:
    Choice *current;
public:
    Iter() { current=0; }
    Iter(Choice *c) { current = c; }
    Iter(List l) { current = l.getTail(); }
    Choice *operator++();
    Choice *operator--();
    Iter &operator =(const Iter &iter)
        { current = iter.current; return *this; }
    Iter &operator =(Choice *ch)
        { current = ch; return *this; }
};

Choice *Iter::operator++()
{
    if (current)
    {
        Choice *temp = current;
        current = current->prev;
        return temp;
    }
    else
        return 0;
}

Choice *Iter::operator--()
{
    if (current)
    {
        Choice *temp = current;
```

```
        current = current->next;
        return temp;
    }
    else
        return 0;
}

main()
{
    List lst("zero");
    lst.add("one");
    List save = lst.getHead();
    lst.add("two");
    lst.add("three");
    save.add("Where will this go?");

    Choice *cl;
    cout << "==========lst: forward from head\n";
    Iter it = lst.getHead();
    while ( (cl = ++it) != 0 )
        cout << cl->getStr() << "\n";
    cout << "==========lst: backward from tail\n";
    it=lst.getTail();
    while ( (cl = --it) != 0 )
        cout << cl->getStr() << "\n";
    cout << "==========save:  forward from head\n";
    it=save.getHead();
    while ( (cl = ++it) != 0 )
        cout << cl->getStr() << "\n";
    cout << "==========save: backward from head\n";
    it=save.getHead();
    while ( (cl = --it) != 0 )
        cout << cl->getStr() << "\n";
    cout << "==========save: forward from tail\n";
    it=save.getTail();
    while ( (cl = ++it) != 0 )
        cout << cl->getStr() << "\n";
    cout << "==========save: backward from tail\n";
    it=save.getTail();
    while ( (cl = --it) != 0 )
        cout << cl->getStr() << "\n";
    cout << "==========\n";
}
```

Compile and run Program P8-6 now. The output shows the increased flexibility in using the **List** and **Iter** classes.

```
==========lst: forward from head
zero
Where will this go?
```

```
one
two
three
==========lst: backward from tail
three
two
one
Where will this go?
zero
==========save:  forward from head
zero
Where will this go?
one
two
three
==========save: backward from head
zero
==========save: forward from tail
Where will this go?
one
two
three
==========save: backward from tail
Where will this go?
zero
==========
```

The main thing to notice is that after elements "zero" and "one" are added to **lst**, a new list is created. This list is called **save**. Recall that the **List** constructor can receive zero, one, or two arguments. The constructor for **save** is given a single argument, which is the head of the existing list denoted by **lst.getHead**. Since the tail argument is not supplied to the constructor, it takes on the same value as the head. This means that the element "zero" is pointed to by both **head** and **tail** in the new **save** list. Recall that when a new element is added to a list, it is added after the member that the tail currently points to.

The building of the first list, **lst**, is completed by adding "two" and "three" to the end of the list. Now the **save** list calls the **List::add** function with "Where will this go?" as an argument. The output verifies that this new element is actually inserted between the "zero" and "one" elements in the **lst** list. The **save** list has a head that points to "zero" and a tail that points to "Where will this go?". This is what is expected since "zero" was the tail of **save** prior to adding the new element.

Now the **lst** List is printed twice; once by setting the iterator **it** to point to the head of the list and moving forward, and once by setting **it** to the tail of the list and moving backward. Then the **save** list is printed in four different ways: first, from the head through the end of the list moving forward; next, from the head to the beginning of the list moving backward. The next two loops start at the tail and move forward and backward, respectively. This shows that the iterator depends on the terminals of the list indicated by **prev = = 0** at the end of the list and **next = = 0** at the beginning of the list.

The iterator could just as easily have been written to stop when the value **it** returns was equal to **getTail** at the end of the list or **getHead** at the beginning of the list. Different results would have been produced if the **Iter** class had been implemented this way. But the way that **Iter** is now implemented makes it easy for a new **Iter** to gain access to a subset of an existing list as well as to the complete list.

The **String** class developed in this chapter, as well as the enhancements made to the **Iter** class, will prove invaluable in the next chapter when you apply these classes to sorting lists and developing applicators that actually modify lists in some specified manner.

From now on, before opening any new projects, be sure to close any open projects and clear the desktop (ALT-SPACEBAR **C**).

9 Applicators for File Lists and Directories

Applicators are a powerful form of control abstraction. Like the iterators discussed in Chapters 7 and 8, applicators walk through linked lists of objects. The difference is that while iterators simply return pointers to give access to list elements, applicators actually change the list or perform an operation on list members. Applicators come in two flavors: those that alter list order, and those that alter list members. Both types of applicators will be developed in this chapter. The primary example will be the sorting of lists. Different techniques for comparing and sorting the elements of a list will be analyzed.

Since you are becoming familiar with C++ language concepts, this chapter will focus more on using the Borland C++ programming platform. Rather than simply loading programs and following their explanation before running them, you will be asked to implement more modifications. This chapter includes a little bit more about using the editor, including the use of the clipboard for copying text, and the use of the project manager for compiling multiple source file programs.

A Simple Applicator

To start, let's modify the last program from Chapter 8. Before invoking the Borland C++ programming environment, be sure you have logged to the appropriate disk directory for this chapter (\DT\CH9). To load Program P8-6, enter **..\CH8\P8-6** as the filename. Rename the program MY9-1.CPP using **File/Save** as (ALT-F A).

The first thing you are going to do is add an applicator function to print the contents of a list. You have seen similar code over and over again in the **main** functions of programs in Chapters 7 and 8.

```
void listPrint(List &lst)
{
    Choice *cl;
    Iter it = lst.getHead();
    while ( (cl = ++it) != 0 )
        cout << cl->getStr() << "\n";
}
```

It might seem like a trick at first to call this function an applicator. After all, there is nothing new here. You are simply packaging the code to print a list inside a function. The **listPrint** function gets a list as an argument. It then declares a local variable, **it**, which is set to the head of the list. Then a pointer to a **Choice** object is declared. The entire list is printed using the iterator to walk through the list. One of the definitions of an applicator is that it applies some function to each member of a collection or list. In this case, the function being applied to each member is to extract a pointer to its **String** component and to pass that value on to the **cout** operator function, which in turn prints the **String**.

The easiest way to make the **listPrint** function is to copy existing code from the **main** function inside MY9-1.CPP. Next, add the necessary text to turn the copied code into a function. The quickest way to do this is to have the Clipboard window and the Edit window visible simultaneously. Use the search function to find **main**. (ALT-S F **main**.) Press CTRL-Z a number of times to scroll the text in the Edit window until the **main** function appears at the top. Now resize the Edit window containing MY9-1.CPP. There are two ways to do this. If you have a mouse, position the mouse cursor on the lower-right corner of the window. Press the left mouse button and hold it down. While continuing to hold the mouse button, move the mouse upward until the window takes up about half the screen. Then let go of the mouse button.

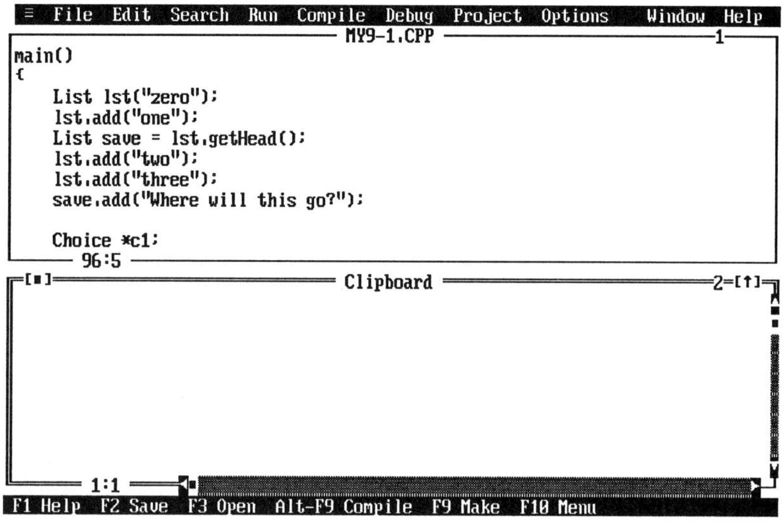

Figure 9-1. *Clipboard window after resize*

If you don't have a mouse, select the **S**ize/**M**ove option inside the Window menu. You can invoke this menu by pressing ALT-W. The shortcut for invoking the **W**indow/**S**ize/**M**ove command is CTRL-F5. When the **S**ize/**M**ove command is active, the current window is highlighted. Use the arrow keys to move the window. Use the arrow keys while depressing the SHIFT key to resize the window. To move the lower border of the window so that it takes up half the screen, press the UP ARROW key about four or five times while keeping the SHIFT key depressed. Press RETURN when you are through resizing the window.

Now open the Clipboard window with the **E**dit/**S**how clipboard command (ALT-E S). Resize the Clipboard window so it fits in the lower half of this screen. Select **W**indow/**S**ize/Move. Experiment with the ARROW keys to move the Clipboard and SHIFT-ARROW keys to resize the Clipboard until it fits in the lower half of the screen. Press RETURN. Your screen should now look like Figure 9-1.

You can rotate through all open windows by pressing the F6 key. Notice that the active window always has double-line borders. All other windows have single-line borders. Make the Edit window active. Scroll down in the Edit window by pressing CTRL-Z until you see the declaration:

```
Choice *cl;
```

Now copy the next five lines to the clipboard:

```
Choice *cl;
cout << "==========lst: forward from head\n";
Iter it = lst.getHead();
while ( (cl = ++it) != 0 )
    cout << cl->getStr() << "\n";
```

Again, you have two choices depending on whether you have a mouse. If you do, position the mouse cursor on column 1 of the first of these lines. Depress the left mouse button and, while holding it down, drag the mouse downward through the first column until all five lines are highlighted. Release the mouse button. Now move the mouse cursor up to the main menu bar and press the left button while the mouse cursor is on Edit. When the menu appears, move the mouse down to the Copy command; then press and release the left button again. The highlighted text is immediately copied to the Clipboard window. Your screen should now look like Figure 9-2.

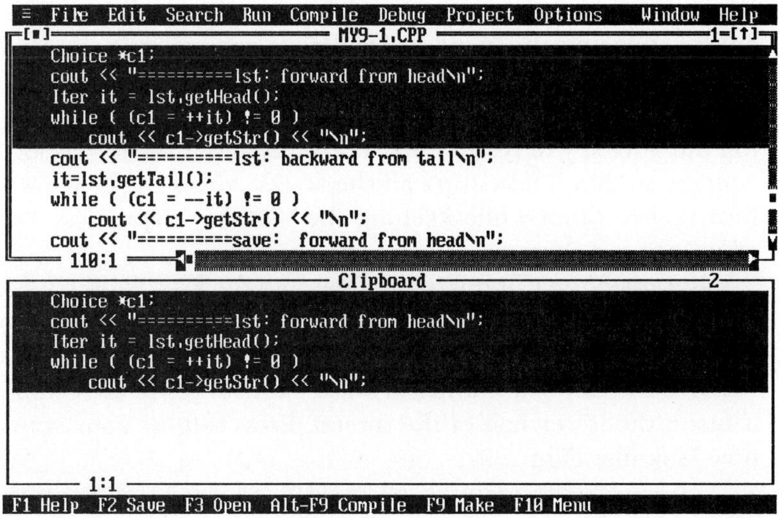

Figure 9-2. *Clipboard window after copy*

For those of you who don't have a mouse, you can achieve the same effect by moving the cursor to the beginning of the first line to be copied. Press CTRL-K B. Now move the cursor down one line past the last line to be copied. Press CTRL-K K. The text about to be copied is now highlighted. Use the **E**dit/**C**opy command (ALT-E C) to copy the highlighted text to the clipboard.

You can now go into the clipboard and edit the text to turn it into the **listPrint** applicator function you want to define. Press F6 until the Clipboard window becomes active. (Mouse users can simply click the left mouse button on the window border.) The first thing to do is delete the **cout** statement immediately following the declaration of the Choice object. You simply don't need this line. Move the cursor to the second line in the Clipboard window and press CTRL-Y. Now move the cursor back up to the beginning of the first line. Press CTRL-N to insert a new line, and type these two lines:

```
void listPrint(List &lst)
{
```

Go to the end of the clipboard buffer (CTRL-PGDN) and insert the closing brace. The complete function definition in the Clipboard window looks like this:

```
void listPrint(List &lst)
{
    Choice *cl;
    Iter it = lst.getHead();
    while ( (cl = ++it) != 0 )
        cout << cl->getStr() << "\n";
}
```

The next thing to do is to move this code to the appropriate spot in MY9-1.CPP. Make this file the active window (F6). Then search backward for **main** (**S**earch/**F**ind). When the dialogue box for Find appears, tab down to the direction field. Use the DOWN ARROW key to mark backward and press RETURN. The cursor should appear at the beginning of the definition for the function **main**. Move back to the Clipboard window. Make sure all of the **listPrint** function is highlighted, including the new text you just typed. Move back to the Edit window with the cursor on the *m* in **main**. Press CTRL-N to open up a line, and paste the **listPrint** function into the window right above **main**. Use the **E**dit/**P**aste command (ALT-E P). The text is inserted as expected just above **main**. If it annoys you that the copied text is always highlighted, you can press CTRL-K H to get rid of the highlighting.

You have two choices as far as the clipboard is concerned. You can leave the text in the clipboard for future reference and editing. Or, you can highlight it and delete it with the **E**dit/**C**lear command. Whenever text is either cut or copied from an Edit window, it is always appended to the clipboard. Only the text from the most recent cut or copy is highlighted inside the clipboard. Any subsequent paste will only copy the highlighted text from the clipboard to the desired Edit window.

Now, any time you want to print a list from the beginning to the end, you can replace the code

```
Choice *cl;
Iter it = lst.getHead();
while ( (cl = ++it) != 0 )
    cout << cl->getStr() << "\n";
```

with

```
listPrint(lst);
```

Using **listPrint** is less flexible than printing the list explicitly with an iterator, because it goes only forward through a list and always prints the entire list. But this is what you will want to do most frequently. If you return to Chapter 8 and study the output from Program P8-6, you will see that printing forward from the head of the **lst** and **save** lists produces exactly the same result. To change this, initialize **save** to point to the tail of **lst**. Change the line

```
List save = lst.getHead();
```

inside **main** to

```
List save = lst.getTail();
```

You can replace all the code that handles the printing of the two lists in **main** with four lines. Edit the definition of **main** to look like this:

```
main()
{
    List lst("zero");
    lst.add("one");
    List save = lst.getTail();
    lst.add("two");
    lst.add("three");
    save.add("Where will this go?");

    cout << "==========lst: forward from head\n";
    listPrint(lst);
    cout << "==========save:  forward from head\n";
    listPrint(save);
}
```

This change eliminates the declaration of **Choice *cl** inside **main** as it is no longer needed.

Once you have made all these changes, save the program (F2). You are ready to compile and test. Like the program it was derived from, MY9-1.CPP must use the **String** class. This means that the program must include the header file STRCLASS.H and must link to STRCLASS .CPP. Set up these linkage dependencies in a project manager file called MY9-1.PRJ. First create the project file with the **P**roject/**O**pen project command. When the Load Project File window appears, type **MY9-1** into the input field and press RETURN.

Select **P**roject/**A**dd item or press the insert key (INS) for a shortcut. Type ***.CPP** for the filename specification. A list of files matching the specification appears. Type **M** and notice that the file list scrolls to a name beginning with M. With MY9-1.CPP highlighted, press RETURN. Now type **S** to move the highlight bar to the first filename that starts with S. With STRCLASS.CPP highlighted, press RETURN. Press ESC to close the window. The Project Items list now contains this:

```
Project Items

STRCLASS.CPP
MY9-1.CPP
```

You can open any of the files in the Project Items list by highlighting the filename and pressing RETURN, or you can use the mouse to point at the filename and double click the left button. Open STRCLASS.CPP this way. An Edit window is immediately opened which contains the file.

Now invoke the compiler with **C**ompile/**M**ake EXE file (F9). Then run the program (**R**un/**R**un or CTRL-F9). If you have implemented all these changes properly, the output will look like this when you run the program:

```
==========1st: forward from head
zero
one
Where will this go?
two
three
==========save:  forward from head
one
Where will this go?
two
three
```

Applicators for Ordering Lists

The next applicator you will add to this program will sort lists. The following function is a sorting applicator. When this function is applied to its list argument, it changes the order of the list elements so that they are sorted alphabetically.

```
void listSort(List &l)
{
    Choice *head = l.getHead();
    for (Choice *i=head->prev; i; i=i->prev)
    {
        String si = i->str;
        for (Choice *j=i->next; j && si < (j->str); j=j->next)
            j->prev->str = j->str;
        if (j)
            j->prev->str = si;
        else
            head->str = si;
    }
}
```

The sort applicator uses two **Choice** pointers, **i** and **j**, to point to list members. The pointer **i** is initialized to the second element of the list. The outer **for** loop walks **i** down toward the end of the list. On each pass, **i** makes a temporary copy of its **String** component in **si**. The inner **for** loop sets **j** to point to one element before **i**. While **i** walks forward through the list in the outer loop, **j** walks backward in the inner loop. As long as the temporary **String** in **si** is less than the **String** in the object pointed to by **j**, **j** copies its **String** to the following element in the list:

```
j->prev->str = j->str;
```

The **j** pointer then moves backward one list element. What **j** is trying to do is find the place at the front of the list where it should insert **si**. This technique is called a *bubble sort* because the item in question, **si**, bubbles up toward the top of the list until it finds its appropriate level. After each pass through the outer loop, it is guaranteed that every item from **i** backward through the beginning of the list will be properly sorted.

Meanwhile, back in the inner loop, the **j** pointer keeps walking toward the beginning of the list until it finds a value that is less than the temporary **String**, **si**, or until it walks past the head of the list. If **j** walks off the head of the list, **si** is placed at the head of the list because the value of **si** is less than all items before **i** in the list. Otherwise, **si** is placed immediately after the item that caused the expression

```
si < (j->str)
```

to fail.

Type this function into MY9-1.CPP, immediately after the **listPrint** function and just before **main**. If you don't want to type in all these changes, a complete listing of the program, including all modifications made so far, is on the disk under the name P9-1.CPP. You are going to test the sort applicator on a list of animal names. You can delete all the code inside of **main** and replace it with the following:

```
main()
{
    List lst;
    lst.add("weasel");
    lst.add("bat");
    lst.add("zebra");
```

```
    lst.add("possum");
    lst.add("dog");
    lst.add("cat");
    lst.add("aardvark");
    lst.add("orangutan");

    cout << "==========before sort\n";
    listPrint(lst);
    listSort(lst);
    cout << "==========after sort\n";
    listPrint(lst);
    cout << "==========\n";
}
```

Save the program and compile it. Selecting **C**ompile/**M**ake EXE automatically uses the current project specification to build the executable file. Now look in the Message window. If you cannot see the strings in the Message window, blow the window up to full screen size by selecting it (F6) and pressing F5.

What happened? The Message window contains the error message:

```
Error...'str' is not accessible in function listSort.
```

The **str** member of the **Choice** class is private. This means that **str** cannot be accessed in an expression like

```
String s1 = i->str
```

unless the function containing this expression is a member function or a friend function of the class **Choice**.

To make this work, you can make **listSort** a friend of the **Choice** class. Do this by adding the following line to the **Choice** class just before the closing brace:

```
friend void listSort(List &l);
```

Compile again. Now you get one warning message and one error message:

```
Warning...: Style of function definition is now obsolete
Error...: , expected
```

The compiler thinks the word *List* is the name of a variable, and not a type. This would be legal in the old style of function argument definitions supported by the original Kernighan and Ritchie (K & R) C. For C++ and ANSI C the style is obsolete, but is still supported so that older code will continue to work. Because the **List** class is declared after the declaration of **listSort**, the compiler does not know that **List** is a type. It thinks it is a variable name in the old K & R style and is now looking for a second argument (indicated by a comma) or the end of the argument list (indicated by a closing parenthesis). Since it finds neither, the compiler signals an error.

To solve this, you need a forward declaration for the **List** class, which must come before the declaration of the **Choice** class. The following line will do the job:

```
class List;  // Forward declaration of List
             // required for declaration of listSort.
```

Place this on the line immediately before

```
class Choice
{
//...
};
```

Compile and run the program now. Look at the output to verify the order of the list before and after sorting. The program is working correctly if the second list is in alphabetical order. If you are having trouble getting the program to compile, you might check your file against Program P9-1, which is listed here for your convenience. You can also find the file on the disk.

P9-1
```
#include <string.h>
#include <iostream.h>
#include "strclass.h"

class List;  // Forward declaration of List
             // required for declaration of listSort.

class Choice
{
private:
    String str;
```

```
public:
    Choice *next;
    Choice *prev;
    Choice(const String &s) : str(s) { }
    ~Choice() { }
    const String &getStr() { return str; }
    friend void listSort(List &l);
};

class List
{
private:
    Choice *tail;
    Choice *head;
public:
    List(Choice *h=0, Choice *t=0)
        { head=h; tail = t ? t : h; }
    List (const String &s) { tail=0; add(s); head=tail; }
    void add(const String &s);
    void add(const char *s);
    Choice *getTail() { return tail; }
    Choice *getHead() { return head; }
};

void List::add(const String &s)
{
    Choice *temp = new Choice(s);
    if (!tail)
    {
        temp->prev = temp->next = 0;
    }
    else if (!tail->prev)
    {
        temp->prev = 0;
        temp->next = tail;
        tail->prev = temp;
    }
    else
    {
        temp->prev = tail->prev;
        temp->next = tail;
        tail->prev->next = temp;
        tail->prev = temp;
    }
    tail = temp;
    if (!head)          // Only true when adding first
        head = tail;    // element to an empty list.
}

void List::add(const char *s) { add(String(s)); }

class Iter
{
```

```
private:
    Choice *current;
public:
    Iter() { current=0; }
    Iter(Choice *c) { current = c; }
    Iter(List l) { current = l.getTail(); }
    Choice *operator++();
    Choice *operator--();
    Iter &operator =(const Iter &iter)
        { current = iter.current; return *this; }
    Iter &operator =(Choice *ch)
        { current = ch; return *this; }
};

Choice *Iter::operator++()
{
    if (current)
    {
        Choice *temp = current;
        current = current->prev;
        return temp;
    }
    else
        return 0;
}

Choice *Iter::operator--()
{
    if (current)
    {
        Choice *temp = current;
        current = current->next;
        return temp;
    }
    else
        return 0;
}

void listPrint(List &lst)
{
    Choice *cl;
    Iter it = lst.getHead();
    while ( (cl = ++it) != 0 )
        cout << cl->getStr() << "\n";
}

void listSort(List &l)
{
    Choice *head = l.getHead();
    for (Choice *i=head->prev; i; i=i->prev)
    {
        String si = i->str;
        for (Choice *j=i->next; j && si < (j->str); j=j->next)
            j->prev->str = j->str;
```

```
            if (j)
                j->prev->str = si;
            else
                head->str = si;
        }
}

main()
{
    List lst;
    lst.add("weasel");
    lst.add("bat");
    lst.add("zebra");
    lst.add("possum");
    lst.add("dog");
    lst.add("cat");
    lst.add("aardvark");
    lst.add("orangutan");

    cout << "==========before sort\n";
    listPrint(lst);
    listSort(lst);
    cout << "==========after sort\n";
    listPrint(lst);
    cout << "==========\n";
}
```

Applicators for Changing List Elements

There is a second type of applicator that, rather than changing the order of a list, manipulates the values of list elements. For example, suppose you want to change all the **Choice** elements in a list to uppercase. This can be done with a very simple applicator.

```
void listUpr(List &l)
{
    Choice *c = l.getTail();
    Iter it = l;
    while ( (c = --it) != 0 )
        strupr(c->getStr());
}
```

Add this code to Program MY9-1.CPP between **listSort** and **main**. In **main**, change the call

```
listSort(lst);
```

to

```
listUpr(list);
```

You might also want to change the two **cout** messages to reflect the new function name:

```
cout << "==========before listUpr\n";
listPrint(lst);
listUpr(lst);
cout << "==========after listUpr\n";
listPrint(lst);
```

Now compile and run the program. Instead of sorting the list, the program converts all **Choice** elements to uppercase.

A Reusable List Applicator

It is conceivable that you might want to do many different things to a list. You might want to change its components to uppercase and then back to lowercase. You might want to add strings to the end of existing choices. If you had a list of filenames, you might want to mark the names that match a certain pattern. Taking this idea a step further, you might want a list applicator that copies all the marked files in the list to a specified directory. To achieve this end, you can generalize the concept of an applicator.

One form of an applicator comes directly from the LISP programming language where the function **apply** takes two arguments: a function name and a list. When **apply** is called with these two arguments, the function is applied to each element in the list. You can produce this kind of result for lists in C++ by defining a function that gets two arguments. The first argument is a list and the second argument is a pointer to a function. The function receives a **Choice** object and manipulates this **Choice** object in some way. The **listApply** function itself uses an iterator to walk through the list that is passed as an argument. For each member of the list, **listApply** invokes the function that is passed to it and the argument to that function is the current **Choice** object. All functions that are passed to **listApply** must have exactly the same prototype as the prototype for the function pointer argument. Here is a list of three possibilities:

```
void choiceUpr(Choice &c)
{
    strupr(c.getStr());
}

void choiceLwr(Choice &c)
{
    strlwr(c.getStr());
}

void choiceMakeGreat(Choice &c)
{
    String temp(c.getStr() + "s are great");
    c.setStr(temp);
}
```

Add the code for these three functions just before **main**. The **setStr** function is a new member function that you need to add to the **Choice** class. Here is the definition:

```
void setStr(const String &s) { str = s; }
```

Make this change to MY9-1.CPP. Then change the name to MY9-2, using **File/Save** as and typing **MY9-2**. Create a new project file, MY9-2.PRJ, that includes MY9-2.CPP and STRCLASS.CPP. Now you are ready to add the **listApply** function just before the definition of **main**.

```
void listApply(List &l, void(*fp) (Choice &c))
{
    Choice *c = l.getTail();
    Iter it = l;
    while ( (c = --it) != 0 )
        fp(*c);
}
```

The second argument to **listApply** is a pointer to a function. Pointers to functions will be covered in more depth a little later in the chapter. For now, suffice it to say that any functions passed to this argument must have the same prototype as the function pointer in the argument list. Insert **listApply** just before **main**. Then, inside **main**, after the list is built, replace

```
cout << "==========before listUpr\n";
listPrint(lst);
listUpr(lst);
cout << "==========after listUpr\n";
listPrint(lst);
cout << "==========\n";
```

with

```
cout << "==========\n";
listPrint(lst);

cout << "==========\n";
listApply(lst, choiceUpr);
listPrint(lst);

cout << "==========\n";
listApply(lst, choiceLwr);
listPrint(lst);

cout << "==========\n";
listApply(lst, choiceMakeGreat);
listPrint(lst);

cout << "==========\n";
```

Run the program. If the screen scrolls too quickly, use F8 to step through it. Press ALT-F5 to view the output. Your text should match Program P9-2.CPP on disk.

A Class for Retrieving File Information

One of the objects most frequently manipulated by computer programs is a file. You need to get information from files such as name, date and time of creation, size, and so forth. You also need to make copies of files, rename files, and delete files. And you frequently want to copy groups of files from one directory to another. To support these activities, a list composed of file elements is handy.

To build such file lists, you need a definition for file objects. Such a definition is provided on the disk in a file called FILEINFO.CPP. The class implemented by this file is called **FileInfo**. The declaration for the class is in the header file FILEINFO.H. This file is on the disk and is shown here:

```
#ifndef __FileInfo__
#define __FileInfo__
#include <dir.h>
#include "strclass.h"
class FileInfo
{
private:
    String driveStr, dirStr, fnameStr, extStr, dateStr, timeStr;
    String fullpathStr;
    ffblk fileblock;
public:
    FileInfo(const String &filename);
    const String &drive()    const { return driveStr; }
    const String &dir()      const { return dirStr; }
    const String &fname()    const { return fnameStr; }
    const String &ext()      const { return extStr; }
    const String &date()     const { return dateStr; }
    const String &time()     const { return timeStr; }
    const String &fullpath() const { return fullpathStr; }
    char attribute()         const { return fileblock.ff_attrib; }
    long size()              const { return fileblock.ff_fsize; }
};
#endif
```

Notice that each of the member functions is followed by the keyword **const**. A **const** member function should be used for a **const** object.

A **const** member function guarantees that it will not change any of the instance variables inside of the object. If a **const** object invokes a member function that is not declared **const**, Borland C++ generates a warning. Normally such a reference would be an error, but **const** functions are relatively new. To avoid breaking old C++ code, the violation was reduced from an error to a warning. After an adequate adjustment period the warning will probably be changed to an error, so be ready. Start adding the **const** keyword to member functions that you know will not change object member variables.

This discussion will not go into great detail on the implementation of this class. You can study the code in FILEINFO.CPP if you are interested in implementation details. Instead, the discussion focuses on how to use the **FileInfo** class. To use a class, the only thing you need to study is the public section of the class declaration.

Looking at FILEINFO.H, you can see that a **FileInfo** object has a single constructor, which gets a **String** as an argument. You cannot tell this from the information provided in the declaration, but the string used by the constructor will accept a complete filename or a filename that includes the standard DOS wildcards, * and ?. If a name with wildcards is given, the name built by the **FileInfo** object is the first file found in the current directory that matches the wildcard pattern. If a file cannot be found that matches the constructor string, all private member strings are set to null and all private integer members are set to zero.

All the member functions after the constructor are for retrieving information about a file. You can get the drive, the directory, the filename, the extension, the date, the time, and the full pathname for the specified file. All these member functions return references to a **String**. You can also get a character that represents the attributes of the current file. Attributes tell you whether a file is read-only, hidden, a system file, or a file directory, or whether the file has been archived with a DOS BACKUP command since it was last modified.

Using the **FileInfo** class is similar to using the **String** class. All you need to do is include the header file at the top of the program, and then write a program that uses the member functions of the **FileInfo** class.

```
#include "fileinfo.h"
```

Then you must link your program to FILEINFO.CPP with the project manager. Actually, since the **FileInfo** class is built using objects from the **String** class, you will have to link to both STRING.CPP and FILEINFO.CPP. However, since the line

```
#include "strclass.h"
```

appears in FILEINFO.H, there is no need to include this line a second time in your program. Now you are going to build a program and a project file that use the **FileInfo** class. Open a new file in the editor (**F**ile/**N**ew). Type the following code in the new file:

```
#include <iostream.h>
#include "fileinfo.h"

main()
{
    String fname = "fileinfo.h";
    FileInfo f(fname);
    cout << f.fname() + f.ext();
    cout << "\t" + f.date();
    cout << "\t" + f.time();
    cout << "\n";
}
```

Now save the file with the name MY9-3.CPP using the **F**ile/**Sa**ve as command.

Select a new project manager file called MY9-3.PRJ (use the **P**roject/**O**pen project command). Prepare to add items to the new project file (**P**roject/**A**dd item). Now add three files to the project items list: MY9-3.CPP, STRCLASS.CPP, and FILEINFO.CPP. Press F9 to compile the program. When you run the program a **FileInfo** object, **f**, is created and initialized with the string "fileinfo.h." Run the program to see that it prints the filename and extension concatenated as a single string, followed by the date and the time.

```
FILEINFO.H     11-25-89   23:26:04
```

This is a good start, but if you print a list of such filenames, they probably will not all line up, because some filenames might extend beyond the tab at eight characters.

To fix this, use the iostream member functions for output formatting. You can use **ios::width** to set the field width for the next item printed to an output stream. This member function will only change the width for the next item. After the item is printed the width state variable returns to its default value.

You can also use the **ios::setf** function to change state variables for an output stream. Changes to stream state through **ios::setf** are permanent and remain in effect until another call to **ios::setf** changes the affected state variables. You can use **ios::setf** to change the default output justification from right to left.

The iostream class also provides three manipulators, **ios::dec**, **ios::hex**, and **ios::oct**, to change the default output base for numbers. The effect of these three manipulators is also permanent. Once you set the output base to hex, for example, all numbers will be printed in hex until the base is explicitly changed.

The following listing shows how these output formatting functions can be used for the **cout** output stream.

```
#include <iostream.h>
#include "fileinfo.h"

main()
{
    String fname = "fileinfo.h";
    FileInfo f(fname);

    cout.setf(ios::left,ios::adjustfield);     // left justify
    cout.width(14);                            // field width
    cout << f.fname()+f.ext();
    cout.setf(ios::right,ios::adjustfield);    // right justify
    cout.width(10);  cout << f.size();
    cout.width(10);  cout << f.date();
    cout.width(10);  cout << f.time();
    cout.width(10);  cout << hex << (int)f.attribute();
    cout << "\n";
}
```

To be on the safe side, it would be wise to change the default number base back to decimal after the file attribute is printed in hex.

```
cout << dec;
```

But since the program ends before any more numbers are printed, changing the base back to decimal isn't strictly necessary.

Make the modifications to the main function and run the program. The output is beginning to look like the output produced by the DOS DIR command.

```
FILEINFO.H           790  11-25-89  23:26:04      20
```

File Attributes

The last number in the output is curious. It is the value returned by the attribute of the file printed in hex. The file attribute uses individual bits of a **char** to determine the attributes of a file. To see what those bits are, open up the file DOS.H, which is in the default include directory. The full pathname for the file is \TC\INCLUDE\DOS.H or \BORLANDC\INCLUDE\DOS.H. Your directory may be different if you modified it during installation. Make sure that you save the current file before opening DOS.H. Now search for the string "FA_" (make sure that the search direction is set to forward). You should find the following six lines:

```
#define FA_RDONLY   0x01    /* Read only attribute */
#define FA_HIDDEN   0x02    /* Hidden file */
#define FA_SYSTEM   0x04    /* System file */
#define FA_LABEL    0x08    /* Volume label */
#define FA_DIREC    0x10    /* Directory */
#define FA_ARCH     0x20    /* Archive */
```

Notice these are all powers of two, making it possible to express any combination of attributes in a 1-byte value. What you need is an output function that prints a letter if the bit associated with the attribute is on, and prints a dash otherwise. Copy these six lines to the clipboard and then close the window containing DOS.H. Replace the line in **main** that prints the attribute

```
cout.width(10);  cout << hex << (int)f.attribute();
```

with

```
cout << "   ";
cout << ((f. attribute() & FA_RDONLY) ? 'r' : '-');
```

You will need one **cout** statement for each of the file attributes listed in the clipboard (except LABEL). One quick way to do this is to copy the **cout** statement and delete FA_RDONLY so that you have

```
cout << ((f.attribute() & FA_) ? 'r' : '-');
```

Open the clipboard, resize it, and move it to the bottom of the screen. Now make four copies of the last statement and copy the symbolic names for the attributes directly from the clipboard into the **cout** statements. You should have one **cout** statement for each of the following:

```
FA_RDONLY
FA_HIDDEN
FA_SYSTEM
FA_DIREC
FA_ARCH
```

Change 'r' for each attribute. You must also put the following include at the top of the file:

```
#include <dos.h>
```

Now save the file. MY9-3.CPP should now look like this:

```
#include <iostream.h>
#include <dos.h>
#include "fileinfo.h"

main()
{
    String fname = "fileinfo.h";
    FileInfo f(fname);

    cout.setf(ios::left,ios::adjustfield);      // left justify
    cout.width(14);                             // field width
    cout << f.fname()+f.ext();
    cout.setf(ios::right,ios::adjustfield);     // right justify
    cout.width(10);  cout << f.size();
    cout.width(10);  cout << f.date();
    cout.width(10);  cout << f.time();

    cout << "   ";
    cout << ((f.attribute() & FA_RDONLY) ? 'r' : '-');
    cout << ((f.attribute() & FA_HIDDEN) ? 'h' : '-');
    cout << ((f.attribute() & FA_SYSTEM) ? 's' : '-');
    cout << ((f.attribute() & FA_DIREC)  ? 'd' : '-');
    cout << ((f.attribute() & FA_ARCH)   ? 'a' : '-');

    cout << "\n";
}
```

Now when you run the program, the file attribute information is a little more readable.

```
FILEINFO.H           790  11-25-89  23:26:04  ----a
```

This does not test out all the possible attribute combinations. To do that you need to specify different filenames for which the attributes are known. It would be inefficient to have to recompile the program every time you wanted to change the filename. So you need to modify the program to accept an optional filename as a command line argument. First, modify **main** so that it can access the command line. Change

```
main()
```

to

```
main(int argc, char *argv[])
```

The first argument is the number of arguments in the command line. There is always at least one argument—the name of the program. The second argument is an array of character strings corresponding to the command line arguments. The first string is at **argv[0]**. So, in the case of this program, **argv[0]** will always equal "MY9-3.EXE." You need to change the program so that if one command line argument is given (making two arguments including the program name), the argument is used as the filename passed to the **FileInfo** constructor. Change the two lines

```
String fname = "fileinfo.h";
FileInfo f(fname);
```

to read

```
String fname;
if (argc == 2)
    fname = argv[1];
else
    fname = "fileinfo.h";
FileInfo f(fname);
```

This code says that if a command line argument is given (two arguments including the program name), set **fname** equal to the first argument. Otherwise, set **fname** to the default filename, which is "fileinfo.h." As before, **fname** is used to construct the **FileInfo** object, **f**. Before running the program, you can specify the command line argument, **strclass.cpp**, inside of the Borland C++ programmer's platform (**R**un/Arguments).

The output now looks like this:

```
STRCLASS.CPP         2775  11-27-89  22:15:25  ----a
```

You might want to try various filename arguments to see different results. For instance, try a single period (.) for the current directory, or two periods (..) for the parent directory. Also try shelling out to DOS with **File/DOS** Shell, and setting the read-only and archive attributes of STRCLASS.CPP with the following DOS command:

```
attrib strclass.cpp +r -a
```

Now return to Borland C++ by typing **exit** and see how the attributes print out for STRCLASS.CPP. When you are through, make sure you reset STRCLASS.CPP back to its original attributes in DOS with

```
attrib strclass.cpp -r +a
```

Using Inheritance to Add Functionality to a Class

It would be nice if the **FileInfo** class had a built-in output operator, < <, to print a **FileInfo** object in the format just specified. You could always add a new member function to the **FileInfo** definition. But if you acquired this class from a third party who supplied only the interface specification in the header file and not the source code for the implementation, you would have to do something different. Here is a possibility. You can derive a new class, **FileItem**, from the **FileInfo** class. If the inherited class specifies **public** in its declaration, it will inherit all the public member functions of the parent class. Just before **main** add a **FileItem** class as follows:

```
class FileItem : public FileInfo
{
public:
    FileItem(const String &filename) : FileInfo(filename) { }
    friend ostream &operator<<(ostream &os, const FileItem &f);
};

ostream &operator<<(ostream &os, const FileItem &f)
{
}
```

Rename the file to MY9-4.CPP. Create a project, MY9-4.PRJ. Add the files MY9-4.CPP, STRCLASS.CPP, and FILEINFO.CPP.

Now fill in the body of the **operator< <** function. You already have all the code you need to do this. Simply search for the first **cout** statement in **main**. With the cursor in the first column of this line, press CTRL-K B to mark the beginning of a block. Now move the cursor down about 15 lines so that it is on the closing brace in the function **main**. Press CTRL-K K to mark the end of the block. All of the **cout** statements for printing file information are now highlighted, and they are ready to move inside the definition for the **operator< <** function. Search backward for "operator< <". Press the DOWN ARROW key twice followed by HOME so that the cursor is on the line with the return statement. Now press CTRL-K V. This moves the highlighted code from **main** to the **operator< <** function.

There is still a little more work to do. With the cursor at the beginning of the **operator< <** function, you will need to change all occurrences of **cout** to **os**. The ostream, **os**, is the first argument passed to the **operator< <** function. This makes it possible to send the output to any ostream: **cout**, **cerr**, or a user-defined output stream. Press CTRL-Q A. For the search string, type **cout**. Press TAB. For the replacement string, type **os**. Change direction to forward. Select Change **All** (ALT-A). Respond Yes for each of the ten **cout** strings found.

Now you can print **FileItems** to an output stream just as you can **Strings**. Add the following line just before the closing brace in **main**:

```
    cout<< f;
}
```

Also change **f**'s type in **main** from **FileInfo** to **FileItem**. Just for polish, you can add the following six lines just after the opening brace in **main**. Many C programs use this technique to guard against the user typing the wrong number of command line arguments.

```
if (argc > 2)
{
     String programName = argv[0];
     cout << "usage: " << programName << " [fileName]\n";
     return(1);
}
```

Notice that by using the **String** object **programName** and setting it equal to **argv[0]** you can reuse this code in any program, and it will always print the proper filename because **argv[0]** refers to the name of the currently running program. Compile and run the program now. Run and test it against various filenames. Then try giving it two arguments, either by specifying two arguments inside the Borland C++ programmer's platform, or by shelling out to DOS and calling the program directly with a command like

```
my9-3 a b
```

The complete listing with all changes for MY9-3.CPP is included here for your reference. You can use it to check that you have properly implemented all the changes to this point. You can also find this file on the disk under the name P9-3.CPP.

P9-3

```
#include <iostream.h>
#include <stdlib.h>
#include <dos.h>
#include "fileinfo.h"

class FileItem : public FileInfo
{
public:
    FileItem(const String &filename) : FileInfo(filename) { }
    friend ostream &operator<<(ostream &os, const FileItem &f);
};

ostream &operator<<(ostream &os, const FileItem &f)
{
    // ===== print file name, size, date, and time =====
    os.setf(ios::left,ios::adjustfield);     // left justify
    os.width(14);                            // field width
    os << f.fname()+f.ext();
    os.setf(ios::right,ios::adjustfield);    // right justify
    os.width(10);  os << f.size();
    os.width(10);  os << f.date();
    os.width(10);  os << f.time();

    // ===== print attribute settings =====
    os << "  ";
```

```
    os << ((f.attribute() & FA_RDONLY) ? 'r' : '-');
    os << ((f.attribute() & FA_HIDDEN) ? 'h' : '-');
    os << ((f.attribute() & FA_SYSTEM) ? 's' : '-');
    os << ((f.attribute() & FA_DIREC)  ? 'd' : '-');
    os << ((f.attribute() & FA_ARCH)   ? 'a' : '-');
    cout << "\n";
    return os;
}

main(int argc, char *argv[])
{
    String fname;
    if (argc > 2)
    {
        String programName = argv[0];
        cout << "usage: " << programName << " [fileName]\n";
        exit(1);
    }
    if (argc == 2)
        fname = argv[1];
    else
        fname = "fileinfo.h";

    FileItem f(fname);
    cout << f;
}
```

A List of Filenames

So far you have seen several types of lists: a list of **char *s**, a list of **Strings**, and a list of menu **Choices**. Now you can build on the **FileItem** class to make a new kind of list. A list of filenames is a directory. You should be able to create a list of **FileItems** in the same way that you created a list of **Choice** objects back in Program P8-6.

Rather than adapting **List** and **Iter** to every new class of element that you create, why not develop generic list-building and list-processing classes? Create a project, P9-4.PRJ. Add the files, P9-4.CPP, STRCLASS .CPP, and FILEINFO.CPP. Load Program P9-4.

P9-4

```
#include <string.h>
#include <iostream.h>
#include <dos.h>
```

```
#include "fileinfo.h"

class FileItem : public FileInfo
{
public:
    FileItem(const String &filename) : FileInfo(filename) { }
    friend ostream &operator<<(ostream &os, const FileItem &f);
};

ostream &operator<<(ostream &os, const FileItem &f)
{
    // ===== print file name, size, date, and time =====
    os.setf(ios::left,ios::adjustfield);    // left justify
    os.width(14);                           // field width
    os << f.fname()+f.ext();
    os.setf(ios::right,ios::adjustfield);   // right justify
    os.width(10);  os << f.size();
    os.width(10);  os << f.date();
    os.width(10);  os << f.time();

    // ===== print attribute settings =====
    os << "  ";
    os << ((f.attribute() & FA_RDONLY) ? 'r' : '-');
    os << ((f.attribute() & FA_HIDDEN) ? 'h' : '-');
    os << ((f.attribute() & FA_SYSTEM) ? 's' : '-');
    os << ((f.attribute() & FA_DIREC)  ? 'd' : '-');
    os << ((f.attribute() & FA_ARCH)   ? 'a' : '-');
    os << "\n";
    return os;
}

typedef FileItem ETYPE;

class Node
{
public:
    ETYPE el;
    Node *next;
    Node *prev;
    Node(ETYPE e) :  el(e) { }
};

class List
{
private:
    Node *tail;
    Node *head;
public:
    List(Node *h=0, Node *t=0)
        { head = h; tail = t ? t : h; }
    List (const ETYPE e) { tail=0; add(e); head=tail; }
    ~List();
```

```
    void add(const ETYPE e);
    Node *getTail() { return tail; }
    Node *getHead() { return head; }
    void sort(int (*compare) (const ETYPE &e1, const ETYPE &e2));
};

List::~List()
{
    Node *n = head;
    while(n)
    {
        Node  *o = n->next;
        delete n;
        n = o;
    }
}

void List::add(const ETYPE e)
{
    Node *temp = new Node((ETYPE)e);
    if (!tail)
    {
        temp->prev = temp->next = 0;
    }
    else if (!tail->prev)
    {
        temp->prev = 0;
        temp->next = tail;
        tail->prev = temp;
    }
    else
    {
        temp->prev = tail->prev;
        temp->next = tail;
        tail->prev->next = temp;
        tail->prev = temp;
    }
    tail = temp;
    if (!head)           // Only true when adding first
        head = tail;     // element to an empty list.
}

void List::sort(int (*compare) (const ETYPE &e1, const ETYPE &e2))
{
    Node *head = getHead();
    for (Node *i=head->prev; i; i=i->prev)
    {
        Node temp = *i;
        for (Node *j=i->next;
             j && compare(temp.el, j->el) < 0;
             j=j->next)
               j->prev->el = j->el;
```

```
        if (j)
            j->prev->el = temp.el;
        else
            head->el = temp.el;
    }
}

class Iter
{
private:
    Node *current;
public:
    Iter() { current=0; }
    Iter(Node *c) { current = c; }
    Iter(List l) { current = l.getTail(); }
    Node *operator++();
    Node *operator--();
    Iter &operator =(const Iter &iter)
        { current = iter.current; return *this; }
    Iter &operator =(Node *c)
        { current = c; return *this; }
};

Node *Iter::operator++()
{
    if (current)
    {
        Node *temp = current;
        current = current->prev;
        return temp;
    }
    else
        return 0;
}

Node *Iter::operator--()
{
    if (current)
    {
        Node *temp = current;
        current = current->next;
        return temp;
    }
    else
        return 0;
}

int cmpName(const FileItem &f1, const FileItem &f2)
{
    int ret;
    if ((ret = strcmp(f1.fname(), f2.fname())) != 0)
        return ret;
```

```
    if ((ret = strcmp(f1.ext(), f2.ext())) != 0)
        return ret;
    return ret;
}

int cmpExt(const FileItem &f1, const FileItem &f2)
{
    int ret;
    if ((ret = strcmp(f1.ext(), f2.ext())) != 0)
        return ret;
    if ((ret = strcmp(f1.fname(), f2.fname())) != 0)
        return ret;
    return ret;
}

int cmpTime(const FileItem &f1, const FileItem &f2)
{
    int ret;
    if ((ret = strcmp(f1.date(), f2.date())) != 0)
        return ret;
    if ((ret = strcmp(f1.time(), f2.time())) != 0)
        return ret;
    return ret;
}

void listPrint(List &l)
{
    Iter it = l.getHead();
    Node *n;
    while ( (n = ++it) != 0 )
        cout << n->el;
}

main()
{
    List lst;
    lst.add("fileinfo.h");
    lst.add("strclass.h");
    lst.add("fileinfo.cpp");
    lst.add("strclass.cpp");
    lst.add("..");              // parent directory
    lst.add(".");               // current directory
    lst.add("p9-?.cpp");
    lst.add("xxxxxxxx.xxx");    // file which does not exist
    lst.add("*.obj");

    cout << "==========\n";
    listPrint(lst);

    cout << "==========sort by name\n";
```

```
    lst.sort(cmpName);
    listPrint(lst);

    cout << "==========sort by extension\n";
    lst.sort(cmpExt);
    listPrint(lst);

    cout << "==========sort by time\n";
    lst.sort(cmpTime);
    listPrint(lst);

    cout << "==========\n";
}
```

The first class that appears in this program is the **FileItem** class developed in MY9-3.CPP. Following the class declaration and definition is a **typedef** statement.

```
typedef FileItem ETYPE;
```

ETYPE stands for element type, and in this situation can be used to declare variables of type **FileItem**. By introducing **ETYPE** through a **typedef** statement, you can build list and iterator classes that are based on **ETYPE**s instead of on specific classes. Then, if you want, you can change the **typedef** to another type, such as **Choice** or **String**, without having to change any of the list-building or list-processing classes. In fact, if you compare Program P9-4 with Program P8-6, you will find that the implementation of the List and Iter classes is nearly identical. The only difference is that the word *Choice* is replaced by *ETYPE*.

The key to this generic implementation is the new **Node** class. In the implementation of **Choice** in Program P8-6, the **Choice** class contains pointers to the previous and next list elements. The **Node** class factors out these linkages. The **Node** class consists of four public members: a constructor, an element of type **ETYPE**, and pointers to the previous and next elements in the list. This means that you can now build any type of object and put it in the list without having to build linkage information directly into that object. To use any object that you create in or with the generic **List** or **Iter** classes, all you need to do is redefine **ETYPE**.

```
typedef MyClass ETYPE;
```

The List class in Program P9-4 provides an additional member function, **List::sort**. This member function is another form of applicator. It is nearly identical to **ListSort** in Program P9-1. There is no reason that an applicator cannot be a member function. In fact, it usually makes sense for applicators to be member functions of the objects on which they operate. This **sort** function has a unique twist in that it will sort lists in a different order depending on the argument given to the **sort** member function. Look carefully at the declaration for **List::sort**:

```
void sort(int (*compare) (const ETYPE &e1,
                          const ETYPE &e2));
```

This declaration says that the **sort** function gets a single argument. The argument is a pointer to a function. The function is called inside of **sort** to compare two list elements when determining the sort order. The function that is passed as an argument itself receives two arguments and returns an integer. The arguments received by the function are both of **ETYPE**. The value returned by the function indicates whether the first argument is less than, equal to, or greater than the second argument.

The function that is passed to **sort** is analogous to the **strcmp** standard C string comparison function. If the first argument is less than the second argument, the value returned is negative. If the first argument is equal to the second argument, the value returned is 0. If the first argument is greater than the second argument, the value returned is positive.

This provides a mechanism for sorting lists of files by different criteria. For example, you can sort a list by filename, by file extension, or by date and time. All you need to do is provide a separate comparison function for each of the possible ways to sort the list. The prototypes of these comparison functions must match the prototype for the function pointer argument in **List::sort**. Here are three examples:

```
int cmpName(const FileItem &f1, const FileItem &f2)
{
    int ret;
    if ((ret = strcmp(f1.fname(), f2.fname())) != 0)
        return ret;
    if ((ret = strcmp(f1.ext(), f2.ext())) != 0)
        return ret;
    return ret;
}
```

```
int cmpExt(const FileItem &f1, const FileItem &f2)
{
    int ret;
    if ((ret = strcmp(f1.ext(), f2.ext())) != 0)
        return ret;
    if ((ret = strcmp(f1.fname(), f2.fname())) != 0)
        return ret;
    return ret;
}

int cmpTime(const FileItem &f1, const FileItem &f2)
{
    int ret;
    if ((ret = strcmp(f1.date(), f2.date())) != 0)
        return ret;
    if ((ret = strcmp(f1.time(), f2.time())) != 0)
        return ret;
    return ret;
}
```

Now when you want to sort by different criteria, simply give the appropriate argument to **List::sort**:

```
lst.sort(cmpName);
lst.sort(cmpExt);
lst.sort(cmpTime);
```

It is up to the programmer to provide functions of the type required by **List::sort** if any sorting is required for the list. The only other assumption made by this implementation is in the **listPrint** function. This function receives an argument which is a list of **ETYPE**s and assumes that **ETYPE** defines an output operator function <<, which it uses to print list elements. If you are using a class that does not implement an **operator<<** function that works with the standard C++ stream classes, consider deriving a class and providing the additional functionality in the derived class.

A list of files is built in **main** in a manner similar to the earlier lists of animals and menu choices. First, a **List** object is declared.

```
List lst;
```

Then elements are added.

```
lst.add("fileinfo.h");
lst.add("strclass.h");
// ...
```

The only difference is that if the argument to **List::add** does not match an existing filename, all information about the file inside the **FileInfo** class is set to null strings or 0 value integers.

Compile and run Program P9-4. Next create a project file composed of P9-4.CPP, STRCLASS.H, and FILEINFO.H. Compare the four ordering sequences of the lists.

```
==========
FILEINFO.H         790  11-25-89  23:26:04  ----a
STRCLASS.H        1028  12-07-89  04:02:17  ----a
FILEINFO.CPP      1465  11-27-89  22:15:25  ----a
STRCLASS.CPP      2775  11-27-89  22:15:25  ----a
DT                   0  08-22-89  17:02:13  ---d-
CH9                  0  11-19-89  18:44:27  ---d-
P9-2.CPP          2586  12-07-89  03:52:12  ----a
                     0                      -----
STRCLASS.OBJ      1499  12-07-89  03:55:02  ----a
==========sort by name
                     0                      -----
CH9                  0  11-19-89  18:44:27  ---d-
DT                   0  08-22-89  17:02:13  ---d-
FILEINFO.CPP      1465  11-27-89  22:15:25  ----a
FILEINFO.H         790  11-25-89  23:26:04  ----a
P9-2.CPP          2586  12-07-89  03:52:12  ----a
STRCLASS.CPP      2775  11-27-89  22:15:25  ----a
STRCLASS.H        1028  12-07-89  04:02:17  ----a
STRCLASS.OBJ      1499  12-07-89  03:55:02  ----a
==========sort by extension
                     0                      -----
CH9                  0  11-19-89  18:44:27  ---d-
DT                   0  08-22-89  17:02:13  ---d-
FILEINFO.CPP      1465  11-27-89  22:15:25  ----a
P9-2.CPP          2586  12-07-89  03:52:12  ----a
STRCLASS.CPP      2775  11-27-89  22:15:25  ----a
FILEINFO.H         790  11-25-89  23:26:04  ----a
STRCLASS.H        1028  12-07-89  04:02:17  ----a
STRCLASS.OBJ      1499  12-07-89  03:55:02  ----a
==========sort by time
                     0                      -----
DT                   0  08-22-89  17:02:13  ---d-
CH9                  0  11-19-89  18:44:27  ---d-
FILEINFO.H         790  11-25-89  23:26:04  ----a
FILEINFO.CPP      1465  11-27-89  22:15:25  ----a
STRCLASS.CPP      2775  11-27-89  22:15:25  ----a
P9-2.CPP          2586  12-07-89  03:52:12  ----a
```

```
STRCLASS.OBJ        1499  12-07-89  03:55:02  ----a
STRCLASS.H          1028  12-07-89  04:02:17  ----a
==========
```

Notice the empty filename and time strings for the file that was not found. Again, use F8 to step through the program if the screen scrolls too fast.

A File Directory Class

It would be nice if you did not have to build file lists by hand. There is really no need to. You can use Borland C++'s **findfirst** and **findnext** functions to build file lists for you automatically. The next thing you are going to do is just that. Start by deriving a new class, **DirList**, from the generic **List** class.

```
class DirList : public List
{
private:
    String filespec;
public:
    DirList(const String &fspec);
};

DirList::DirList(const String &fspec)
{
    filespec = fspec;
    ffblk fileblock;
    int done = findfirst(filespec, &fileblock, 0xFF);
    while(!done)
    {
        add(fileblock.ff_name);
        done = findnext(&fileblock);
    }
}
```

Add the previous code to the program immediately after the definition of **List::sort**. The constructor for **DirList** is passed a string, which is retained as a private member of a **DirList** object. The constructor keeps looking for files that match the file specification, including matching wildcards * and ?. Each time it finds a new match, it adds an element to the list by calling the **List:add** function. All the code in **main** that was formerly used to build a list can now be replaced with a single constructor invocation. Replace these lines in **main**

```
List lst;
lst.add("fileinfo.h");
lst.add("strclass.h");
lst.add("fileinfo.cpp");
lst.add("strclass.cpp");
lst.add("..");                // parent directory
lst.add(".");                 // current directory
lst.add("p9-?.cpp");
lst.add("xxxxxxxx.xxx");      // file which does not exist
lst.add("*.obj");
```

with

```
DirList lst = String("p9-*.*");
```

Rename the program MY9-5.CPP. Create a new project, MY9-5.PRJ, with the file items MY9-5.CPP, FILEINFO.CPP, and STRCLASS.CPP. Compile and run the program. Your output should look something like the following:

```
==========
P9-7.CPP            5048  12-05-89  01:40:08  ----a
P9-1.CPP            3095  12-07-89  20:25:27  ----a
P9-2.OBJ            1588  12-07-89  03:55:12  ----a
P9-2.EXE           14590  12-07-89  03:55:15  ----a
P9-3.OBJ            2137  12-07-89  05:10:19  ----a
P9-4.OBJ            1627  12-07-89  03:56:06  ----a
P9-5.OBJ            5986  12-07-89  05:53:21  ----a
P9-3.CPP            3664  12-07-89  05:10:03  ----a
P9-4.EXE           18002  12-07-89  03:56:10  ----a
P9-4.CPP            1291  12-07-89  03:12:25  ----a
P9-6.OBJ            4400  12-09-89  23:14:06  ----a
P9-5.EXE           21164  12-07-89  05:53:25  ----a
P9-7.OBJ            4113  12-07-89  03:57:03  ----a
P9-6.EXE           19842  12-09-89  23:14:10  ----a
P9-7.EXE           19588  12-07-89  03:57:07  ----a
P9-3.EXE           14902  12-07-89  05:10:22  ----a
P9-2.CPP            2586  12-07-89  03:52:12  ----a
P9-1.OBJ            1793  12-09-89  23:16:19  ----a
P9-5.CPP            4896  12-07-89  06:10:09  ----a
P9-6.CPP            4826  12-09-89  23:13:26  ----a
P9-1.EXE           14664  12-09-89  23:16:23  ----a
```

```
==========sort by name
P9-1.CPP            3095  12-07-89  20:25:27  ----a
P9-1.EXE           14664  12-09-89  23:16:23  ----a
P9-1.OBJ            1793  12-09-89  23:16:19  ----a
P9-2.CPP            2586  12-07-89  03:52:12  ----a
P9-2.EXE           14590  12-07-89  03:55:15  ----a
P9-2.OBJ            1588  12-07-89  03:55:12  ----a
P9-3.CPP            3664  12-07-89  05:10:03  ----a
P9-3.EXE           14902  12-07-89  05:10:22  ----a
P9-3.OBJ            2137  12-07-89  05:10:19  ----a
P9-4.CPP            1291  12-07-89  03:12:25  ----a
P9-4.EXE           18002  12-07-89  03:56:10  ----a
P9-4.OBJ            1627  12-07-89  03:56:06  ----a
P9-5.CPP            4896  12-07-89  06:10:09  ----a
P9-5.EXE           21164  12-07-89  05:53:25  ----a
P9-5.OBJ            5986  12-07-89  05:53:21  ----a
P9-6.CPP            4826  12-09-89  23:13:26  ----a
P9-6.EXE           19842  12-09-89  23:14:10  ----a
P9-6.OBJ            4400  12-09-89  23:14:06  ----a
P9-7.CPP            5048  12-05-89  01:40:08  ----a
P9-7.EXE           19588  12-07-89  03:57:07  ----a
P9-7.OBJ            4113  12-07-89  03:57:03  ----a
==========sort by extension
P9-1.CPP            3095  12-07-89  20:25:27  ----a
P9-2.CPP            2586  12-07-89  03:52:12  ----a
P9-3.CPP            3664  12-07-89  05:10:03  ----a
P9-4.CPP            1291  12-07-89  03:12:25  ----a
P9-5.CPP            4896  12-07-89  06:10:09  ----a
P9-6.CPP            4826  12-09-89  23:13:26  ----a
P9-7.CPP            5048  12-05-89  01:40:08  ----a
P9-1.EXE           14664  12-09-89  23:16:23  ----a
P9-2.EXE           14590  12-07-89  03:55:15  ----a
P9-3.EXE           14902  12-07-89  05:10:22  ----a
P9-4.EXE           18002  12-07-89  03:56:10  ----a
P9-5.EXE           21164  12-07-89  05:53:25  ----a
P9-6.EXE           19842  12-09-89  23:14:10  ----a
P9-7.EXE           19588  12-07-89  03:57:07  ----a
P9-1.OBJ            1793  12-09-89  23:16:19  ----a
P9-2.OBJ            1588  12-07-89  03:55:12  ----a
P9-3.OBJ            2137  12-07-89  05:10:19  ----a
P9-4.OBJ            1627  12-07-89  03:56:06  ----a
P9-5.OBJ            5986  12-07-89  05:53:21  ----a
P9-6.OBJ            4400  12-09-89  23:14:06  ----a
P9-7.OBJ            4113  12-07-89  03:57:03  ----a
==========sort by time
P9-7.CPP            5048  12-05-89  01:40:08  ----a
P9-4.CPP            1291  12-07-89  03:12:25  ----a
P9-2.CPP            2586  12-07-89  03:52:12  ----a
P9-2.OBJ            1588  12-07-89  03:55:12  ----a
P9-2.EXE           14590  12-07-89  03:55:15  ----a
P9-4.OBJ            1627  12-07-89  03:56:06  ----a
```

```
P9-4.EXE             18002  12-07-89  03:56:10  ----a
P9-7.OBJ              4113  12-07-89  03:57:03  ----a
P9-7.EXE             19588  12-07-89  03:57:07  ----a
P9-3.CPP              3664  12-07-89  05:10:03  ----a
P9-3.OBJ              2137  12-07-89  05:10:19  ----a
P9-3.EXE             14902  12-07-89  05:10:22  ----a
P9-5.OBJ              5986  12-07-89  05:53:21  ----a
P9-5.EXE             21164  12-07-89  05:53:25  ----a
P9-5.CPP              4896  12-07-89  06:10:09  ----a
P9-1.CPP              3095  12-07-89  20:25:27  ----a
P9-6.CPP              4826  12-09-89  23:13:26  ----a
P9-6.OBJ              4400  12-09-89  23:14:06  ----a
P9-6.EXE             19842  12-09-89  23:14:10  ----a
P9-1.OBJ              1793  12-09-89  23:16:19  ----a
P9-1.EXE             14664  12-09-89  23:16:23  ----a
==========
```

If you want to verify your program against a working version, you can look at the program on the disk named Program P9-5.CPP. If the screen scrolls too fast, use F8 to step through the program.

A Sorted Directory Tree

Program P9-6 is here mainly for fun. It shows what you can do with a small amount of code if you have the support of a good set of class definitions. Create a project, P9-6.PRJ, consisting of P9-6.CPP, STRCLASS.CPP, and FILEINFO.CPP.

P9-6

```
#include <string.h>
#include <iostream.h>
#include <dos.h>
#include "strclass.h"
#include "fileinfo.h"

typedef FileInfo ETYPE;

class Node
{
public:
    ETYPE el;
    Node *next;
    Node *prev;
    Node(ETYPE &e) : el(e) { }
};
```

```
class List
{
private:
    Node *tail;
    Node *head;
public:
    List(Node *h=0, Node *t=0)
        { head = h; tail = t ? t : h; }
    List (const ETYPE e) { tail=0; add(e); head=tail; }
    ~List();
    void add(const ETYPE e);
    Node *getTail() { return tail; }
    Node *getHead() { return head; }
    void sort(int (*compare) (const ETYPE &e1, const ETYPE &e2));
};

List::~List()
{
    Node *n = head;
    while(n)
    {
        Node  *o = n->next;
        delete n;
        n = o;
    }
}

void List::add(const ETYPE e)
{
    Node *temp = new Node(ETYPE(e));
    if (!tail)
    {
        temp->prev = temp->next = 0;
    }
    else if (!tail->prev)
    {
        temp->prev = 0;
        temp->next = tail;
        tail->prev = temp;
    }
    else
    {
        temp->prev = tail->prev;
        temp->next = tail;
        tail->prev->next = temp;
        tail->prev = temp;
    }
    tail = temp;
    if (!head)          // Only true when adding first
        head = tail;    // element to an empty list.
}
```

```
void List::sort(int (*compare) (const ETYPE &e1, const ETYPE &e2))
{
    Node *head = getHead();
    for (Node *i=head->prev; i; i=i->prev)
    {
        ETYPE temp = i->el;
        for (Node *j=i->next;
             j && compare(temp, j->el) < 0;
             j=j->next)
                j->prev->el = j->el;
        if (j)
            j->prev->el = temp;
        else
            head->el = temp;
    }
}

class DirList : public List
{
private:
    String filespec;
public:
    DirList(const String &fspec);
};

DirList::DirList(const String &fspec)
{
    filespec = fspec;
    ffblk fileblock;
    int done = findfirst(filespec, &fileblock, 0xFF);
    while(!done)
    {
        if (fileblock.ff_attrib & FA_DIREC &&
            fileblock.ff_name[0] != '.')
        {
            add(fileblock.ff_name);
        }
        done = findnext(&fileblock);
    }
}

class Iter
{
private:
    Node *current;
public:
    Iter() { current=0; }
    Iter(Node *c) { current = c; }
    Iter(List l) { current = l.getTail(); }
    Node *operator++();
    Node *operator--();
    Iter &operator =(const Iter &iter)
```

```
        { current = iter.current; return *this; }
    Iter &operator =(Node *c)
        { current = c; return *this; }
};

Node *Iter::operator++()
{
    if (current)
    {
        Node *temp = current;
        current = current->prev;
        return temp;
    }
    else
        return 0;
}

Node *Iter::operator--()
{
    if (current)
    {
        Node *temp = current;
        current = current->next;
        return temp;
    }
    else
        return 0;
}

int cmpName(const FileInfo &f1, const FileInfo &f2)
{
    int ret;
    if ((ret = strcmp(f1.fname(), f2.fname())) != 0)
        return ret;
    if ((ret = strcmp(f1.ext(), f2.ext())) != 0)
        return ret;
    return ret;
}

int cmpExt(const FileInfo &f1, const FileInfo &f2)
{
    int ret;
    if ((ret = strcmp(f1.ext(), f2.ext())) != 0)
        return ret;
    if ((ret = strcmp(f1.fname(), f2.fname())) != 0)
        return ret;
    return ret;
}

int cmpTime(const FileInfo &f1, const FileInfo &f2)
{
    int ret;
```

```
    if ((ret = strcmp(f1.date(), f2.date())) != 0)
        return ret;
    if ((ret = strcmp(f1.time(), f2.time())) != 0)
        return ret;
    return ret;
}

const Left = 0xB3;
const CenterLeft = 0xC3;
const Top = 0xC4;
const BottomLeft = 0xC0;
const Spacing = 4;

int PrintLeadingChar[] =
{
    1, 1, 1, 1, 1, 1, 1, 1, 1, 1,
    1, 1, 1, 1, 1, 1, 1, 1, 1, 1
};

void line(int i)
{
    while(i-- > 0)
        for (int j=0; j<Spacing-1; j++)
            cout.put(Top);
}

void indent(int level)
{
    for (int i = 0; i < level; i++)
    {
        if (PrintLeadingChar[i])
            cout.put(Left);
        else
            cout.put(' ');
        for (int j=0; j<Spacing-1; j++)
            cout.put(' ');
    }
}

void dirTree(const char *dirStr)
{
    static int NestLevel = 0;
    DirList dir = dirStr;
    if (!dir.getHead()) return;  // return if list empty
    dir.sort(cmpName);
    Iter itl = dir.getHead();
    Node *f;
    while ( (f = ++itl) != 0 )
    {
        char *dirName = f->el.fullpath();
```

```
        int last = (f == dir.getTail());  // end of list
        PrintLeadingChar[NestLevel] = last ? 0 : 1;
        indent(NestLevel);
        cout.put(last ? BottomLeft : CenterLeft);
        line(1);
        cout.width(12);
        cout.setf(ios::left, ios::adjustfield);
        cout << dirName << "\n";
        chdir(dirName);
        NestLevel++;
        dirTree("*.*");
        chdir("..");
        NestLevel--;
    }
}

main()
{
    char currentDirectory[MAXPATH];
    getcwd(currentDirectory, MAXPATH);
    chdir("\\");
    dirTree("*.*");
    chdir(currentDirectory);
    return 0;
}
```

This program uses the generic **List**, **Iter**, and **DirList** classes developed in Programs P9-4 and P9-5. The program prints a visual tree of all the subdirectories of the directory from which the program is run. Most of the work is done by the recursive function **dirTree**. The basic algorithm is the same as that used in the last program in Chapter 5 (Program P5-6). You will notice that the code for this version of **dirTree** is shorter because the work of building the directory lists is all handled by the **DirList** constructor.

The basic algorithm for **dirTree**, which receives a file specification **String** as an argument, is

```
dirTree
    Build a list of all subdirectories
    Sort the list
    With an iterator walk through each list element
    For each subdirectory in the list
        Print the name
```

Change to the subdirectory
Call dirTree recursively
Change back to parent directory

One modification is required in order to be sure that the program does not run out of space when printing directory trees from the root directory of a large hard disk with a lot of files. The constructor for **DirList** is modified so that it does not add every file it finds to the list it is creating. Instead, a conditional statement is added so that only files that have the directory attribute set are added to the list. The modified constructor looks like this:

```
DirList::DirList(const String &fspec)
{
    filespec = fspec;
    ffblk fileblock;
    int done = findfirst(filespec, &fileblock, 0xFF);
    while(!done)
    {
        if (fileblock.ff_attrib & FA_DIREC &&
            fileblock.ff_name[0] != '.') // new condition
        {
            add(fileblock.ff_name);
        }
        done = findnext(&fileblock);
    }
}
```

One of the more interesting elements of the program is the way the indenting is handled. There is a static local variable inside of **dirTree** called **NestLevel**. A static local variable retains its value from one invocation of a function to the next. Such a variable can be used to see how many recursive calls have been made to a function. By seeing how many levels deep the recursion has nested, you can determine how far to indent the directory names being printed.

Create a project file, P9-6.PRJ, composed of P9-6.CPP, STRCLASS .CPP, and FILEINFO.CPP. Compile and run the program. Try running the program from different directories by modifying the line,

```
chdir("\\");
```

in main. A typical output looks like this:

```
├────QUATTRO
├────SK
├────TC
│    ├────INCLUDE
│    │    └────SYS
│    └────LIB
├────TEMP
├────TODO
├────TYPESET
│    └────SAVE
└────USR
     ├────BIN
     │    └────SAVE
     ├────GREG
     ├────GUEST
     └────HELP
```

The program uses four special IBM graphics characters to print lines connecting the tree nodes: Left, CenterLeft, Top, and BottomLeft. The same technique was used to print menu borders in Chapter 6. The tricky part of the code is determining what graphic character to print for connecting a given node. For example, if the last directory in a list has no subdirectories, then no connecting vertical bar should be printed directly below that directory name at the same level of nesting. That is the only hint you get.

See if you can figure out how the code works. Try changing the indentation and character-printing logic to see what happens. One interesting challenge would be to pass the parent directory name for the entire tree as a command line argument. Try to think of other interesting features to add.

Object-Oriented Programming: Building Systems from Reusable Components

Part Three

I stood on the shoulders of giants.
—Newton

10 Reusing Code: Inheritance

Reusing code is what inheritance is all about. Structured programming languages try to achieve this goal through libraries. Libraries capture the most commonly used operations and data structures and make them available for reuse. In order to be reusable, the functions in a library must be general. They need to foresee all the special cases to which they will be applied. This is typically where they fall down—while **printf** is nice, you can't write to **stdout** in a graphics application. So a more general form of **printf** is provided, called **sprintf**, to format strings in memory. You can then use your own output routine to print the strings. If you are dealing with character-attribute pairs, rather than straight C strings (**char** *'s), you want to do the same kind of formatting on them that **printf** does, but the basic data structure of the string is different. There should be some way to modify **printf**.

This is where you run out of luck. You probably don't have the source code for **printf**, and even if you do, it is no trivial project to adapt it to handle application-specific data types. You might break the code while modifying it. A module that took years to build and standardize can be broken in seconds with little effort. Even worse, the functionality you add to **printf** will be unique to your implementation: your standard library will not be standard anymore. Furthermore, using very general routines is not without cost. Whenever you use a library function that must by definition be general, you are probably pulling a lot of unused code into your executable program file. Wouldn't it be nice if you could be selective about the features of a module used by your program? What is needed is a method of extending, restricting, or otherwise modifying the behavior of a library feature without modifying the library itself.

Unfortunately, structured languages lack the tools for extending and modifying the features provided in core modules. Changing core libraries is a slow, evolutionary process. Changes are made selectively after careful deliberation. Standard libraries are critical building blocks, which must provide a stable and transportable set of features on which applications depend. This makes it very hard to build on the work of others because there is always some feature that you need in your application that the implementor did not foresee. As a result, every day, programmers are rewriting list handlers, stacks, queues, special sorting routines, and graphics primitives like line-drawing and area-fill routines, all based on exactly the same algorithms. The specific applications differ enough—because of hardware constraints or application-specific data types—that they cannot be generalized and subsequently standardized. As one developer put it, "Instead of standing on one another's shoulders we wind up standing on one another's toes."

Tools for Code Reuse

Object-oriented programming languages like Smalltalk, Eiffel, and C++ provide solutions for the problem of reusability. The tools are inheritance, polymorphism, and dynamic binding.

You've seen examples of inheritance. For example, "I want my window class to be like a rectangle, but I want it to draw a border and paint the inside blue;" or, "I want my list to handle menu choice objects instead of string objects." Inheritance lets you reuse or modify any of the public features of a base class without changing the base class itself.

Polymorphism is a companion of inheritance. If you have the ability to derive a menu or a dialog box from a basic window, then you need a general way of handling the common features of the window family. For instance, you might use a list to keep track of all the windows and menus currently open on the screen. Polymorphic arrays and other types of collections let you put all objects derived from a common ancestor into the same data structure. If the desktop configuration is changed (say, a user moves a window with the mouse), you can walk down the list with an iterator and tell each window or menu to print itself, effectively refreshing the entire desktop.

Dynamic or *late binding* is a specific form of polymorphism. It has to do with the way that a call to a class method is linked or directed to the code that defines that method. In many cases, this linking or binding can be resolved when the program is compiled. If you have the source code for a menu and a dialog box, and both are derived from a window class, you can use a (polymorphic) window pointer to point to either of them. Furthermore, if all three classes define a print method, late binding determines which print routine will be invoked.

```
Window *pWindow;          // polymorphic pointer
Menu menu;                // derived from Window
DialogBox aDialogBox;     // also derived from Window
pWindow = &menu;
pWindow->print();
pWindow = &aDialogBox
pWindow->print();
```

Should the print statements invoke the method for **Window::print**, or **Menu::print** and **DialogBox::print**?

Some references can be resolved when the program is compiled; others cannot be resolved until the program is run. The linking of caller to callee at run time is called late or dynamic binding. Third-party class libraries frequently use late binding to provide "hooks" for users of the class to patch new types into the framework of the base class methods. These hooks can be made available by defining certain base class functions as virtual, meaning that they will wait until run time to determine which derived class method to call.

This makes it possible for code written yesterday to call a method that will be written tomorrow—without recompiling the original source. Not having source code is no longer an obstacle to modifying the behavior of third-party libraries. Dynamic binding also helps class providers avoid having to rewrite base class methods every time a new derived type is added. Interactive systems, where the user controls the flow of events through keyboard and mouse input, place special demands on programs, which are often handled most conveniently through dynamic binding.

This chapter covers the reuse of code in general and explains how inheritance, polymorphism, and dynamic binding support the reuse of code. You will see how easy it is to build applications when you have a good set of reusable support classes that can handle a variety of polymorphic objects and user-defined data types.

Looking Ahead: Inheritance, Polymorphism, and Reusable Container Classes

Chapters 10 through 12 introduce tools that support the reuse of code. Chapter 10 covers inheritance as a tool for modifying the behavior of existing code and for extending or restricting the interface to existing classes. Chapter 11 discusses multiple inheritance or classes that are derived from more than one parent. Chapter 12 covers polymorphism and dynamic binding. Chapter 12 then goes on to show specific uses of polymorphism in generic container classes provided by the DiskTutor.

Always keep in mind, while you are working through these three chapters, the concept of reusing code and building on the work of others. It is not so important that you memorize every new C++ language feature that is introduced. Focus on the general concepts. You can always look up the specific use and availability of features that support the general concepts in any of the excellent reference works available for C++.

The harder issues to grasp are more abstract. If you know you want to extend the capabilities of a base class and that inheritance is the primary tool for doing so, you know where to begin looking for the language features that support this activity: private versus public inheritance, overriding inherited methods, resolving ambiguous references, and initializing base classes. You will be much further along if you start with a simple working example program and a general idea of where you want to go than if you try to memorize a list of rules for using specific language features.

With that in mind, let's begin with the notion of code reuse in general.

Reusing Code Without Inheritance

Although inheritance provides the primary mechanism for reusing existing code, you don't always need inheritance to reuse code. You can boost your productivity through classes already available. All you need are some existing classes from which you can create objects. This approach is not really object-oriented even though you are using objects. To use provided classes without modification has no great advantage over using the traditional libraries provided for structured languages.

Here is an example of code reuse without inheritance. Suppose, for example, your goal is to simulate the behavior of a digital watch or a clock/calendar utility. You could start thinking about using the PC's timer, and how you could use it to construct the internal workings of a clock, or you could do a little better by using MS-DOS's built-in clock support. The problem with this is that it is not portable across operating systems.

Even if that were not an issue for your application, the format provided by MS-DOS may not be consistent with that required by your application. For instance, you might need to deal with dates prior to 1980, the first year supported by the DOS clock. It is no small task to find the number of days between any two dates from this century or to determine the day of the week for a particular date, especially when leap year comes into play. You could go to a higher level of abstraction and use UNIX-compatible date routines such as **gettime**, **getdate**, **gmtime**, and so on. You could even use the conversions provided by Borland C++, such as **dostounix** and **unixtodos**. But you still have to build up a program from these lower-level abstractions.

You can get a big head start simply by reusing code already provided for handling time and dates in the DiskTutor Time class.

Using Existing Classes

The **Time** class in DiskTutor is very similar to the **Time** class provided by Smalltalk. Rather than describing its complete interface, let's just look at Program P10-1, which uses Time. Before starting the Borland C++ IDE, remember to log to the appropriate directory for this chapter (\DT\CH10).

P10-1

```
#include "timec.h"
#include <conio.h>
main()
{
    Time now;
    cout << "It is now " << now
         << " (" << now.seconds() << " seconds) "
         << "\n";
    for (;;)
    {
        now.update();
        cout<< now << "\n";
        int c=getch();
        if  (c=='Q' || c=='q')
        break;
    }
}
```

All you need do to use the **Time** class is to add the line

```
#include "timec.h"
```

at the top of your program.

To create an instance of class **Time**, use something similar to

```
Time now;
```

This creates an object called **now**, which is set to the current date and time. The value contained in **now** retains the time at which the object was created unless the programmer specifically updates it with either

```
now = Time();
```

which invokes **Time**'s constructor and assigns the current time to either **now**, or

```
now.update();
```

One reason for having a time object retain its value is so that a program can remember dates and times. This makes it easy to add and subtract times and dates from one another. You could even find the number of seconds between June 9, 1956, and now.

Open a project called P10-l and add two files: P10-1.CPP and DT.LIB. Open the main file, P10-1.CPP. Run this program now. You will see something like this:

```
It is now 12-Mar-90  7:09:46 pm (2814739786 seconds)
```

Notice that the program stops after printing the initial time. Each time you press a key, **now** is updated to the current time.

```
12-Mar-90  7:09:46 pm
12-Mar-90  7:09:47 pm
12-Mar-90  7:09:47 pm
12-Mar-90  7:09:47 pm
12-Mar-90  7:09:47 pm
12-Mar-90  7:09:47 pm
12-Mar-90  7:09:49 pm
```

Pressing Q will exit the program. Notice that **Time** knows about **cout** and can be printed to a stream with the simple statement

```
cout << now;
```

This is a good start for a digital watch. All you have to do is keep updating the time and displaying **now** at the same position on the screen. A few simple changes to this program will make it look more like the display on a real digital watch. First, delete the following **cout** statement:

```
cout << "It is now " << now
     << " (" << now.seconds() << " seconds) "
     << "\n";
```

Next, add a statement to clear the screen and another statement to change the endless **for** loop to a **while** statement that terminates when a key is pressed. Change

```
for (;;)
```

to

```
clrscr();
while(!kbhit())
```

Now, whenever the time is printed, you will want to position the cursor to the upper-left corner of the screen. Add the following statement just before the **cout** statement inside the loop:

```
gotoxy(1,1);
```

Delete the code that waits for a keypress and exits if a `Q` is entered:

```
int c=getch();
if (c=='Q' || c=='q')
    break;
```

The program should now look like this:

```
#include "timec.h"
#include <conio.h>
main()
{
    Time now;
    clrscr();
    while(!kbhit())
    {
        now.update();
        gotoxy(1,1);
        cout << now << "\n";
    }
}
```

Run the program now. The clock appears in the upper-left corner of the screen and continually updates itself.

```
12-Mar-90  7:23:37 pm
```

The loop has been changed from an endless **for** loop to a **while** loop that exits as soon as a key is pressed. The screen is cleared before entering the loop. On each pass through the loop, **now** is updated, the cursor is positioned to the upper-left corner of the screen, and the time is printed. As you watch the seconds of your life tick away, think about how much time you saved by using an existing class instead of writing your own. Press any key to exit.

There are other features in the **Time** class, but the main point is that you have a good start here for building a digital watch simulation. The question is, can the **Time** class be easily adapted for a specific design? What if you want to change the date format or print the watch in a window and control it with buttons? In order to answer these questions, let's take a closer look at the mechanism of inheritance.

The main thing to observe in reusing a class without inheritance is how to do it. No special tools are required. It is the same thing you would do if you were using a set of library functions to build a program. You would go to the manual or use the on-line help system to give you the prototypes and descriptions of the functions you need. For classes, all you need is the class interface. Often, these are provided as documentation. If not, simply look at the header file. Look first for constructors to see how to create an object of this class. Next, look at the names of all the methods. A well-designed class should give you a pretty good idea of how it is used just from the method names and the names and types of the method arguments.

Reading Interface Specifications

When you first study a class, don't look at the implementation (the .CPP file). Usually, the interface (declaration) is found in a header file (.H). Also, you should ignore the private sections of class declarations. It is not that there are any dark secrets in the private section. It is just that there is enough to digest from the protected and public sections that you don't need extra confusing details that are irrelevant to the use of the class.

If that is true, then why are the private sections listed in header files? Recall that a class is adapted from the C **struct**, which defines how much storage an object will occupy. It is permissible to leave private methods out of the class declaration, but if you leave out instance variable declarations, the compiler will not know how much space to set aside for an object or **struct** when an instance is created. In fact, the values in the private section of the header provided to the user of the class don't even have to be the same types as the definition used by the supplier to build the library. The only thing that matters is that the variables occupy exactly the same amount of storage space.

Sometimes, classes are designed for one-time use, in which case both the interface (declaration) and the implementation (definition) are found in the same file as the program that uses the class. The interface and the implementation are sometimes one and the same. In this case, all methods are completely defined in the class declaration.

This is a complete interface and implementation with one constructor and one method:

```
class Integer
{
     int val;
public:
     Integer(int i) { val=i; }
     int value() { return value; }
};
```

ElapsedTime: An Example Interface In addition to the **Time** class, the DiskTutor provides an **ElapsedTime** class. Here is the interface:

```
#ifndef ETIME_H
#define ETIME_H

////////////////////////////////////////////////////////////////
// class ElapsedTime (declaration)
////////////////////////////////////////////////////////////////
class ElapsedTime
{
private:
    long elapsedTime;
    long lastTime;
    long thisTime;
    int timerOn;
protected:
    int isOn();
public:
    ElapsedTime();
    void update();
    void on();
    void off();
    void reset();
```

```
    int hours();
    int minutes();
    int seconds();
    int hundredths();
    long totalSeconds();

    void display();
    void state();
};

#endif
```

It is not hard to guess how to use this class. The constructor takes no arguments, so you know how to create an **ElapsedTime** object:

```
ElapsedTime et;
```

There are several types of operations for most classes, but almost all have operations for changing the state in some way (manipulators) as well as operations that merely give information (access operators). The manipulators provided for **ElapsedTime** objects are **update**, **on**, **off**, and **reset**. Elapsed timers behave like stopwatches, so it makes sense that they have a state that knows whether they are on or off and ways of turning the stopwatch on and off. In addition, stopwatches must be set back to zero. The **reset** method does this.

By looking at the access methods, you can see how to get information about the number of elapsed hours, minutes, seconds, and hundredths of seconds. You can also get information about the total number of elapsed seconds, which is useful for comparing one elapsed timer against another. Finally, there are two methods for displaying information about the timer on the screen. The **display** method prints the timer on the screen through **cout** in a standard format. The **state** method is provided with many of the classes developed for the DiskTutor. This method dumps the values of all the private instance variables in the class to the **stdout** device. The primary purpose of **state** is for debugging.

Although you don't need to know about the private instance variables of a class in order to use it, in developing derived classes it is often useful to be able to dump the state of the base class to see that it contains the values you expect. For this reason, the **state** methods have been left in several of the classes. Normally, these methods would be removed from production code with conditional compilation directives to reduce the code size.

Program P10-2 uses the **ElapsedTime** class.

P10-2

```
#include <iostream.h>
#include "etime.h"
#include <conio.h>

main()
{
    clrscr();

    ElapsedTime et;
    while(!kbhit())
    {

        et.update();
        gotoxy(1,1);
        cout << "Elapsed Time: ";
        et.display();
    }
}
```

The program looks almost exactly the same as the modifications you made to Program P10-1. The only difference is that

```
#include "timec.h"
```

is replaced with

```
#include "etime.h"
```

and the variable name and declaration have been changed from

```
Time now;
```

to

```
ElapsedTime et;
```

with subsequent variable name changes in the other statements. Close Project P10-1. Answer No if the Borland C++ IDE asks if you want to save the modified version of P10-1.CPP. In order to run Program P10-2, you will have to make a project file composed of P10-2, ETIME.CPP, and DT.LIB. Do that now. Then compile and run the program.

As long as you do not press a key, the elapsed time will be displayed in the upper-left corner of the screen in the following format:

```
Elapsed Time:  0:00:02.38
```

Press any key when you have seen enough. Of the four components of the typical digital watch (clock, stopwatch, timer, and alarm), you have two already (clock and stopwatch), without doing any programming. In the next section you will develop a more specialized timer based on the class provided by the DiskTutor. As you go along, you will see why inheritance is indispensable for reusing code that does not already do exactly what you want it to—even if you don't have the source code.

Inheritance

You are now going to modify Program P10-2 to create a new class, **Timer**, which is inherited from **ElapsedTime**. If file P10-2.CPP is not already open, open it by selecting the filename in the Project window and pressing RETURN. Or double-click on the filename if you have a mouse. First, add the following three lines just before **main**.

```
class Timer : public ElapsedTime
{
};
```

This declares the new class **Timer**, and indicates that it is derived from **ElapsedTime**. No constructor or methods are provided for the new class at this point. Now, instead of declaring an object of class **ElapsedTime**, you want a **Timer** object. So change

```
ElapsedTime et;
```

to

```
Timer aTimer;
```

You have changed the name of the timer from **et** to **aTimer**, so now you will have to change all subsequent occurrences of **et** to **aTimer**. Do so now with the editor's global find and replace command (ALT S R). Select the Change All button after specifying the search string and the replacement.

Your program should now look like this:

```
#include <iostream.h>
#include "etime.h"
#include <conio.h>

class Timer : public ElapsedTime
{
};

main()
{
    clrscr();

    Timer aTimer;
    while(!kbhit())
    {
        aTimer.update();
        gotoxy(1,1);
        cout << "Elapsed Time: ";
        aTimer.display();
    }
}
```

Save the program now as MYTIMER.CPP. You will use this file as the basis of a StopWatch class in a program to be built later in the chapter. Use the **File/Save** as command to change the name. Now make a second copy of the file. Use the **File/Save** as command again to rename the file MY10-2.CPP so that MYTIMER will not be affected by the modifications you are about to make. Since you have changed the name of the source file, you will also have to create a new project file. Do so now. Close Project P10-2 and create a project file called MY10-2 and add to it the files MY10-2.CPP, ETIME.CPP, and DT.LIB. Open MY10-2.CPP.

Run the program now. Not surprisingly, the result is exactly the same as Program P10-2. But it does show two things. First, a derived class behaves exactly like its parent class when the **public** keyword is included in the inheritance specification. Second, it shows that you do not always have to create a new constructor when you create a new inherited class. If the base class provides a constructor with no arguments, then the inherited class need not provide one. The parent's constructor will be used in such a case.

Inheritance for Modifying Class Behavior

Inheritance is a tool for modifying the behavior of an existing class. Suppose a class does almost, but not exactly, what you want it to do. In a language that does not provide inheritance, you have to toss out the baby with the bath water even if the language supports user-defined types. If a library subroutine does not give you exactly what you want, you either have to work around it or build your own routine from scratch. In doing so, you will probably duplicate 90 percent of the code already in the library routine, adding extra bulk to the final program.

Inheritance lets you create a new class that behaves just like the old class but differs only in ways that you specify. Inheritance can be used to either extend or restrict the features of an existing class. Extension is used when the features of the base class are not powerful enough for the application at hand. Restriction is used when the base class includes everything but the kitchen sink and you want to provide a reusable class with a simplified interface so people don't get confused. Restriction is also used when you want to take out some features of the base class that could do damage. For example, you may not want to let class users remove events from an event queue, even though you will allow them to add events. You could derive a **UserEventQueue** class from **EventQueue** and not implement a method for **remove**. In some cases, you don't extend or restrict behavior as much as you modify it—making the timer count down instead of up, for example.

Timer: Enhancing the ElapsedTime Class

The **Timer** class is going to behave a little bit differently than the **ElapsedTime** class. The **ElapsedTime** class starts at zero and counts upward. The **Timer** class will start with a time interval specified by a user of the class and will count down to zero. First, you need a private instance variable for the interval of time the **Timer** is supposed to count. Next, you need a constructor that accepts an interval as an argument so it can be specified by the class user when a **Timer** object is created. Finally, you need an access method so you can find out how much time is left. All this is accomplished by adding four lines to the **Timer** class so that it looks like this:

```
class Timer : public ElapsedTime
{
    long interval;
public:
    Timer(long anInterval) { interval = anInterval; }
    long timeLeft() { return interval - totalSeconds(); }
};
```

Add four lines to MY10-2.CPP inside the declaration for the **Timer** class so it looks like the listing above. Since the constructor now takes an argument, you have to change the declaration for the instance variable **aTimer** from

```
Timer aTimer;
```

to

```
Timer aTimer(15);        // count down fifteen seconds
```

Finally, you need to add code to print out the time left in the timer. For now, leave the code that prints the elapsed time so you can compare the two values. Just after the statement

```
aTimer.display();
```

add the following statements:

```
gotoxy(1,3);
cout << "Time Left: "
     << aTimer.timeLeft()
     << "     \n";  // 5 spaces
```

Here is what the program should look like now.

```
#include <iostream.h>
#include "etime.h"
#include <conio.h>

class Timer : public ElapsedTime
{
    long interval;
public:
    Timer(long anInterval) { interval = anInterval; }
    long timeLeft() { return interval - totalSeconds(); }
};

main()
{
    clrscr();

    Timer aTimer(15);        // count down fifteen seconds
    while(!kbhit())
    {
        aTimer.update();
        gotoxy(1,1);
        cout << "Elapsed Time: ";
        aTimer.display();
        gotoxy(1,3);
        cout << "Time Left: "
             << aTimer.timeLeft()
             << "     \n";  // 5 spaces
    }
}
```

Save your modifications, keeping the same filename (MY10-2.CPP), and run the program.

The timer starts off with a count of 15 seconds and seems to keep accurate time. It is counting downward as expected, but what happens when zero is reached? The value goes negative. That may or may not be what you want. In most digital watches the timer stops when the time reaches zero, so you probably want the timer to turn itself off when it gets to zero. Better yet, it would be nice if some kind of alarm went off. But one thing at a time. Getting the timer to shut itself off will be a good first step. At first glance this looks easy. All you have to do is wait until the expression

```
timeLeft()==0
```

is true. Then you turn off the timer:

```
off();
```

All you need is a statement like this:

```
if (timeLeft()==0)
   off();
```

But think about it for a minute. Where would you put such a control statement? You could put it inside the **while** loop in **main**, as follows:

```
while(!kbhit())
{
     if (timeLeft()==0)
         aTimer.off();
}
```

But this puts the burden of checking the time left and turning off the timer on the user or client of the **Timer** class. What good is a timer that you have to keep looking at so you can shut it off when it reaches zero? The timer is supposed to tell you when it reaches zero.

When you modify the behavior of an inherited class, keep the modifications as few and as simple as possible. You want to automate maintenance of the timer's state. Why not use the **update** method inherited from **ElapsedTime** to check for a zero count as well as for updating the elapsed time?

Remember that in a real situation you probably would have bought this code from a third party or had it supplied to you by someone from another programming team responsible for its development. Even though it is on disk here, you should pretend you don't have the source code for the implementation. Even if you could modify the source, it would not help in this case because **ElapsedTime::update** would not have access to either the private variable, **interval**, or the public method, **timeLeft**, in the **Timer** class.

Overriding Inherited Methods

The answer is to override the public method, **update**, which **Timer** inherits from **ElapsedTime**. You override an inherited method simply by writing a new definition for it in the inherited class. If you don't write a new method, the parent's method is automatically available when the **public** keyword is included in the inheritance specification for the derived class.

You might ask why the **ElapsedTime::update** method is necessary at all. Why should the client of either **Timer** or **ElapsedTime** have to explicitly call an **update** method? There are three reasons for this.

First, by guaranteeing that the state of a timer does not change unless the user tells it to, you avoid problems of how to synchronize the values returned by the methods **hours, minutes, seconds, hundredths**, and **totalTime**. If the timer was updated continually, two successive calls (for example, calling **seconds** and then calling **totalSeconds**) would return inconsistent values.

Second, short of writing an interrupt handler, there is no way to have the timer updated automatically. Third, writing several different process-oriented classes shows some interesting ways that you can simulate a parallel processing environment in a programming environment that does not explicitly support it.

How do you override the **update** method that the **Timer** class inherits from **ElapsedTime**? Simply write a new method with exactly the same name. (Don't make this change to your program.)

```
void update()    // overrides inherited update method
{
    ElapsedTime::update();        // call inherited method
    if (timeLeft() <= 0)
        off();                    // call inherited method
}
```

The first thing the overriding method does is call the overridden method of the parent class (**ElapsedTime**). An overridden method has no obligation to call the parent method it overrides, but in this case it is a convenient way to tackle the problem of updating the timer. Note the use of the parent or base class name followed by **::** to resolve the scope of the call. If some kind of scope resolution operator is not given, the first statement in **update** would be a recursive call to itself and the program would be stuck in an infinite loop. Note that in most cases it is permissible to omit the base class name.

```
::update();       // go to scope outside current scope
```

This tells the call to look for an **update** function that is outside the current scope—in this case, the class **scope** for **ElapsedTime**—to resolve the call. The preferred explicit style includes the parent class name, giving the reader extra information and costing nothing.

Next, **Timer::update** checks to see if the timer has gone past zero. If so, it turns off the timer by sending the **off** message to **ElapsedTime**. Notice that the call to the **ElapsedTime::off** method requires neither an explicit nor an implicit scope resolution modifier because only the parent class, **ElapsedTime**, defines an **off** method.

How Overriding Works In the class declaration for **Timer** in MY10-2.CPP, the method of inheritance for **Timer** is public:

```
class Timer : public ElapsedTime
```

This means that all class members that were public in **ElapsedTime** will be public members of **Timer**. Therefore, an object that is an instance of the **Timer** class

```
Timer aTimer(15);
```

can specifically invoke inherited public methods without having to define them:

```
aTimer.display();
cout <<  "seconds: " << aTimer.seconds();
aTimer.off();
```

Also, for public inheritance, protected members of the parent class are available to the child class as private members. The member function **isOn** in **ElapsedTime** is an example. Here is how **Timer** might use **isOn**:

```
Timer::toggle()     // inherited protected method isOn
{                   // appears as a private
    if (isOn())     // method of Timer
        off();
    else
        on();
}
```

(This code fragment is an example and not a modification you should make to the current program.)

The following reference to **isOn**, however, would cause a compile-time error.

```
main()
{
    Timer aTimer(15);
    if (aTimer.isOn())      // error: aTimer can't
        //...               // reference private member
}                           // of Timer class
```

Finally, private members of a parent class inherited through private inheritance are unavailable to the child class.

```
long Timer::timeLeft()
{
    return elapsedTime-interval;  // error: can't
                                  // access private
                                  // member of parent
}
```

If the private member **elapsedTime** was made available to the inheriting class (by making it protected), the preceding code would be legal but would produce a meaningless value because the units for **elapsedTime** are timer ticks (1/18.2 of a second), while the units for **interval** are seconds—something like adding apples and oranges. A user of the **ElapsedTime** class does not need to know that elapsed time is represented internally as timer ticks and should not count on it in any way. The implementation could be changed at a later date and use a floating-point value to keep track of time in milliseconds. To prevent this kind of misuse of **ElapsedTime** by its heirs, it is declared private. Making the variable private broadcasts this message to class users: "Don't mess with this if you want to avoid trouble later."

What happens if the inheritance is not public—that is, if the keyword **public** is left out of the declaration?

```
class Timer : ElapsedTime
{
    //...
}
```

In such a case, private members of **ElapsedTime** are unavailable to instances of the **Timer** class. Also, protected members of **ElapsedTime** are unavailable to the child class, **Timer.** Only members that are declared public in the parent class, **ElapsedTime,** are available to the child class, and they will act as private members of the child class.

If the keyword **public** was eliminated from the inheritance specification in the declaration for **Timer** in Program MY10-2, the following reference would be illegal:

```
main()
{
    Timer aTimer(15);
    aTimer.display();        // compile-time error:
                             // aTimer can't access
                             // private member of Timer
}
```

This is because code defined inside the function **main** is outside the scope of the **Timer** class. However, code defined within a method for the **Timer** class is within the scope of the class and therefore can reference the class's private members.

```
Timer::update()
{
    ElapsedTime::update()    // legal reference
}
```

The reference is legal here because the scope of the reference is the class **Timer**. All code defined within the methods of the **Timer** class is considered to be within the scope of the class. Even though the function **ElapsedTime::update** is now considered a private member of **Timer** (due to the private inheritance specification), it can still be called from methods defined by the **Timer** class. Classes that are created through private inheritance are useful if you want to restrict rather than extend the interface of a class. The **StopWatch** class, which appears later in this chapter, provides an example of an interface that is restricted through private inheritance.

Now go ahead and modify the **Timer** class by adding the code to override the **update** method.

```
void update()    // overrides inherited update method
{
    ElapsedTime::update();        // call inherited method
    if (timeLeft() <= 0)
        off();                    // call inherited method
}
```

Type this code just after the definition for the **timeLeft** function.

The entire program should now look like this:

```
#include <iostream.h>
#include "etime.h"
#include <conio.h>

class Timer : public ElapsedTime
{
    long interval;
public:
    Timer(long anInterval) { interval = anInterval; }
    long timeLeft() { return interval - totalSeconds(); }
    void update()    // overrides inherited update method
    {
        ElapsedTime::update();        // call inherited method
        if (timeLeft() <= 0)
            off();                    // call inherited method
    }
};

main()
{
    clrscr();

    Timer aTimer(15);          // count down fifteen seconds
    while(!kbhit())
    {
        aTimer.update();
        gotoxy(1,1);
        cout << "Elapsed Time: ";
        aTimer.display();
        gotoxy(1,3);
        cout << "Time Left: "
```

```
                << aTimer.timeLeft()
                << "     \n"; // 5 spaces
    }
}
```

Save the program, compile it, and run it. The timer should now shut itself off when it reaches zero.

Inheritance for Extending Class Features

The last modification you are going to make will add an alarm to the newly created **Timer** class. This is an example of how you might not only want to modify the behavior of a class, but also to extend the features provided by the base class. The alarm for the **Timer** class will go off when the time runs down to zero. The alarm will sound for a specified duration. You also need a way to shut the alarm off if the noise is bugging you and you don't want to wait for the alarm's duration setting to run out.

Add the following two private member declarations to the **Timer** class just before the public section.

```
long alarmDuration;
int alarmOn;
```

Now you need to modify the constructor to accept an additional argument specifying the alarm duration. The constructor should also initialize the two new private member variables.

```
Timer(long anInterval, long alarmTime=5)
{
    interval = anInterval;
    alarmDuration = alarmTime;
    alarmOn=0;
}
```

Note that a default argument is specified for the alarm duration so that you can still declare an instance of **Timer** as you have done all along:

```
Timer aTimer(15);
```

This would set the default duration for the alarm, which is 5 seconds. You could set the alarm to last 30 seconds as follows:

```
Timer aTimer(15, 30);
```

It will take a little work to modify the **Timer::update** method. You still want to call the parent's method to update the parent's timer, so leave the first statement in the method unchanged.

```
ElapsedTime::update();       // call inherited method
```

However, the following two statements will need to be replaced:

```
if (timeLeft() <= 0)
    off();                   // call inherited method
```

Delete these two lines and replace them with the following:

```
if (alarmOn)
{
    putch('\a');             // ANSI C alert character
    if (timeLeft() + alarmDuration <= 0)
    {
        alarmOn=0;
        off();               // call inherited method
    }
}
if (isOn() && timeLeft() <= 0)
    alarmOn=1;
```

Now the timer is no longer turned off when **timeLeft** is less than or equal to zero. Instead, the method waits until the combined value of **timeLeft** and **alarmDuration** is less than or equal to zero. If this is true, both the alarm and the timer are turned off.

```
alarmOn=0;
off();                 // call inherited method
```

On each call to **Timer::update** the alarm is sounded if it is turned on.

```
if (alarmOn)
{
    putch('\a');            // ANSI C alert character
    //...
}
```

Also, on each call to **Timer::update**, the alarm is switched on if the parent's timer is on and if the time left in the counter is less than or equal to zero.

```
if (isOn() && timeLeft() <= 0)
    alarmOn=1;
```

Finally, modify the statement that prints out the value of the timer so that it does not print a negative value while the alarm is sounding, since **update** no longer switches off the timer until the alarm is over. Change the line that reads

```
<< aTimer.timeLeft()
```

to

```
<< (aTimer.timeLeft() <= 0L ? 0L : aTimer.timeLeft())
```

Save the program and verify that it now looks like this:

```
#include <iostream.h>
#include "etime.h"
#include <conio.h>

class Timer : public ElapsedTime
{
    long interval;
    long alarmDuration;
    int alarmOn;
public:
    Timer(long anInterval, long alarmTime=5)
    {
        interval = anInterval;
        alarmDuration = alarmTime;
        alarmOn=0;
    }
    long timeLeft() { return interval - totalSeconds(); }
    void update()   // overrides inherited update method
    {
        ElapsedTime::update();      // call inherited method
        if (alarmOn)
        {
            putch('\a');            // ANSI C alert character
            if (timeLeft() + alarmDuration <= 0)
```

```
                {
                    alarmOn=0;
                    off();              // call inherited method
                }
        }
        if (isOn() && timeLeft() <= 0)
            alarmOn=1;
        }
};

main()
{
    clrscr();

    Timer aTimer(15);         // count down fifteen seconds
    while(!kbhit())
    {
        aTimer.update();
        gotoxy(1,1);
        cout << "Elapsed Time: ";
        aTimer.display();
        gotoxy(1,3);
        cout << "Time Left: "
             << (aTimer.timeLeft() <= 0L ? 0L : aTimer.timeLeft())
             << "     \n";  // 5 spaces
    }
}
```

You could put a control statement around

```
aTimer.display();
```

that would stop the timer from being printed once it had run below zero and the alarm was sounding. But leave it in for now so you can see that the alarm is ringing for the right period of time. Run the program now and sit on the edge of your seat, waiting for the alarm to go off. Press any key when you have had enough. Close Project MY10-2.

Inheritance for Restricting Class Features

Inheritance can be used to limit the number of features available in the original base class. In this section you will load and modify the program MYTIMER.CPP, which you saved way back in the section introducing inheritance. You are going to modify MYTIMER to develop a new class called **StopWatch** that is inherited from the **ElapsedTime** class.

Go ahead and load Program MYTIMER.CPP now. Use the **File/Save as** command to rename the file to STWATCH.CPP. Now, execute a global find and replace, changing all occurrences of "Timer" to "StopWatch."

The program should now look like this:

```
#include <iostream.h>
#include "etime.h"
#include <conio.h>

class StopWatch : public ElapsedTime
{
};

main()
{
    clrscr();

    StopWatch aStopWatch;
    while(!kbhit())
    {
        aStopWatch.update();
        gotoxy(1,1);
        cout << "Elapsed Time: ";
        aStopWatch.display();
    }
}
```

Make a project called STWATCH. Add three files: STWATCH.CPP, ETIME.CPP, and DT.LIB. Compile and run the program. Not surprisingly, it works just like MYTIMER. The next step will fix that.

Remove the keyword **public** from the class declaration so it looks identical to this:

```
class StopWatch : ElapsedTime
```

Now, when you compile, you should get the following two error messages:

```
'ElapsedTime::update' is not accessible in function main
'ElapsedTime::display' is not accessible in function main
```

Removing the **public** keyword from the inheritance specification for **StopWatch** made **update** and **display** into private methods. They can no longer be accessed outside the scope of the class. That is how you restrict the interface. But suppose you want to use these two methods and only limit access to other methods inherited from **ElapsedTime**. The first thing you might try is adding the following three lines inside the declaration for **StopWatch**.

```
public:
    void update();
    void display();
```

Now try compiling. This time, the program compiles, but the linker complains:

```
Error: Undefined symbol 'StopWatch::display()'
Error: Undefined symbol 'StopWatch::update()'
```

You might think that the added lines would simply indicate that you wanted to change the status of the inherited methods, **update** and **display**, from private to public. But what you really did was to declare methods that override the inherited methods. The compiler accepts this, but since it does not find a definition for the overridden methods, it assumes that the definitions are in another file. The linker, however, shows that this is not the case. What you would have to do in order to simply restrict the new interface would be to define two methods that explicitly call the parent methods.

```
void update()
{
     ElapsedTime::update();
}

void display()
{
     ElapsedTime::display();
}
```

The cost of this extra code is nothing at run time because methods defined inside a class declaration are expanded as inline macros. This means that the compiler replaces a call to **StopWatch::update** with a call to **ElapsedTime::update** before converting the call to machine language.

Rather than making these changes, you are going to provide users of class **StopWatch** with a single method, **display**, which is going to both update the timer and display it. Change the declaration of **StopWatch** to look like this:

```
class StopWatch : ElapsedTime
{
public:
    void display()
    {
        ElapsedTime::update();
        ElapsedTime::display();
    }
};
```

Now delete the line

```
aStopWatch.update();
```

Here is a full listing of the program.

```
#include <iostream.h>
#include "etime.h"
#include <conio.h>

class StopWatch : ElapsedTime
{
public:
    void display()
    {

        ElapsedTime::update();
        ElapsedTime::display();
    }
};
main()
{
    clrscr();

    StopWatch aStopWatch;
    while(!kbhit())
    {
        gotoxy(1,1);
        cout << "Elapsed Time: ";
        aStopWatch.display();
    }
}
```

By combining the **update** and **display** operations into a single method, you relieve users of the class from having to make the distinction. As mentioned earlier, there are advantages in forcing the programmer to explicitly distinguish updating a timer from displaying it. But if you don't buy that argument, the technique of restricted inheritance gives you a way out. You can have a timer that is updated automatically every time you print it. If you do this, users of the class cannot access methods for **hours**, **minutes**, **seconds**, and so forth. But maybe you don't want them to. Run the program now to see that calling the **display** method automatically updates the timer.

Adapting Classes to Print to Devices Other than ostream

One problem with the previous implementation of **StopWatch** is that it is tied to an ostream style of output, namely **cout**. How would you use **StopWatch** in a window system that does not support stream I/O? You could give the class user a pointer to a string that formats the stop watch output in a desired style. You don't want the class user to worry about calling **update**; you want that handled automatically. Furthermore, you don't want to give the class user access to the **display** or **state** methods included in the original **ElapsedTime** class mainly for diagnostics during development.

Here is an approach. The first step will be to provide the requested display formatting without providing a method for returning a pointer to the formatted string.

Suppose you want to take this a step further and show the time in a different format, eliminating hours altogether and showing tenths instead of hundredths. You could accommodate all these criteria and still use a restricted interface providing only a subset of the original methods. To do this, modify the display method of the **StopWatch** class to look like this:

```
class StopWatch : ElapsedTime
{
public:
```

```
    void display()
    {
        ElapsedTime::update();
        char buf[100];
        // display minutes, seconds, and tenths
        sprintf(buf, "%2d:%02d.%1d", // %1=numeral one
                minutes(),
                seconds(),
                (hundreths()+5) / 10);  // round & truncate
    cout << buf;
    }
};
```

Add the line #include <stdio.h> just after #include <conio.h> to include the prototype for sprintf. The entire program is printed here for your reference.

```
#include <iostream.h>
#include "etime.h"
#include <conio.h>
#include <stdio.h>

class StopWatch : ElapsedTime
{
public:
    void display()
    {
        ElapsedTime::update();
        char buf[100];
        // display minutes, seconds, and tenths
        sprintf(buf, "%2d:%02d.%1d",
                minutes(),
                seconds(),
                (hundreths()+5) / 10);  // round & truncate
        cout << buf;
    }
};

main()
{
    clrscr();

    StopWatch aStopWatch;
    while(!kbhit())
    {
        gotoxy(1,1);
        cout << "Elapsed Time: ";
        aStopWatch.display();
    }
}
```

Run the program to see a different **StopWatch** time format.

Now that the formatting is set up the way you want it, you can get back to the problem of displaying the time in a window instead of an output stream. Do this by changing the method, **update**, to the definition for a conversion operator function that returns a pointer to a string. Change the line

```
void display()
```

to

```
operator char*()
```

Next, modify the display format to give a little more information by changing

```
sprintf(buf, "%2d:%02d.%1d",
```

to

```
sprintf(buf, "minutes: %2d seconds: %02d tenths %1d",
```

Next, instead of printing the string

```
cout << buf;
```

you want to allocate storage for it, copy the string to the new storage, and return a pointer to the copy:

```
char *p = new char[strlen(buf)+1];
strcpy(p,buf);
return p;
```

Replace the **cout** statement with these three lines now. This technique is a bit out of the ordinary. Normally, it is the responsibility of the class that creates storage for an object to also delete that object and return its storage to the heap. In this situation, it is not practical for **StopWatch** to destroy the string. Here is a case where the requirements justify breaking the convention. Otherwise, you would have to build knowledge into the **StopWatch** class about the output systems that are going to be using **StopWatch**. Such specific knowledge would make **StopWatch** less useful as a general-purpose utility. It is important to remember that when the situation justifies violating a convention like this, you must warn users of the class—both in the code and in the documentation—that it is their responsibility to destroy the string returned by the cast (conversion operator function).

Printing the **StopWatch** display now requires three statements instead of two. Replace

```
cout << "Elapsed Time: ";
aStopWatch.display();
```

with

```
char *pTimeString = aStopWatch;
cout << "Elapsed Time: " << pTimeString << "\n";
delete pTimeString;
```

Add the line #include <string.h> just before the line #include <stdio.h>. Here is what you should have now:

```
#include <iostream.h>
#include "etime.h"
#include <conio.h>
#include <string.h>  // for strlen and strcpy prototypes
#include <stdio.h>

class StopWatch : ElapsedTime
{
public:
    operator char*()
    {
        ElapsedTime::update();
        char buf[100];
        // display minutes, seconds, and tenths
        sprintf(buf, "minutes: %2d seconds: %02d tenths %ld",
                minutes(),
                seconds(),
                (hundreths()+5) / 10);  // round & truncate
        char *p = new char[strlen(buf)+1];
        strcpy(p,buf);
        return p;
    }
};

main()
{
```

```
    clrscr();

    StopWatch aStopWatch;
    while(!kbhit())
    {
        gotoxy(1,1);
        char *pTimeString = aStopWatch;
        cout << "Elapsed Time: " << pTimeString << "\n";
        delete pTimeString;
    }
}
```

Running the program won't produce output that is much different from what you have seen already. But these changes are preparations for the following program, which uses the DiskTutor's screen display tools to display the stopwatch in a window.

Preview: Using Display Classes for I/O

You can add the modifications for the following program yourself to STWATCH.CPP, or you can create a new project for Program P10-3. If you modify STWATCH.CPP yourself, be sure to replace P10-3.CPP with STWATCH.CPP when you create the project file. The main thing to note is that the definition for **StopWatch** is the same as in the previous example. The following line is added to the top of the program to provide declarations for the display classes.

```
#include "display.h"
```

Rather than worrying about the details of using the display classes—introduced more formally in Chapter 14—you should just run the program and see what these classes will do for you. Here is Program P10-3 in full.

P10-3

```
#include "display.h"
#include "etime.h"
#include <conio.h>
#include <string.h>  // for strlen and strcpy prototypes
#include stdio.h
```

```
class StopWatch : ElapsedTime
{
public:
    operator char*()
    {
        ElapsedTime::update();
        char buf[100];
        // display minutes, seconds, and tenths
        sprintf(buf, "minutes: %2d seconds: %02d tenths %1d",
                minutes(),
                seconds(),
                (hundreths()+5) / 10);  // round & truncate
        char *p = new char[strlen(buf)+1];
        strcpy(p,buf);
        return p;
    }
};

main()
{
    Display.fill(Chat(0xb1,0x2f));
    StopWatch aStopWatch;
    char *pTimeString = aStopWatch;
    int width = strlen(pTimeString);
    delete pTimeString;

    DisplayMedium box(Rectangle(1, 2, width+2, 3));
    box.color(YELLOW + (BLUE<<4));
    box.display();
    box.border(FRAME1, WHITE + (RED<<4));
    gotoxy(2+(width+2-strlen("Elapsed Time"))/2,3);
    textattr(WHITE + (RED<<4));
    cputs("Elapsed Time");

    _setcursortype(_NOCURSOR);
    while(!kbhit())
    {
        gotoxy(3,4);
        char *pTimeString = aStopWatch;
        textattr(YELLOW + (BLUE<<4));
        cputs(pTimeString);
        delete pTimeString;
    }
    clrscr();
    _setcursortype(_NORMALCURSOR);
}
```

Create a project, P10-3, and add four files: P10-3.CPP, ETIME.CPP, DT.LIB, and DTUI.LIB. If you keep your existing project (STWATCH .PRJ), you must add DTUI.LIB to the project list. Load Program

P10-3 (or type in the changes). Now run the program. The backdrop of the display is set to a special shading character and then a window is opened with the label "Elapsed Time" appearing as the title. Finally, the program enters the loop that you have seen over and over throughout the modifications of the various clock and watch programs.

As you can see, the visual display is an improvement on the iostream display technique.

```
┌───────────Elapsed Time───────────┐
│minutes:  1 seconds: 19 tenths 2│
└──────────────────────────────────┘
```

This program shows that tools developed for the iostream system can easily be converted for other input/output systems like the display classes. Finally, the display classes provide another example of how you can get complex applications up and running with very few lines of code. Chapter 14 will cover the display classes and window system provided by the DiskTutor in more detail. But for now, flexibility in the reuse of code is the thing to be aware of.

11 Code Reuse: Multiple Inheritance

Sometimes, it is useful to build classes that inherit the characteristics of more than one parent class. The concept of inheritance was introduced in Chapter 6, where the **Window** class was derived from **Rectangle**. Subsequently, a **Menu** class was developed, which used both **Window** and **List** classes to implement a pop-up menu.

Candidates for Multiple Inheritance

As you may recall, **Menu** was implemented as a list of choices. More precisely, a menu contained a pointer to the head of a list of objects, which were instances of the class **Choice**. A special **List** class was implemented to maintain lists of **Choice** objects.

Furthermore, a menu maintained an origin and a width. The height for a menu was determined from the number of **Choice** objects added to the menu. Height and width could be grouped together into a single point and called either **extent** or **corner**, depending on preference. Interestingly enough, these values maintained by **Menu** are exactly the same properties required to define a window.

The method **Menu::getChoice** used in Chapter 6 hints at this knowledge by creating a window, **w**, in its first statement, as follows:

```
int Menu::getChoice()
{
    Window w(org, org+Point(width+2, nentries+1);
    //...
}
```

Looking for Duplicated Effort

There is some duplication of code here. Both the **Menu** object and the **Window** object it creates maintain two distinct points defining the area occupied by the menu. In this particular application, the **Window** class inherited the properties of **Rectangle**; however, the **Menu** class had no parents. Why couldn't **Menu** be derived from **Rectangle** or **Window**?

The **List** class used by **Menu** could also be built in a way that would make its code more reusable. You have seen a number of lists so far. The **Menu** class introduces a circular list to keep track of menu choices in Chapter 6. Then a noncircular **List** class is developed in Chapter 7. This implementation differs from that of Chapter 6 although it still maintains nodes of **Choice** objects. Lists turn out to be so useful that they wind up being implemented over and over again in slightly different forms. Chapters 7 and 8 discuss the use of iterators for processing lists. Chapter 9 introduces applicators for modifying lists and implements yet another list class to handle file information (the **FileInfo** and **FileItem** classes). This implementation is more generic than previous lists and is adapted to handle directories (**DirList**).

Reusing Code to Avoid Duplication

You could go on adapting the **List** class to each new application, but there is a better way. DiskTutor provides generic classes for data structures (like lists) that are required by many programs. These classes will be introduced more thoroughly in Chapter 13, but for now you can take for granted a generic **LinkedList** class that will handle objects of many different types. An instance of the **LinkedList** class provided by the DiskTutor can hold points, rectangles, strings, and windows as well as other objects. In fact, much of the code used to manage the linked list of **Choice** strings in the original **Menu** class was derived from the **LinkedList** class provided by the DiskTutor.

A **Window** class can also be implemented in a more reusable manner than the version implemented in Chapter 6. The DiskTutor provides a powerful **Window** class, supporting all the features of the earlier version and more. If the name of the game is code reuse, why can't you reuse the code in the generic **LinkedList** and **Window** classes to build menus? In fact, you can.

Multiple Inheritance Increases the Potential for Reuse

You can declare a new class, **Menu**, that inherits both the characteristics of a window and a linked list. The DiskTutor provides a **Menu** class that does this. This section will not go into the full implementation at this point because the **Menu** class will be more easily understood once you work through a simpler implementation of a class based on multiple inheritance. But to whet your appetite, here is one possible way to declare a **Menu** class.

```
Class Menu : public Window, LinkedList
{
     //...
};
```

Specifying Multiple Parents

The comma-separated list that follows the colon is the list of all classes from which **Menu** will inherit methods and instance variables. There are two classes here, but there can be more. The syntax of the language does not specify a limit, but you will not want to specify so many parent classes that you cannot keep track of all the class members.

Inheritance for Each Parent May Be Private or Public

As with single inheritance, it is possible to specify public or private inheritance from the parent class. If neither the keyword **public** nor **private** precedes the parent class name, private inheritance is assumed.

As explained in Chapter 10, public inheritance indicates that the parent's public members appear as public members to the child. The parent's protected members become private members of the child. Private members of the parent are unavailable to the child.

In the case of private inheritance, the parent's public members become private members of the child. Neither protected nor private members of the parent can be accessed by a child created through private inheritance.

In the previous example, the **Menu** class is able to access all the public methods of the **Window** class, which includes functions like **open**, **displayAt**, and **move**. Such a menu inherits the parent's ability to be moved with the mouse or special keyboard commands.

The private inheritance specification in **Menu** for the **LinkedList** parent means that the public methods of **LinkedList** will become private methods of **Menu**. These methods can only be accessed within the scope of the **Menu** class. In other words, **LinkedList** methods—such as **add**, **remove**, **first**, **last**, and so on—can only be invoked inside of new method definitions created for the **Menu** class.

Design Strategies for Multiple Inheritance

As with single inheritance, classes developed with multiple inheritance can apply techniques for modifying, extending, or restricting the features provided by their parents.

Selecting Parents

The typical process for designing a class with multiple inheritance is first to determine what features the new class has in common with existing classes. The next step is to determine how the new class should be different from the parent classes. The first step is the key to the declaration, specifically to the inheritance specification. The second step is the key to the implementation.

SnoozeClock: An Example of Multiple Inheritance

Let's make further discussion of multiple inheritance concrete by applying the concepts to the development of a **SnoozeClock** class. **SnoozeClock** inherits properties from the **ElapsedTime** class discussed in the previous chapter. **SnoozeClock** also inherits from **AlarmClock**, which is introduced in this chapter. **AlarmClock** is a class provided especially for this example. **AlarmClock** is in turn derived from the **Time** class.

The interface for **ElapsedTime** was provided in the previous chapter. If you need a refresher, go back and review that listing now. The interface for **AlarmClock** is provided in Program P11-1. The implementation is included in the program as well, but ignore it for now. At some point it might be beneficial to examine the implementation of both

ElapsedTime and **AlarmClock**. For now, treat them as code supplied by a third party—that is, pretend that only the interface is supplied.

Before you can use multiple inheritance, you have to know the features of the base classes that are useful for your application. The best way to familiarize yourself with an interface is to study an example of how the class is used. Let's look at the first program for this chapter, which provides the **AlarmClock** class and shows how to use it. Again, before invoking the Borland C++ IDE and loading any programs, make sure you have logged to the appropriate directory for this chapter (\DT\CH11).

P11-1

```
#include <iostream.h>
#include <stdio.h>
#include <string.h>
#include <conio.h>
#include "timec.h"

//////////////////////////////////////////////////////////////
// class AlarmClock (declaration)
//////////////////////////////////////////////////////////////
class AlarmClock : Time
{
    long alarmDuration;
    int armed;
    char buf[10];
protected:
    void setForTomorrow();
    int alarmIsRinging();
public:
    AlarmClock(int hr, int min=0, long duration=10)
    : Time(hr, min), alarmDuration(duration), armed(1) { }
    void update();
    void arm() { armed=1; }
    void disarm() { armed=0; }
    int isArmed() { return armed; }
    void touch();
    char* alarmString();
    char* timeString();
    // diagnostic
    void state()
    {
        cout << "====AlarmClock state====\n";
        Time::printOn(cout);
        cout << "\nduration: " << alarmDuration;
        cout << "\narmed: " << armed;
        cout << "\n";
    }
};
```

```
/////////////////////////////////////////////////////////////
// class AlarmClock (definition)
/////////////////////////////////////////////////////////////
const long secondsInDay = 24L*60L*60L;
void AlarmClock::setForTomorrow()
{
    // advance no more than 24 hours ahead
    if (*this < Time())
        *this += secondsInDay;  // same time tomorrow
}
inline int AlarmClock::alarmIsRinging()
{
    return (isArmed() &&
            Time() >= *this &&
            Time() <= (*this + alarmDuration));
}
void AlarmClock::update()
{
    if (alarmIsRinging())
    {
        cout << "RING";
    }
    else
        cout << "    ";
    if (Time() > *this + alarmDuration)
        setForTomorrow();
}
void AlarmClock::touch()
{
    if (alarmIsRinging())
        setForTomorrow();
}
char* AlarmClock::alarmString()
{
    sprintf(buf, "%2d:%02d",
                 Time::hour(),
                 Time::minute());
    return buf;
}
char* AlarmClock::timeString()
{
    Time now;
    sprintf(buf, "%2d:%02d:%02d",
                 now.hour(),
                 now.minute(),
                 now.second());
    return buf;
}

main()
{
    Time now;
    AlarmClock anAlarmClock(now.hour(), now.minute()+1);
```

```
    clrscr();
    int more=1;
    while(more)
    {
        gotoxy(1,1);
        cout << "Time:   " << anAlarmClock.timeString();
        gotoxy(1,2);
        cout << "Alarm: " << anAlarmClock.alarmString();
        gotoxy(1,3);
        anAlarmClock.update();
        gotoxy(1,15);
        anAlarmClock.state();
        if (kbhit())
        {
            int c=getch();
            switch(c)
            {
                case 'q':
                case 'Q':   more=0; break;
                case 't':
                case 'T':   anAlarmClock.touch(); break;
            }
        }
    }
    cout << "\ngoodbye, world\n\n";
}
```

To run Program P11-1.CPP, create a project file called P11-1.PRJ. Add two files to the project: P11-1.CPP and DT.LIB. Create the project now and open the file P11-1.CPP, by moving the highlight bar in the project window over the file name and pressing RETURN. Or double click the left mouse button with the mouse pointer on the filename.

An example of a clock program was provided in Program P10-1 in the previous chapter. That program took an instance of class **Time** and continually updated the instance, printing it to the screen. The format, as you will recall, was

```
12-Mar-90  7:09:49 pm
```

The **AlarmClock** class inherits from **Time** and modifies some of its features. For example, the date is no longer available directly through the features of **AlarmClock** (although the date can be seen when an instance of **AlarmClock** prints its state). Also, instances of **AlarmClock** return strings that represent a 24-hour clock rather than a clock divided into two twelve-hour periods distinguished by A.M. and P.M. The choice of the 24-hour clock is arbitrary but shows how little effort it takes to modify the features provided by a parent class.

Studying the Features of Potential Parents

Before running the program, study the interface for **AlarmClock**.

```
/////////////////////////////////////////////////////////////////
// class AlarmClock (declaration)
/////////////////////////////////////////////////////////////////
class AlarmClock : Time
{
    long alarmDuration;
    int armed;
    char buf[10];
protected:
    void setForTomorrow();
    int alarmIsRinging();
public:
    AlarmClock(int hr, int min=0, long duration=10)
    : Time(hr, min), alarmDuration(duration), armed(1) { }
    void update();
    void arm() { armed=1; }
    void disarm() { armed=0; }
    int isArmed() { return armed; }
    void touch();
    char* alarmString();
    char* timeString();
    // diagnostic
    void state()
    {
        cout << "====AlarmClock state====\n";
        Time::printOn(cout);
        cout << "\nduration: " << alarmDuration;
        cout << "\narmed: " << armed;
        cout << "\n";
    }
};
```

The main thing to notice about the interface of **AlarmClock** is that it is designed to imitate the behavior of a clock that you might use to wake up each morning. The **Time** class was far too general to provide this type of interface. Thus, an **AlarmClock** can be armed or disarmed. You can ask whether it is armed. Furthermore, it is possible to set the alarm time through the **hour** and **minute** arguments provided by the constructor. For example,

```
AlarmClock anAlarmClock (6,30)
```

creates an **AlarmClock** object called **anAlarmClock** and sets the time for the alarm to 6:30 A.M. Twenty-four-hour time is used to set the alarm; **anAlarmClock** can subsequently be assigned a new value by invoking **AlarmClock**'s constructor.

```
anAlarmClock = AlarmClock(10,30);
// reset alarm to a reasonable hour
```

The time of day cannot be reset in this version of **AlarmClock** since that information is provided by the DOS system clock. While the **Time** class had the disadvantage of not being easily printed to a non-iostream device like a window, **AlarmClock** returns formatted strings representing the time of day,

```
char* timeString ();
```

and the time of the alarm:

```
char* alarmString.
```

Both of these strings are held in a private buffer internal to the class, so the class user need not worry about returning storage for the string to the heap when the string is no longer needed. Returning a string allows the formatted output string to be sent to any device or function that can handle standard C strings.

Note, however, that the same buffer is used to store both the time and alarm strings and that subsequent calls to either of these string methods automatically destroys the previous contents of the buffer. Therefore, any routine that needs to preserve such a string should make its own copy.

The alarm will go off daily at the specified alarm time. It will stay on for the period of time specified in the third constructor argument,

duration, which defaults to ten seconds. The argument type for duration is **long**, so theoretically you could set the duration for about a century. Practically speaking, you will only be able to set it for ten years or so because this figure has to be added to the current time, which is represented as the number of seconds since January 1, 1901. This means that **Time** will no longer be able to represent an accurate date somewhere shortly after the turn of this century.

Instead of actually sounding the bell, the alarm clock rings by printing "RING" on the screen. While this is happening, invoking the touch method will turn off the ringer by advancing the time for the next alarm to the same time tomorrow. You can invoke the **touch** method during the ten seconds the alarm rings in Program P11-1 by pressing the T key.

Using the AlarmClock Class

Look at the code in **main** now to see how the **AlarmClock** class is used.

```
main()
{
    Time now;
    AlarmClock anAlarmClock(now.hour(), now.minute()+1);
    clrscr();
    int more=1;
    while(more)
    {
        gotoxy(1,1);
        cout << "Time:  " << anAlarmClock.timeString();
        gotoxy(1,2);
        cout << "Alarm: " << anAlarmClock.alarmString();
        gotoxy(1,3);
        anAlarmClock.update();
        gotoxy(1,15);
        anAlarmClock.state();
        if (kbhit())
        {
            int c=getch();
            switch(c)
            {
                case 'q':
                case 'Q':   more=0; break;
                case 't':
```

```
                case 'T':    anAlarmClock.touch(); break;
            }
        }
    }
    cout << "\ngoodbye, world\n\n";
}
```

First, an instance of **Time** called **now** is created. This object is used to set the time of the alarm in the following line.

```
AlarmClock anAlarmClock(now.hour(), now.minute()+1);
```

creates an instance of **AlarmClock** called **anAlarmClock** and sets it to go off within the next minute.

Next, the screen is cleared and the program enters a **while** loop, which continues as long as the value of **more** is true (nonzero).

```
int more=1;
while(more)
{
    //...
}
```

Cursor positioning is used to print the formatted strings for the time of day and the time of the alarm in the upper-left corner of the screen.

```
gotoxy(1,1);
cout << "Time:  " << anAlarmClock.timeString();
gotoxy(1,2);
cout << "Alarm: " << anAlarmClock.alarmString();
```

Next, the alarm is updated:

```
anAlarmClock.update();
```

This is the method that causes the alarm to sound if the time is right. Next, the diagnostic method **state** is called, printing the alarm clock's internal instance variables to the screen, so you can see what is going on inside of **anAlarm**. Note that **state** prints the date as well as the time in A.M./P.M. format. When you run the program, keep an eye on the date as you press T to touch and consequently turn off the alarm. The date should change as you do so.

The final statement inside the loop is a conditional that checks to see if a key has been pressed. If so, it reads and processes the key.

```
if (kbhit())
        {
            int c=getch();
            switch(c)
            {
                case 'q':
                case 'Q':    more=0; break;
                case 't':
                case 'T':    anAlarmClock.touch(); break;
            }
        }
```

Pressing either upper- or lowercase Q sets the variable **more** to zero, terminating the **while** loop and subsequently the program. Pressing upper- or lowercase T sends the **touch** message to **anAlarm**. If the alarm is ringing, the **touch** message advances the alarm to go off at the same time tomorrow.

Run the program now. When the program starts, the screen looks like this:

```
Time:    1:08:57
Alarm:   1:09

====AlarmClock state====
17-Mar-90  1:09:00 am
duration: 10
armed: 1
```

Since the alarm is set to one minute later than the current time when the program starts, you won't have to wait long. **Time** will vary because alarm time is rounded to the nearest minute. Be patient. When the seconds approach 59 and wrap back around to 00 you will see the following change in the screen.

```
Time:    1:09:02
Alarm:   1:09
RING

====AlarmClock state====
17-Mar-90  1:09:00 am
duration: 10
armed: 1
```

At this point you can either press T to disable the alarm, or wait for it to run out—ten seconds by default. Either way, you will have to press Q when you want to quit the program.

Program P11-1 provides a convenient starting point for a study of multiple inheritance. Now that you have an understanding of the interface and usage of the **AlarmClock** class, you are ready to use it as a base class from which new classes can be derived.

A Class with Two Parents

While **AlarmClock** serves as another example of modification and specialization through inheritance, its main purpose here is to serve as one of two parents for a new class. The new class will inherit publicly from the **AlarmClock** class and privately from the **ElapsedTime** class introduced in Chapter 10. If you need a refresher on the interface for **ElapsedTime**, you will find the header file ETIME.H, containing the interface for **ElapsedTime**, printed in that chapter.

Mapping Out Class Features Before Coding or What Is a SnoozeClock, Anyway?

The goal here is to modify the **AlarmClock** class and, through multiple inheritance, create a snooze alarm that will let you get a little extra sleep in the morning when you need it. Most people are familiar with snooze alarms. A snooze alarm is an alarm clock with a special button in addition to the regular button used to shut off the alarm. When the alarm goes off in the morning, you can hit either of these two buttons. If you hit the regular alarm button, the alarm shuts off and is reset to go on at the same time tomorrow. If you press the snooze button instead, the alarm stops, but just for a little while—ten or twenty minutes—to let you sleep a little longer. At the end of that period the alarm comes on again. At this point you have the same choice as when the alarm first came on: to snooze or not to snooze. You can either shut off the alarm until the regular time tomorrow, or you can snooze again. In fact, you can keep snoozing all day long as long as you keep pressing the snooze button every ten or twenty minutes. The snooze alarm is one of the great inventions of modern science.

While the **AlarmClock** class provides all the features of a simple alarm clock, the **ElapsedTime** class provides the extra features needed to build a snoozer on top of a regular alarm clock.

Starting with a Simple Class Declaration

Here is the declaration for a new class called **SnoozeClock**.

```
//////////////////////////////////////////////////////////////
// class SnoozeClock (declaration)
//////////////////////////////////////////////////////////////
class SnoozeClock : public AlarmClock, ElapsedTime
{
    long snoozeDuration;
public:
    SnoozeClock(int hr, int min=0, long duration=10,
                long snoozeTime=5);
};
```

Rename Program P11-1 to MY11-1 with the **F**ile/**S**ave as command. Now add the preceding code to the file after the last method definition for **AlarmClock** (**Alarm Clock::timeString**) and just before **main**.

Defining Constructors First

This code declares the class and a constructor for the class. However, it provides no implementation for the constructor.

The constructor definition follows:

```
//////////////////////////////////////////////////////////////////
// class SnoozeClock (definition)
//////////////////////////////////////////////////////////////////
SnoozeClock::SnoozeClock(int hr, int min,
                         long duration,
                         long snoozeTime)
    : AlarmClock(hr, min, duration),
      snoozeDuration(snoozeTime),
{
}
```

This code, including the three lines of comments identifying the subsequent code as definitions for **SnoozeClock**, should be placed immediately after the **SnoozeClock** class declaration and just before **main**. The two expressions in the constructor that follow the colon header and precede the opening brace of the constructor's definition are constructor initializers. The first,

```
AlarmClock(hr, min, duration)
```

calls the constructor for the **AlarmClock** base class. It is not necessary to directly invoke the constructor for **ElapsedTime**, though it is a parent as well. **ElapsedTime** provides a constructor requiring no arguments. If no base class constructor is specified by a child, the compiler assumes that a base class requiring no arguments exists and calls that constructor automatically. If such a constructor is not defined in the base class, the compiler will complain. It is necessary to explicitly call the **AlarmClock** constructor since the **AlarmClock** class does not provide a constructor with no arguments.

The second initializer in **SnoozeClock**'s constructor,

```
snoozeDuration(snoozeTime)
```

initializes **SnoozeClock**'s private instance variable, **snoozeDuration**, with **snoozeTime**—the value passed to **SnoozeClock** as the fourth constructor argument.

Adapting Existing Programs to Test New Classes

You now have all you need to get started with a basic definition. Next, you need a way to test **SnoozeClock**. An easy way to do this is to change the code in **main** to use an instance of **SnoozeClock** instead of an instance of **AlarmClock**.

First, change the declaration for **anAlarmClock** from

```
AlarmClock anAlarmClock(now.hour(), now.minute()+1);
```

to

```
SnoozeClock aSnoozer(now.hour(), now.minute()+1);
```

Now globally find and replace from this declaration through to the end of the file, changing all occurrences of **anAlarmClock** to **aSnoozer**.

You need to add an include file with declarations for **ElapsedTime** since that is one of the parents of **SnoozeClock**. Put the line

```
#include "etime.h"
```

just after

```
#include "timec.h"
```

near the top of the file.

Finally, you need to make a project file since the program needs to link to the object file created by ETIME.CPP. Create a new project called MY11-1. Now add three files to the project list: MY11-1.CPP, ETIME .CPP, and DT.LIB. Reopen MY11-1.CPP.

Testing Additions

Exit the project manager, save the program, and then compile. Unfortunately, if you have followed all the steps carefully, you get these two compiler errors:

```
Field 'update' is ambiguous in 'SnoozeClock' in function main
Field 'state' is ambiguous in 'SnoozeClock' in function main
```

Parents with Common Method Names

Don't panic. Ambiguous method names are exactly what we want to highlight at this point. This is a common problem with multiple inheritance, especially if you are at all consistent about the names you give to methods that serve common purposes like **print**, **show**, **hide**, **update**, and **state**.

Both **AlarmClock** and **ElapsedTime** define the methods **update** and **state**. The compiler is pretty lenient about gripes related to multiple inheritance. If a child class inherits from two or more parents with a common method name, the compiler will issue an ambiguous name error only if you try to call the common method through the child class. If no reference is made to the common method by the child, no error is signaled. Look again at **main** to see if you can find the culprits.

They are

```
//...
aSnoozer.update();
gotoxy(1,15);
aSnoozer.state();
//...
```

You could try commenting out the two offending lines by preceding them with comment tokens, like this:

```
//aSnoozer.update();
gotoxy(1,15);
//aSnoozer.state();
```

Now the program should compile, link, and run but you have lost a lot of useful information. If you have compiled the program and you are running it now, press Q to exit. Then go back and remove the two comment tokens you just inserted. There is a better way to resolve ambiguous references to multiple parents.

Resolving Ambiguous References First, add declarations for two new methods to the **SnoozeClock** class.

```
void update();
void state();
```

Place these two lines immediately after the constructor in the declaration section. Now, add these definitions:

```
void SnoozeClock::update()
{
    AlarmClock::update();
    ElapsedTime::update();
}

void SnoozeClock::state()
{
    AlarmClock::state();
    ElapsedTime::state();
}
```

Put this code immediately after the definition for the constructor and just before **main**.

The class should now look like this:

```
////////////////////////////////////////////////////////////
// class SnoozeClock (declaration)
////////////////////////////////////////////////////////////
class SnoozeClock : public AlarmClock, ElapsedTime
{
    long snoozeDuration;
public:
    SnoozeClock(int hr, int min=0, long duration=10,
                long snoozeTime=5);
    void update();
    void state();
};

////////////////////////////////////////////////////////////
// class SnoozeClock (definition)
////////////////////////////////////////////////////////////
SnoozeClock::SnoozeClock(int hr, int min=0,
                         long duration=10,
                         long snoozeTime=5)
    : AlarmClock(hr, min, duration),
      snoozeDuration(snoozeTime),
```

```
{
}

void SnoozeClock::update()
{
    AlarmClock::update();
    ElapsedTime::update();
}

void SnoozeClock::state()
{
    AlarmClock::state();
    ElapsedTime::state();
}
```

The definitions for **update** and **state** show that you can have it all. You can invoke an ambiguous method in either parent by providing a scope resolution modifier indicating exactly which parent to reference.

Invoking Overridden Parent Methods Is Optional There is nothing that forces a child method to call a parent method that the child overrides. For instance, the **SnoozeClock::state** method could just as easily be defined like this:

```
void SnoozeClock::state()
{
    cout << "snoozeDuration: "
         << snoozeDuration
         << "\n";
}
```

The child method can also call only one parent method, like this:

```
void SnoozeClock::update()
{
     Alarm Clock::update();
}
```

For now, leave **update** and **state** each calling two parent methods. Save, compile, and run the program.

The program output is like the original P11-1 except that extra state information is printed for **ElapsedTime**. Notice that the elapsed timer count starts as soon as **aSnoozer** is created.

```
Time:    1:10:03
Alarm:   1:10
RING

====AlarmClock state====
17-Mar-90  1:10:00 am
duration: 10
armed: 1
====ElapsedTime state====
elapsedTime:        519    28.52     0:00:28.83
thisTime: 519
lastTime: 519
timerOn: 1
```

Getting a Class Working Before Expanding Features

This is a step forward. What you need at this point is to use the features provided by the **ElapsedTime** class to add the snooze alarm to the basic alarm clock provided by the **AlarmClock** class.

Thinking Through Additional Interface Requirements

First, you need to determine the conditions that will indicate when the snoozer has been turned on and when the snoozer should start ringing. These are two different conditions. You might call the state that the **SnoozeClock** enters when the snooze button is pushed *snooze mode*. You can only make the clock enter snooze mode when the alarm is ringing (actually, when either of two alarms is ringing: either the regular clock alarm, or the snooze alarm). Start off by adding the following two protected methods, which supply snooze state information. Put the methods just before the keyword **public** in the declaration of **SnoozeClock**.

```
protected:
    int snoozeIsRinging();
    int snoozeIsOn();
```

At some point you will have to flesh out the definitions for these state methods. But first you have to decide exactly what to do to maintain information about the two states. Right inside the constructor, you can use the elapsed time timer itself to keep track of the states **snoozeIsRinging** and **snoozeIsOn**.

By default, an instance of **ElapsedTime** starts ticking away the moment it is created. But if you turn the timer off immediately in the constructor and set it back to zero, as follows,

```
ElapsedTime::off();
ElapsedTime::reset();
```

you can use **ElapsedTime** itself to keep track of both states. If the value returned by **ElapsedTime::totalSeconds** equals zero, then the snoozer has not been switched on. To enter snooze mode, you simply turn on the timer by calling **ElapsedTime::on**. This looks like a good way to go, so add the preceding two lines inside the braces of the definition of the constructor. The constructor should now look like this:

```
SnoozeClock::SnoozeClock(int hr, int min,
                         long duration,
                         long snoozeTime)
    : AlarmClock(hr, min, duration),
      snoozeDuration(snoozeTime),
{
    ElapsedTime::off();
    ElapsedTime::reset();
}
```

How do you know when the snoozer should ring? You already have an instance variable to keep track of how long the snoozer should wait between the time it is activated and the time the alarm should sound: **snoozeDuration**. Here is one possible definition for **snoozeIsRinging**:

```
inline int SnoozeClock::snoozeIsRinging()
{
    return
    ElapsedTime::totalSeconds() > snoozeDuration;
}
```

This method returns 1 if your snooze time is up, 0 otherwise. Add the entire method just before the constructor definition. The definition for **snoozeIsOn** is very similar.

```
inline int SnoozeClock::snoozeIsOn()
{
    return
    ElapsedTime::totalSeconds() > 0;
}
```

Add this method as well—immediately after the definition for **snoozeIsRinging** and just before the constructor. Now you need a way to initiate snooze mode. Most clocks let you do this only under two conditions: either the regular alarm is ringing or the snooze alarm is ringing. You cannot tell the clock to shut up if it is not making any noise. Call this method **snooze**. Add a declaration for the method immediately after the declaration for **state** inside the **SnoozeClock** class.

```
void state();
void snooze();
```

Distinguishing Internal Methods from External Methods

A user of **SnoozeClock** does not need to ask whether the snoozer is on or whether the snoozer is ringing. It is up to the instance object to communicate these states to the user through whatever output channel is available (by printing strings to the screen or sounding the bell). Such methods are declared protected, so instances of **SnoozeClock** cannot access them. On the other hand, the class user does need to communicate, through instance variables, the desire to snooze or shut off the alarm altogether. For this reason a snooze feature is added as a public method.

You can define the **snooze** method as follows. Put the code immediately after the definition of **state**, just before **main**.

```
void SnoozeClock::snooze()
{
    if (alarmIsRinging() || snoozeIsRinging())
    {
        ElapsedTime::reset();
        ElapsedTime::on();
        AlarmClock::touch();      // turn off clock alarm
    }
}
```

Finally, you need a way to activate snooze mode from the keyboard. The S key is a good choice. Add the following two cases inside the switch in **main** immediately after **case** 'T'.

```
case 's':
case 'S':   aSnoozer.snooze(); break;
```

That should do it for a first pass. Here is what you should have for the class declaration:

```
////////////////////////////////////////////////////////////
// class SnoozeClock (declaration)
////////////////////////////////////////////////////////////
class SnoozeClock : public AlarmClock, ElapsedTime
{
    long snoozeDuration;
protected:
    int snoozeIsRinging();
    int snoozeIsOn();
public:
    SnoozeClock(int hr, int min=0, long duration=10,
                long snoozeTime=5);
    void update();
    void state();
    void snooze();
};
```

The class definition has grown somewhat.

```
////////////////////////////////////////////////////////////
// class SnoozeClock (definition)
////////////////////////////////////////////////////////////
inline int SnoozeClock::snoozeIsRinging()
{
    return
    ElapsedTime::totalSeconds() > snoozeDuration;
```

```
}

inline int SnoozeClock::snoozeIsOn()
{
    return
    ElapsedTime::totalSeconds() > 0;
}

SnoozeClock::SnoozeClock(int hr, int min,
                         long duration,
                         long snoozeTime)
    : AlarmClock(hr, min, duration),
      snoozeDuration(snoozeTime),
{
    ElapsedTime::off();
    ElapsedTime::reset();
}

void SnoozeClock::update()
{
    AlarmClock::update();
    ElapsedTime::update();
}

void SnoozeClock::state()
{
    AlarmClock::state();
    ElapsedTime::state();
}

void SnoozeClock::snooze()
{
    if (alarmIsRinging() || snoozeIsRinging())
    {
        ElapsedTime::reset();
        ElapsedTime::on();
        AlarmClock::touch();    // turn off clock alarm
    }
}
```

Finally, the **switch** statement inside **main** should contain six cases.

```
switch(c)
{
    case 'q':
    case 'Q':   more=0; break;
    case 't':
    case 'T':   aSnoozer.touch(); break;
```

```
        case 's':
        case 'S':    aSnoozer.snooze(); break;
}
```

Testing Features as You Add Them

Save, compile, and run the program. At first it might appear that there is not enough information to tell whether everything is working. As before, the alarm clock will print the string "RING" on the screen when the time of day reaches the alarm time. This message will stay up for ten seconds, which is the alarm duration as you can see in the **AlarmClock** state information. Notice that the elapsed time counter does not start now until snooze mode is selected.

```
Time:    1:11:04
Alarm:   1:11

====AlarmClock state====
18-Mar-90  1:11:00 am
duration: 10
armed: 1
====ElapsedTime state====
elapsedTime:          22      1.21      0:00:01.22
thisTime: 741
lastTime: 741
timerOn: 1
```

It is only during this ten-second period that pressing the S key will have any effect. Try pressing S before the clock alarm goes off. Nothing happens. However, if you press S while the clock alarm is ringing, the **ElapsedTime** component starts ticking away. That is exactly what you want. You have entered snooze mode. But don't go to sleep yet. There are still some details to work out.

First, even though you can turn on the snoozer, you still cannot turn it off. But that hardly matters because you have not made the alarm ring yet when the snooze period is over. Compared to the last set of changes you made, these two additions will be trivial. Stop the program now by pressing Q.

Adding Finishing Touches

Probably the best way to handle turning off the snoozer is to use the same touch control that turns off the alarm. By definition, the snoozer alarm and the clock alarm will never sound simultaneously. Furthermore, once the alarm has been turned off, it will not sound again until the following day. No matter how many times you touch the clock alarm after it has sounded and been turned off, you will never change its state. This means that you can touch the clock alarm every time you touch the snooze alarm. The thing to do is override the **touch** method inherited by **SnoozeClock** from **AlarmClock**. First, add this declaration inside the **SnoozeClock** class immediately after the declaration for **snooze**:

```
void snooze();
void touch();
```

Turning Off the Snoozer

Now you can define the method. Add it immediately after the definition for **snooze** and just before **main**.

```
void SnoozeClock::touch()
{
    AlarmClock::touch();          // turn off clock alarm
    ElapsedTime::off();           // stop counting
    ElapsedTime::reset();         // reset to zero
}
```

Calling **touch** turns off the clock alarm and terminates snooze mode by turning off the **ElapsedTime** component and resetting it to zero. The user must distinguish between pressing T, which means "Enough, I'm getting up already," and S: "Well maybe I'll sleep for another five seconds."

Sounding the Snooze Alarm

The last thing to add is the code that actually sounds the snooze alarm when your five seconds are up. You are going to be nice to your office mates by printing a message indicating the snooze alarm is sounding rather than sounding a bell. Of course, you can always replace the output statement,

```
cout << "SOUND SNOOZE ALARM";
```

with

```
putch('\a');     // print ANSI C alarm character
```

Here is the peacekeeper's version. Add this code to the **update** method immediately after the call to **ElapsedTime::update** and just before the closing brace.

```
if (snoozeIsOn())
   cout << "\nSNOOZE MODE\n";
else
   cout << "\n           \n";

if (snoozeIsRinging())
   cout << "SOUND SNOOZE ALARM";
else
   cout << "                  ";
```

The entire definition for **update** now looks like this:

```
void SnoozeClock::update()
{
    AlarmClock::update();
    ElapsedTime::update();
    if (snoozeIsOn())
        cout << "\nSNOOZE MODE\n";
    else
        cout << "\n           \n";

    if (snoozeIsRinging())
        cout << "SOUND SNOOZE ALARM";
    else
        cout << "                  ";
}
```

The names chosen for the state-accessing methods—**snoozeIsOn** and **snoozeIsRinging**—make the code very readable. Every time **update** is called, if snooze mode is on, the method prints the string "SNOOZE MODE"; otherwise, it wipes out the snooze mode message with a blank string. Next, if the snooze alarm should be ringing, the string "SOUND SNOOZE ALARM" is printed; otherwise, it is overwritten with blanks.

Test, Test, and Then Test

Now you have everything you need to snooze. Save the program and then run it. First, you will see the alarm go off at the appointed time.

```
Time:    1:12:01
Alarm:   1:12
RING

====AlarmClock state====
17-Mar-90  1:12:00 am
duration: 10
armed: 1
====ElapsedTime state====
elapsedTime:          0     0.00      0:00:00.00
thisTime: 0
lastTime: 0
timerOn: 0
```

If you press S while the alarm is ringing, the clock enters snooze mode.

```
Time:    1:12:05
Alarm:   1:12

SNOOZE MODE

====AlarmClock state====
18-Mar-90  1:12:00 am
duration: 10
armed: 1
====ElapsedTime state====
elapsedTime:         27     1.48      0:00:01.50
thisTime: 695
lastTime: 695
timerOn: 1
```

The elapsed timer counter starts. After five seconds the snooze alarm sounds.

```
Time:    1:12:11
Alarm:   1:12

SNOOZE MODE
SOUND SNOOZE ALARM

====AlarmClock state====
18-Mar-90  1:12:00 am
duration: 10
armed: 1
====ElapsedTime state====
elapsedTime:        138     7.58     0:00:07.66
thisTime: 806
lastTime: 806
timerOn: 1
```

At this point you can press S again. Notice when you do that the snooze alarm is turned off and the state information for **ElapsedTime** shows the **count** reset to zero. The other option available—only while the snooze alarm is sounding—is to press T, for touch, in which case **snooze** is disabled until the alarm clock goes off again tomorrow. You can also press Q at any time, in which case you exit the program.

The default duration for the snooze alarm is 24 hours, so don't wait for it to shut off by itself unless you can sleep through anything.

The program is presented here in its entirety and is also available on the disk under the name P11-2.CPP, if you want to compare your program against a working version. If you want to run this version of the program, create a project file called P11-2.PRJ. Add three files to the project: P11-2.CPP, ETIME.CPP, and DT.LIB. Once you've done this, you can compile and run the program.

P11-2

```
#include <iostream.h>
#include <stdio.h>
#include <string.h>
#include <conio.h>
#include "timec.h"
#include "etime.h"

////////////////////////////////////////////////////////////
// class AlarmClock (declaration)
////////////////////////////////////////////////////////////
class AlarmClock : Time
```

```
{
    long alarmDuration;
    int armed;
    char buf[10];
protected:
    void setForTomorrow();
    int alarmIsRinging();
public:
    AlarmClock(int hr, int min=0, long duration=10)
    : Time(hr, min), alarmDuration(duration), armed(1) { }
    void update();
    void arm() { armed=1; }
    void disarm() { armed=0; }
    int isArmed() { return armed; }
    void touch();
    char* alarmString();
    char* timeString();
    // diagnostic
    void state()
    {
        cout << "====AlarmClock state====\n";
        Time::printOn(cout);
        cout << "\nduration: " << alarmDuration;
        cout << "\narmed: " << armed;
        cout << "\n";
    }
};
/////////////////////////////////////////////////////////////
// class AlarmClock (definition)
/////////////////////////////////////////////////////////////
const long secondsInDay = 24L*60L*60L;
void AlarmClock::setForTomorrow()
{
    // advance no more than 24 hours ahead
    if (*this < Time())
        *this += secondsInDay;  // same time tomorrow
}
inline int AlarmClock::alarmIsRinging()
{
    return (isArmed() &&
            Time() >= *this &&
             Time() <= (*this + alarmDuration));
}
void AlarmClock::update()
{
    if (alarmIsRinging())
    {
        cout << "RING";
    }
    else
        cout << "    ";
    if (Time() > *this + alarmDuration)
```

```
        setForTomorrow();
}
void AlarmClock::touch()
{
    if (alarmIsRinging())
        setForTomorrow();
}
char* AlarmClock::alarmString()
{
    sprintf(buf, "%2d:%02d",
                Time::hour(),
                Time::minute());
    return buf;
}
char* AlarmClock::timeString()
{
    Time now;
    sprintf(buf, "%2d:%02d:%02d",
                now.hour(),
                now.minute(),
                now.second());
    return buf;
}

///////////////////////////////////////////////////////////////
// class SnoozeClock (declaration)
///////////////////////////////////////////////////////////////
class SnoozeClock : public AlarmClock, ElapsedTime
{
    long snoozeDuration;
protected:
    int snoozeIsRinging();
    int snoozeIsOn();
public:
    SnoozeClock(int hr, int min=0, long duration=10,
                long snoozeTime=5);
    void update();
    void state();
    void snooze();
    void touch();
};

///////////////////////////////////////////////////////////////
// class SnoozeClock (definition)
///////////////////////////////////////////////////////////////
inline int SnoozeClock::snoozeIsRinging()
{
    return
    ElapsedTime::totalSeconds() > snoozeDuration;
}

inline int SnoozeClock::snoozeIsOn()
```

```
{
    return
    ElapsedTime::totalSeconds() > 0;
}

SnoozeClock::SnoozeClock(int hr, int min,
                         long duration,
                         long snoozeTime)
    : AlarmClock(hr, min, duration),
      snoozeDuration(snoozeTime),
{
    ElapsedTime::off();
    ElapsedTime::reset();
}

void SnoozeClock::update()
{
    AlarmClock::update();
    ElapsedTime::update();
    if (snoozeIsOn())
        cout << "\nSNOOZE MODE\n";
    else
        cout << "\n           \n";

    if (snoozeIsRinging())
        cout << "SOUND SNOOZE ALARM";
    else
        cout << "                  ";
}

void SnoozeClock::state()
{
    AlarmClock::state();
    ElapsedTime::state();
}

void SnoozeClock::snooze()
{
    if (alarmIsRinging() || snoozeIsRinging())
    {
        ElapsedTime::reset();
        ElapsedTime::on();
        AlarmClock::touch();     // turn off clock alarm
    }
}

void SnoozeClock::touch()
{
    AlarmClock::touch();         // turn off clock alarm
    ElapsedTime::off();          // stop counting
    ElapsedTime::reset();        // reset to zero
}
```

```
main()
{
    Time now;
    SnoozeClock aSnoozer(now.hour(), now.minute()+1);
    clrscr();
    int more=1;
    while(more)
    {
        gotoxy(1,1);
        cout << "Time:  " << aSnoozer.timeString();
        gotoxy(1,2);
        cout << "Alarm: " << aSnoozer.alarmString();
        gotoxy(1,3);
        aSnoozer.update();
        gotoxy(1,15);
        aSnoozer.state();
        if (kbhit())
        {
            int c=getch();
            switch(c)
            {
                case 'q':
                case 'Q':   more=0; break;
                case 't':
                case 'T':   aSnoozer.touch(); break;
                case 's':
                case 'S':   aSnoozer.snooze(); break;
            }
        }
    }
    cout << "\ngoodbye, world\n\n";
}
```

Evaluation and Redesign

There is an old saying in the software industry: "Plan to throw the first system away. You will anyway."

The wisdom of this aphorism is ignored time and again with disastrous consequences. It is rare to get a design right the second time—even more rare to get it right on the first shot. Be prepared to work through your design and implementation several times.

Knowing When a Class Design Is Complete

One question frequently asked about designing classes is "How do you know when you're finished?" You can keep reworking and improving a class indefinitely.

The truthful answer is that you don't know until someone uses the class. But no one can use it until you design and implement it. The practical way out of this circle is to decide early on whether you are designing a class for others to reuse or whether you are designing a class to get a specific application up and running as quickly as possible. You can never get away from the distinction between class users and class providers introduced by object-oriented programming.

If you are designing a class for other developers, it is worth the extra time and effort required to think through designs thoroughly and test alternative implementations. Incorporate as much feedback as possible from early users of the class. Make no mistake: this process takes a long time. You can save yourself a lot of sweat if you decide your class does not need to be a Swiss army knife. You probably fall in this category if your clients are end users of executable software rather than programmers in search of support tools. If this is the case, resist the temptation to perfect classes that may never be reused.

You Decide: Class User or Class Provider?

Chapter 12 discusses the distinction between class users (often called clients) and class providers in detail. For now, keep it clear in your mind on which side of the street you are working.

Multiple inheritance is always closely associated with reusing the work of others. However, in reusing classes you could still be developing additional reusable classes for others, or simply building a final product. **SnoozeClock** is an example of a quick final product rather than a generally reusable class.

12 Code Reuse: Polymorphism

In biology, polymorphism refers to variation in form and function found among members of a common species. Take bees for example. The queen bee is much larger than both the worker and drone bees. Her special function is propagation. Other bees are typically smaller and have specialized tasks or functions ranging from construction of honeycomb cells, to gathering pollen, to attending the queen. Even the shapes and organs of bees from the same hive may be different. For instance, only the pollen gathering bees have pollen sacks on their hind legs. Despite differences in shape and function, the bees in a given hive are all members of the same species. The term polymorphism connotes both the characteristics shared in common by a species—such as bees—as well as the properties by which members of a species differ.

Polymorphism comes from the terms *poly,* or many, and *morph,* meaning shape or form. Just as members of a species of animal may be polymorphic, so might a species of object. You may already know that in the hierarchy of biological nomenclature, a species is more specific than a class. In other words, the term *class* is more general and appears closer to the root of the genealogical tree. Object-oriented programming has borrowed the terms class and species because a parallel can be drawn between the biological hierarchy and the hierarchy of objects used to build a programming system. While a shape is a class defining the characteristics of an object, a shape can also be considered a species that defines the common properties shared by its children—triangle, rectangle, square, pentagon, hexagon, octagon, polygon, and circle.

In object-oriented programming, polymorphism defines common methods as well as common states for a species of object. An example of state might be the center point of a shape used to indicate its position on the screen. Common methods of the **Shape** class might include **display**, **move**, and **hide**.

```
class Shape
{
   int x, y;
public:
    void display();
    void move();
    void hide();
};
```

You have seen how useful inheritance can be in building new classes based on the operations provided by existing classes like **Shape**. The only new code that needs to be added to a derived class is the behavior that distinguishes it from its parent. But polymorphism provides another reason for basing a set of similar objects on a common base class.

Polymorphism provides a handle whereby objects of different types can be processed by a single method or function designed to handle all objects descending from the common parent. Further polymorphic objects can be stored in a common array or data structure. Polymorphic objects can be compared and assigned to one another based on the features they have in common.

Assignment of one polymorphic object to another is possible provided the direction of assignment is from the specific to the general. Both objects must have a common ancestor defining common data members.

```
generalObject = specificObject;  // assignment
```

The general object takes on the value of the more specific object, retaining only the values of fields common to both. The result is a loss of information specific to the source object. Furthermore, the specific object must define all the fields found in the general object. This is guaranteed in the declaration of the common ancestor or base class.

For this kind of assignment to work, the general object must be a complete subset of the specific object. If the general object defines any fields not found in the specific object, assignment will not work: the compiler will signal an error. This makes sense because there would be no way to determine the value of a field unique to the general object after the assignment.

Note that comparison of different objects is possible provided that the base class defines a comparison method.

```
class Shape
{
    //...
public:
    int operator==()
    //...
};

main()
{
    Circle aCircle(5,10, 3);  // Shape is base
    Square aSquare(5,10, 2, 4);
    if (aCircle == aSquare)    // Shape is base
        collision(aCircle, aSquare);
    //...
}
```

In most cases of assignment and comparison, the general object would be an instance of the polymorphic base class itself, although it could be an instance of a class derived from that same base class. Again, for this to work, the object on the left side of the assignment cannot define any data members that are not also defined in the object on the right side of the assignment. It would be permissible for the derived class to add methods, or override methods of its parent without affecting the assignment operation, as assignment is only applied to state or instance variables.

The common fields of two classes characterize the polymorphism shared by two objects. In fact, it is precisely this set of fields, as well as a common set of methods, that you must look for when defining the highest level class found in a hierarchy of polymorphic objects.

Program P12-1 should clarify some of these concepts. Be sure you have logged to the DiskTutor directory for Chapter 12 before starting Borland C++ and loading Program P12-1.

P12-1

```
#include <iostream.h>

class Shape
{
public:
    void print()
    {
        cout << "I am a shape\n";
    }
};

class Triangle : public Shape
{
public:
    void print()
    {
        cout << "I am a triangle\n";
    }
};

class Circle : public Shape
{
public:
    void print()
    {
        cout << "I am a circle\n";
    }
};

main()
{
    Shape aShape;
    Triangle aTriangle;
    Circle aCircle;

    aShape.print();
    aTriangle.print();
    aCircle.print();

    cout << "===================\n";
    Shape *p;

    p = &aShape;
    p->print();
```

```
    p = &aTriangle;
    p->print();

    p = &aCircle;
    p->print();
}
```

Load Program P12-1 now. The program is much simpler than it looks at first. It declares three classes: **Shape**, **Triangle**, and **Circle**. Each of these classes defines a single method, **print**. Both **Triangle** and **Circle** are derived from **Shape**, making **Shape** the common base class that defines the polymorphism. Program P12-1 represents a situation where none of the classes have any data members, but each class provides its own definition of **print**. This means that both **Triangle** and **Circle** override the parent print method provided by **Shape**. So far, there is nothing in Program P12-1 that you have not already encountered in other examples of inheritance.

Look now at the code in **main**. The first three statements declare objects of the three respective types:

```
Shape aShape;
Triangle aTriangle;
Circle aCircle;
```

The next three statements invoke the print method for each of the three objects:

```
aShape.print();
aTriangle.print();
aCircle.print();
```

Now you are getting to the point where polymorphism becomes significant. A dividing line is printed on the screen by the subsequent **cout** statement to mark this transition. Next, a pointer to an object of class **Shape** is declared.

```
cout << "===================\n";
Shape *p;
```

The next six statements are paired. You really have one single operation being applied to each of the three objects. First, the pointer

p is assigned to point to the object (**aShape**, **aTriangle**, **aCircle**), and then the print method is invoked through the pointer. The fact that either **aTriangle** or **aCircle** can be pointed to by a pointer of type **Shape** is evidence of polymorphism.

```
p = &aShape;
p = &aTriangle;
p = &aCircle;
```

If these types were not all compatible with the base class **Shape**, the compiler would signal an error. See if you can guess what the output for the program will be before you run it.

Compile and run the program now. Are you surprised? Did you think you would get a different form of output after each assignment? Here is what your output should look like:

```
I am a shape
I am a triangle
I am a circle
====================
I am a shape
I am a shape
I am a shape
```

A lot of people expect the last three lines to look like the first three. It might seem logical that the print method invoked should be the one associated with the object pointed to, but this is not so. The print method invoked is the one associated with the pointer **p**, which points to a **Shape**. What actually happens is that the compiler casts the address of each object as a pointer to a **Shape** when the assignment is made.

```
p = &aTriangle; // casts address of aTriangle
                // as a pointer to a Shape
```

This casting is possible because of the common polymorphic definitions of **Shape** and **Triangle**. Suppose you actually want to invoke the method associated with the object pointed to rather than the method for the parent class. There is a way to do this.

Just to get a preview of things to come, you should make one small change to this program. At the top of the file, inside the declaration for the **Shape** class, you should add a single keyword. The keyword is **virtual**. This word should go just before the declaration of **Shape::print**. Change the line

```
void print()
```

to

```
virtual void print()
```

Do this only in the **Shape** class. You do not need to change **Triangle** or **Circle**.

Once the change is made, compile and run the program. The output now looks like this:

```
I am a shape
I am a triangle
I am a circle
====================
I am a shape
I am a triangle
I am a circle
```

This is probably closer to the result you expected from the first program. The keyword **virtual** implements a mechanism referred to as dynamic binding. Dynamic binding is probably the single feature that most distinguishes object-oriented programming from procedural programming.

However, before going into that, let's look at some other issues of polymorphic assignment. Before continuing, save the program modification under the name MY12-1.CPP using the **File**/**Save** as command. Even though the change was minor, you will be returning to this example shortly.

It might seem that the only reason assignment is possible to members of different data types is because you are assigning pointers or because none of the objects define any data members. Let's look at Program P12-2, where that is not the case. Load Program P12-2.

P12-2

```
#include <iostream.h>

class Shape
{
protected:
public:
    int x, y;
    Shape(int xVal, int yVal) : x(xVal), y(yVal) { }
    virtual void print()
    {
        cout << "I am a shape\n";
        cout << "x: " << x;
        cout << "\ty: " << y;
        cout << "\n";
    }
};

class Circle : public Shape
{
protected:
    int r;
public:
    Circle(int xVal, int yVal, int rVal=1)
    : Shape(xVal, yVal), r(rVal) { }
    void print()
    {
        cout << "I am a circle\n";
        cout << "x: " << x;
        cout << "\ty: " << y;
        cout << "\tr: " << r;
        cout << "\n";
    }
};

main()
{
    Shape aShape(1,2);
    Circle aCircle(3,4,5);

    aShape.print();
    aCircle.print();
    cout << "===================\n";
    aShape = aCircle;  // polymorphic assignment
    aShape.print();    // info specific to circle is lost
}
```

Program P12-2 adds data to the basic **Shape** class defined originally in Program P12-1. **Circle**, as before, is derived from **Shape**, but now adds its own specific data member, **r**, to represent the radius. The

Triangle class has been omitted. The print methods for **Shape** and **Circle** now provide information about the new data members as well as indicating whether the **Shape** or **Circle print** method has been invoked.

The main purpose of Program P12-2 is to show the effect of assigning a specialized polymorphic object (**aCircle**) to a more generalized one (**aShape**). Notice in **main** that instead of declaring a pointer to a **Shape** object and assigning it to point to **Circle**,

```
cout << "====================\n";
Shape *p;
//...
p = &aCircle;
p->print();
```

Program P12-2 declares a variable, **aShape,** as an instance of **Shape**. In Program P12-2, the assignment in question is made from one instance to another rather than from an address to a pointer.

```
Shape aShape(1,2);
Circle aCircle(3,4,5);
//...
aShape = aCircle;   // polymorphic assignment
```

What would you now expect to be the result of

```
aShape.print();
```

Run the program now. You should get the following output:

```
I am a shape
x: 1 y: 2
I am a circle
x: 3 y: 4 r: 5
====================
I am a shape
x: 3 y: 4
```

The **x** and **y** values of **aCircle** are assigned to **Shape**. There is no **r** data member in **aShape**, so the **r** value in **aCircle** is ignored by the assignment. Notice that the result is the same even if the **print** method is declared virtual. Go ahead and add the keyword **virtual** before the word **void** in the declaration for **Shape::print** as you did in Program P12-1. Compile and run. You should get the same output.

Many people are under the impression that virtual functions and dynamic binding are what make polymorphism possible. (Virtual functions and dynamic binding will be discussed in more detail in one of the following sections.) But programs P12-1 and P12-2 show that polymorphism can be employed independently of virtual functions and dynamic binding.

Another thing to notice about Program P12-2 is that the assignment cannot be reversed. Try it. Change the lines

```
aShape = aCircle;
aShape.print();
```

to

```
aCircle = aShape;
aCircle.print();
```

Compile after you have made these changes. The compiler generates the following error:

```
Could not find a match for 'Circle::Circle (Shape)'
```

Under certain circumstances you might really want to assign **aShape** to a circle. Say that all you want to do with the assignment is to give the circle a new position based on the position of another object derived from **Shape**. You could do this by adding an assignment operator to the **Circle** class.

```
Circle& operator=(Shape aShape)
{
    x=aShape.x;
    y=aShape.y;
    return *this;
}
```

That is the only code required to solve the problem. The language could have been defined in a way that would do the same thing. In other words, the implicit assignment provided by classes could have been defined to copy to only fields that classes share in common. However, the purpose of the restriction is to protect you from yourself and to warn you when you might be losing necessary information. There are usually ways around protections imposed by the compiler when the situation calls for them.

Go ahead and add the method just listed inside the declaration for **Circle**. The entire declaration now looks like this:

```
class Circle : public Shape
{
protected:
    int r;
public:
    Circle(int xVal, int yVal, int rVal=1)  // default r
added
    : Shape(xVal, yVal), r(rVal) { }
    void print()
    {
        cout << "I am a circle\n";
        cout << "x: " << x;
        cout << "\ty: " << y;
        cout << "\tr: " << r;
        cout << "\n";
    }
    Circle& operator=(Shape aShape)
    {
        x=aShape.x;
        y=aShape.y;
        return *this;
    }
};
```

Now the program should compile without errors. Run the program and you will get the following output:

```
I am a shape
x: 1 y: 2
I am a circle
x: 3 y: 4 r: 5
====================
I am a circle
x: 1 y: 2 r: 5
```

Only the **x** and **y** values of **aCircle** are changed by the assignment; **r** retains its original value.

Dynamic Binding and Virtual Functions

There was a hint of what virtual functions are about back in the modification you made to Program P12-1, that you saved as MY12-1.CPP. Clear the desktop and load Program MY12-1 now. If you remember, before you added the keyword **virtual** to the print method in **Shape**, all objects, when printed indirectly through a pointer to a **Shape** object, produced exactly the same result.

```
I am a shape
I am a shape
I am a shape
```

However, making the print method for **Shape** virtual produced a different result.

```
I am a shape
I am a triangle
I am a circle
```

This change in behavior is brought about by a mechanism called dynamic binding.

Note that declaring a function virtual does not mean that it must be redefined by a child class. To verify this, add a new **Polygon** class to Program MY12-1 just before **main**.

```
class Polygon : public Shape
{
};
```

Add four lines to **main**. The first line declares a **Polygon**:

```
Polygon aPolygon;
```

The next line prints a **Polygon** object:

```
aPolygon.print();
```

These two lines assign **p** to point to a **Polygon** object and print the **Polygon** indirectly through the pointer:

```
p = &aPolygon;
p->print();
```

The whole definition for **main** should look like this:

```
main()
{
    Shape aShape;
    Triangle aTriangle;
    Circle aCircle;
    Polygon aPolygon;

    aShape.print();
    aTriangle.print();
    aCircle.print();
    aPolygon.print();

    cout << "===================\n";
    Shape *p;

    p = &aShape;
    p->print();

    p = &aTriangle;
    p->print();

    p = &aCircle;
    p->print();

    p = &aPolygon;
    p->print();
}
```

Compile and run the program. Here is what you will see.

```
I am a shape
I am a triangle
I am a circle
I am a shape
===================
I am a shape
I am a triangle
I am a circle
I am a shape
```

Not surprisingly, **aPolygon** prints out as though it were a shape because the print method inherited from **Shape** is not overridden. The whole point of this exercise is to show that declaring a function virtual (**Shape::print** in this case) does not affect the scope of inheritance. It only changes how the linkages between calls and function definitions are resolved.

What Is Binding?

The linkages between function calls and function definitions are often referred to as *bindings*. A linker is a form of binding mechanism, but most linkers support only one restricted type of binding. In object-oriented programming, binding is a more general term than linking. The main issue about bindings is whether they are resolved at the time the program is compiled or at the time the program is run.

Binding Resolved at Compile Time

Most structured languages do not make the distinction because all bindings are resolved at compile time. For the purpose of the discussion on binding, think of compile time as referring to both compiling and linking in a single step. The compiler creates object files. The linker takes object files and libraries and arranges them in a particular order, creating an executable file. Before the linker does its job, some function calls and data references in a particular object file will be unresolved.

For example, if code in module 1 calls a function defined in module 2 or defined in one of the libraries, the compiler cannot supply all the information required to resolve the call. That is why prototypes are used. Prototypes tell the compiler that somewhere outside the file currently being compiled, there exists a function or data object referred to by the current file. In the case of a function, the compiler inserts a call instruction in the object file, but puts a dummy stub in place of the address of the target function. It is up to the linker to fill in the stub when it knows the address of the target function.

As the linker collects and orders all object and library modules into a single file, it builds a table of the addresses of all global functions and data. Once all modules have been ordered and all addresses entered in the table, the linker goes back to the unresolved address stubs and fills in the correct addresses. Once the executable file is created, the symbol table containing all the global addresses is thrown out. Since all binding references have been resolved, the table is no longer needed.

Binding Resolved at Run Time

There are times when program structuring and code reuse are facilitated by providing a mechanism for binding calls to target method definitions at run time. In these cases a function call can be linked or bound to any one of a specified set of function definitions. The program cannot know which one of the functions will be called when it is compiled. This situation arises frequently in interactive event-driven programs like window systems, where input from the user is directed through mouse and keyboard devices. The program does not know what actions it will carry out until the user issues commands.

Since the program cannot know until run time which method definition will be bound to a given call, a table of addresses of potential bindings must be retained by the executable file. Furthermore, a dispatch mechanism must be provided to look up the target candidates for a particular call in the table. Based on the type of the object to which the call is being applied, the dispatcher directs the call to the appropriate target function address.

This dispatch mechanism is called *run-time binding, late binding,* or *dynamic binding.* In contrast, *compile-time binding* is often referred to as *early binding* or *static binding.* The specific C++ feature that supports dynamic binding is the virtual function. If you think carefully about the declaration for the pointer **p** in MY12-1, you can reason why declaring **print** as virtual changes the output.

```
Shape *p;
```

The only type information retained by **p** is with respect to **Shape**. The compiler knows that **p** is a pointer that points to a **Shape** object, so the natural conclusion for the compiler to arrive at when it sees a statement like the following,

```
p->print();
```

is that the object pointed to is a **Shape** and that the print method for shape should be invoked. For non-virtual methods this is all the compiler can do. The object pointed to knows nothing about its own type—whether it is a **Shape**, a **Circle**, or a **Rectangle**. Remember that for statically bound methods, the linker throws out the symbol table when it is finished building the executable program. Polymorphism makes these objects type compatible and thus capable of being assigned to one another; however, polymorphism does not automatically indicate dynamic binding.

By adding the keyword **virtual** to the declaration of a function in a polymorphic base class, you indicate to the compiler that the type information about a method in a base class, as well as any derived methods that override it, should be resolved at run time. Run-time binding is therefore slightly more costly because type information about objects that have dynamic or virtual methods must be retained in the executable program. C++ manages this information in a very efficient manner by maintaining a virtual function lookup table with the addresses of virtual functions, so very few extra indirect memory references are required to resolve bindings at run time. Most programs will not notice any difference between compile-time and run-time resolutions.

Dynamic Binding in Polymorphic Class Hierarchies

The next set of example programs expands on the concepts of polymorphism and dynamic binding. Program P12-3 introduces a polymorphic base class, **Body**, that serves as the common definition for simulating bodies in motion on the computer screen. Load Program P12-3.

P12-3

```
#include <conio.h>
#include <dos.h>          // for geninterrupt

unsigned int oldcursor, nocursor = 0x2000;

inline void gotoxy0(int x, int y)    // zero based gotoxy
```

```
{
    gotoxy(x+1, y+1);
}

void setCursor(unsigned int shape)
{
    _AH = 1;
    _CX = shape;
    geninterrupt(0x10);
}

unsigned int getCursor(void)
{
    _AH=3;
    _BH=0;
    geninterrupt(0x10);
    return _CX;
}

//////////////////////////////////////////////////////////////
// class Body
//////////////////////////////////////////////////////////////
class Body
{
protected:
    int xPos;
    int yPos;
    char symbol;
public:
    Body(int x, int y, char c)
    : xPos(x), yPos(y), symbol(c)
    {
    }
    virtual void show()
    {
        gotoxy0(xPos, yPos);
        putch(symbol);
    }
    virtual void hide()
    {
        gotoxy0(xPos, yPos);
        putch(' ');
    }
    virtual void move()
    {
    }
};

//////////////////////////////////////////////////////////////
// class LinearBody
//////////////////////////////////////////////////////////////
class LinearBody : public Body
```

```
{
private:
    int deltaX;
    int deltaY;
public:
    LinearBody(int x, int y, char c, int dx, int dy)
    :   Body(x,y,c), deltaX(dx), deltaY(dy) { }
    virtual void move()
    {
        hide();
        xPos += deltaX;
        yPos += deltaY;
        show();
    }
};

main()
{
    oldcursor=getCursor();
    setCursor(nocursor);
    clrscr();
    LinearBody lBody = LinearBody(0,24, 'L', 1,-1);
    lBody.show();
    for (int i=0; i<24; i++)
    {
        Body aBody=Body(i,i, 'B');
        aBody.show();
        getch();
        aBody.hide();
        lBody.move();
    }
    getch();
    clrscr();
    setCursor(oldcursor);
}
```

Application: Simulating Bodies in Motion

Before analyzing the program as a whole, take a look at the declaration for **Body**.

```
////////////////////////////////////////////////////////////////
// class Body
////////////////////////////////////////////////////////////////
```

```
class Body
{
protected:
    int xPos;
    int yPos;
    char symbol;
public:
    Body(int x, int y, char c)
    : xPos(x), yPos(y), symbol(c)
    {
    }
    virtual void show()
    {
        gotoxy0(xPos, yPos);
        putch(symbol);
    }
    virtual void hide()
    {
        gotoxy0(xPos, yPos);
        putch(' ');
    }
    virtual void move()
    {
    }
};
```

Body declares three protected members: **xPos**, **yPos**, and **symbol**. The intended use of an object derived from body is to print a symbol representing a particular body at a specified location on the screen. **Body**, as a base class, represents this symbol as a single character; however, there is no reason that a subsequent derived class could not change the representation of a screen object to a string or even a graphic bitmap.

Two methods of **Body** describe the minimum functionality required to display and hide a **Body** object on the screen.

```
virtual void show()
{
    gotoxy0(xPos, yPos);
    putch(symbol);
}
virtual void hide()
{
    gotoxy0(xPos, yPos);
    putch(' ');
}
```

Notice that these functions are both virtual to signify that dynamic binding is applied to objects that call **show** or **hide**. Dynamic binding causes objects that are descendants of **Body** to be bound to the appropriate versions of **show** and **hide** when the program is run. Both methods position the cursor to the location specified by the protected instance variables and then print a character. The **show** method prints the symbol associated with the body. The **hide** method prints a blank character, which serves to erase the body from the screen.

Body provides a third method, **move**.

```
virtual void move()
{
}
```

Move is a virtual method, just like **show** and **hide**. However, the definition of **move** is empty, so nothing happens when **Body::move** is invoked. This might seem odd, but it is quite common for a base class to define a virtual method that does nothing. It is usually intended that derived classes define their own version of virtual functions like **move**. Defining **move** as a virtual function in the base class provides a dispatch mechanism for run-time binding to the associated method of a derived class. Furthermore, the empty definition in the base class provides a safety net in the form of default behavior in case a programmer forgets to override the definition of **move** in a derived class.

The constructor for **Body** accepts three arguments, corresponding to the position and symbol used to represent a body. The protected instance variables are assigned the values of these arguments through a constructor initializer.

```
Body(int x, int y, char c)
: xPos(x), yPos(y), symbol(c)
{
}
```

Characteristics of Polymorphic Base Classes

There are two traits of **Body** that signal to the astute programmer that it is intended as a base class for other classes. First, the virtual methods in general signify that derived classes will probably override their definitions. Specifically, a virtual function with a do-nothing definition is an indicator of an abstract-base class, a class whose main purpose is polymorphic—that is, a class whose main purpose is to define common properties and operations of derived classes. Second, the declaration of protected variables is a signal that a class is designed to be inherited. Recall that protected members become private members of a derived class. If these members were not intended to be used by inherited classes, they would be declared as private.

How would an abstract-base class be used? The intended purpose of **Body** is to provide an abstract base for bodies that are programmed to move about on the screen. But since no meaningful definition for **move** is provided, an inherited class must be created to provide a more useful behavior.

Consider the declaration for a new class derived from **Body**, called **LinearBody**.

```
//////////////////////////////////////////////////////////////
// class LinearBody
//////////////////////////////////////////////////////////////
class LinearBody : public Body
{
private:
    int deltaX;
    int deltaY;
public:
    LinearBody(int x, int y, char c, int dx, int dy)
    :   Body(x,y,c), deltaX(dx), deltaY(dy) { }
    virtual void move()
    {
        hide();
        xPos += deltaX;
        yPos += deltaY;
        show();
    }
};
```

The purpose of **LinearBody** is to provide an easy way to define speed and direction for objects that are intended to move in a straight line. The constructor for **LinearBody** requires two more arguments than the constructor for **Body**. These extra arguments, **dx** and **dy**, indicate the relative amounts by which the position of the body will change on each call to **LinearBody::move**. The values are retained in the private instance variables, **deltaX** and **deltaY**.

The only method defined by **LinearBody** is **move**. **LinearBody** accepts the default method definitions for **show** and **hide**, but overrides **Body**'s do-nothing definition for **move**. The definition for **move** is straightforward.

```
virtual void move()
{
    hide();
    xPos += deltaX;
    yPos += deltaY;
    show();
}
```

First, the body is hidden. Next, the position of the body is adjusted by adding the relative offsets **deltaX** and **deltaY**. Finally, the body is redrawn at the new position by calling **show**.

Before analyzing **main**, compile, and run the program. Two symbols appear on the screen. Press a key and watch as the two symbols are moved. The symbol "B" represents a **Body** while the symbol "L" represents a **LinearBody**. Each time you press the SPACEBAR, the two symbols move until both of them walk completely off the screen.

But wait a minute. If the class **Body** has a do-nothing definition for **move**, how is it that the "B" can move at all? Take a look at **main**.

```
main()
{
    oldcursor=getCursor();
    setCursor(nocursor);
    clrscr();
    LinearBody lBody = LinearBody(0,24, 'L', 1,-1);
    lBody.show();
    for (int i=0; i<24; i++)
    {
        Body aBody=Body(i,i, 'B');
        aBody.show();
        getch();
        aBody.hide();
        lBody.move();
    }
    getch();
    clrscr();
```

```
    setCursor(oldcursor);
}
```

The declarations bear out that the "L" is a linear body that is programmed to change its x position by 1 (move right) and its y position by −1 (move up) on each call to **move**.

```
LinearBody lBody = LinearBody(0,24, 'L', 1,-1);
```

The starting position for **lBody** is the lower-left corner of the screen (0,24).

Meanwhile, the declaration for the "B" symbol reveals that it is a **Body**.

```
Body aBody=Body(i,i, 'B');
```

This declaration combines a constructor initialization with an assignment. Furthermore, the assignment takes place inside a loop, that iterates 24 times.

The constructor initializer for **Body** takes the loop control variable, **i**, as both the x and y position of the object that is assigned to **aBody**. Even though **Body** provides no internal method that actually moves a body, the programmer can change the position of the body through assignment. This is less in the spirit of object-oriented programming because the programmer is forced to retain information about and update the position of **aBody** rather than encapsulating that knowledge inside the body itself. Nevertheless, it does work.

Immediately after **aBody** is assigned its new position, **aBody.show** is called to display it. The program waits for a keypress. Next, **aBody.hide** is called to make **aBody** invisible before its position is changed and it is shown again. Ignore **lBody** for now. Program control winds up back at the top of the **for** loop where **aBody** is assigned a new position, which is one x value greater (right) and one y value greater (down) than on the last pass. The programmer is effectively manipulating **aBody** to behave like a linear body, moving from the upper-left toward the lower-right corner of the screen. After 24 passes through the loop, the "B" moves off the bottom of the screen, the loop terminates, and the program ends.

It takes three statements for **aBody** to achieve the same result as a single statement for **lBody** inside the loop.

```
lBody.move();
```

This is because the class **LinearBody** has done most of the work for the programmer by specifying a general behavior for all linear bodies. All the programmer need do is supply the original position, the direction, and the speed.

At this point, there is nothing in Program P12-3 that shows the utility of polymorphism, since the program would not change in behavior if **show**, **hide**, and **move** were not declared as virtual methods in **Body**.

Advantages of Dynamic Binding

Load Program 12-4. Program P12-4 shows one of the advantages of encapsulating knowledge about motion inside an object, rather than forcing the programmer to manage that knowledge and apply it to the object. First, by encapsulating knowledge of behavior in a class definition, the programmer does not need to write special code for each type of object being manipulated. Second, by eliminating the need for special-case handling, objects of different types can be placed in a common data structure and manipulated through pointers. Distinctive behavior for objects is retained through dynamic binding.

P12-4

```
#include <conio.h>
#include <dos.h>          // for geninterrupt
#include <stdlib.h>       // for rand

const MINX=0;
const MINY=0;
const MAXX=79;
const MAXY=23;

unsigned int oldcursor, nocursor = 0x2000;

inline void gotoxy0(int x, int y)     // zero based gotoxy
{
    gotoxy(x+1, y+1);
}

void setCursor(unsigned int shape)
{
    _AH = 1;
```

```
    _CX = shape;
    geninterrupt(0x10);
}

unsigned int getCursor(void)
{
    _AH=3;
    _BH=0;
    geninterrupt(0x10);
    return _CX;
}

/////////////////////////////////////////////////////////////////
// class Body
/////////////////////////////////////////////////////////////////
class Body
{
protected:
    int xPos;
    int yPos;
    char symbol;
public:
    Body(int x, int y, char c)
    : xPos(x), yPos(y), symbol(c)
    {
    }
    virtual void show()
    {
        gotoxy0(xPos, yPos);
        putch(symbol);
    }
    virtual void hide()
    {
        gotoxy0(xPos, yPos);
        putch(' ');
    }
    virtual void move()
    {
    }
};

/////////////////////////////////////////////////////////////////
// class LinearBody
/////////////////////////////////////////////////////////////////
class LinearBody : public Body
{
private:
    int deltaX;
    int deltaY;
public:
    LinearBody(int x, int y, char c, int dx, int dy)
    :   Body(x,y,c), deltaX(dx), deltaY(dy) { }
```

```
    virtual void move()
    {
        hide();
        xPos += deltaX;
        yPos += deltaY;
        if (xPos < 0) xPos = MAXX;
        if (xPos > MAXX) xPos = 0;
        if (yPos < 0) yPos = MAXY;
        if (yPos > MAXY) yPos = 0;
        show();
    }
};

main()
{
    oldcursor=getCursor();
    setCursor(nocursor);
    clrscr();

    typedef Body *pBody;
    const maxBody=10;
    pBody array[maxBody];
    int nBodies=0;
    array[nBodies++] = new LinearBody(0,24, 'L', 1,-1);
    array[nBodies++] = new LinearBody(0,12, 'l', 2,0);
    array[nBodies++] = new Body(0,0, 'B');

    for (int j=0; j<nBodies; j++)  // display all bodies
        array[j]->show();
    for (int i=0; i<24; i++)
    {
        getch();
        for (int j=0; j<nBodies; j++)  // move all bodies
            array[j]->move();
    }
    getch();
    clrscr();
    setCursor(oldcursor);
}
```

Rather than keeping track of each body by creating a unique identifier, Program P12-4 declares an array of polymorphic pointers to keep track of each body on the screen. To do this, a **typedef** is declared.

```
typedef Body *pBody;
```

This declares **pBody** to be a synonym for the type "pointer to Body." An array of pointers is then declared that is large enough to hold all the bodies.

```
const maxBody=10;
pBody array[maxBody];
```

The variable **nBodies** is used to keep track of the number of bodies currently in **array**.

```
int nBodies=0;
```

Next, two **LinearBodies** and a single **Body** are created, each with a unique starting position and identifying symbol. Linear bodies specify speed and direction as well.

```
array[nBodies++] = new LinearBody(0,24, 'L', 1,-1);
array[nBodies++] = new LinearBody(0,12, 'l', 2,0);
array[nBodies++] = new Body(0,0, 'B');
```

You want to see the initial positions of the bodies before they are moved. The following loop accomplishes this:

```
for (int j=0; j<nBodies; j++)  // display all bodies
    array[j]->show();
```

It now requires two loops to control the motion of the bodies.

The outer loop controls the number of times the bodies are moved before the program terminates.

```
for (int i=0; i<24; i++)
{
    //...
}
```

The inner loop is similar to the loop that shows the bodies before they are initially moved. The method **show** is replaced by **move**.

```
for (int j=0; j<nBodies; j++)  // move all bodies
    array[j]->move();
```

Compile and run Program P12-4. Upon entry to the outer loop all three bodies are visible. On each keypress the bodies advance to their next relative position. This goes on for 24 keypresses until the program terminates. Notice that the "B" at the top of the screen does not move. That is because "B" is a **Body** and not a **LinearBody**. Remember that the definition for **Body::Move** does nothing.

```
virtual void move()
{
}
```

Program P12-4 removed the calls that explicitly moved "B" in Program P12-3.

```
Body aBody=Body(1,1, 'B');
aBody.show();
// ...
aBody.hide();
```

So "B" just sits there.

Extending Polymorphic Hierarchies

To make the discussion of polymorphism and dynamic binding as clear as possible, you are going to add the declaration for a new type of body to Program P12-4.

```
////////////////////////////////////////////////////////////////
// class RandomBody
////////////////////////////////////////////////////////////////
class RandomBody : public Body
{
public:
    RandomBody(int x, int y, char c)
    : Body(x, y, c) { }
    void move()
    {
        hide();
        xPos += (rand()%5-2);
        yPos += (rand()%5-2);
        if (xPos < 0) xPos = MAXX;
        if (xPos > MAXX) xPos = 0;
```

```
        if (yPos < 0) yPos = MAXY;
        if (yPos > MAXY) yPos = 0;
        show();
    }
};
```

This class inherits publicly from **Body** and overrides the **move** method. The constructor for **RandomBody** takes the same number of arguments as the constructor for **Body**. The **move** method simply modifies the x position by adding to it a random number between −2 and 2.

The y position is adjusted similarly. Before making any adjustments, the object is hidden. After the adjustment in position, four **if** statements make sure that if the body walks off any end of the screen, it wraps around to the opposite end. Thus, if an object goes beyond the bottom of the screen, its new position becomes the top. The same applies for horizontal movement. Though it was not mentioned, these same four lines were added to the implementation of **LinearBody::move**, which precedes the declaration for **RandomBody**. This relieves the programmer from worrying about either **LinearBodies** or **RandomBodies** floating off the screen edges. Once the final position is determined, the body is redisplayed through the show method.

Add the declaration for **RandomBody** to P12-4 just before **main**. Next, add a new **RandomBody** to the array of bodies.

```
array[nBodies++] = new RandomBody(79,0,'r');
```

Note that the ++ operator is applied to **nBodies** to maintain the correct value for the total number of bodies now in the system.

Also, change "B" from a **Body**

```
array[nBodies++] = new Body(0,0, 'B');
```

to a **LinearBody**:

```
array[nBodies++] = new LinearBody(0,0, 'B', 1,1);
```

Verify that your program creates and adds a total of four bodies to **array**.

```
array[nBodies++] = new LinearBody(0,24, 'L', 1,-1);
array[nBodies++] = new LinearBody(0,12, 'l', 2,0);
array[nBodies++] = new LinearBody(0,0, 'B', 1,1);
array[nBodies++] = new RandomBody(79,0,'r');
```

Now, change the outer loop to keep running until a key is pressed. Change

```
for (int i=0; i<24; i++)
{
    getch();
```

to

```
while (!kbhit())
{
    delay(100);
```

The call to **getch** should be replaced with the call to **delay**, which waits for 100 milliseconds or 1/10 second on each pass through the loop. The **while** loop automates the movement of the bodies, and the **delay** keeps everything from happening so fast that you cannot see it.

Save your changes. Your program should look like this:

```
#include <conio.h>
#include <dos.h>        // for geninterrupt
#include <stdlib.h>     // for rand

const MINX=0;
const MINY=0;
const MAXX=79;
const MAXY=23;

unsigned int oldcursor, nocursor = 0x2000;

inline void gotoxy0(int x, int y)     // zero based gotoxy
{
    gotoxy(x+1, y+1);
}

void setCursor(unsigned int shape)
{
    _AH = 1;
    _CX = shape;
    geninterrupt(0x10);
}
```

```
unsigned int getCursor(void)
{
    _AH=3;
    _BH=0;
    geninterrupt(0x10);
    return _CX;
}

////////////////////////////////////////////////////////////
// class Body
////////////////////////////////////////////////////////////
class Body
{
protected:
    int xPos;
    int yPos;
    char symbol;
public:
    Body(int x, int y, char c)
    : xPos(x), yPos(y), symbol(c)
    {
    }
    virtual void show()
    {
        gotoxy0(xPos, yPos);
        putch(symbol);
    }
    virtual void hide()
    {
        gotoxy0(xPos, yPos);
        putch(' ');
    }
    virtual void move()
    {
    }
};

////////////////////////////////////////////////////////////
// class LinearBody
////////////////////////////////////////////////////////////
class LinearBody : public Body
{
private:
    int deltaX;
    int deltaY;
public:
    LinearBody(int x, int y, char c, int dx, int dy)
    :   Body(x,y,c), deltaX(dx), deltaY(dy) { }
    virtual void move()
    {
        hide();
```

```
        xPos += deltaX;
        yPos += deltaY;
        if (xPos < 0) xPos = MAXX;
        if (xPos > MAXX) xPos = 0;
        if (yPos < 0) yPos = MAXY;
        if (yPos > MAXY) yPos = 0;
        show();
    }
};

/////////////////////////////////////////////////////////////
// class RandomBody
/////////////////////////////////////////////////////////////
class RandomBody : public Body
{
public:
    RandomBody(int x, int y, char c)
    : Body(x, y, c) { }
    void move()
    {
        hide();
        xPos += (rand()%5-2);
        yPos += (rand()%5-2);
        if (xPos < 0) xPos = MAXX;
        if (xPos > MAXX) xPos = 0;
        if (yPos < 0) yPos = MAXY;
        if (yPos > MAXY) yPos = 0;
        show();
    }
};

main()
{
    oldcursor=getCursor();
    setCursor(nocursor);
    clrscr();

    typedef Body *pBody;
    const maxBody=10;
    pBody array[maxBody];
    int nBodies=0;
    array[nBodies++] = new LinearBody(0,24, 'L', 1,-1);
    array[nBodies++] = new LinearBody(0,12, 'l', 2,0);
    array[nBodies++] = new LinearBody(0,0, 'B', 1,1);
    array[nBodies++] = new RandomBody(79,0,'r');

    for (int j=0; j<nBodies; j++)  // display all bodies
        array[j]->show();
    while (!kbhit())
    {
```

```
        delay(100);
        for (int j=0; j<nBodies; j++)  // move all bodies
            array[j]->move();
    }
    getch();
    clrscr();
    setCursor(oldcursor);
}
```

Save your modifications for later; change the name to MY12-4.CPP. Compile and run the program.

Now, in addition to the three **LinearBodies**, you have a **RandomBody**. The random body can go wherever it livens up your screen. Press any key when you are satisfied.

Seeing the Effects of Dynamic Binding

One small change should drive a stake into the heart of any lingering doubts you have about virtual functions and dynamic binding. Find the definition for **Body::move** and comment out the keyword **virtual** by surrounding it with comment tokens, **/* . . . */**. Change

```
/////////////////////////////////////////////////////////////
// class Body
/////////////////////////////////////////////////////////////
class Body
{
    //...
    virtual void move()
    {
    }
};
```

so that the line declaring **move** now reads

```
/* virtual */ void move()
```

Body::Move is no longer virtual. What will happen when you run the program now? Try it.

Your happily moving bodies are not moving so happily anymore. Because dynamic binding is no longer specified in the parent class, **Body**, the compiler assumes it has all the information it needs about the objects in **array** at compile time. It assumes that they will all be of type **Body**. Thus, each

```
array[j]->move();
```

call binds at compile time to the method **Body::move**. But this is a do-nothing function. All your bodies just sit around like bumps on a log.

If you study the declarations that create each of the objects, you can see why the computer cannot know the actual types of any of the bodies until run time.

```
typedef Body *pBody;
//...
pBody array[maxBody];
//...
array[nBodies++] = new LinearBody(0,24, 'L', 1,-1);
array[nBodies++] = new LinearBody(0,12, 'l', 2,0);
array[nBodies++] = new LinearBody(0,0, 'B', 1,1);
array[nBodies++] = new RandomBody(79,0,'r');
```

Since **new** is a run-time global operator, the objects pointed to by the **array** do not exist until the program is run. Furthermore, even if the program did know the types of **array**'s elements, there is no place in **array** to store the information. The **array** merely stores the pointers returned by **new**. Pointers have no type information at run time. By removing the virtual declaration from **Body::move**, you change the status of all **move** methods that inherit from **Body** and override it from dynamic (run-time) to static (compile-time) methods. This means that any object pointed to by an element of **array** is assumed to be equivalent to a **Body**, and any call such as

```
array[j]->move();
```

will be bound at compile time to **Body::move**.

Before moving on, save Program MY12-4. Do not put the keyword **virtual** back yet. A subsequent exercise will pick up where MY12-4 leaves off.

Application: Saturn Fly-By

You can take the concept of polymorphic bodies a considerable distance by defining behaviors for all kinds of bodies inherited from **Body**. For instance, you can program falling bodies that slowly drop from the top of the screen and stop moving when they hit the bottom. You can design orbiting bodies that move in a circle around a center point. You can define pursuing bodies that follow other bodies around the screen.

Program P12-5 does all this and more, implementing a small dynamic model of the solar system. It includes bodies called Planets that are programmed to imitate the relative motions, distances, and speeds of the six planets closest to the sun. The program contains old friends like linear bodies, which now look like meteors dashing about the solar system. A random body buzzes around looking as though it needs a place to land. Finally, a pursuing body is programmed to track the course of Saturn, much like the Voyager probes launched by NASA.

As you run the program, consider the starting point of the Voyager probe and the path that the programming causes it to follow in its quest to fly by Saturn. See if you can think of a way of saving fuel and time. The purpose of simulations is to give researchers insight into problems like these. In fact, a considerable amount of money was spent at the Jet Propulsion Laboratory in Pasadena simulating with computer graphics how Saturn would appear as the Voyager probe flew by.

Load Program P12-5 and run it. Try to see how many times the earth revolves before Voyager catches up with Saturn. If someone does not come up with a better algorithm than the one defined in **PursuingBody**, most of the design team will be retired by the time Voyager reaches Saturn. At least they won't be responsible for what happens afterward. Figure 12-1 shows Voyager II in hot pursuit of Saturn.

Do not let the size of the program fool you. While Program P12-5 is considerably larger than Program P12-4, the overall structure is exactly

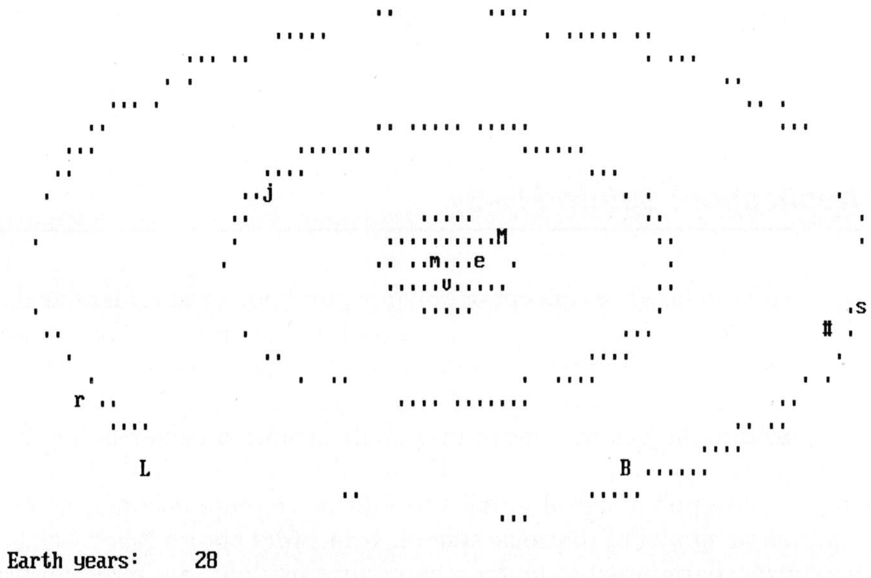

Figure 12-1. *Voyager II Saturn Fly-By*

the same. First, the base class for **Body** is defined. Then, a number of classes derived from **Body** are defined. The code at the start of **main** is exactly the same. An array of pointers to **Body** is declared. The only difference is the size of the array.

```
main()
{
    oldcursor=getCursor();
    setCursor(nocursor);
    textattr(0x07)
    clrscr();

    ////////////////////////////////////////
    // array elements point to active bodies
    // programmer must maintain nBodies
    // to reflect current number of active
    // bodies in array
    ////////////////////////////////////////
    typedef Body *pBody;
    const maxBody=20;
    pBody array[maxBody];
    int nBodies=0;
```

Bodies are added to **array**, just as they were in Program P12-4, only now certain bodies have more sophisticated constructors.

```
///////////////////////////
// constructor prints data
// for each planet
// as it is created
///////////////////////////
array[nBodies++] = new Planet("Mecury",
                              58.0,
                              4850,
                              (88.0/365.0),
                              'm');
array[nBodies++] = new Planet("Venus",
                              108.0,
                              12104,
                              (225.0/365.0),
                              'v');
array[nBodies++] = new Planet("Earth",
                              149.5,
                              12756,
                              1,
                              'e');
```

The arguments to a constructor for a **Planet** are the planet's name, its distance from the sun, its diameter, the number of earth years per orbit, and the symbol used to display the body on the screen.

After the first six planets are declared and added to **array**, the exact same code that appeared in Program P12-4 is used to simulate meteors.

```
/////////////////////////
// throw in some meteors
// and a random body
/////////////////////////
array[nBodies++] = new LinearBody(0,24, 'L', 1,-1);
array[nBodies++] = new LinearBody(79,0, 'B', -2,-1);
array[nBodies++] = new RandomBody(79,0,'r');
```

The technique for displaying all bodies in the array is the same.

```
clrscr();
for (int j=0; j<nBodies; j++)  // display all bodies
    array[j]->show();
```

The main controlling loop is borrowed directly from P12-4 without modification.

```
////////////////////////////////
// main program loop
// keep moving all bodies in
// array until a key is pressed
////////////////////////////////
while (!kbhit())
{
    //////////////////////////////
    // general purpose code:
    // manages all objects in
    // array and prints number of
    // elapsed earth years since
    // start of simulation
    //////////////////////////////
    delay(10);
    for (int j=0; j<nBodies; j++)   // move all bodies
        array[j]->move();
    //...
    //...
    //...
}
////////////////////////////
// end of main program loop
////////////////////////////
getch();
clrscr();
setCursor(oldcursor);
```

Two extra statements appear on each iteration to print the number of earth years elapsed since the start of the simulation.

```
gotoxy0(0,24);
cprintf("Earth years: %6d", earth.orbits());
```

The only significant difference between Program P12-5 and Program P12-4 is the code to control the Voyager space probe. This code is required to launch Voyager and then to change its destination periodically when it reaches its target. First, the code for the launch.

```
////////////////////////
// special purpose code:
// manages voyager probe
```

```
// and modifies targets
/////////////////////////
if (!voyager.tracking())  // voyager has no target
{
    //////////////////////////////////////
    // launch voyager on 2nd earth orbit
    //////////////////////////////////////
    if (earth.orbits() == 2)
    {
        ///////////////////////////////////
        // first target to track is saturn
        ///////////////////////////////////
        targetIndex = saturnIndex;
        voyagerIndex = nBodies;

        ////////////////////////////////////////
        //        launch probe:
        // start at current position of earth
        // char specifies probe's symbol
        // track object in array[targetIndex]
        // percent of top speed, range: 0 - 100
        ////////////////////////////////////////
        voyager = PursuingBody(earth.x(), earth.y(),
                               '#',
                               *array[targetIndex],
                               10);

        ////////////////////////////////////////
        // add voyager to array of active bodies
        ////////////////////////////////////////
        array[nBodies++] = &voyager;
    }
}
```

The original launch occurs if Voyager is not currently tracking anything, and the simulation has reached the second solar orbit for earth. The original target is Saturn. The index number in **array** for Saturn was saved in the variable **saturnIndex** when Saturn was created. That value is now assigned to **targetIndex**, that is used to give Voyager a target body to pursue. The Voyager probe is given data for its mission through a **PursuingBody** constructor. (The voyager object was created with a null constructor—meaning that it should not track anything—just after Saturn was created and just before entering the main control loop.) The index position in **array** for voyager is remembered in the variable, **voyagerIndex**. The arguments for the **PursuingBody** assignment constructor give the starting position, the symbol for Voyager, a pointer to a target body, and an initial speed, which is a percentage of the maximum possible speed for a **PursuingBody**.

This is all the code necessary to send Voyager to Saturn. The rest is all for fun. Perhaps NASA scientists decided to make good use of the probe once it was out there. The code immediately following the launch tests to see if Voyager has reached its current target.

```
else if (voyager.missionAccomplished())
{
    ///////////////////////////////
    // voyager catches its target
    ///////////////////////////////
    gotoxy0(0,0);   cputs("Gotcha");
    delay(1500);
    gotoxy0(0,0);   cputs("      ");

    int x = array[targetIndex]->x();
    int y = array[targetIndex]->y();

    array[targetIndex]->hide();
    delete array[targetIndex];

    if (targetIndex >= 1)
    {
        ////////////////////////////////////////
        // old target becomes a falling body
        // new target: next lower array element
        ////////////////////////////////////////
        array[targetIndex] =
            new FallingBody(x-2, y-2, '*');
        voyager.target(*array[targetIndex-1]);
    }
```

The only logical explanation for this code is an undetected virus. The code momentarily stops the solar system and prints a success message. Then the target body is hidden and removed from **array**. It is then replaced with a **FallingBody**, and Voyager is assigned to pursue the next lower element in **array**. That would be the next planet inward toward the sun. This continues, planet by planet. Mercury, however, decides to bolt when it sees the fate of Venus.

```
if (targetIndex == 1)
{
    ///////////////////////////////
    // mercury gets smart
```

```
    // args to RunningBody:
    //    origin (x, y)
    //    symbol
    //    initial direction (x, y)
    //    speed
    ///////////////////////////////
    array[0]->hide();
    array[0] = new RunningBody(x-4, y, 'm',
                               -1,  0, 100);
    voyager.target(*array[0]);
    voyager.speed(70);  // try 80 for fun
}
```

The following code will not be executed unless you modify the program, because at the current rates, Mercury can outrun Voyager for some time.

```
else if (targetIndex == 0)
{
    ///////////////////////
    // mercury gets caught
    ///////////////////////
    voyager.target(*(Body*)NULL);
    array[targetIndex] =
       new FallingBody(x-2, y-2, '*');
    array[voyagerIndex] =
       new LinearBody(x-2,y,'#',1,0,50);
}
```

This code turns Mercury into a **FallingBody**, sets the target for Voyager to null (no target) and replaces the pointer to Voyager with a pointer to a **LinearBody**, forever doomed to wander an empty solar system.

You might try some experiments with the Voyager simulation. Try changing the initial launch speed from 10 to 100 percent. The probe is also fast enough to catch the wayward Mercury if you crank its speed up to 80 percent. As another experiment, similar to the modification you made to Program MY12-4, try changing the virtual function **Body::move** to a normal static function by commenting out the word **virtual**.

```
class Body
{
    //...
```

```
    /* virtual */ move()
    //...
};
```

If you are not 100 percent sure what will happen, you should try it so there is no doubt.

Here is a challenge: see if you can direct Voyager to arrive at Saturn in five years. That is two years longer than it took for Voyager II. Do it without defining any new classes, without modifying the **PursuingBody** class, and without changing Voyager's launch speed of 10 percent. (Yes, it is possible.) You cannot change the launch site to any location other than earth.

Polymorphism, Dynamic Binding, and Encapsulation

Encapsulation is often presented as a generalization for the term *data hiding*. For instance, inside the class **Body**, the representation of the body's position and symbol are hidden from a user of the class.

```
//////////////////////////////////////////////////////////////
// class Body
//////////////////////////////////////////////////////////////
class Body
{
protected:
    int xPos;
    int yPos;
    char symbol;
public:
    //...
};
```

In addition, a given set of operations is associated with the data inside an object. It is said that the data and methods are *encapsulated* inside the object. Encapsulation is thought of as a protective shell wrapped around a process with a state. Encapsulation isolates the process (object) as much as possible from the outside world, protecting it from accidental modification. Encapsulation also protects users of a class from changes in the internal representation of the object's state. This protection is provided by the restricted access of the public interface to the object. Encapsulation thus establishes a partition or wall between the internal representation of an object and the world outside, freeing components on both sides of the wall from worry about what goes on on the other side. The interface negotiates all interactions across the partition.

Two Types of Encapsulation

This is one form of encapsulation. The term *encapsulation* has a broader meaning as well. While in the previous example, encapsulation applies to the division between the inside and outside of an object, the broader sense of encapsulation applies to the decentralization of knowledge about overall system organization. The reasons for either form of encapsulation are the same: minimize the number of interdependencies among system components. If this is accomplished, changes to one part of the system do not force changes in other parts.

Encapsulation of Knowledge About System Structure

In the broader sense, encapsulation refers to the number and names of classes in a polymorphic hierarchy and the knowledge required for a system component to process instances of those classes. In this sense, encapsulation connotes the partitioning of a system and tries to ensure that knowledge about one part of the system does not needlessly spill over into another part. This second form of encapsulation requires the support of dynamic binding.

For example, consider the type hierarchy found in the planets program, P12-5.

```
Class Hierarchy
Body

├──────── FallingBody
├──────── PursuingBody
├──────── OrbitingBody
│         └──────── Planet
├──────── RandomBody
└──────── LinearBody
          └──────── RunningBody
```

Seven types are specified in this hierarchy exclusive of the base class, **Body**. Instances of all seven types appear in Program P12-5. Focus on just the **move** method implemented for each of these body types. With polymorphism it is possible to store a pointer to any type of body in a single array so that only one control structure is required to move all the bodies in the system. There is no object or function that needs to know about every possible type of body that may appear. As far as the **move** method is concerned, each object knows how to move itself. Even **main** does not know which **move** method needs to be bound to each particular object in the array of bodies. This partitioning of knowledge about the type hierarchy is possible because of dynamic binding. The virtual base method for **move** takes responsibility for binding a given polymorphic object to the proper **move** method at run time.

You saw what resulted from removing the keyword **virtual** from the declaration of **Body::move**: the motion of all bodies stopped because dynamic binding was no longer specified.

Extending Polymorphic Class Hierarchies Without Dynamic Binding

Think about how you would have to move each of the bodies in a polymorphic array if dynamic binding were not supported. Either **main** or **Body::move** would have to retain specific information about each type of body that an array element could possibly point to. Furthermore, each body would have to retain type information about itself so that the binding of objects to **move** methods could be handled by a **switch** statement inside either **main** or **Body::move**.

First, a common header file would have to declare an enumerated type.

```
enum bodyType
{
    body,
    fallingBody,
    pursuingBody,
    orbitingBody
    planet,
    randomBody,
    linearBody,
    runningBody
};
```

Now **Body** would have to define a public field to retain type information about each object.

```
class Body
{
    //...
public:
    bodyType thisType;
    //...
};
```

Constructors for **Body** and each class derived from **Body** would have to set **thisType**.

```
Body::Body (...)
{  //...
   thisType = body;
   //...
}

LinearBody::LinearBody (...)
{  //...
   thisType = linearBody;
   //...
}

RandomBody::RandomBody (...)
{
    //...
    thisType = randomBody;
}
// ..., etc.
```

Now, with each body retaining type information, either **main** or **Body::move** could be programmed to handle the binding at compile time.

```
main
{
    //...
    pBody array[maxBody];
    int nBodies=0;
    //...
    array[nBodies++] = new Planet("Mecury",
                               58.0,
                               4850,
                               (88.0/365.0),
                               'm');
    //..., etc.
    while (!kbhit())
    {
        delay(10);
        for (int j=0; j<nBodies; j++)  // move all bodies
            switch (array[j]->thisType)
            {
            case body:
                ((Body*) array[j])->move();
                break
            case linearBody:
                ((LinearBody*) array[j])->move();
                break;
            case randomBody:
                ((RandomBody*) array[j])->move();
                break;
            case fallingBody:
                //...
            case orbitingBody:
                //...
            case Planet:
                //...
            case pursuingBody:
                //...
            case runningBody:
                //...
            default:
                cerr << "error unknown body type\'n';
            }
        //...
    }
    //...
}
```

That is a lot of extra work just to handle one of the three virtual functions defined in **Body**. It is not uncommon to have 10 or 20 virtual functions in a polymorphic hierarchy of 20 or more classes.

Exercises for the Unconvinced If you feel you have a handle on all this, you can skip the following exercise. Otherwise, read on. You are going to modify Program MY12-4 once again. This time you are going to make all the bodies move without using virtual functions. The changes will put the dispatcher to the appropriate versions of **move** inside of **main**. Before making any changes, load and run MY12-4 now. Make sure the bodies do not move. This should be the case if you followed the previous exercise, which had you comment out the word **virtual** in the declaration of **Body::move**. If the bodies move now, go back and comment out the keyword **virtual** and run the program again until they just sit there. There are only three classes defined in this program, so the example will be significantly easier than the code shown for the planets program. First add an enumeration to the top of the file, just before the declaration for the **Body** class.

```
enum bodyType { body, linearBody, randomBody };
```

Note that each symbol in the enumeration begins with a lowercase letter to distinguish it from the corresponding class name, which is otherwise identical. Add a declaration to keep track of the type for each body. This will be a public instance variable inside **Body**. Just after the keyword **public** in the declaration for **Body**, add a single line declaring **thisType**.

```
public:
    bodyType thisType;
```

Now the constructors must be modified to assign one of the enumerated types to the value for **thisType**. This requires the addition of a single line to all three constructors.

```
 //...
thisType = body;
//...
```

```
thisType = linearBody;
//...
thisType = randomBody ;
//...
```

The declaration for body now looks like this:

```
enum bodyType { body, linearBody, randomBody };
////////////////////////////////////////////////////////////
// class Body
////////////////////////////////////////////////////////////
class Body
{
protected:
    int xPos;
    int yPos;
    char symbol;
public:
    bodyType thisType;
    Body(int x, int y, char c)
    : xPos(x), yPos(y), symbol(c),
    {
        thisType = body;
    }
    /* virtual */ void show()
    {
        gotoxy0(xPos, yPos);
        putch(symbol);
    }
    /* virtual */ void hide()
    {
        gotoxy0(xPos, yPos);
        putch(' ');
    }
    /* virtual */ void move()
    {
    }
};
```

The constructors for **LinearBody** and **RandomBody** should also be checked.

```
// LinearBody constructor
    LinearBody(int x, int y, char c, int dx, int dy)
    :   Body(x,y,c), deltaX(dx), deltaY(dy)
    {
        thisType = linearBody;
```

```
    }
// RandomBody constructor
    RandomBody(int x, int y, char c)
    : Body(x, y, c)
    {
        thisType = randomBody;
    }
```

Now for the fun part. You have to change the single **move** command inside the **for** statement in **main**.

```
for (int j=0; j<nBodies; j++)  // move all bodies
    array[j]->move();
```

For the compile-time dispatching to work properly, you have to switch on the type of object, and based on the type, decide whether to call **Body::move**, **LinearBody::move**, or **RandomBody::move**. Change the line

```
array[j]->move();
```

to

```
switch(array[j]->thisType)
{
case body:
            ((Body*)array[j])->move();
            break;
case linearBody:
            ((LinearBody*)array[j])->move();
            break;
case randomBody:
            ((RandomBody*)array[j])->move();
            break;
default:
            // error
            cprintf("Unknown body type\r\n");
}
```

Once you have double-checked your work, compile and run the program. The program should compile and run properly now. In fact, it should behave just as it did before you made all the changes. Why go to all this trouble when dynamic binding will do it all for you? You did not create dispatches to call **show** and **hide**, which were also virtual functions. It is not required in this program because none of the inherited classes override the definitions for **show** and **hide**, even though they are virtual. Several classes in the planets program do override these functions. If you are still not convinced, try the exercises at the end of the chapter.

Dispatching Calls in the Base Class The number of modifications required is even greater if you decide to handle the dispatching in the base class. If **Body::move** handled the dispatching, it would have to know about every type derived from it. This means that forward declarations for all classes in the hierarchy must precede the definition of any dispatching function in **Body**.

This choice is forced by systems that do not provide dynamic binding. You must either dispatch calls in a global function like **main**, or in the base class of the polymorphic hierarchy. Do the providers of a class library implement the dispatching mechanism? They probably should, but they cannot unless they provide a library that is impossible to extend, or unless they supply source code. Even with the source code, you still have a can of worms. All the source code that the supplier took years to implement and debug can be broken in seconds when you go to modify one of the dispatch mechanisms. The other alternative is for you to handle the dispatching yourself in **main**, or another function that you define. The class provider likes this: the provider is off the hook. But now you have to learn about every potential type that must be handled by the dispatch mechanism.

You can almost predict that, given the choice between studying someone else's code and starting from scratch, programmers will start from scratch. Who hasn't thought, "I can rewrite it faster than I can untangle this mess."

The problem is that all continuity in development and stability in code is lost every time a module is rewritten from scratch; and just possibly, we do not understand the issues as well as the original designer.

Assume that you decide to handle the dispatching of calls to move inside **Body** rather than **main**. If information hiding is a goal, it seems logical to protect **main** from knowledge of the dispatch mechanism and the types in the hierarchy.

On the disk is a program that implements the dispatch mechanism for the previous example in **Body::move** rather than in **main**. If you compile and run it, it behaves no differently although it required significant modification. The program is P12-6.CPP and if you want to see the details, study it when you have some time. Try adding some new types of bodies to the system.

New Class Definitions Force Recompilation of Base Classes Think about the trouble caused by adding a new type, regardless of whether the static dispatch mechanism is handled in a global function like **main** or in a base class like **Body**.

Consider that you must provide a dispatch mechanism for all virtual methods in a given polymorphic class hierarchy. In the case of planets, you would still have to duplicate the **switch** statement, probably inside **Body::show** and **Body::hide**, to handle all types in the hierarchy. Just for the sake of keeping the clutter out of global functions, it seems more sensible to concentrate the dispatch mechanism inside the base class.

But now what happens if you want to add a new type to the hierarchy? Say that you need to define a **Moon** class to simulate bodies that revolve around planets. First, you have to find the header file with the enumeration declaring all the body types and add the new one.

```
enum bodyType { ..., moon};
```

After declaring and defining the **Moon** class, you must go back to every method dispatcher that is type dependent and add a new **case** inside the **switch** statement.

```
// Body:move
      case moon:
         ((Moon*)this)->move();
         break;

// Body::hide
      case moon:
         ((Moon*)this)->hide();
         break;

// Body::show
      case moon:
         ((Moon*)this)->show();
         break;
```

You would also have to remember to initialize **thisType** in the constructor for the new **Moon** class.

```
Moon::Moon (...)
{
    //...
    thisType = moon;
}
```

This is something that could easily be forgotten, since there is nothing built into C++ that forces you to initialize instance variables. Forgetting to do so in this case would cause a run-time error, possibly a call to the wrong method, which would be hard to nail down.

In the course of a typical development process you will add many new class declarations to a polymorphic hierarchy. The number of dependencies throughout the system tends to grow exponentially as the number of types grows linearly.

This precludes a class like **Body**—and especially a more elaborate class like **OrbitingBody** or **Planet**—from being provided by a third party library without source code. The entire source code for the library would have to be recompiled every time you added a new class. Without source code, the library cannot be extended to add required classes not foreseen by the original designer.

Lack of support for polymorphism and dynamic binding forces knowledge of the overall structure of a class hierarchy upward toward the root of the hierarchy. Ironically, the root or base class will always be coded first, at the time when the least information is available about the overall structure of the hierarchy. Furthermore, the addition of any new type means that *all* source code must be recompiled. This is not so with dynamic binding. As long as a header file with the declaration for the base class is provided, only the source file containing the new class definitions needs to be compiled.

Alternately, structural knowledge can be shifted to the class user and dispatching can be handled in a function like **main**, as shown in an earlier listing. But that forces the user to know about each and every type in the library that is part of the polymorphic hierarchy. All methods requiring special treatment for binding must be known as well. But isn't the reason for buying a class library in the first place to avoid handling those kinds of details? Making the user build a dispatch mechanism pushes the responsibility for defining the general behavior of what would be a virtual method out of the hands of the class provider and places it in the hands of the class user. So why buy a library?

Dynamic Binding Decentralizes Knowledge About the Structure of Polymorphic Type Hierarchies

Dynamic binding eliminates the need for any one component to have overall structural knowledge of a given class hierarchy. A virtual function dispatch table is built automatically by the compiler for any functions that override a virtual base method. At run time, this table supplies all the information required to bind a call from a polymorphic object to the correct method for handling that object. This is the most powerful aspect of dynamic binding. In this form of encapsulation lies the single greatest difference between traditional programming and object-oriented programming. For example, if the methods for **show**, **hide**, and **move** inside **Body** are virtual, **Body** does not need to know either the number or the type names of its descendants in order to match a given object with its proper method. Polymorphism and dynamic binding make third-party libraries truly reusable even if source code is not provided.

With dynamic binding, type knowledge is said to be decentralized or encapsulated within each class definition. This form of encapsulation is more general than the encapsulation referring to the packaging of data and operations within a single entity known as an object. A base module or library provides basic functionality for reuse by descendants and indicates which methods should be dynamically bound. By declaring methods as virtual, the base class supplies an automated dispatch mechanism that works for any object of a class that inherits from the base class. This dispatch mechanism binds polymorphic objects to the appropriate methods, even for classes built long after the base module is delivered and even if source code for the base class is not available.

The dynamic dispatch mechanism makes it possible to handle objects with common characteristics in a generic manner and avoids special case code. In the following chapter, you will see how polymorphism and dynamic binding make it possible to build generic container classes, which provide powerful processing capabilities for managing generic objects.

Exercises for the Still Unconvinced

1. Rework the planets program, P12-5, to run without the support of virtual functions

- **a.** with the dispatch mechanisms coded in **main**
- **b.** with the dispatch mechanisms coded in the **Body** class

2. Go for the moon. Add a **Moon** class to both of the programs in Exercise 1. Modify the appropriate dispatch mechanisms to handle the new class.

13 Polymorphic Collections and Containers

You have studied the tools that make code reuse possible. Now you can put code reuse to work.

You have probably heard the terms *collection* and *container* in various articles and discussions on object-oriented programming. These terms might sound esoteric at first, but they are simply basic data structures that contain common elements. Examples of containers include lists, stacks, queues, collections, and sets. If containers are nothing more than lists or arrays, why give them a special name?

What distinguishes collections and containers from aggregate data structures available in traditional languages is polymorphism. Although it is possible in a language like C or Pascal to declare a basic record or structure

```
struct Point
{
    int x;
    int y;
};
```

and then declare an array of structures

```
struct Point arrayOfPoints[10];
```

you still don't have what is referred to in the object-oriented world as a collection.

True, you can put different instances of **Point** objects in the array or you can even write a set of list processing routines that operate on **Point** elements. In fact, this is what was done with the **List** and **Menu** classes in Chapters 6 through 9. The problem with this approach is that only objects of the type declared in the structure can be stored in the list or in the array.

Containers, on the other hand, have elements that are polymorphic; that is, they can contain any one of a set of objects derived from a polymorphic base class. The reason it is so hard to convey the advantages and differences introduced by container classes in short magazine articles is that readers must first have a firm grasp of the contribution of polymorphism and dynamic binding to the reuse of code.

Without polymorphism, new container classes have to be built for each new type of element. You saw this when the **List** class introduced in Chapter 6 was adapted to operate on the **String** class, and later on the **Choice** class, and then later again on the **FileInfo** class. However, if all of your elements are derived from one basic class, then you can build stacks, queues, arrays, and other collections that can contain anything from points, rectangles, and strings to complex structures like planets or windows on a desktop.

In Smalltalk, all classes are ultimately derived from a single base class called **Object**. The DiskTutor container classes adopt this technique for implementing generic container classes. The DiskTutor class library contains a base class called **Object** and all classes in the library are derived from **Object**. This chapter will go into more detail later on the declaration of **Object** and how deriving all classes from **Object** makes possible the implementation of polymorphic containers. For now, the next section simply surveys the most commonly used container classes.

In order to compile and run programs in this chapter, which use the DiskTutor class library, you must use the small memory model. This is the default memory model set when you install either Turbo C++ or Borland C++.

Note: *Project files for this chapter*

Programs P13-1.CPP through P13-16.CPP all require project files to link and run correctly. Each of these programs must link to the DiskTutor container class library called DT.LIB. For example, in order to compile and run program P13-1, you must create a project file containing two files,

P13-1.CPP and DT.LIB.

Likewise, Program P13-2 requires a project composed of two files,

P13-2.CPP and DT.LIB.

The remaining fourteen example programs each require a unique project file consisting of

P13-XX.CPP and DT.LIB.

For convention's sake, it's best to make the name of the project correspond to the main program filename. The project name for P13-1.CPP would be P13-1.PRJ, and the project name for Program P13-16.CPP would be P13-16.PRJ.

As you read through the text, you will be asked to run each of the sixteen example programs. When asked to run a program you should stop and make a project file that consists of the main program, P13-*XX*.CPP, and DT.LIB. You should know how to make project files by now. As a reminder: select **P**roject **O**pen (ALT-P O) and type in the project's name, P13-*XX*, followed by RETURN. Next, add items to the project by pressing the INS key with the Project Window active. Type in the names of the files you wish to add, or select from a list of CPP files by entering ***.CPP.**

> ***Note:*** *(continued)*
>
> When you are asked to load a program simply to view it, first create the project file. Then, open the main program file and inside the Project Window, highlight the main program filename (P13-*XX*.CPP) and press RETURN. Alternately, you can double click on the filename with the left mouse button. When you are through running an example program, select **P**roject **C**lose (ALT-P C), before moving on to the next example.
>
> Three bonus programs are also included in this chapter to show how to put container classes to work. Each of these bonus programs will give special instructions for creating project files at the appropriate time.

Overview of Container Classes

This section introduces the basic container classes: **Set**, **Bag**, **OrderedCltn**, and **SortedCltn**. **Set**s are collections of items that can have no duplicate elements. Program P13-1 shows how to use the **Set** class. Be sure to log to the appropriate directory (\DT\CH13) before invoking Borland C++ and loading Program P13-1.

P13-1

```
#include "point.h"
#include "set.h"

main()
{
    cout << "Set of 3 points\n";
    Point A(1,1);
    Point B(1,2);
    Point C(1,3);

    Set s;
    s.add(A);
    s.add(B);
    s.add(C);
    cout << s;
}
```

Load Program P13-1 now. This program declares three points—**A**, **B**, and **C**—and then adds each of them to a set.

```
Set s;
```

Finally, the entire set is printed.

```
cout << s;
```

You can see that sets are very easy to use. All that is required is the inclusion of the file declaring the **Set** class.

```
#include "set.h"
```

You must also include any header files required by the elements you will be adding to the set. In this case, you are only adding points, so only the POINT.H header file is required in addition to SET.H. Items are added to a set with the add method.

```
s.add(A);
s.add(B);
s.add(C);
```

Run the program now. You should get the following output:

```
Set of 3 points
Set[
(1 @ 1)
(1 @ 2)
(1 @ 3)]
```

One nice thing about collections is that they all override the << insert operator. In fact, all classes in the DiskTutor class library override the << insert operator. This gives you a way of looking at the internal variables of any object without doing any extra programming.

Since all the point objects in Program P13-1 are eventually added to the set **s**, you really don't need to give each of them names. The declaration

```
Point A(1,1);
```

creates a point on the stack and gives it a name, **A**. The only reason to keep this name is to use it to add the point to the set.

```
s.add(A);
```

However, it is possible to allocate the object on the heap with the **new** operator. If **new** is used, there is no need to name the point at all. It can be created and added to the set with a single statement.

```
s.add(*new Point (1,1));
```

This allocates a new **Point** object on the heap and adds the object to the set **s**.

P13-2
```
#include "point.h"
#include "set.h"
main()
{
    cout << "Set of 3 points\n";
    Set s;
    s.add(*new Point (1,1));
    s.add(*new Point (1,2));
    s.add(*new Point (1,3));
    cout << s;
}
```

Load and run Program P13-2 now and observe that it produces the same output as Program P13-1. The only difference is that all three points are now created on the heap instead of the stack.

Program P13-3 shows that a set can contain different types of elements.

P13-3
```
#include "point.h"
#include "strclass.h"
#include "rect.h"
#include "set.h"

main()
{
    Set s;
    s.add(*new String("A string, 3 points, and a rectangle"));
    s.add(*new Point (1,1));
    s.add(*new Point (1,2));
    s.add(*new Point (1,3));
    s.add(*new Rectangle(1,1,80,25));
```

```
    cout << s;
}
```

Program P13-3 adds a string and a rectangle to set **s** in addition to the original three points. Note that this requires the inclusion of two extra header files to declare classes for **String** and **Rectangle**.

```
#include "strclass.h"
#include "rect.h"
```

It is now no more difficult to add a string

```
s.add(*new String("A string, 3 points, and a rectangle"));
```

or a rectangle

```
s.add(*new Rectangle(1,1,80,25));
```

than a point. Run the program and you should get the following output:

```
Set[
(1 @ 1)
A string, 3 points, and a rectangle
(1 @ 2)
(1 @ 1) corner: (80 @ 25)
(1 @ 3)]
```

You might be surprised that the elements do not appear in the same order that they are added to the set. There is nothing about a set that guarantees the order in which its elements are stored. In fact, the ordering of elements is one of the properties that distinguish general collections like bags and sets from a more specific class of collections referred to as *ordered collections.* The ordering of elements in sets and bags is determined by a hashing algorithm, which tries to evenly distribute newly added elements inside the collection. This is an implementation issue that is not of concern here, as long as you know that ordering is not guaranteed in sets or bags and that it is merely coincidental that the output of the first two programs shows an ordering that corresponds to the order in which elements were added to the collection.

Bags Versus Sets

The property that distinguishes a set from a bag is that a set can contain no duplicate elements. Consider Program P13-4.

P13-4
```
#include "point.h"
#include "set.h"

main()
{
    Set container;
    container.add(*new Point (1,1));
    container.add(*new Point (1,2));
    container.add(*new Point (1,3));
    container.add(*new Point (1,1));
    cout << container;
}
```

Program P13-4 tries to add a duplicate element. Note that both the first and the last element added are the same. So what will the output be? Load and run the program now.

```
Set[
(1 @ 1)
(1 @ 2)
(1 @ 3)]
```

The duplicate is eliminated from the set automatically. You might, however, want a collection in which duplicates are allowed. In that case you need a bag. Program P13-5 changes the declaration of **s** from a set to a bag.

P13-5
```
#include "point.h"
#include "bag.h"

main()
{
    Bag container;
    container.add(*new Point (1,1));
    container.add(*new Point (1,2));
    container.add(*new Point (1,3));
    container.add(*new Point (1,1));
    cout << container;
}
```

Load and run the program now, and you should get the following output:

```
Bag[
AssocInt((1 @ 1)=2)
AssocInt((1 @ 2)=1)
AssocInt((1 @ 3)=1)]
```

Associations

The output might not be exactly what you expected, but it probably gives the same information. Instead of reporting point (**1 @ 1**) twice, the output reports two copies of (**1 @ 1**) in the collection. If you preferred to have each item listed out on an individual line, you would use a collection instead of a bag. **AssocInt** is a new concept. Bags are implemented as associations. An association connects one type of object with another. The dictionary that might be found on your desk is a collection of associations in which a word is associated with a definition. **AssocInt** is a special form of association that associates any object with an integer. In the case of a bag, objects are associated with an integer that represents the number of occurrences of an object in the bag. Bags would be useful for counting duplicate items. For example, a bag could be used to count the number of words in a file or input stream. Program P13-6 does this.

P13-6

```
#include "point.h"
#include "strclass.h"
#include "bag.h"

main()
{
    Bag container;
    char buf[100];
    cout << "Type some words.\n";
    cout << "Press Ctrl-Z when through.\n";
    while (cin >> buf)
    {
        container.add(*new String(buf));
    }
    cout << "==========\n";
    cout << container;
}
```

This program waits for input from the standard input device. As long as the input has not reached the end of the file, the next word is read into a buffer.

```
while (cin >> buf)
```

Each new line is then added to the bag.

```
container.add(*new String(buf));
```

When the end of the file is reached, the contents of the bag are printed.

```
cout << container;
```

Load and run the program. In response to the input prompt, type

```
to be or not to be
```

followed by RETURN, CTRL-Z, and another RETURN.

The CTRL-Z tells the program that the end of input has been reached. After you press the final RETURN, your screen should look like this:

```
Type some words.
Press Ctrl-Z when through.
to be or not to be
^Z
==========
Bag[
AssocInt(not=1)
AssocInt(or=1)
AssocInt(to=2)
AssocInt(be=2)]
```

With almost no programming effort, you have a word counting program. It is trivial to change the output to a more acceptable format by using iterators to print all the elements of a collection. In fact, you will see this in a later example. For now, let's look at iterators.

Iterators

Look at Program P13-7.

P13-7
```
#include "point.h"
#include "set.h"
#include <conio.h>

void gotoxy(Point p)
{
    gotoxy(p.x(), p.y());
}

main()
{
    Set container;
    container.add(*new Point (1,1));
    container.add(*new Point (80,1));
    container.add(*new Point (80,24));
    container.add(*new Point (1,24));
    container.add(*new Point (40,12));

    cout << container;
    getch();
    clrscr();
    DO(container, Point*, p)
        gotoxy(*p);
        putch('*');
        getch();
    DONE
    clrscr();
}
```

This program creates a set of five points corresponding to the four corners and center point of the screen. The set is printed as usual. Up to this point there is nothing new.

```
Set container;
container.add(*new Point (1,1));
container.add(*new Point (80,1));
container.add(*new Point (80,24));
container.add(*new Point (1,24));
container.add(*new Point (40,12));

cout << container;
getch();
```

Now the program waits for a keypress, after which the screen is cleared. Then, two special macros are used to iterate over the collection. The basic form of the iteration is

```
DO(container, Point*, p)
    //...
DONE
```

Both DO and DONE are macros defined in ITERATOR.H. A detailed explanation is irrelevant to the usage of the macros. However, you may wonder why it is not necessary to put braces either after DO or before DONE. They are unnecessary because the macros automatically insert them for you. Nevertheless, it would not be an error to include extra braces to make the iterator look more like a normal control structure.

The DO macro takes three arguments. The first argument is the name of the collection over which the iteration is to take place. The second argument should be a pointer to the type of object expected to be returned for each element of the collection. The third argument is a variable name corresponding to the type specified in argument two. Use the name to refer to the object in the current phase of the iteration. The second argument can be specific, as in the case of **Point***, if you know that all objects will be of this type. It is also possible to use a more general type for the second argument, such as **Object***. The only requirement for the type used for the second argument is that the class referred to must define whatever methods will be invoked inside the iteration.

For example, if you wish to invoke the **origin** method defined for class **Point**, the second argument to DO must be a **Point*** rather than an **Object*** because

```
cout << p->origin();
```

is legal if **p** is a pointer to a **Point** and illegal if **p** is a pointer to an **Object**. No **origin** method is defined for the **Object** class. The net effect of the iteration is to position the cursor to the current point and print an * at that location. Note the definition

```
void gotoxy(Point p)
{
    gotoxy(p.x(), p.y());
}
```

at the top of the file. This definition overloads the normal **gotoxy** function declared in CONIO.H and accepts a point in place of two explicit coordinates. This makes it easier to position points with the simple statement

```
gotoxy(*p);
```

Load and run the program now. First, the set of points is printed.

```
Set[
(1 @ 1)
(40 @ 12)
(80 @ 24)
(80 @ 1)
(1 @ 24)]
```

The order of elements in the set is not the same as the order in which they were added. Sometimes this makes a difference. The order of elements here is the same order in which the elements will be processed by the iterator. Each time you press a key, the point corresponding to the successive element in the set will be printed on the screen. Note the order in which each of the asterisks appears. By changing the type of the basic collection, you can change this order.

Ordered Collections

For an example of ordered collections, look at Program P13-8.

P13-8

```
#include "point.h"
#include "ordcltn.h"
#include <conio.h>

void gotoxy(Point p)
{
    gotoxy(p.x(), p.y());
}

main()
{
    OrderedCltn container;
```

```
    container.add(*new Point (1,1));
    container.add(*new Point (80,1));
    container.add(*new Point (80,24));
    container.add(*new Point (1,24));
    container.add(*new Point (40,12));

    cout << container;
    getch();
    clrscr();
    DO(container, Point*, p)
        gotoxy(*p);
        putch('*');
        getch();
    DONE
    clrscr();
}
```

The only difference between this program and Program P13-7 is that **container** is now declared as an ordered collection,

```
OrderedCltn container;
```

instead of as a set.

Load and run the program. Now when the collection is printed, it looks like this:

```
OrderedCltn[
(1 @ 1)
(80 @ 1)
(80 @ 24)
(1 @ 24)
(40 @ 12)]
```

The order of elements is the same as the order in which they were added. A basic property of ordered collections is that they retain order. Each time you press a key, the points will be drawn in the order specified by the program. This would be crucial if your goal were to connect each of the dots using a graphics function like **lineto**.

Sorted Collections

Another form of ordered collection is a *sorted collection*. A sorted collection maintains order among elements according to a method defined in the element's class. In the DiskTutor class library, all objects define a method, **compare**, which is used to order objects of the same type within a collection. Have a look at Program P13-9.

P13-9
```
#include "point.h"
#include "sortcltn.h"
#include <conio.h>

void gotoxy(Point p)
{
    gotoxy(p.x(), p.y());
}

main()
{
    SortedCltn container;
    container.add(*new Point (1,1));
    container.add(*new Point (80,1));
    container.add(*new Point (80,24));
    container.add(*new Point (1,24));
    container.add(*new Point (40,12));

    cout << container;
    getch();
    clrscr();
    DO(container, Point*, p)
        gotoxy(*p);
        putch('*');
        getch();
    DONE
    clrscr();
}
```

The only thing that distinguishes P13-9 from P13-8 or P13-7 is that **container** is now declared as a sorted collection.

```
SortedCltn container;
```

Load and run the program. Now, when the container is printed, the order is as follows:

```
SortedCltn[
(1 @ 1)
(80 @ 1)
(40 @ 12)
(1 @ 24)
(80 @ 24)]
```

Points sort in an order such that y values are considered before x values. The natural arrangement of a sorted collection of points starts at the upper-left corner of the screen, moving from left to right. After all points in a given line are processed, the points in successive lines are processed. This is the ordering that you would expect from an x,y coordinate system: the x variable varies faster than the y variable. This is the way that the points are drawn on the screen each time you press a key.

Just as with sets, bags, and ordered collections, sorted collections can contain any objects derived from the **Object** base class. This is one of the reasons for declaring a **String** class. Since **String** is derived from **Object**, it shares polymorphic attributes that allow it to be placed in a collection. This is not true of the basic data types automatically provided by C++, such as **char**, **char***, **int**, **long**, **float**, and so on. This means that you could not put strings represented as **char***'s inside of polymorphic collections. Program P13-10 shows a way to sort a collection of strings (without using a sort applicator as in Chapter 9) to sort a list of animal names.

P13-10

```
#include "sortcltn.h"
#include "strclass.h"
#include <conio.h>

main()
{
    SortedCltn container;
    container.add(*new String("weasel"));
    container.add(*new String("bat"));
    container.add(*new String("zebra"));
    container.add(*new String("possum"));
    container.add(*new String("dog"));
    container.add(*new String("cat"));
    container.add(*new String("aardvark"));
    container.add(*new String("orangutan"));

    cout << container;
}
```

It is no longer necessary to explicitly invoke an applicator to sort the collection. If you know you want a sorted collection, simply declare your container as a **SortedCltn**. Each item is sorted automatically as it is added to the collection. Load and run the program now. You should see the following output:

```
SortedCltn[
aardvark
bat
cat
dog
orangutan
possum
weasel
zebra]
```

The output is nearly identical to that produced by the program in Chapter 9. Containers provide the additional benefit of printing the collection name and surrounding the elements with square brackets, [. . .]. As indicated earlier, if that is not what you want, you can output the elements of the collection in any order desired. This will be covered later.

Converting Collections

It is possible to convert collections from one type to another. For instance, if your original collection is an ordered collection, you can create a new collection from the original. The new collection can be a bag, a set, a sorted collection, or other types of collections not yet introduced. Program 13-11 shows how this is done.

P13-11

```
#include "strclass.h"
#include "ordcltn.h"
#include "bag.h"
#include "set.h"
#include "sortcltn.h"
#include <conio.h>

main()
{
    OrderedCltn container;
    container.add(*new String("one"));
    container.add(*new String("two"));
    container.add(*new String("three"));

    container.add(*new String("one"));
    container.add(*new String("two"));
    container.add(*new String("three"));
```

```
    container.add(*new String("one"));
    container.add(*new String("two"));
    container.add(*new String("three"));

    cout << "==== container ====\n";
    cout << container;
    getch();
    cout << "==== container.asBag() ====\n";
    cout << container.asBag();
    getch();
    cout << "==== container.asSet() ====\n";
    cout << container.asSet();
    getch();
    cout << "==== container.asSortedCltn() ====\n";
    cout << container.asSortedCltn();
    cout << "====================\n";
    getch();
}
```

The original collection is declared as an **OrderedCltn**.

```
OrderedCltn container;
```

Nine strings are added to the container with two sets of duplicates. The output from Program P13-11 not only shows the results of converting one container type to another, but also shows how the properties of each container type influence the order and the contents of the collection. Printing the container as a bag is straightforward.

```
cout << container.asBag();
```

It would be equally possible to declare a bag and assign it the contents of the ordered collection.

```
Bag aBag = container.asBag();
cout << aBag;
```

However, there is no need to do this if you simply want to print out the container as a bag. You would use an assignment like this if you wanted to perform some operation on **aBag** before printing it. It is just as simple to print an **OrderedCltn** as a **Set** or as a **SortedCltn**.

```
cout << container.asSet();
//...
cout << container.asSortedCltn();
```

Load and run the program. You should see the following output for the ordered collection:

```
==== container ====
OrderedCltn[
one
two
three
one
two
three
one
two
three]
```

Note that the ordered collection retains the order in which the items were added. The program now waits for a keypress before printing the container as a bag. Press a key and you will see

```
==== container.asBag() ====
Bag[
AssocInt(two=3)
AssocInt(one=3)
AssocInt(three=3)]
```

The bag prints a more consolidated version of the contents, even though it loses ordering information. Another keypress produces

```
==== container.asSet() ====
Set[
two
one
three]
```

The set gives you the least information. Not only do you lose order, you lose the number of elements in the original collection. Sets are useful for weeding out unneeded information. Press another key to see the sorted collection.

```
==== container.asSortedCltn() ====
SortedCltn[
one
one
one
three
three
three
two
two
two]
================================
```

The order of the elements is determined by the **compare** function defined in the **String** class. By now you should have a pretty good handle on the distinguishing properties of the basic collection classes.

Objects That Can Determine Their Type

Sometimes it is useful to mix different classes of elements in a collection in a regular pattern. For instance, it might be useful to alternate points and strings. Then, when the collection is processed with an iterator, alternative actions can be specified depending on the type of the element. All classes in DT.LIB have methods for determining some of their properties. Remember from Chapter 12 that polymorphic collections are implemented using pointers to a common base class. In the case of collections, the base class is the **Object** class. Once an object is placed in a polymorphic collection, the compiler can no longer determine the object's type. However, virtual functions give you a way out.

A Class Called Class

In the DiskTutor container class library, all classes have a global variable associated with them. The variable is derived from a class called **Class**. Each instance of **Class** keeps track of the name of a particular class and implements virtual methods that allow a pointer to an object to determine the type of the object as well as the type of the object's base class.

Other virtual methods provided by instances of **Class** allow objects to determine if they are derived from a specific ancestor class.

You will learn a little more about the **Class** class later when you learn how to declare new objects that are compatible with the DiskTutor collection classes. For now, the only thing you need to know about **Class** is that every class declares an instance of **Class**, which has a name very similar to the name of the class. If this sounds confusing, it might be because it is hard to see how **Class** can be a class. It is actually very straightforward:

```
class Class
{
    //...
};
```

Class is declared just like any other class. The initial capital distinguishes it from the reserved C++ keyword. You can also declare instances of **Class**.

```
Class class_Point;
```

This declares an instance of **Class** whose name is **class_Point**. The actual declaration is a little more complicated, but the basic idea still holds. Every class—like **Point, Rectangle**, and **Set**—has an instance of **Class** associated with it. The name of that instance can be determined from the name of the class with which it is associated. For example, the following table shows the instances of **Class** associated with **Point, Rectangle**, and **Set**.

Name of Class	**Associated Instance of Class**
Point	point_Class
Rectangle	rectangle_Class
Set	set_Class

Among other things, **point_Class**, for example, contains a string "Point." Likewise, **rectangle_Class** and **set_Class**, respectively, contain the strings "Rectangle" and "Set." A similar string is retained for every class. That is how it is possible for containers to print out their names in addition to their elements.

```
Set[
(1 @ 1)
(1 @ 2)
(1 @ 3)]
```

Every class derived from the **Object** class has a virtual method called **isA**. When this method is called for a given object, usually in conjunction with a pointer, the value returned is a pointer to a **Class** object. For instance, consider the following:

```
OrderedCltn container;

container.add(*new Point (55,10));
//...
```

On the first pass through an iterator, declared as

```
DO(container, Object*, o)
    Class *pClass = o->isA();
    //...
DONE
```

the **pClass** will be set to point to **point_Class**, the instance of **Class** associated with **Point**. Had the first object in container been a **String**

```
container.add(*new String("Tricks?"));
```

pClass would have been set to point to **string_Class**, which is associated with **String**. Given a pointer to a **Class** object, a program can obtain a pointer to the object's base class

```
Class pBase = pClass->baseClass();
```

or the name of the class

```
char *name = pClass->className()
```

Thus, given a pointer to any **Object**, it is possible to determine its name, its base class, and the number of bytes of storage it will occupy.

```
cout << "class name: "
     << (o->isA()->className())
     << "\n";
cout << "base name : "
     << (o->isA()->baseClass()->className())
     << "\n";
cout << "size of object: "
     << (o->isA()->size())
     << "\n";
```

There is another method provided by all classes derived from **Object** that tells whether the object is ultimately derived from another class:

```
if (o->isKindOf(class_Point))
```

The method **isKindOf** is a virtual function defined in the **Object** class. It is overridden by every class derived from **Object**. Even if a class is not the immediate heir to a given base class, **isKindOf** will tell you if its argument is an ancestor of the object in question. For example, given three classes, each in turn derived from the other

```
class A : Object
{
   //...
}

class B : A
{
   //...
};

class C : B
{
   //...
};
```

the conditional expression in the following listing would be true.

```
C instanceOfC;
//...
if (instanceOfC.isKindOf(a_Class))
    //...
```

The number of levels between an heir and a base class does not matter as long as tracing upward through the hierarchy ultimately locates the argument to **isKindOf**. Program P13-12 shows a case where you might mix elements in an ordered collection and use **isKindOf** to determine how to process each of the elements inside an iterator.

P13-12
```
#include "point.h"
#include "strclass.h"
#include "ordcltn.h"
#include <conio.h>

void gotoxy(Point p)
{
    gotoxy(p.x(), p.y());
}

main()
{
    OrderedCltn container;

    container.add(*new Point (55,10));
    container.add(*new String("Tricks?"));
    container.add(*new Point (15,6));
    container.add(*new String("world."));
    container.add(*new Point (50,8));
    container.add(*new String("How's"));
    container.add(*new Point (10,4));
    container.add(*new String("Hello,"));

    cout << container;
    getch();
    clrscr();
    DO(container, Object*, o)
        if (o->isKindOf(class_Point))
            gotoxy(*(Point*)o);
        else
        {
            cout << *o;
            getch();
        }
    DONE
    gotoxy(1,20);
}
```

The program uses both strings and points in a collection to indicate the positions on the screen where a successive string should be printed.

After four points and four strings are added to the collection, the collection is printed. An iterator processes each member of the collection. If the element is a point, the cursor is positioned to that location.

```
DO(container, Object*, o)
    if (o->isKindOf(class_Point))
        gotoxy(*(Point*)o);
    //...
```

Otherwise, the element is printed and the program waits for a keypress before continuing.

```
//...
    else
    {
        cout << *o;
        getch();
    }
DONE
```

Load the program. See if you can predict the output. After an honest effort, run the program. First you will see the collection printed.

```
OrderedCltn[
(55 @ 10)
Tricks?
(15 @ 6)
world.
(50 @ 8)
How's
(10 @ 4)
Hello,]
```

Now, press a key and the first string appears at the indicated location. Three more keypresses and the mystery is resolved, as shown in Figure 13-1.

Although collections make this kind of loose data structuring possible, it is not always advisable. Often, loose structure is acceptable for quick prototyping, eliminating the need to build special data structures for a given application. More frequently, polymorphic containers are used to process collections whose elements have more in common than strings and points. The planets program in the previous chapter is a

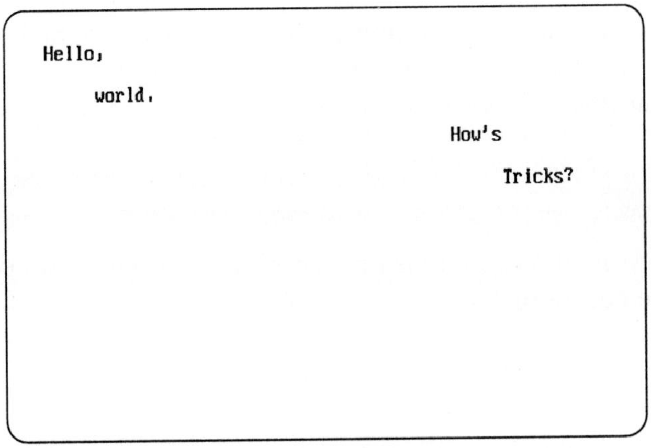

Figure 13-1. *Output for Program P13-12*

good example. All classes derived from **Body** define a **move** method. An ordered collection can be used to manage all the active bodies in a simulation. This makes it easier to add and remove elements from the collection. Using a collection frees you from worrying about replacing elements removed from an array, or moving all bodies down to fill a hole created when an object is destroyed.

Collections for Playing Cards

The next set of examples involves playing cards. Card games provide many opportunities to use collections. A deck of cards is a collection of cards. Shuffling a deck can be thought of as random reordering of a collection. A card hand is also a collection of cards. A program that simulates a game of cards must provide a mechanism for removing cards from one collection and putting them into another, as when a dealer distributes cards to each player or when each player returns a card hand to the game deck. Furthermore, a game like blackjack can be simulated as a collection of players plus a dealer.

Even the cards themselves can use collections. The problem of drawing a card can be addressed by thinking of its representation as a collection of pips. Pips are the markings on a card that indicate the suit and rank of a card. Let's explore some of these notions.

Consider the problem of printing a graphic representation of a card on the screen. First, you need a way to draw the background of the card. This is done easily, given information about the width, height, color, and position of the card. If a card is represented by a rectangle, **r**, declared as the following,

```
Rectangle r(0,0,cardWidth,cardHeight);
```

then a red window can be used to draw a heart or a diamond,

```
textattr(YELLOW + (RED<<4));
window0(x,y,r.width(),r.height());
```

and a blue window can be used to draw the background for a spade or a club.

```
textattr(YELLOW + (BLUE<<4));
window0(x,y,r.width(),r.height());
```

Next, you need a way to draw pips. Card pips can be drawn on the screen using special IBM PC graphics characters. An enumeration can be used to give symbolic names to these characters:

```
enum
{
    heartChar='\x03',
    diamondChar='\x04',
    clubChar='\x05',
    spadeChar='\x06'
};
```

Close study of a typical card deck reveals that a pip generally occupies one of three columns. A varying number of rows can be used, but two columns of five rows will handle the largest number of pips required (for a card having a rank of ten). Kings, queens, and jacks will be represented with one pip, which appears at the card's center. A simple **for** loop can be used to draw all the possible pip locations on a card.

```
for(int i=0; i<cardWidth; i++)
    for (int j=0; j<cardHeight; j++)
        { gotoxy0(i,j); putch(heartChar); }
```

Program P13-13 uses all these techniques to draw two cards.

P13-13

```
#include "point.h"
#include "rect.h"
#include <conio.h>

const cardWidth=3;
const cardHeight=5;
enum
{
    heartChar='\x03',
    diamondChar='\x04',
    clubChar='\x05',
    spadeChar='\x06'
};

/////////////////////////////////////////////////////////////
// video support routines
/////////////////////////////////////////////////////////////
void window0(int x, int y, int w, int h)
{
    window(x+1, y+1, x+w, y+h);
}

void gotoxy0(int x, int y)
{
    gotoxy(x+1, y+1);
}

void gotoxy0(Point& p)
{
    gotoxy0(p.x(), p.y());
}

main()
{
    textattr('\x71');     // blue on grey
    clrscr();
    Rectangle r(0,0,cardWidth,cardHeight);
    int x=10;    // position for card 1
```

```
    int y=2;
    textattr(YELLOW + (RED<<4));
    window0(x,y,r.width(),r.height());
    clrscr();
    window0(x,y,r.width(),r.height()+1);  // adjust height
                                          // so window doesn't
                                          // scroll when a char
                                          // is written to the
                                          // lower right  corner
    for(int i=0; i<cardWidth; i++)
        for (int j=0; j<cardHeight; j++)
            { gotoxy0(i,j); putch(heartChar); }
    x=40;         // new position for card 2
    textattr(YELLOW + (BLUE<<4));
    window0(x,y,r.width(),r.height());
    clrscr();
    window0(x,y,r.width(),r.height()+1);  // adjust height
    for(i=0; i<cardWidth; i++)
        for (j=0; j<cardHeight; j++)
            { gotoxy0(i,j); putch(spadeChar); }
    window0(0,0,79,24);      // reset output to full screen
    gotoxy0(0,20);
    getch();
}
```

Both cards fill in all pip positions with a special graphics character. The first card is red and fills in 15 pip positions with a heart. The second card is blue and fills in all 15 pip positions with a spade. Note the use of the two global constants, **cardWidth** and **cardHeight**, which make it easy to modify the size of a card.

Load and run the program now. As you can see in Figure 13-2, the two rectangles on the screen are sorry excuses for playing cards. The proportions are way off, but at least the general principles have been laid down. It should be fairly easy to make the cards wider, giving them more realistic proportions. Simply redefine the constants. While you are doing that, why not leave enough room to draw a nice frame border around the card?

```
const cardWidth=11;
const cardHeight=7;
```

Although this takes care of the problem of proportion, the **for** loop can now no longer be used to draw the pips.

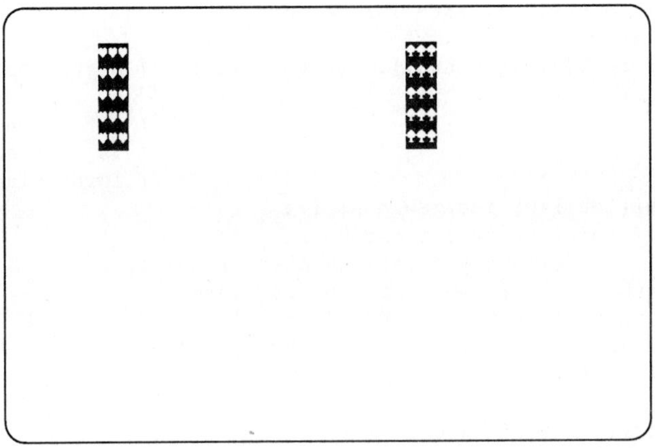

Figure 13-2. *Output for Program P13-13*

```
for(int i=0; i<cardWidth; i++)
    for (int j=0; j<cardHeight; j++)
        { gotoxy0(i,j); putch(heartChar); }
```

This loop will now draw 77 pips instead of 15, which is not what you want. You need to adapt your pip drawing technique. The easiest way to do this is to enumerate the three columns that can contain pips.

```
enum { left=2, middle=5, right=8 };
```

The values assigned to these symbols leave enough room for a card frame border. The function used to draw a frame around a card is adapted from Chapter 6 and is called **drawFrame**.

```
void drawFrame(int x, int y, int w, int h)
{
    // top
    gotoxy0(x,y);
    putch(TopLeft);
    for (int i=0; i<w-2; i++)
        putch(Top);
    putch(TopRight);
```

```
    // right
    for (i=0; i<h-2; i++)
    {
        gotoxy0(x+w-1,y+i+1);
        putch(Right);
    }

    // bottom
    gotoxy0(x,y+h-1);
    putch(BottomLeft);
    for (i=0; i<w-2; i++)
        putch(Bottom);
    putch(BottomRight);

    // left
    for (i=0; i<h-2; i++)
    {
        gotoxy0(x,y+i+1);
        putch(Left);
    }
}
```

Note that all x,y coordinates in the card programs in this chapter are zero-based. Three special video support routines are provided to make this possible.

```
///////////////////////////////////////////////////////////////
// video support routines
///////////////////////////////////////////////////////////////
void window0(int x, int y, int w, int h)
{
    window(x+1, y+1, x+w, y+h);
}

void gotoxy0(int x, int y)
{
    gotoxy(x+1, y+1);
}

void gotoxy0(Point& p)
{
    gotoxy0(p.x(), p.y());
}
```

Program P13-14 incorporates all of these ideas, and the cards that it draws are a little more convincing.

P13-14

```
#include "point.h"
#include "rect.h"
#include <conio.h>

const cardWidth=11;
const cardHeight=7;
enum { left=2, middle=5, right=8 };
enum
{
    heartChar='\x03',
    diamondChar='\x04',
    clubChar='\x05',
    spadeChar='\x06'
};

////////////////////////////////////////////////////////////
// video support routines
////////////////////////////////////////////////////////////
void window0(int x, int y, int w, int h)
{
    window(x+1, y+1, x+w, y+h);
}

void gotoxy0(int x, int y)
{
    gotoxy(x+1, y+1);
}

void gotoxy0(Point& p)
{
    gotoxy0(p.x(), p.y());
}

enum Frame
{
    TopLeft=218,    Top=196,    TopRight=191,
    Left=179,                   Right=179,
    BottomLeft=192, Bottom=196, BottomRight=217
};

void drawFrame(int x, int y, int w, int h)
{
    // top
    gotoxy0(x,y);
    putch(TopLeft);
    for (int i=0; i<w-2; i++)
        putch(Top);
    putch(TopRight);

    // right
```

```
    for (i=0; i<h-2; i++)
    {
        gotoxy0(x+w-1,y+i+1);
        putch(Right);
    }

    // bottom
    gotoxy0(x,y+h-1);
    putch(BottomLeft);
    for (i=0; i<w-2; i++)
        putch(Bottom);
    putch(BottomRight);

    // left
    for (i=0; i<h-2; i++)
    {
        gotoxy0(x,y+i+1);
        putch(Left);
    }
}

main()
{
    textattr('\x71');      // blue on grey
    clrscr();
    Rectangle r(0,0,cardWidth,cardHeight);
    int x=10;    // position for card 1
    int y=2;
    textattr(YELLOW + (RED<<4));
    window0(x,y,r.width(),r.height());
    clrscr();
    window0(x,y,r.width(),r.height()+1);// adjust for scroll
    drawFrame(0,0,r.width(),r.height());
    gotoxy0(middle,3);  putch(heartChar);

    x=40;          // new position for card 2
    textattr(YELLOW + (BLUE<<4));
    window0(x,y,r.width(),r.height());
    clrscr();
    window0(x,y,r.width(),r.height()+1);// adjust for scroll
    drawFrame(0,0,r.width(),r.height());
    gotoxy0(left,1);  putch(spadeChar);
    gotoxy0(right,5); putch(spadeChar);

    window0(0,0,79,24);   // reset output to full screen
    gotoxy0(0,20);
    getch();
}
```

This program draws an ace of hearts and a two of spades. Load and run the program now to see the improvement. You can see in Figure

13-3 that the proportions are better. The pips are more spread out. But, it takes two statements to draw each pip.

```
// ace
gotoxy0(middle,3);  putch(heartChar);
//...
// 2
gotoxy0(left,1);  putch(spadeChar);
gotoxy0(right,5); putch(spadeChar);
```

Furthermore, if you try to find a regular pattern by which you can determine pip layout from card rank, you will soon be disappointed. An array of coordinates might seem like one possibility, but even this is awkward because the array for each card will be a different size.

Card Pips as a Set of Points

It turns out that one of the easiest ways to associate a set of pips with a given card rank is by using 13 different collections of pips. The pip

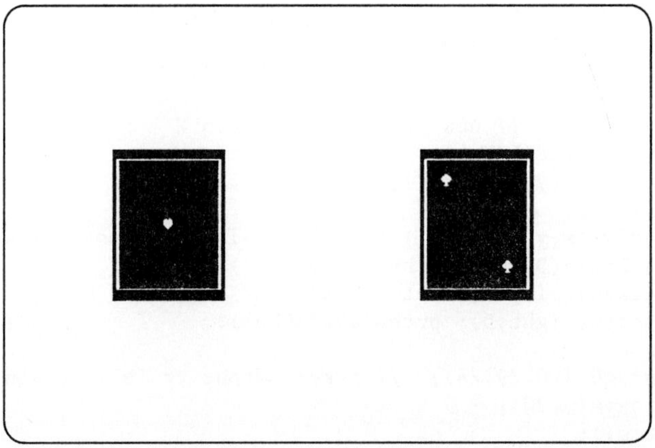

Figure 13-3. *Output for Program P13-14*

collection for each card can be represented as a set of points. All points in the set are relative to the upper-left corner of the card. Here is how you could create the pip set for a card with a rank of five.

```
Set pips5;       // pip set for 5
// ==== add points to pip set for 5 ====
pips5.add(*new Point(left,1));
pips5.add(*new Point(left,5));

pips5.add(*new Point(middle,3));

pips5.add(*new Point(right,1));
pips5.add(*new Point(right,5));
```

Now all you need is a function that takes two arguments: a pip set, and a character representing the card suit.

```
void drawPips(Set &cardPipSet, char pipChar)
{
    DO(cardPipSet, Point*, p)
        gotoxy0(*p);
        putch(pipChar);
    DONE
}
```

Note that the overloaded function **gotoxy0** will accept either two integers or a single point. This makes it easy to position the cursor using the iterator macros of the DiskTutor class library.

Program P13-15 creates pip sets for cards of ranks five and seven. It then draws a five of hearts and a seven of spades on the screen using the **drawPips** function.

P13-15

```
#include "point.h"
#include "rect.h"
#include "set.h"
#include <conio.h>

const cardWidth=11;
const cardHeight=7;
enum { left=2, middle=5, right=8 };
enum
{
    heartChar='\x03',
    diamondChar='\x04',
    clubChar='\x05',
```

```
    spadeChar='\x06'
};

////////////////////////////////////////////////////////////
// video support routines
////////////////////////////////////////////////////////////
void window0(int x, int y, int w, int h)
{
    window(x+1, y+1, x+w, y+h);
}

void gotoxy0(int x, int y)
{
    gotoxy(x+1, y+1);
}

void gotoxy0(Point& p)
{
    gotoxy0(p.x(), p.y());
}

enum Frame
{
    TopLeft=218,    Top=196,   TopRight=191,
    Left=179,                  Right=179,
    BottomLeft=192, Bottom=196, BottomRight=217
};

void drawFrame(int x, int y, int w, int h)
{
    // top
    gotoxy0(x,y);
    putch(TopLeft);
    for (int i=0; i<w-2; i++)
        putch(Top);
    putch(TopRight);

    // right
    for (i=0; i<h-2; i++)
    {
        gotoxy0(x+w-1,y+i+1);
        putch(Right);
    }

    // bottom
    gotoxy0(x,y+h-1);
    putch(BottomLeft);
    for (i=0; i<w-2; i++)
        putch(Bottom);
    putch(BottomRight);

    // left
```

```
    for (i=0; i<h-2; i++)
    {
        gotoxy0(x,y+i+1);
        putch(Left);
    }
}

void drawPips(Set &cardPipSet, char pipChar)
{
    DO(cardPipSet, Point*, p)
        gotoxy0(*p);
        putch(pipChar);
    DONE
}

main()
{
    textattr('\x71');     // blue on grey
    clrscr();
    Rectangle r(0,0,cardWidth,cardHeight);

    Set pips5;       // pip set for 5
    Set pips7;       // pip set for 7
    // ==== add points to pip set for 5 ====
    pips5.add(*new Point(left,1));
    pips5.add(*new Point(left,5));

    pips5.add(*new Point(middle,3));

    pips5.add(*new Point(right,1));
    pips5.add(*new Point(right,5));

    // ==== add points to pip set for 7 ====
    pips7.add(*new Point(left,1));
    pips7.add(*new Point(left,3));
    pips7.add(*new Point(left,5));

    pips7.add(*new Point(middle,3));

    pips7.add(*new Point(right,1));
    pips7.add(*new Point(right,3));
    pips7.add(*new Point(right,5));

    int x=10;    // position for card 1
    int y=2;
    textattr(YELLOW + (RED<<4));
    window0(x,y,r.width(),r.height());
    clrscr();
    window0(x,y,r.width(),r.height()+1); // adjust for scroll
    drawFrame(0,0,r.width(),r.height());
    drawPips(pips5, heartChar);

    x=40;        // new position for card 2
```

```
    textattr(YELLOW + (BLUE<<4));
    window0(x,y,r.width(),r.height());
    clrscr();
    window0(x,y,r.width(),r.height()+1) // adjust for scroll
    drawFrame(0,0,r.width(),r.height());
    drawPips(pips7, spadeChar);

    window0(0,0,79,24);  // reset output to full screen
    gotoxy0(0,20);
    getch();
}
```

Load and run the program now. The result is shown in Figure 13-4. The output keeps getting better.

Card Names as Ordered Collections of Strings

Now you need a way to associate a card name with a rank. Strings make a good choice for this. There are other possibilities, but the main issue

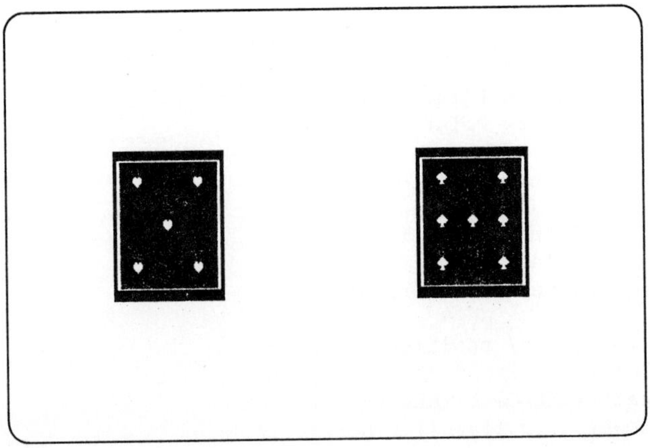

Figure 13-4. *Output for Program P13-15*

with card names is that the order of retrieval must match the rank number. Sets cannot be used, because sets do not guarantee the order of a collection. If you execute the statement,

```
cout << cardNames[13];
```

you want the output to be "King" and not some random element from **cardNames**. This restriction did not apply to pips, because the order in which pips are drawn does not matter. Creating an ordered collection of card names is straightforward.

```
OrderedCltn cardNames;
cardNames.add(*nil);
cardNames.add(*new String("1"));
cardNames.add(*new String("2"));
cardNames.add(*new String("3"));
cardNames.add(*new String("4"));
cardNames.add(*new String("5"));
cardNames.add(*new String("6"));
cardNames.add(*new String("7"));
cardNames.add(*new String("8"));
cardNames.add(*new String("9"));
cardNames.add(*new String("10"));
cardNames.add(*new String("Jack"));
cardNames.add(*new String("Queen"));
cardNames.add(*new String("King"));
```

Ordered collections provide an access operator, **operator[](int)**, which returns a pointer to an object. All collections also provide a **size** method, which returns the number of elements currently in the collection. Together, these two methods provide an alternative to iterators for processing the elements of an ordered collection.

```
cout << "cardNames.size()==>"
     << cardNames.size()
     << "\n";
// Access is possible without an iterator
for (int i=0; i<cardNames.size(); i++)
{
     cout << "cardNames[" << i << "] ==>"
          << *cardNames[i]
          << "\n";
}
```

Since cards are ranked from one to thirteen, it makes sense to put the first card name in **cardNames[1]**. This is achieved by adding the object ***nil** first.

```
//...
cardNames.add(*nil);
cardNames.add(*new String("1"));
//...
```

The DiskTutor class library defines a single **Nil** object, which is a global instance variable. **Nil** signifies nothing, or no object, and is used in the context of an empty array element or an object pointer which is undefined. A global pointer, **nil** (lowercase n) is provided to point to **Nil** (uppercase N). The expression ***nil** returns the **Nil** object. Any object pointer that has an unspecified value should be set to **nil**. In this example, the reference

```
cardNames[0]
```

would return the **Nil** object. The **Nil** object can be referenced, but it should never be created with **new** or destroyed with **delete**.

Program P13-16 creates a collection of card names and uses this collection to add the card names to the two cards drawn in Program P13-15.

P13-16

```
#include "point.h"
#include "rect.h"
#include "set.h"
#include "ordcltn.h"
#include "strclass.h"
#include <conio.h>

const cardWidth=11;
const cardHeight=7;
enum { left=2, middle=5, right=8 };
enum
{
    heartChar='\x03',
    diamondChar='\x04',
    clubChar='\x05',
    spadeChar='\x06'
};

/////////////////////////////////////////////////////////////////
// video support routines
/////////////////////////////////////////////////////////////////
void window0(int x, int y, int w, int h)
```

```
{
    window(x+1, y+1, x+w, y+h);
}

void gotoxy0(int x, int y)
{
    gotoxy(x+1, y+1);
}

void gotoxy0(Point& p)
{
    gotoxy0(p.x(), p.y());
}

enum Frame
{
    TopLeft=218,    Top=196,    TopRight=191,
    Left=179,                   Right=179,
    BottomLeft=192, Bottom=196, BottomRight=217
};

void drawFrame(int x, int y, int w, int h)
{
    // top
    gotoxy0(x,y);
    putch(TopLeft);
    for (int i=0; i<w-2; i++)
        putch(Top);
    putch(TopRight);

    // right
    for (i=0; i<h-2; i++)
    {
        gotoxy0(x+w-1,y+i+1);
        putch(Right);
    }

    // bottom
    gotoxy0(x,y+h-1);
    putch(BottomLeft);
    for (i=0; i<w-2; i++)
        putch(Bottom);
    putch(BottomRight);

    // left
    for (i=0; i<h-2; i++)
    {
        gotoxy0(x,y+i+1);
        putch(Left);
    }
}
```

```
void drawPips(Set &cardPipSet, char pipChar, String& nameString)
{
    DO(cardPipSet, Point*, p)
        gotoxy0(*p);
        putch(pipChar);
    DONE
    gotoxy0((cardWidth-1)-nameString.size(), 0);
    cprintf(nameString);
    putch(pipChar);
    gotoxy0(0, (cardHeight-1));
    putch(pipChar);
    cprintf(nameString);
}

main()
{
    while(kbhit()) getch();  // eat pending keypresses
    OrderedCltn cardNames;
    cardNames.add(*nil);
    cardNames.add(*new String("1"));
    cardNames.add(*new String("2"));
    cardNames.add(*new String("3"));
    cardNames.add(*new String("4"));
    cardNames.add(*new String("5"));
    cardNames.add(*new String("6"));
    cardNames.add(*new String("7"));
    cardNames.add(*new String("8"));
    cardNames.add(*new String("9"));
    cardNames.add(*new String("10"));
    cardNames.add(*new String("Jack"));
    cardNames.add(*new String("Queen"));
    cardNames.add(*new String("King"));

    cout << "cardNames.size()==>"
         << cardNames.size()
         << "\n";
    // Access is possible without an iterator
    for (int i=0; i<cardNames.size(); i++)
    {
     cout << "cardNames[" << i << "] ==>"
             << *cardNames[i]
             << "\n";
    }
    getch();

    textattr('\x71');     // blue on grey
    clrscr();
    Rectangle r(0,0,cardWidth,cardHeight);

    Set pips5;       // pip set for 5
    Set pips7;       // pip set for 7
```

```
    // ==== add points to pip set for 5 ====
    pips5.add(*new Point(left,1));
    pips5.add(*new Point(left,5));

    pips5.add(*new Point(middle,3));

    pips5.add(*new Point(right,1));
    pips5.add(*new Point(right,5));

    // ==== add points to pip set for 7 ====
    pips7.add(*new Point(left,1));
    pips7.add(*new Point(left,3));
    pips7.add(*new Point(left,5));

    pips7.add(*new Point(middle,3));

    pips7.add(*new Point(right,1));
    pips7.add(*new Point(right,3));
    pips7.add(*new Point(right,5));

    int x=10;    // position for card 1
    int y=2;
    textattr(YELLOW + (RED<<4));
    window0(x,y,r.width(),r.height());
    clrscr();
    window0(x,y,r.width(),r.height()+1); // adjust for scroll
    drawFrame(0,0,r.width(),r.height());
    drawPips(pips5, heartChar, *(String*)cardNames[5]);

    x=40;        // new position for card 2
    textattr(YELLOW + (BLUE<<4));
    window0(x,y,r.width(),r.height());
    clrscr();
    window0(x,y,r.width(),r.height()+1); // adjust for scroll
    drawFrame(0,0,r.width(),r.height());
    drawPips(pips7, spadeChar, *(String*)cardNames[7]);

    window0(0,0,79,24);    // reset output to full screen
    gotoxy0(0,20);
    getch();
}
```

The **drawPips** function has been modified to accept a third argument, a string representing the card name.

```
void drawPips(Set &cardPipSet, char pipChar, String& nameString)
{
    DO(cardPipSet, Point*, p)
        gotoxy0(*p);
        putch(pipChar);
```

```
    DONE
    gotoxy0((cardWidth-1)-nameString.size(), 0);
    cprintf(nameString);
    putch(pipChar);
    gotoxy0(0, (cardHeight-1));
    putch(pipChar);
    cprintf(nameString);
}
```

All the code that follows DONE is also new. This code prints extra pips in the upper-right and lower-left corners of the card, and prints the card name string in both these locations as well. Load the program now.

When you first compile and run the program, the size of the **cardNames** collection is printed, followed by each element of the collection.

```
cardNames.size()==>14
cardNames[0] ==>NIL
cardNames[1] ==>1
cardNames[2] ==>2
cardNames[3] ==>3
cardNames[4] ==>4
cardNames[5] ==>5
cardNames[6] ==>6
cardNames[7] ==>7
cardNames[8] ==>8
cardNames[9] ==>9
cardNames[10] ==>10
cardNames[11] ==>Jack
cardNames[12] ==>Queen
cardNames[13] ==>King
```

Note that the **nil** object automatically knows how to print itself in an output stream. Press any key at this point, and as shown in Figure 13-5, you will see the same two cards as in the last program. Now, however, the string names appear to indicate the card names.

Playing with a Full Deck

The CARDPIPS.CPP program found on your disk will draw all 52 cards in a typical deck. It does this through a new class called **CardPainter**. The declaration for this class can be found in DRWCRD.H. Create a project file, CARDPIPS.PRJ.

Add the following files to the project:

CARDPIPS.CPP
DRWCRD1.CPP
DRWCRD2.CPP
DT.LIB

When you compile the program, the project manager automatically keeps track of all files associated with the project, including header files. This makes it easy to browse through all files required to build a project.

Compile the program now. Before running the program, let's examine some of the source files. Make sure the highlight bar in the project window is on CARDPIPS.CPP. You can load header files by opening the Project Manager menu and selecting Include files (ALT-P I). When the list of header files appears, select DRWCRD.H, either by double clicking on it with the mouse or by moving the highlight bar to the entry and pressing RETURN. The DRWCRD.H file is shown here.

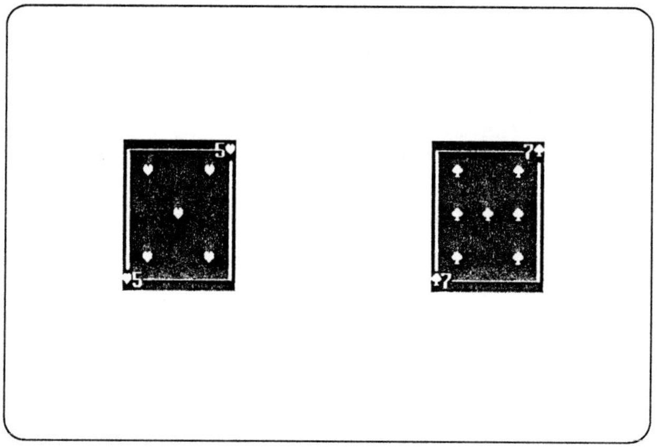

Figure 13-5. *Output for Program P13-16*

```
FILE DRWCRD.H

#ifndef DRWCRD_H
#define DRWCRD_H

const cardsInSuit = 13;
const cardWidth=11;
const cardHeight=7;

class ArrayOb;
class Rectangle;
class Set;
class String;
//////////////////////////////////////////////////////////////
// class CardPainter (declaration)
//////////////////////////////////////////////////////////////
class CardPainter
{
public:
    // class constants
    enum { spade, heart, club, diamond };
    enum { left=2, middle=5, right=8 };
    enum
    {
        heartChar='\x03', diamondChar='\x04',
        clubChar='\x05',  spadeChar='\x06'
    };
private:
    ArrayOb& v;                    // array of Objects
    Rectangle& r;                  // bounding box
    char suitChar(int aSuit);
public:
    CardPainter();
    void print();
    Set& pipSet(int i);
    String& symbol(int i);
    void drwcrd(int x, int y,
                  int rank, int suit, int faceUp=1);
};

//////////////////////////////////////////////////////////////
// Only one instance of CardPainter should
// be declared for a given application.
//////////////////////////////////////////////////////////////
extern CardPainter aCardPainter;

void drawCard(int x, int y, int rank, int suit, int faceUp=1);

//////////////////////////////////////////////////////////////
// video support routines
//////////////////////////////////////////////////////////////
```

```
void window0(int x, int y, int w, int h);
void gotoxy0(int x, int y);
class Point;
void gotoxy0(Point& p);
void drawFrame(int x, int y, int w, int h);
#endif
```

Some interesting tricks appear in the declaration for the **CardPainter** class. For instance, all the enumerations that were formerly global are now public members of the class.

```
class CardPainter
{
public:
    // class constants
    enum { spade, heart, club, diamond };
    enum { left=2, middle=5, right=8 };
    enum
    {
        heartChar='\x03', diamondChar='\x04',
        clubChar='\x05',  spadeChar='\x06'
    };
    //...
};
```

This changes the scope of the enumerations so that they don't conflict with any symbols having the same names that might appear in other files. Any program that includes this file as a header can have access to these enumerations by using the scope resolution operator.

```
if (suit == CardPainter::spade)
    //...
```

Two private variables are used to represent card dimensions, pip sets, and card names.

```
private:
    ArrayOb& v;                  // array of Objects
    Rectangle& r;                // bounding box
```

The array **v** introduces a new type, **ArrayOb**. **ArrayOb** is used to declare an array of pointers to objects. An array is a fixed-size collection.

If you are going to represent pip sets as collections, you need to bundle all of these collections somehow. A fixed-size array is convenient because there will always be 13 cards and 13 sets of pips. If the size of **v** is set to 13, then each pointer in the array can be set to point to one pip set.

It would also be nice to start the array index at one rather than at zero, as was done with the collection of card-name strings. Rather than wasting the contents of **v[0]** by setting it to nil, why not set **v[0]** to hold an ordered collection of card names? You are really exercising polymorphism here by dealing with arrays, ordered collections, sets, points, and strings; these are all contained inside one object, **v**. The array **v** is a polymorphic array whose first element, **v[0]**, is an ordered collection of strings. The rest of the elements of **v**, **v[1-13]**, are sets of points representing pip locations. You will see how all of this is set up when you examine the constructor declared in DRWCRD1.CPP.

But first let's take a look at the methods available in **CardPainter**. Here is a list:

```
private:
    char suitChar(int aSuit);
public:
    CardPainter();
    void print();
    Set& pipSet(int i);
    String& symbol(int i);
    void drawCard(int x, int y,
                  int rank, int suit, int faceUp=1);
```

The private method **suitChar** converts from an enumerated suit type (spade, heart, club, or diamond) to the IBM PC character used to print the pip for the corresponding suit. This method is private because it is only used by other methods of class **CardPainter**. The constructor for **CardPainter** takes no arguments. The print method is used for diagnostics to see the collection of names and pip sets. The **pipSet** method will return a set of pips corresponding to a rank number, which is given as an argument. The **symbol** method returns a string representing the card name given a card rank.

The last method, **drawCard**, does all the work. It will draw a card of specified rank and suit at the indicated position. It automatically determines the correct color, draws a frame and a pip set, and prints a name appropriate for the card. The last argument for this function is given a default value. Most cards will be face up. However, in the case of a blackjack game or a poker game, certain cards will be dealt face down. If this is desired, a zero value can be given for the last argument. The card will then be drawn with a light blue background and a blue frame. No card name or pips will be printed on the card.

Let's look at how the constructor sets up the array of card names and pip sets. Open the project window (ALT-W P) and select the file DRWCRD1.CPP, either by double clicking with the mouse or by highlighting the entry and pressing RETURN. The DRWCRD1.CPP file is shown here.

```
FILE DRWCRD1.CPP

#include "drwcrd.h"
#include "point.h"
#include "rect.h"
#include "set.h"
#include "ordcltn.h"
#include "arrayob.h"
#include "strclass.h"

///////////////////////////////////////////////////////////////
// CardPainter constructor
//     creates all subcollections
//     contained by Object array v
//
//     v[0]      Contains a collection of
//               strings representing the
//               names of each of the cards.
//               v[0] is an OrderedCltn because
//               the order in which the Strings
//               are stored matters since the
//               order provides a way to look
//               up the string by a rank number.
//
//     v[1-13]   Each of these collections contains
//               a set of points indicating the position
//               of pips to be drawn on a card. The order
//               of retrieval does not matter so these
//               collections are implemented as Sets.
//               It doesn't matter what order the pips are
//               drawn in, as long as every member of the
//               set is drawn.
///////////////////////////////////////////////////////////////
CardPainter::CardPainter()
: v(*new ArrayOb(cardsInSuit+1)),
  r(*new Rectangle(0,0,cardWidth,cardHeight))
```

```
{
    int i=0;
    v[i] = new OrderedCltn();
    ((Collection*)v[i])->add(*nil);
    ((Collection*)v[i])->add(*new String("1"));
    ((Collection*)v[i])->add(*new String("2"));
    ((Collection*)v[i])->add(*new String("3"));
    ((Collection*)v[i])->add(*new String("4"));
    ((Collection*)v[i])->add(*new String("5"));
    ((Collection*)v[i])->add(*new String("6"));
    ((Collection*)v[i])->add(*new String("7"));
    ((Collection*)v[i])->add(*new String("8"));
    ((Collection*)v[i])->add(*new String("9"));
    ((Collection*)v[i])->add(*new String("10"));
    ((Collection*)v[i])->add(*new String("Jack"));
    ((Collection*)v[i])->add(*new String("Queen"));
    ((Collection*)v[i])->add(*new String("King"));

    for (i=1; i<=cardsInSuit; i++)
        v[i] = new Set;
    // ==== ace ====
    i = 1;
    ((Collection*)v[i])->add(*new Point(middle,3));
    // ==== 2 ====
    i = 2;
    ((Collection*)v[i])->add(*new Point(left,1));
    ((Collection*)v[i])->add(*new Point(right,5));
    // ==== 3 ====
    i = 3;
    ((Collection*)v[i])->add(*new Point(left,1));
    ((Collection*)v[i])->add(*new Point(middle,3));
    ((Collection*)v[i])->add(*new Point(right,5));
    // ==== 4 ====
    i = 4;
    ((Collection*)v[i])->add(*new Point(left,1));
    ((Collection*)v[i])->add(*new Point(left,5));

    ((Collection*)v[i])->add(*new Point(right,1));
    ((Collection*)v[i])->add(*new Point(right,5));

    // ==== 5 ====
    i = 5;
    ((Collection*)v[i])->add(*new Point(left,1));
    ((Collection*)v[i])->add(*new Point(left,5));

    ((Collection*)v[i])->add(*new Point(middle,3));

    ((Collection*)v[i])->add(*new Point(right,1));
    ((Collection*)v[i])->add(*new Point(right,5));

    // ==== 6 ====
    i = 6;
```

```
((Collection*)v[i])->add(*new Point(left,1));
((Collection*)v[i])->add(*new Point(left,3));
((Collection*)v[i])->add(*new Point(left,5));

((Collection*)v[i])->add(*new Point(right,1));
((Collection*)v[i])->add(*new Point(right,3));
((Collection*)v[i])->add(*new Point(right,5));

// ==== 7 ====
i = 7;
((Collection*)v[i])->add(*new Point(left,1));
((Collection*)v[i])->add(*new Point(left,3));
((Collection*)v[i])->add(*new Point(left,5));

((Collection*)v[i])->add(*new Point(middle,3));

((Collection*)v[i])->add(*new Point(right,1));
((Collection*)v[i])->add(*new Point(right,3));
((Collection*)v[i])->add(*new Point(right,5));

// ==== 8 ====
i = 8;
((Collection*)v[i])->add(*new Point(left,1));
((Collection*)v[i])->add(*new Point(left,3));
((Collection*)v[i])->add(*new Point(left,5));

((Collection*)v[i])->add(*new Point(middle,2));
((Collection*)v[i])->add(*new Point(middle,4));

((Collection*)v[i])->add(*new Point(right,1));
((Collection*)v[i])->add(*new Point(right,3));
((Collection*)v[i])->add(*new Point(right,5));

// ==== 9 ====
i = 9;
((Collection*)v[i])->add(*new Point(left,1));
((Collection*)v[i])->add(*new Point(left,3));
((Collection*)v[i])->add(*new Point(left,5));

((Collection*)v[i])->add(*new Point(middle,1));
((Collection*)v[i])->add(*new Point(middle,3));
((Collection*)v[i])->add(*new Point(middle,5));

((Collection*)v[i])->add(*new Point(right,1));
((Collection*)v[i])->add(*new Point(right,3));
((Collection*)v[i])->add(*new Point(right,5));

// ==== 10 ====
i = 10;
((Collection*)v[i])->add(*new Point(left,1));
((Collection*)v[i])->add(*new Point(left,2));
((Collection*)v[i])->add(*new Point(left,3));
```

```
    ((Collection*)v[i])->add(*new Point(left,4));
    ((Collection*)v[i])->add(*new Point(left,5));

    ((Collection*)v[i])->add(*new Point(right,1));
    ((Collection*)v[i])->add(*new Point(right,2));
    ((Collection*)v[i])->add(*new Point(right,3));
    ((Collection*)v[i])->add(*new Point(right,4));
    ((Collection*)v[i])->add(*new Point(right,5));

    // ==== 11 J ====
    i = 11;
    ((Collection*)v[i])->add(*new Point(middle,3));

    // ==== 12 Q ====
    i = 12;
    ((Collection*)v[i])->add(*new Point(middle,3));

    // ==== 13 K ====
    i = 13;
    ((Collection*)v[i])->add(*new Point(middle,3));
}
```

This is a long file, but it only does two things, both of which are handled by the constructor for **CardPainter**. First, two expressions are evaluated in the constructor initializer.

```
CardPainter::CardPainter()
: v(*new ArrayOb(cardsInSuit+1)),
  r(*new Rectangle(0,0,cardWidth,cardHeight))
{
```

The first initializer sets **v** to reference a new object array, which is large enough to hold 13 pip sets and one collection of card names. The second initializer sets a rectangle, which is used to obtain dimensions for a card. Setting up the collection of card names is a little different from what you might expect.

```
int i=0;
v[i] = new OrderedCltn();
((Collection*)v[i])->add(*nil);
((Collection*)v[i])->add(*new String("1"));
((Collection*)v[i])->add(*new String("2"));
((Collection*)v[i])->add(*new String("3"));
((Collection*)v[i])->add(*new String("4"));
((Collection*)v[i])->add(*new String("5"));
((Collection*)v[i])->add(*new String("6"));
```

```
((Collection*)v[i])->add(*new String("7"));
((Collection*)v[i])->add(*new String("8"));
((Collection*)v[i])->add(*new String("9"));
((Collection*)v[i])->add(*new String("10"));
((Collection*)v[i])->add(*new String("Jack"));
((Collection*)v[i])->add(*new String("Queen"));
((Collection*)v[i])->add(*new String("King"));
```

First, an index value, **i**, is set to reference **v[0]**. The next statement creates a new ordered collection and sets **v[0]** to point to that collection.

```
v[i] = new OrderedCltn();
```

This collection will eventually contain the card names. The unexpected twist is that each time **v[i]** is referenced, it is cast as a pointer to a **Collection** rather than an **OrderedCltn**. **Collection** is a super class of **OrderedCltn**. Furthermore, a **Collection** can always determine its type through the **isA** method provided for all objects. Only **Collection** objects have **add** methods. Objects like **Point**, **Rectangle**, and **String** do not. If **v[i]** is not cast as a **Collection**, then it returns a pointer to an **Object** and no add method is defined for **Object**. Thus, a statement like

```
v[i]->add(*new String("1"));
```

would produce a compiler error. It would be equally correct in this particular situation to cast **v[i]** as a pointer to a set.

```
((Set*)v[i])->add(*new String("1"));
```

However, the **Collection** class is the most general container class and encompasses all forms of collections. Casting **v[i]** as a collection allows a consistent way of representing addition of all different types of collections to the array **v**. That way, if you later change the type of class used to represent pips or card names, you don't have to change all the references to **v[i]**. Here is a hierarchy of the collection classes provided by DiskTutor:

```
Collection
    Bag
    Set
    SeqCltn     (sequenceable collection)
```

```
LinkedList
OrderedCltn
   SortedCltn
Stack
Queue
```

A similar technique is used to add collections of pips to the object array.

```
// ==== 3 ====
i = 3;
((Collection*)v[i])->add(*new Point(left,1));
((Collection*)v[i])->add(*new Point(middle,3));
((Collection*)v[i])->add(*new Point(right,5));
```

It is only necessary to show one example since all the others effectively do the same thing. This covers all code included in the constructor and in file DRWCRD1.CPP.

Rather than concerning yourself with all the definitions for the various methods, simply note that the methods other than the constructor appear in DRWCRD2.CPP. All the code in DRWCRD1.CPP and DRWCRD2.CPP could just as easily have been included in a single file. However, because of the size of the constructor, the code was broken up. Once files get larger than one or two hundred lines, it is a good idea to break them up. This will speed up compile time by minimizing the amount of code that has to be recompiled when functions are modified. A listing of file DRWCRD2.CPP is provided here for your reference. However, it is not important to understand all the details in order to use a **CardPainter** object.

```
FILE DRWCRD2.CPP

#include "drwcrd.h"
#include "point.h"
#include "rect.h"
#include "set.h"
#include "ordcltn.h"
#include "arrayob.h"
#include "strclass.h"
#include <conio.h>

/////////////////////////////////////////////////////////////////
// video support routines
/////////////////////////////////////////////////////////////////
void window0(int x, int y, int w, int h)
```

```
{
    window(x+1, y+1, x+w, y+h);
}

void gotoxy0(int x, int y)
{
    gotoxy(x+1, y+1);
}

void gotoxy0(Point& p)
{
    gotoxy0(p.x(), p.y());
}

enum Frame
{
    TopLeft=218,    Top=196,    TopRight=191,
    Left=179,                   Right=179,
    BottomLeft=192, Bottom=196, BottomRight=217
};

void drawFrame(int x, int y, int w, int h)
{
    // top
    gotoxy0(x,y);
    putch(TopLeft);
    for (int i=0; i<w-2; i++)
        putch(Top);
    putch(TopRight);

    // right
    for (i=0; i<h-2; i++)
    {
        gotoxy0(x+w-1,y+i+1);
        putch(Right);
    }

    // bottom
    gotoxy0(x,y+h-1);
    putch(BottomLeft);
    for (i=0; i<w-2; i++)
        putch(Bottom);
    putch(BottomRight);

    // left
    for (i=0; i<h-2; i++)
    {
        gotoxy0(x,y+i+1);
        putch(Left);
    }
}
```

```
//////////////////////////////////////////////////////////////
// class CardPainter (definition)
//////////////////////////////////////////////////////////////
char CardPainter::suitChar(int aSuit)
{
    switch(aSuit)
    {
        case spade   : return spadeChar;
        case heart   : return heartChar;
        case club    : return clubChar;
        case diamond : return diamondChar;
    }
}

String& CardPainter::symbol(int i)
{
    OrderedCltn* p = (OrderedCltn*)v[0];
    return *(String*)(p->at(i));
}

Set& CardPainter::pipSet(int i)
{
    if (v[i]->isKindOf(class_Set))
        return *((Set*)v[i]);
    else
        return (Set&)nil;
}

void CardPainter::print()
{
    cout << "==== CardPainter::print ==\\/==\n";
    for (int i=0; i<=cardsInSuit; i++)
    {
        cout << "v[" << i << "]: ";
        cout << (*v[i]);
        getch();
    }
    cout << "==== CardPainter::print ==/\\==\n";
}

void CardPainter::drawCard(int x, int y,
                       int rank, int suit, int faceUp)
{
    Set& cardPipSet = pipSet(rank);
    String& nameString = symbol(rank);
    char pipChar = suitChar(suit);

    textattr(BLUE + (CYAN<<4));  // color for face down
    if (faceUp)
    {
```

```
        switch(suit)
        {
        case heart   :
        case diamond :  textattr(YELLOW + (RED<<4));  break;
        case spade   :
        case club    :  textattr(YELLOW + (BLUE<<4)); break;
        default      :  cout << "illegal suit";
                        getch();
                        cout << "\n";
                        return;
        }
    }
    window0(x,y,r.width(),r.height());
    clrscr();
    window0(x,y, r.width(),r.height()+1);
    drawFrame(0,0,r.width(),r.height());
    if (faceUp)
    {
        DO(cardPipSet, Point*, p)
            gotoxy0(*p);
            putch(pipChar);
        DONE
        gotoxy0(r.corner().x()-nameString.size(), 0);
        cprintf(nameString);
        putch(pipChar);
        gotoxy0(0, r.corner().y());
        putch(pipChar);
        cprintf(nameString);
    }
    window0(0,0,80,25);
}

/////////////////////////////////////////////////////////////
// Only one instance of CardPainter should
// be declared for a given application.
/////////////////////////////////////////////////////////////
CardPainter aCardPainter;

/////////////////////////////////////////////////////////////
// Public interface to aCardPainter.
// There are times when it makes more sense
// to present the user with a function
// than with an object.
/////////////////////////////////////////////////////////////
void drawCard(int x, int y, int rank, int suit, int faceUp)
{
    aCardPainter.drawCard(x,y,rank,suit, faceUp);
}
```

Let's pay attention now to the main program. Go back to the project manager and open the file CARDPIPS.CPP.

```
FILE CARDPIPS.CPP

#include "drwcrd.h"
#include <conio.h>
#include <dos.h>        // for delay

main()
{
    cputs("hello, world\r\n");
    aCardPainter.print();
    cputs("Press any key for part 2");
    getch();

    textattr('\x71');
    clrscr();
    textattr('\x31');

    while(1)
    {
        textattr('\x31');
        clrscr();
        for (int rank=1; rank<=cardsInSuit; rank++)
            for (int suit=CardPainter::spade;
                 suit<=CardPainter::diamond;
                 suit++)
            {
                int x = suit*(cardWidth+8)+rank-1;
                int y = rank;
                drawCard(x,y,rank,suit);
                delay(150);
                if (kbhit())    // exit on keypress
                {
                    getch();    // eat the key
                    goto end;   // rules are made to be broken
                }
            }
    }
end:                            // label for goto statement
    gotoxy0(0,20);
}
```

All the hard work for the program was done in setting up the **CardPainter** class. Using the class is actually pretty easy. Whenever the DRWCRD files are included in a project, a global variable is automatically created called **aCardPainter**. You don't need to use this object unless you want to use the diagnostic print function, which prints out the contents of the private instance variable **v**. A global function, **drawCard**, is provided so that you don't need to know about the **CardPainter** class to draw playing cards. However, if you want diagnostics, you could use **aCardPainter**.

```
aCardPainter.print();
```

The output produced by this simple statement is pretty long. It prints each of the 14 elements of **v**, one at a time, and waits for a keypress between each element. The contents of the entire array look like this when the program is run:

```
==== CardPainter::print ==\/==
v[0]: OrderedCltn[
NIL
1
2
3
4
5
6
7
8
9
10
Jack
Queen
King]
v[1]: Set[
(5 @ 3)]
v[2]: Set[
(8 @ 5)
(2 @ 1)]
v[3]: Set[
(8 @ 5)
(2 @ 1)
(5 @ 3)]
v[4]: Set[
(8 @ 5)
(8 @ 1)
(2 @ 5)
(2 @ 1)]
v[5]: Set[
(8 @ 5)
(8 @ 1)
(2 @ 5)
```

```
(2 @ 1)
(5 @ 3)]
v[6]: Set[
(8 @ 5)
(8 @ 3)
(8 @ 1)
(2 @ 5)
(2 @ 1)
(2 @ 3)]
v[7]: Set[
(8 @ 5)
(8 @ 3)
(8 @ 1)
(2 @ 5)
(2 @ 1)
(2 @ 3)
(5 @ 3)]
v[8]: Set[
(8 @ 5)
(8 @ 3)
(8 @ 1)
(5 @ 4)
(5 @ 2)
(2 @ 5)
(2 @ 1)
(2 @ 3)]
v[9]: Set[
(5 @ 5)
(8 @ 5)
(8 @ 3)
(8 @ 1)
(2 @ 5)
(2 @ 1)
(2 @ 3)
(5 @ 3)
(5 @ 1)]
v[10]: Set[
(2 @ 2)
(8 @ 5)
(8 @ 3)
(8 @ 1)
(2 @ 5)
(2 @ 1)
(2 @ 3)
(8 @ 4)
(8 @ 2)
(2 @ 4)]
v[11]: Set[
(5 @ 3)]
v[12]: Set[
```

```
(5 @ 3)]
v[13]: Set[
(5 @ 3)]
==== CardPainter::print ==/\==
```

The main processing in CARDPIPS.CPP is done entirely inside the **while** loop. On each pass through the loop, the screen is cleared. Then two **for** loops are used to print every card in the deck. The outer loop controls the rank. The inner loop controls the suit.

```
for (int rank=1; rank<=cardsInSuit; rank++)
    for (int suit=CardPainter::spade;
         suit<=CardPainter::diamond;
         suit++)
    {
        //...
    }
```

This has the effect of printing the ace for each suit followed by the deuce for each suit, and so on until the entire deck is printed. A global function is used to draw each card.

```
drawCard(x,y,rank,suit);
```

This function is declared inside DRWCRD.H. The function knows about the global variable **aCardPainter** and uses **CardPainter**'s **drawCard** method. Sometimes it makes more sense to present the user with a global function than a global object. It might be more natural to think of drawing a card as a function. Either way is correct. It is simply a matter of preference. Since a typical program will use only one method in the **CardPainter** class, it might be easier on the user to eliminate any need to know about the object or the class.

Run the program now. First you will see the contents of the object array as listed by the **CardPainter::print** method. You will have to press a key to see each new array element. After 13 keypresses, the program enters a **while** loop and draws the entire deck of cards. After the deck is drawn, program control passes back to the top of the **while** loop. The screen is then cleared and the deck of cards is printed again, as shown in Figure 13-6.

Figure 13-6. *Output for CARDPIPS program*

You may have noticed that the infamous **goto** statement has crept into this program. There are actually times when a **goto** statement provides a very clean control framework. Exiting from two loops at once is an example. A **break** statement would only exit from the inner loop. If a **goto** statement were not used to pass control to the statement following the **end**: label, some sort of variable would have to be introduced to control the main **while** loop.

```
int more=1;
while(more)
{
    //...
}
```

The reader would then have to look for all the statements that change the value of **more**, in order to follow control flow. In this case, **goto** provides a simple and direct way to break out of the program without delay.

Simulating Card Games

Drawing cards is only half the game. You still need to simulate the process of playing; and even before you do that, you need to figure out how to represent a card, a card deck, and a card hand. The next example program is built from four files. Close the CARDPIPS project and create a project file called CARDGAME.PRJ now.

Add the following files to the project:

CARDGAME.CPP
SAMPLE.CPP
CARD.CPP
DT.LIB

The header files are not listed in the project list. You have two choices when following along here. You can compile the program, in which case the Borland C++ IDE will create a list of all header files used to create the project. Once this list exists, you can use the **P**roject/**I**nclude menu selection to open header files. Alternatively, you can explicitly open the header files with the **F**ile/**O**pen command.

Open CARD.H. Declarations for the three classes—**Card**, **CardDeck**, and **CardHand**—are found in this file. The CARD.H file is shown here.

```
FILE CARD.H

#include "ordcltn.h"

enum Suit { spade, heart, club, diamond };
enum {faceUp, faceDown};
/////////////////////////////////////////////////////////////
// class Card (declaration)
/////////////////////////////////////////////////////////////
class Card : public Object
{
    Suit    cardSuit;
    int     cardRank;
    int     facing;
public:
    Card(Suit suit, int rank, int isFacing = faceUp)
    { cardSuit = suit; cardRank = rank; facing = isFacing; }
    Suit suit() { return cardSuit; }
    int rank() { return  cardRank; }
    int face() { return facing; }
    void face(int isFacing) { facing = isFacing; }
    bool operator==(Card c);

    // override virtual functions declared in Object
```

```
    virtual bool isEqual(const Object&);
    virtual const Class* isA();
    void printOn(ostream& strm);
    virtual unsigned hash();
};

////////////////////////////////////////////////////////////
// class CardDeck (declaration)
////////////////////////////////////////////////////////////
class CardDeck : Object
{
    OrderedCltn *pSuits;
    OrderedCltn *pCards;
public:
    CardDeck();
    Card* next();
    void returnCard(Card& aCard);
    void shuffle();
    bool isEmpty() { return pCards->isEmpty(); }

    // override virtual functions declared in Object
    virtual const Class* isA();
    void printOn(ostream& strm);
    virtual unsigned hash() { return pCards->hash(); }
    virtual unsigned size() { return pCards->size(); }
};

////////////////////////////////////////////////////////////
// class CardHand (declaration)
////////////////////////////////////////////////////////////
class CardHand : public Object
{
    OrderedCltn *pCards;

public:
    CardHand() { pCards = new OrderedCltn; }
    void take(Card& aCard, int isFacing = faceUp);
    void returnAllCardsTo(CardDeck& aCardDeck);
    int points();
    OrderedCltn& asOrderedCltn() { return *pCards; }
    void allFaceUp();

    // override virtual functions declared in Object
    virtual bool isEqual(const Object&);
    virtual const Class* isA();
    void printOn(ostream& strm) { strm << *pCards; }
    virtual unsigned hash() { return pCards->hash(); }
};
```

Representing a Card

You can get a pretty good idea of how these classes work by studying the interfaces. A **Card** object is represented internally by three private instance variables:

```
Suit    cardSuit;
int     cardRank;
int     facing;
```

Suit is an enumerated type, which can be a spade, a heart, a club, or a diamond. The variable **facing** should be set to contain one of two values: **faceUp** or **faceDown**. It is easy to guess what the methods do from their names. The constructor creates a card given a suit and a rank. The argument determining whether the card is face up or face down is given a default value of **faceUp**. Therefore, if the third argument is not supplied, the card is considered to be face up.

The methods **suit**, **rank**, and **face** return the values of the respective instance variables. There is also a second overloaded definition for **face** that takes an integer as an argument. The argument should be either **faceUp** or **faceDown** and changes the way a card faces based on the argument. An **operator==** method is provided to compare cards to one another. The most interesting thing about the **Card** class is that it is derived from **Object**.

```
class Card : public Object
```

Object as a Common Polymorphic Base Class

Any object that you want to place in one of the polymorphic collections provided by DiskTutor must ultimately be derived from class **Object**. This is not as big a restriction as it might seem. It is very easy to derive classes from the **Object** class. The only thing that you need do in addition to the inheritance specification is to override several virtual function definitions declared in **Object**.

```
// override virtual functions declared in Object
virtual bool isEqual(const Object&);
virtual const Class* isA();
void printOn(ostream& strm);
virtual unsigned hash();
```

You don't have to override all the definitions—only the ones you plan to use. If the object is going to be placed in a collection, you must provide definitions for **isA** and **hash**. If you also want to print that collection, you need to provide a definition for **printOn**. Other than these methods, you need only override the specific methods required by your object. There are some other steps that must be taken to complete the definitions, but what you see here is all that is required in the header file. The other steps will be covered in the discussion of CARD.CPP.

Representing a Deck

You can see that the declaration for **CardDeck** represents a deck as an ordered collection of suits and an ordered collection of cards. There is a constructor that creates the deck, a method called **next** that returns the card on top of the deck, and a method called **returnCard** that returns the card given to it as an argument to the deck. There is a method called **shuffle** that puts the cards in random order, and another method called **isEmpty** that you can use to see when all cards in the deck have been dealt.

Class **CardDeck** is also derived from **Object**. It declares the required **isA**, **printOn**, and **hash** methods to override the virtual methods found in **Object**. It also overrides the **size** virtual method declared in **Object**. The **size** method can be used to see how many cards are left in the deck.

Representing a Card Hand

The last class is **CardHand**. **CardHand** is represented as an ordered collection of cards. A card is added to the hand with the **take** method. All cards in a hand can be returned to a deck with the **returnAllCardsTo** method. You can see the total number of points in a hand with the

points method and convert a card hand to an ordered collection using **asOrderedCltn**. This is handy if you need to examine the cards one by one or do some special form of printing. When somebody finally calls your bluff, you can turn all cards in a hand face up with the **allFaceUp** method. **CardHand** is also derived from **Object** and overrides the virtual methods **isEqual**, **isA**, **printOn**, and **hash**. As mentioned earlier, **hash** returns a value to help evenly distribute objects inside collections.

Normally, this would be all you need to know to use cards, decks, and hands. Deriving each of these classes from **Object** allows you to create, for example, a collection of hands that could be used to represent a group of players or even a collection of decks for games that require more than one deck of cards. The use of a collection to represent a card deck is also made possible by using **Object** as a base class for **Card**.

You also need to take a look at the file CARD.CPP. The main reason is to see the extra work required for classes derived from **Object**. Load the file now.

```
FILE CARD.CPP

#include "card.h"
#include "sample.h"
#include <stdlib.h>          // for exit
#include <stdio.h>           // for sprintf

/////////////////////////////////////////////////////////////
// class Card (definition)
/////////////////////////////////////////////////////////////
DEFINE_CLASS(Card,Object);

bool Card::operator==(Card c)
{
    return ( cardSuit == c.cardSuit &&
             cardRank == c.cardRank);
}

unsigned Card::hash()
{
    return (unsigned)this;
}

bool Card::isEqual(const Object& c)
{
    return *this==*(Card*)&c;
}
```

```
void Card::printOn(ostream& strm)
{
    switch(cardRank)
    {
        case 1  :   strm << "ace"; break;
        case 11 :   strm << "jack"; break;
        case 12 :   strm << "queen"; break;
        case 13 :   strm << "king"; break;
        default :   strm << cardRank;
    }
    strm << " of ";
    switch (cardSuit)
    {
        case spade   :  strm << "spades"; break;
        case heart   :  strm << "hearts"; break;
        case club    :  strm << "clubs"; break;
        case diamond :  strm << "diamonds"; break;
    }
    //strm << cardSuit << " "  << cardRank;
}

//////////////////////////////////////////////////////////////
// class CardDeck (definition)
//////////////////////////////////////////////////////////////
DEFINE_CLASS(CardDeck,Object);

CardDeck::CardDeck()
{
    pCards = new OrderedCltn(52);
    for (int suit=spade; suit<=diamond; suit++)
        for (int rank=1; rank<=13; rank++)
            pCards->add(*new Card(suit,rank));
}

Card* CardDeck::next()
{
   return (Card*)pCards->remove(*pCards->first());
}

void CardDeck::returnCard(Card& aCard)
{
    pCards->addLast(aCard);
}

void CardDeck::shuffle()
{
    SampleDelete sample(*pCards);
    OrderedCltn *tempDeck = new OrderedCltn(pCards->size());
    for (int i=0; i<pCards->size(); i++)
    {
```

```
        tempDeck->addLast(*sample.next());
    }
    pCards = tempDeck;
}

void CardDeck::printOn(ostream& strm)
{
    strm << *pCards;
}

/////////////////////////////////////////////////////////////
// class CardHand (definition)
/////////////////////////////////////////////////////////////
DEFINE_CLASS(CardHand,Object);

void CardHand::allFaceUp()
{
    DO(*pCards, Card*, pCard)
        pCard->face(faceUp);
    DONE
}

bool CardHand::isEqual(const Object& ob)
{
    return pCards->isEqual( *((CardHand*)&ob)->pCards );
}

void CardHand::take(Card& aCard, int isFacing)
{
    aCard.face(isFacing);
    pCards->add(aCard);
}

void CardHand::returnAllCardsTo(CardDeck& aCardDeck)
{
    DO(*pCards, Card*, pc)
        aCardDeck.returnCard(*pc);
    DONE
    delete(pCards);
    pCards = new OrderedCltn;
}

int CardHand::points()
{
    int ret=0;
    DO(*pCards, Card*, pc)
        ret += (pc->rank() > 10) ? 10 : pc->rank();
    DONE
    return ret;
}
```

Class Class Retains Type Information at Run Time

The most notable difference between this file and others you have seen is the introduction of the DEFINE_CLASS macro.

```
//////////////////////////////////////////////////////////////////
// class Card (definition)
//////////////////////////////////////////////////////////////////
DEFINE_CLASS(Card,Object);
```

One of these macros must be included for every class derived from **Object**. In addition to the declaration for **Card**, there are corresponding declarations for **CardDeck** and **CardHand**.

```
//...
DEFINE_CLASS(CardDeck,Object);
//...
DEFINE_CLASS(CardHand,Object);
//...
```

The DEFINE_CLASS macro takes two arguments. The first argument is the name of the class. The second argument is the name of the parent class or base class. The DEFINED_CLASS macro can be found in OBJECT.H.

```
//////////////////////////////////////////////////////////////////
// macro DEFINE_CLASS
//////////////////////////////////////////////////////////////////
#define DEFINE_CLASS(classname, basename)                        \
const Class class_##classname = Class( class_##basename,         \
                                       #classname,               \
                                       sizeof(classname));       \
const Class* classname::isA() { return &class_##classname; }
```

Note the use of the \ in the macro definition. Normally, a macro definition lasts until the end of a line; however, the definition can be extended to cover more than one line by making the last character in the line a \. The definition for DEFINE_CLASS spreads out over five lines.

The ## and # symbols are preprocessor tokens indicating string operations performed by the Borland C++ preprocessor. The ## token concatenates two preprocessor strings to create a single string. The # token can be put in front of a macro argument to turn it into a string.

The preprocessor deals in strings. When it encounters the token DEFINE_CLASS followed by an open parenthesis, it takes the two arguments preceding the closing parenthesis and uses them to perform the macro substitution just defined.

As an example, consider the definition

```
DEFINE_CLASS(Card,Object);
```

The preprocessor will make the following substitution before passing the text on to the compiler.

```
const Class class_Card = Class( class_Object,
                                "Card",
                                sizeof(Card));
const Class* Card::isA() { return &class_Card; }
```

The DEFINE_CLASS macro is therefore used as a shorthand for declaring a **Class** class, and an **isA** method for each class derived from **Object**. As mentioned earlier, the **Class** associated with a class can be used to determine its type, its name, and its size given a pointer to an **Object**.

Shuffling a Deck

Most of the other code in CARD.CPP is self-explanatory. The only methods worth special attention are the constructor for the **CardDeck** and the method used to shuffle the deck.

```
CardDeck::CardDeck()
{
    pCards = new OrderedCltn(52);
    for (int suit=spade; suit<=diamond; suit++)
        for (int rank=1; rank<=13; rank++)
            pCards->add(*new Card(suit,rank));
}
```

```
//...
void CardDeck::shuffle()
{
    SampleDelete sample(*pCards);
    OrderedCltn *tempDeck = new OrderedCltn(pCards->size());
    for (int i=0; i<pCards->size(); i++)
    {
        tempDeck->addLast(*sample.next());
    }
    pCards = tempDeck;
}
```

The **CardDeck** creates a new ordered collection of 52 cards. The cards are in perfect order with the spades first followed by hearts, clubs, and diamonds. That is fine for a new deck, but you wouldn't want to play with a deck in that order. The **shuffle** method provides a way to randomly order the deck. The **shuffle** method uses a class called **SampleDelete** to create a duplicate copy of the original deck in a variable called **sample**. Each time ***sample.next** is called, a random card is removed from **sample** and returned to the caller. A shuffled deck is created from **sample** by making a third temporary deck and having **sample** add 52 cards to that deck. The instance variable **pCards** inside the **CardDeck** object is then set to point to this new shuffled deck.

Random Sampling of Collections

SampleDelete is derived from **SampleReplace**. These are two classes used for drawing random samples from ordered collections. The difference is that objects derived from **SampleReplace** are not deleted from the original collection. A good use for **SampleReplace** would be to simulate the roll of dice. To simulate a single die you could have an ordered collection of dot sets similar to the pip sets used for cards. When you ask the **SampleReplace** object to return one of six possible dot sets, you don't want that set removed from that collection. It remains one of six permanent elements. A card is different, on the other hand. When you draw a random card from a collection used to represent a deck, you actually want to remove the card from that collection. In this case you would use **SampleDelete**. The declarations for **SampleDelete** and **SampleReplace** are found in SAMPLE.H.

```
FILE SAMPLE.H

#include "object.h"
class SeqCltn;
class Random;
class OrderedCltn;
class Collection;

////////////////////////////////////////////////////////////
// class SampleReplace (declaration)
////////////////////////////////////////////////////////////
class SampleReplace : Object
{
protected:
    SeqCltn *data;
    Random *rand;
public:
    SampleReplace(SeqCltn& _data);
    Object* next();
    OrderedCltn& next(int n);
    bool isEmpty();
    unsigned size();
    void print();
    virtual const Class* isA();
    virtual void printOn(ostream& strm);
};

////////////////////////////////////////////////////////////
// class SampleDelete (declaration)
////////////////////////////////////////////////////////////
class SampleDelete : public SampleReplace
{
public:
    SampleDelete(Collection& aCollection);
    Object* next();
    virtual const Class* isA();
    virtual void printOn(ostream& strm);
}
```

The definitions for **SampleDelete** and **SampleReplace** are found in SAMPLE.CPP.

```
FILE SAMPLE.CPP

#include "sample.h"
```

```
#include "ordcltn.h"
#include "random.h"

//////////////////////////////////////////////////////////////
// class SampleReplace (definition)
//////////////////////////////////////////////////////////////
DEFINE_CLASS(SampleReplace,Object);

void SampleReplace::print()
{
    cout << *data;
}

SampleReplace::SampleReplace(SeqCltn& d)
{
    data = &d;
    rand = new Random();
}

Object* SampleReplace::next()
{
    if (isEmpty())
    {
        cerr << "error: no values exist in sample space\n";
    }
    return data->at( int( rand->next() * data->size()) );
}

OrderedCltn& SampleReplace::next(int n)
{
    OrderedCltn aCollection(n);
    while (n-- > 0)
    {
        aCollection.addLast(*next());
    }
    return aCollection;
}

bool SampleReplace::isEmpty()
{
    return ( size() == 0 );
}

unsigned SampleReplace::size()
{
    return data->size();
}

void SampleReplace::printOn(ostream& strm)
{
```

```
    strm << *data;
}

//////////////////////////////////////////////////////////////
// class SampleDelete (definition)
//////////////////////////////////////////////////////////////
DEFINE_CLASS(SampleDelete,Object);

SampleDelete::SampleDelete(Collection& aCollection)
: SampleReplace((SeqCltn&)NULL)
{
    data = new OrderedCltn(aCollection.asOrderedCltn());
    rand = new Random();
}

Object* SampleDelete::next()
{
    return data->remove(*(SampleReplace::next()));
}

void SampleDelete::printOn(ostream& strm)
{
    strm << *data;
}
```

Don't spend too much time studying these files. It is more important to know how to use the classes **Card**, **CardDeck**, and **CardHand**.

Simulating Play

Now you need a way to simulate a game. The sample game will be played by four players.

```
OrderedCltn players;
for (int i=0; i<4; i++)
    players.add(*new CardHand);
```

A card deck is created and then shuffled.

```
CardDeck gameCards;
cout << "main: SHUFFLING CARDS\n";
gameCards.shuffle();
```

```
cout << "main: CARDS SHUFFLED\n";
cout << "Cards left in deck==>"
     << gameCards.size() << "\n";
```

The rules of the game are as follows. Each player is dealt a card.

```
DO(players, CardHand*, hand)
    if (hand->points() < 21)
    {
        hand->take(*gameCards.next());
        cout << "Cards left in deck==>"
             << gameCards.size() << "\n";
    }
DONE
```

If the total points in any one of the player's hands is between 18 and 21 points, that player is a winner.

```
DO(players, CardHand*, hand)
    if (hand->points() >= 18  && hand->points() <= 21)
    {
        winners.add(*hand);
    }
DONE
```

On each deal, winners are added to a collection called winners.

```
OrderedCltn winners;
```

Players are only given a new card if they have not gone over 21 points. The game ends as soon as anyone becomes a winner, or if no one is able to take a card.

```
do
{
    deckSizeBeforeDeal = gameCards.size();
    //...
} while(winners.isEmpty() &&
    gameCards.size() < deckSizeBeforeDeal);
```

Once the game is over, the winners are printed along with the total number of points in their hands.

```
DO(winners, CardHand*, hand)
    cout << "==hand==" << players.indexOf(*hand);
    cout <<  "\n";
    hand->printOn(cout);
    cout << " hand->points(): " << hand->points();
    cout << "\n";
DONE
```

That is all that is required to simulate a simple card game. The code for the complete game can be found in CARDGAME.CPP shown here.

```
FILE CARDGAME.CPP

#include "card.h"
#include "ordcltn.h"

main()
{
    OrderedCltn players;
    for (int i=0; i<4; i++)
        players.add(*new CardHand);

    CardDeck gameCards;
    cout << "main: SHUFFLING CARDS\n";
    gameCards.shuffle();
    cout << "main: CARDS SHUFFLED\n";
    cout << "Cards left in deck==>"
         << gameCards.size() << "\n";

    OrderedCltn winners;
    int deckSizeBeforeDeal;
    do
    {
        deckSizeBeforeDeal = gameCards.size();
        cout <<  "====main: dealing 1 card to each hand under 21====\n";
        DO(players, CardHand*, hand)
            if (hand->points() < 21)
            {
                hand->take(*gameCards.next());
                cout << "Cards left in deck==>"
                     << gameCards.size() << "\n";
            }
        DONE
        cout <<  "====main: select winners (if any)====\n";
        DO(players, CardHand*, hand)
            if (hand->points() >= 18  && hand->points() <= 21)
            {
                winners.add(*hand);
            }
```

```
        DONE
    } while(winners.isEmpty() &&
            gameCards.size() < deckSizeBeforeDeal);
    cout << "====WINNERS====\n";
    DO(winners, CardHand*, hand)
        cout << "==hand==" << players.indexOf(*hand);
        cout <<  "\n";
        hand->printOn(cout);
        cout << " hand->points(): " << hand->points();
        cout << "\n";
    DONE
    cout << "\n";
    cout << "Cards left in deck==>"
         << gameCards.size() << "\n";
    cout << "\n";
    cout << "\n";
}
```

Compile and run the program now. Of course, your output won't be exactly the same because the cards will be dealt in a random order. There can be anywhere from zero to four winners. A sample game output will look like this:

```
main: SHUFFLING CARDS
main: CARDS SHUFFLED
Cards left in deck==>52
====main: dealing 1 card to each hand under 21====
Cards left in deck==>51
Cards left in deck==>50
Cards left in deck==>49
Cards left in deck==>48
====main: select winners (if any)====
====main: dealing 1 card to each hand under 21====
Cards left in deck==>47
Cards left in deck==>46
Cards left in deck==>45
Cards left in deck==>44
====main: select winners (if any)====
====WINNERS====
==hand==0
OrderedCltn[
9 of spades
10 of clubs]
 hand->points(): 19
==hand==3
OrderedCltn[
queen of hearts
```

```
jack of spades]
 hand->points(): 20

Cards left in deck==>44
```

Heading for Vegas

There is no reason that you need to settle for this type of output. After going to all the trouble of building a class to draw cards, why not make use of it? The final program of this chapter is built from a project file called BLACKJCK.PRJ.

Close Project CARDGAME.PRJ now. Create a new project file, BLACKJCK.PRJ. Add the following files:

BLACKJCK.CPP
SAMPLE.CPP
CARD.CPP
DRWCRD1.CPP
DRWCRD2.CPP
DT.LIB

This program is a complete simulation of an interactive blackjack game. The project makes use of all the classes developed in this chapter. After creating the project, compile and run the program. The screen shown in Figure 13-7 will appear.

The cards are shuffled. Four hands are dealt at the top of the screen. The dealer hand is shown off to the right with the hole card face down. The dialogue window at the left asks each user in turn if another card is desired. Press Y if you want another card. Any other key will skip the player. When all players skip their turns, a card is handed to the dealer hand as long as the total points in the hand are less than 18. A tie goes to the dealer. Figure 13-8 shows the outcome of a typical game.

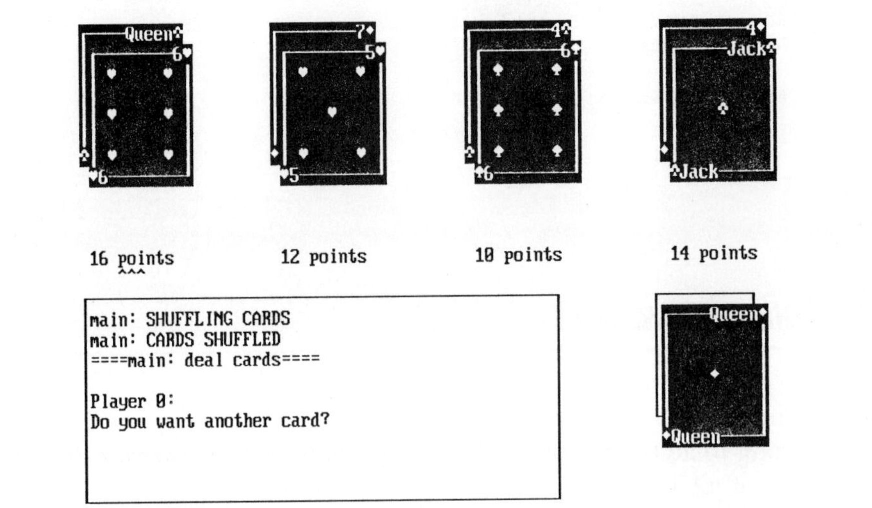

Figure 13-7. *Starting a new blackjack game*

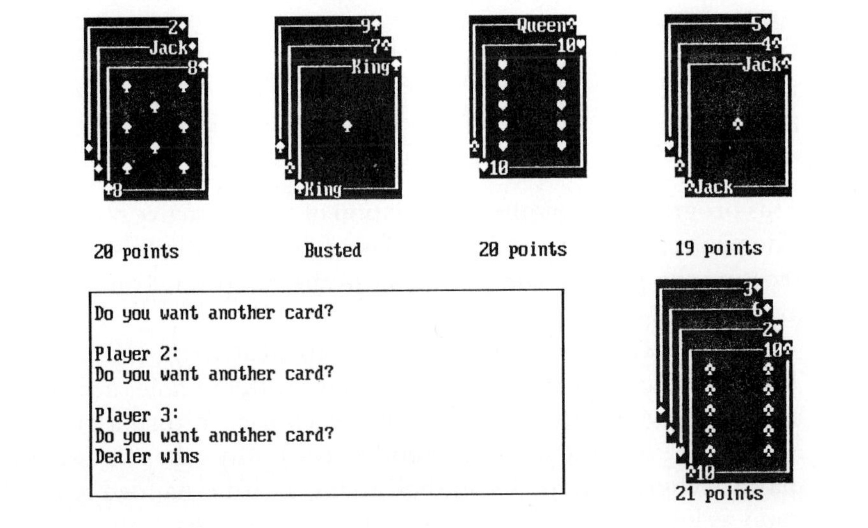

Figure 13-8. *Outcome of a typical game of blackjack*

Programming Challenges

Here are some modifications you might try. Make play continuous. In other words, rather than terminating after each deal, ask the user:

```
"Play again?"
```

If the player answers yes, you will have to return all cards to the game deck. Here is how you return all cards from the dealer's hand to the game deck.

```
dealerHand.ReturnAllCardsTo(gameCards);
```

You will have to figure out how to return all the player hands yourself.

If you want a bigger challenge, try to simulate more realistic play. For instance, aces can have a value of either one or eleven. See if you can come up with an algorithm that automatically adjusts the value to an ace if the player's hand goes over 21 and the hand contains an ace. Default values for aces would be eleven points. Furthermore, you should deal all cards in the original deck before returning used cards. This means that you will have to create a discard pile to hold all used cards until the game deck runs out. At that point the discard pile, the dealer hand, and all player hands should be returned to the game deck. The main code for the blackjack game is in BLACKJCK.CPP, which is included here for your reference. Good luck—and keep your shirt on.

```
FILE BLACKJCK.CPP

#include "card.h"
#include <conio.h>
#include "drwcrd.h"

void wputs(const char* s)
{
    for(; *s; s++)
    {
        if (*s=='\n')
            putch('\r');
        putch(*s);
```

```
    }
}

inline void fullScreen()
{
    window0(0,0,80,25);
}

inline void clearWindow()
{
    window0(0,13,50,11);
    textattr(BLUE + (CYAN<<4));
    clrscr();
    fullScreen();
    drawFrame(0,13,50,11);
}

inline void setWindowOutput()
{
    window0(1,14,48,9);
    textattr(BLUE + (CYAN<<4));
}

int xx=0;
int yy=0;

void windowPrint(const char* s)
{
    setWindowOutput();
    gotoxy0(xx,yy);
    textattr(BLUE + (CYAN<<4));
    wputs(s);
    xx=wherex()-1;
    yy=wherey()-1;
}

void windowPrint(int  i)
{
    window0(1,14,78,9);
    gotoxy0(xx,yy);
    textattr(BLUE + (CYAN<<4));
    cprintf("%d",i);
    xx=wherex()-1;
    yy=wherey()-1;
}

void printHandAt(int x, int y, CardHand& aCardHand)
{
    int i=0;
    OrderedCltn oc = aCardHand.asOrderedCltn();
    DO(oc, Card*, pCard)
        int isFaceUp = (pCard->face() == faceUp);
```

```
        drwcrd(x+i,y+i,
                pCard->rank(),
                pCard->suit(),
                isFaceUp);
        i++;
    DONE
}

main()
{
    fullScreen();
    textattr(BLUE + (LIGHTGRAY<<4));
    clrscr();

    clearWindow();
    fullScreen();

    // play game.
    OrderedCltn players;
    for (int i=0; i<4; i++)
    {
        players.add(*new CardHand);
    }
    CardHand dealerHand;
    CardDeck gameCards;
    windowPrint("main: SHUFFLING CARDS\n");
    gameCards.shuffle();
    windowPrint("main: CARDS SHUFFLED\n");

    int firstCard = 1;
    for (int j=0; j<2; j++)    // deal two cards
    {
        DO(players, CardHand*, hand)
            hand->take(*gameCards.next());
            int xPos = players.indexOf(*hand)*20;
            printHandAt(xPos,0,*hand);
            fullScreen();
            textattr(BLUE + (LIGHTGRAY<<4));
            gotoxy0(xPos, 11);
            if (hand->points() > 21)
                cprintf("   Busted   ");
            else
                cprintf("% 2d points", hand->points());
        DONE
        if (firstCard)
        {
            dealerHand.take(*gameCards.next(), faceDown);
            firstCard = 0;
        }
        else
            dealerHand.take(*gameCards.next());
    }
```

```
// Show dealer's Hand
printHandAt(59,13,dealerHand);
while(kbhit()) getch();  // eat pending keypresses
int allPass = 1;         // true if no one wants a card
do
{
    allPass = 1;  // true until someone takes a card
    // deal new cards, 1 to each player
    windowPrint("====main: deal cards====\n");
    DO(players, CardHand*, hand)
        int answer = 'n';
        do
        {
            if (hand->points() < 21)
            {
                fullScreen();
                textattr(BLUE + (LIGHTGRAY<<4) + BLINK);
                int xPos = players.indexOf(*hand)*20;
                gotoxy0(xPos,12); cprintf("    ^^^");
                windowPrint("\nPlayer ");
                windowPrint(players.indexOf(*hand));
                windowPrint(":\n");
                windowPrint("Do you want another card? ");
                answer = getch();
                windowPrint("\n");
                if (answer == 'y' || answer == 'Y')
                {
                    hand->take(*gameCards.next());
                    allPass = 0; // someone took a card
                    printHandAt(xPos,0,*hand);
                    fullScreen();
                    textattr(BLUE + (LIGHTGRAY<<4));
                    gotoxy0(xPos, 11);
                    if (hand->points() > 21)
                        cprintf("   Busted   ");
                    else
                        cprintf("% 2d points",
                                hand->points());
                    textattr(BLUE + (LIGHTGRAY<<4));
                }
                fullScreen();
                textattr(BLUE + (LIGHTGRAY<<4));
                gotoxy0(xPos,12); cprintf("         ");
            }
        } while ((answer == 'y' || answer == 'Y') &&
                hand->points() < 21);
    DONE
} while( !gameCards.isEmpty() && !allPass );

// do dealer
dealerHand.allFaceUp();
printHandAt(59,13,dealerHand);
```

```
fullScreen();
textattr(BLUE + (LIGHTGRAY<<4));
gotoxy0(60,23);
cprintf("% 2d points", dealerHand.points());
while (dealerHand.points()<18)
{
    dealerHand.take(*gameCards.next());
    printHandAt(59,13,dealerHand);
    fullScreen();
    textattr(BLUE + (LIGHTGRAY<<4));
    gotoxy0(60,23);
    if (dealerHand.points() > 21)
        cprintf("   Busted   ");
    else
    cprintf("% 2d points", dealerHand.points());
}
// look for winners
OrderedCltn winners;
if (dealerHand.points() > 21)
{
    DO(players, CardHand*, hand)
        if (hand->points() <= 21)
        {
            winners.add(*hand);
        }
    DONE
}
else
{
    DO(players, CardHand*, hand)
        if (hand->points() > dealerHand.points() &&
            hand->points() <= 21)
        {
            winners.add(*hand);
        }
    DONE
}
if (winners.isEmpty())
{
    fullScreen();
    gotoxy0(60,23);
    textattr(BLUE + (LIGHTGRAY<<4) + BLINK);
    cprintf("% 2d points", dealerHand.points());
    textattr(BLUE + (LIGHTGRAY<<4));
    windowPrint("Dealer wins\n");
}
// show winners
DO(players, CardHand*, hand)
    if (winners.indexOf(*hand) != -1)
    {
        int xPos = players.indexOf(*hand)*20;
        printHandAt(xPos,0,*hand);
```

```
            fullScreen();
            textattr(BLUE + (LIGHTGRAY<<4) + BLINK);
            gotoxy0(xPos, 11);
            cprintf("% 2d points", hand->points());
        }
    DONE
    textattr(BLUE + (LIGHTGRAY<<4));

    getch();
    fullScreen();
    gotoxy0(0,24);
}
```

14 Object-Oriented Programming Tools for the Design of User Interfaces

This last chapter is not so much an explanation of code as an invitation to explore. The chapter breaks from the tutorial style used in previous chapters. Instead, the programs presented here illustrate the concepts you have learned throughout the rest of the book.

Some general concepts are explained here, but no code is analyzed. If you want to know more about a program or class, the code is available for you to study. The main thing to do in this chapter is run each of the examples and look at the screens. See if there are any programs that interest you. Try modifying the programs and integrating some of the classes with other programs you have written.

DiskTutor User Interface Toolkit

The DiskTutor C++ class library provides the core classes required to build a complete window system. You can create text windows for text or dialog boxes. Input can be obtained through the mouse by clicking on special *hot spots*. Such input would be required to build control classes such as toggle buttons, radio buttons, and text input fields. Message windows and dialog boxes can be built from these basic tools.

Model-View-Controller

Smalltalk and other object-based systems frequently embrace the concept of *model-view-controller*. The notion is to break up all programs into three components. The *model* is the actual application program or the data created by the application program. The *view* is the format used to present the data. For example, data about the current positions of planets in a simulation can be printed out as text, or the relative two-dimensional positions of the planets can be displayed graphically in a window. The same applies to a digital watch. The idea is that while the view is likely to change frequently, depending on the type of hardware as well as the desired perspective of the user, the application will remain constant.

The third component, the *controller,* determines how the user interacts with the application or model. In simulations, the user might not interact at all except to start or stop the simulation. This is how the CARDGAME example in the previous chapter works. You run the program, and winners are selected based on input created from a random number generator rather than from any actions on your part. A flight simulator is at the other end of the spectrum. You can use mouse, joystick, or keyboard to control the underlying model (your position, speed, and direction). The model then communicates with the view to make it look as though you are inside the cockpit of a Cessna or a fighter jet. A flight simulator also provides a good example of how alternative views are possible from the same underlying model. The program can present a view of the data from the pilot's position or from the position of the control tower. Another possible view would be the position of the aircraft on an x,y coordinate system representing a chart or map.

More common examples of using different views to present the same data include switching back and forth between a hex dump and an ASCII representation of a file you are examining. Many PC utilities do this. Another example is using a single data structure to represent a menu. The menu can be shown as a horizontal bar menu, as a pop-up, or as a pull-down menu. Control to the menu can be facilitated by pressing keys that correspond to highlighted characters within the text strings of the menu choices. The menus can just as well be controlled by pressing arrow keys and using RETURN to indicate selection when the desired choice is highlighted. A mouse can be another form of input.

Various forms of look and feel arise when deciding on some of these controller issues. For instance, does the user have to continue to hold down the left mouse button in order to move the highlight bar through a set of menu choices in a menu? If this is the case, then does letting go of the mouse button while a choice is highlighted indicate selection of the highlighted item? Do you need to let go of the mouse button immediately? In such a case, clicking the mouse on a menu entry would indicate selection. Some items perform different operations depending on whether the mouse is clicked only once or clicked twice in rapid succession. If this is the case, controllers need to have event handlers for both single and double mouse clicks.

Some window systems, like many X Window-based toolkits, make a window active for input as soon as the mouse pointer is moved inside a window. Other systems, like the Macintosh, use what are called *listeners.* These windows become active for input when you click on them. The mouse pointer can be moved anywhere on the screen, even outside the active window, but all keyboard input still goes to the active listener.

These look and feel issues have become so important in user interface design that some companies think they have unique proprietary rights to look and feel styles designed for their products.

The DiskTutor C++ interface design tools follow the Smalltalk notion of separating model, view, and controller. The model is provided by the user in the form of an application program such as a digital watch, a planet simulation, or a card game. The controllers monitor user input in the form of keystrokes and mouse events. Each time a key is pressed or a mouse button is pushed, the display is updated and the controller invokes the appropriate methods. The basic form of view provided by the DiskTutor C++ interface toolkit is a text-based window. It would be fairly easy to extend this implementation to a graphics-based system, but even within the context of a text-based system, it is possible to present very different views of data and applications programs. You will see examples of this as you run each of the programs in this chapter.

The Programs

Be sure you are logged to the appropriate DiskTutor directory (\DT\CH14) before invoking Borland C++ and loading any programs. Also be sure you are using the small memory model. This is the default memory model set when you install either Turbo C++ or Borland C++. Program P14-1 shows how to use the **Form** and **ChatBlt** classes. These two classes provide the basic operations required to draw, save, and restore areas on the screen. The **Form** class is borrowed directly from Smalltalk. The **ChatBlt** class is adapted from Smalltalk's **BitBlt** class. Where Smalltalk's **BitBlt** class deals with pixels on the screen, **ChatBlt** works with character-attribute pairs unique to the IBM PC display screen. To run program P14-1 you must create a project file, P14-1.PRJ, consisting of the following files:

P14-1.CPP
DT.LIB
DTUI.LIB

DT.LIB is the library containing the DiskTutor C++ container classes, as well as the **Point** and **Rectangle** classes used to implement windows in the DiskTutor User Interface library. DTUI.LIB is the DiskTutor User Interface library itself, which contains the basic operations needed to create and manipulate windows.

After creating the project, run the program. Figure 14-1 shows a sample output screen from Program 14-1. Program P14-1 shows many different things which can be done with the **Form** and **ChatBlt** classes. This particular screen shows how a window can be drawn with borders, how strings can be displayed in a window, and how any area of the screen can be copied from one location to another. The **Form** class makes it possible to copy only the attributes from a given region (i.e. color) or to copy only the characters from a given region without changing the attributes in the destination area. The default mode for copying is to copy both characters and attributes.

Program P14-2 shows how forms can be used to simulate moveable windows. The global **Display** object is sent messages to color a rectangle

Figure 14-1. *Using **Form** and **ChatBlt** to draw a window and to copy screen areas*

filled with the letter A and draw a border around it. A **Form** object, **o**, is created, automatically saving a copy of the same area of the screen in which the border was drawn. The display module provides an overloaded function, **window**, which accepts a rectangle as an argument. Calling this function causes the Borland C++ built-in **window** function to be called with rectangle converted to four appropriate integer arguments. The **expandBy** message can be sent to any rectangle, and returns a rectangle in which each dimension is adjusted by adding itself to **expandBy's** argument. The **expandBy** method provides a way to reduce the size of a rectangle to compensate for the border around a window. Once the window function is called, normal Borland C++ console functions can be used to send strings to the window. These tools will provide the foundation for the **Window** class used in P14-4.

After a keypress, 1000 test strings are printed to the window. A copy of the window is saved by creating a new **Form**, **p**, with the appropriate rectangle argument. The **Display** object then clears the screen. The first **for** loop alternately displays the forms **o** and **p** in a different location waiting for a keypress in between. The second **for** loop shows how it is possible to simulate movement of a window around the screen without destroying what is underneath. This requires two forms: one to save the covered area and one to save the image of the window being moved. The loop moves the window filled with A's twenty times, restoring the covered area, moving the window, and redisplaying the image on each iteration.

To run Program P14-2 you need to create a project file, P14-2.PRJ, consisting of the following files:

P14-2.CPP
DT.LIB
DTUI.LIB

In Figure 14-2 the window filled with A's is moved by repeatedly pressing the SPACEBAR until it moves off the edge of the screen.

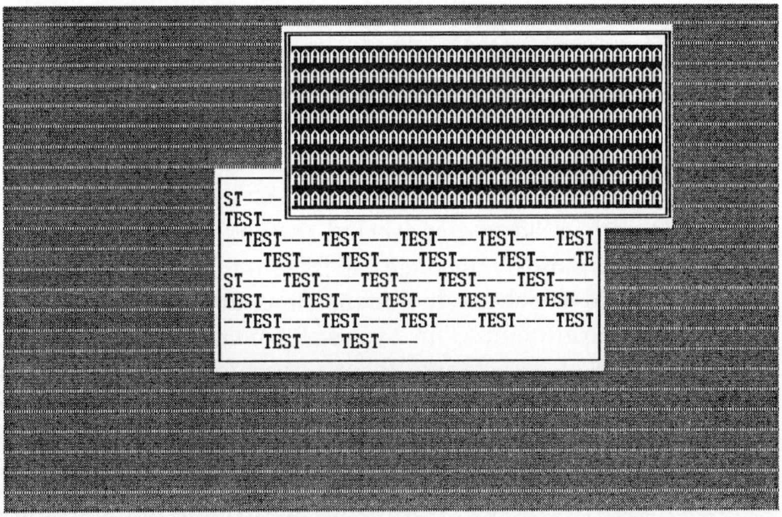

Figure 14-2. *Forms can simulate window movement without destroying covered areas*

Program P14-3 takes moveable windows a step further by encapsulating the above technique for moving windows in a class and adding mouse control. Program P14-3 uses a new class called **ObscuringForm**, which contains two pointers to **Form** objects. These pointers can be used to save a copy of the screen before the window is displayed and to save a copy of the screen after the window is displayed. This makes it possible to move a window quickly around the screen by first restoring what is beneath the window, adjusting the window data to reflect the new screen position, and redisplaying the saved window image.

Program 14-3 will not run without a mouse. There is no harm in trying, however, since the program checks for the presence of a mouse and aborts with an error message if it does not find one. A complete set of mouse operations is provided with source code in the files MOUSE.H and MOUSE.CPP. To run the program create a project file, P14-3.PRJ, consisting of the following files:

P14-3.CPP
DT.LIB
DTUI.LIB
OFORM.CPP
MOUSE.CPP

When the program is run a window appears in the upper left corner of the screen, and a second window appears at the center of the screen. Grab the upper left window by moving the mouse anywhere inside the window. Depress the left mouse button and hold it down. As long as the left mouse button is not released, you can move the mouse anywhere on the screen that you like. Figure 14-3 shows the screen after moving the window down and to the right. Press the right mouse button once. The moveable window disappears temporarily. One hundred test strings are written to the remaining window. Then the moveable window reappears. If you grab the moveable window and move it to the upper right corner of the screen, you should get something like Figure 14-4.

Program P14-4 shows how container classes can help to build a user interface. A **Window** class is provided in the files WINDOW.H and WINDOW.CPP. Since **Window** is a subclass of **Object**, **Window** objects can be placed in containers. Program P14-4 creates an object called **DeskTop**, which is an ordered collection of **Windows**. To run Program P14-4 create a project file, P14-4.PRJ, consisting of the following files:

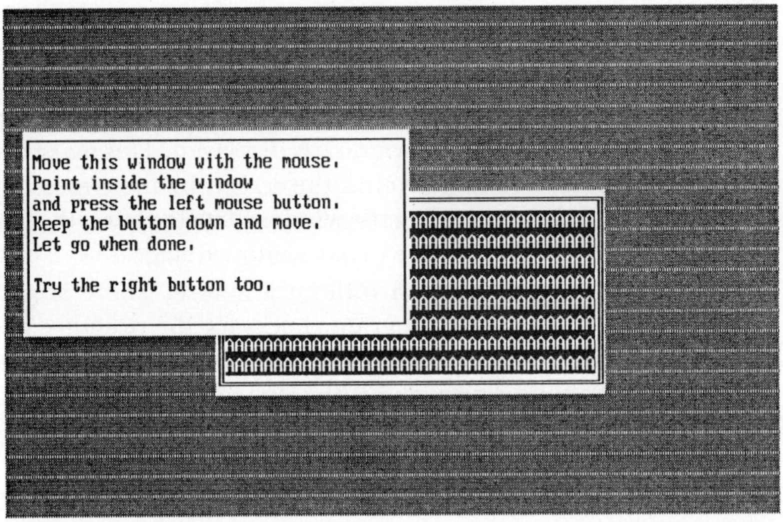

Figure 14-3. *Window for Program P14-3 after being moved with the mouse*

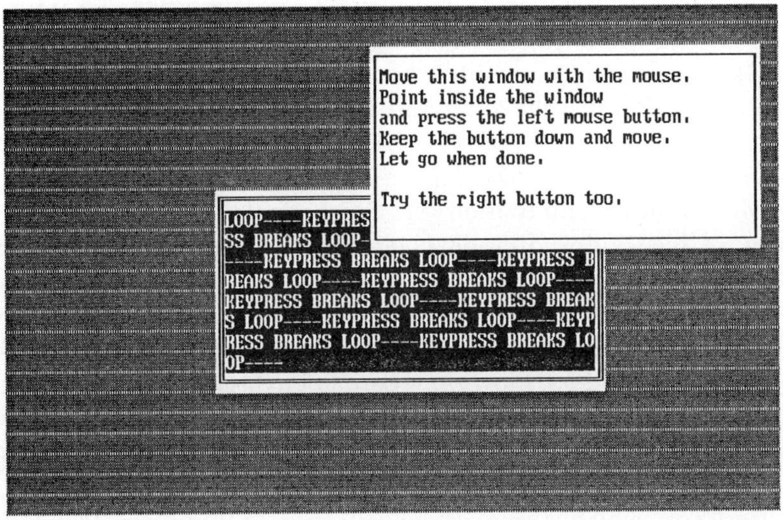

Figure 14-4. *Pressing the right mouse button sends test strings to the second window*

P14-4.CPP
DT.LIB
DTUI.LIB
OFORM.CPP
WINDOW.CPP

Figure 14-5 shows the screen after all windows in the **DeskTop** are opened. One greeting test string is sent to each window. Then the program enters a loop that on each iteration sends a test string to window 2 and a similar test string to window 3. Note that sending a test string to a window causes the window to restore its image, making it appear as a top window, and then selects it as the active output window. If you watch closely, when you run the program you can see each of the windows alternately disappear and reappear as strings are sent to them. Immediately after the screen in Figure 14-5 appears, another loop sends a test string to the three windows in the **DeskTop**, giving you a better chance to see how the **ObscuringForm** class restores rectangular images. Finally, the program uses iterators to cause all of the windows to

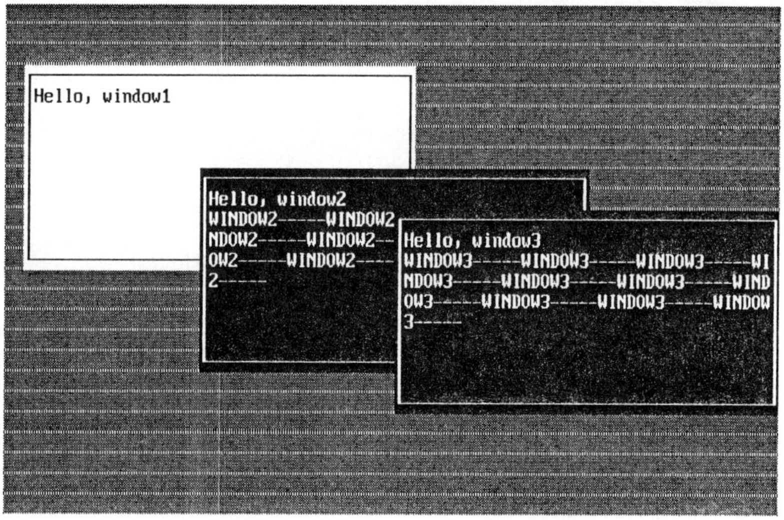

Figure 14-5. *DeskTop: an OrderedCltn of windows*

disappear and then reappear with new strings inside (see Figure 14-6).

Program P14-5 makes the windows contained by **DeskTop** moveable. Each time you press one of the arrow keys on the arrow pad, the active window is moved in the corresponding direction. The active window can be distinguished by a double line border. All other windows have a single line border. To run Program P14-5, create a project file, P14-5.PRJ, containing the following files:

P14-5.CPP
DT.LIB
DTUI.LIB
OFORM.CPP
WINDOW.CPP

You can change the active window by pressing the SPACEBAR or RETURN. Figure 14-7 shows what the screen will look like after pressing the SPACEBAR twice. Since the program starts out with the last window displayed

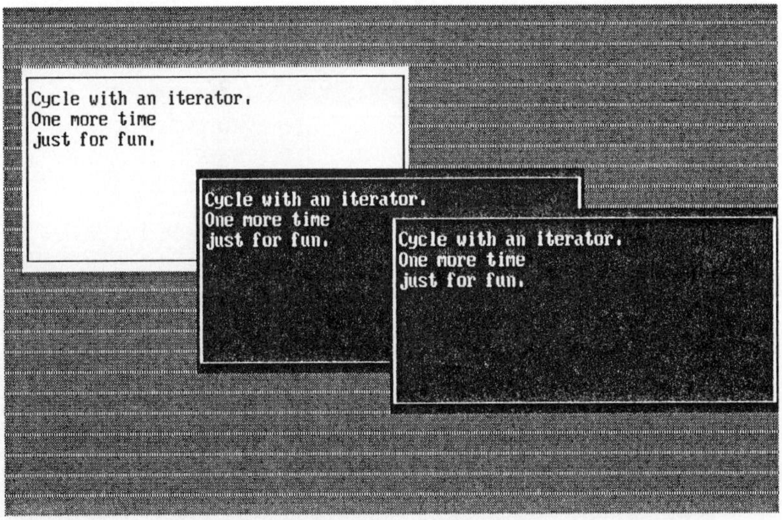

Figure 14-6. *Display **DeskTop** windows with an iterator*

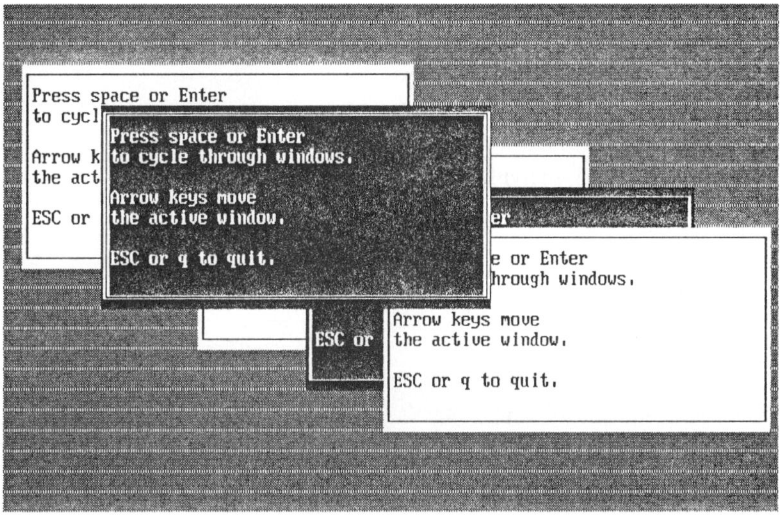

Figure 14-7. *Collection of five moveable windows*

being the active window, pressing the SPACEBAR once makes the window in the upper left corner the active window. Pressing it again makes the second window active. Try moving the windows around with the arrow keys. Figure 14-8 shows a possible configuration after moving each of the windows.

Programs P14-6 and P14-7 show the benefits of breaking a program down into the model-view-controller components. The model is the actual application program or the data being manipulated. The view is the way the data is displayed. For example, it is possible to display the data that represents a menu using either TTY output or screen-oriented window output. The data for the menu does not change just because the view changes, nor do the methods for manipulating the menu. The menu is referred to as the model. You can add choices to a menu or manipulate the current choice by sending the ++ or -- messages.

The controller connects the model to the view and also connects the model and view to the user. The controller generally handles input, interprets it, and passes the appropriate control messages to the model and the view. For example, the controller can be completely keyboard

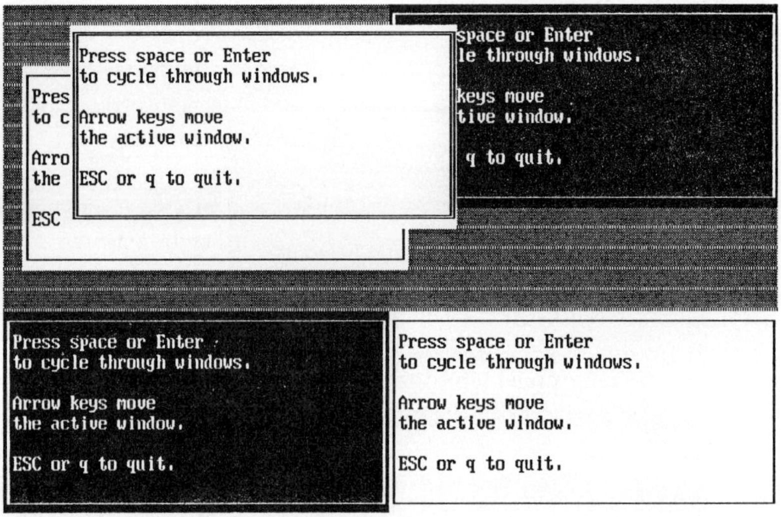

Figure 14-8. *Possible configuration after moving windows in Program P14-5*

driven, or it can get all its input from a mouse. It can also be a combination of the two. Or a controller might get all input from a file or a serial port. The model and the view need not change because the type of controller is changed. Programs P14-6 and P14-7 show how this is possible.

P14-6 implements a menu model. The program also uses two different views to display the data inside the model. A single keyboard controller is used for either view. To run Program P14-6, create a project file, P14-6.PRJ, containing the following files:

P14-6.CPP
DT.LIB
DTUI.LIB
OFORM.CPP
WINDOW.CPP
MENU.CPP
MVIEW.CPP
MCONTROL.CPP

When you run Program P14-6, you will first see a TTY output screen that looks like Figure 14-9. Since the **Menu** class is derived from class **Object**, it can be printed on a standard iostream using the << operator. This makes it easy to test the menu model as you develop it. Look at the **Menu::printOn** method to see how a menu is displayed. All choices in the menu are printed, and three asterisks are printed beside the current menu choice.

The elements of a menu are **Choices**. **Choices** are objects containing a string and a pointer to a function. This allows an action to be associated with a **Choice** string. If the **select** message is sent to a **Choice** object, the action associated with that object is executed. If no action is specified when a **Choice** object is created, the action pointer is set to null and no action will take place when the **Choice** object receives a **select** message. When a **Menu** object receives a **select** message, the currently active menu **Choice** is sent a **select** message. You can see how all this works when you run Program P14-6. Press the DOWN ARROW key once. The screen scrolls as the updated menu is being printed. Notice that now the asterisk appears by the second choice in the menu. The keyboard controller reads keys as you type them. If a DOWN ARROW is pressed, the

```
StreamMenuController now active
*pMenu==>Menu [
***Open ...      F3
   New
   Save          F2
   Save as ...
   Save all
   Change dir ...
   Print
   Get info ...
   Dos Shell
   Quit        Alt-X]
```

Figure 14-9. *Testing the menu model with a TTY view (asterisks indicate current choice)*

controller sends a ++ message to the menu. If an UP ARROW is pressed, the controller sends a -- message to the menu. If RETURN is pressed, the controller sends a **select** message to the menu. Press RETURN and you will see the message

```
hello from action2
```

appear at the bottom of the screen. This message is coming from the **action2** function, which was specified for the second menu choice when it was added to the menu. Your screen should look like Figure 14-10.

The **action2** function retains control until a key is pressed. Once a key is pressed, control returns to the main controller. Try scrolling up and down the menu by pressing the UP and DOWN ARROW keys. Try out different actions by pressing return on each of the choices. Note that the

```
   Save as ...
   Save all
   Change dir ...
   Print
   Get info ...
   Dos Shell
   Quit         Alt-X]


*pMenu==>Menu [
   Open ...         F3
***New
   Save             F2
   Save as ...
   Save all
   Change dir ...
   Print
   Get info ...
   Dos Shell
   Quit         Alt-X]

    hello from action2
```

Figure 14-10. *Pressing RETURN with the second menu choice active causes the* ***action2*** *function to be executed*

choices that had no action specified when they were created do nothing when they are selected. The controller lets you exit by pressing RETURN when the Quit menu choice is active. Alternately you can press ESC or Q at any time.

Once you select Quit, a new view is associated with the menu. The new view is a more sophisticated window-oriented view. Figure 14-11 shows this view.

The program behaves exactly as it did before when the TTY view handled program output. Try experimenting by moving the menu choice bar up and down and pressing RETURN with various choices highlighted. Specifically, try pressing RETURN with the second choice highlighted. You should see output like that in Figure 14-11. The **action2** function is still called when the **select** message is sent to the menu with the second choice active.

Program P14-7 exchanges controllers rather than views. Program P14-7 uses the same menu model as that in Program P14-6. Different

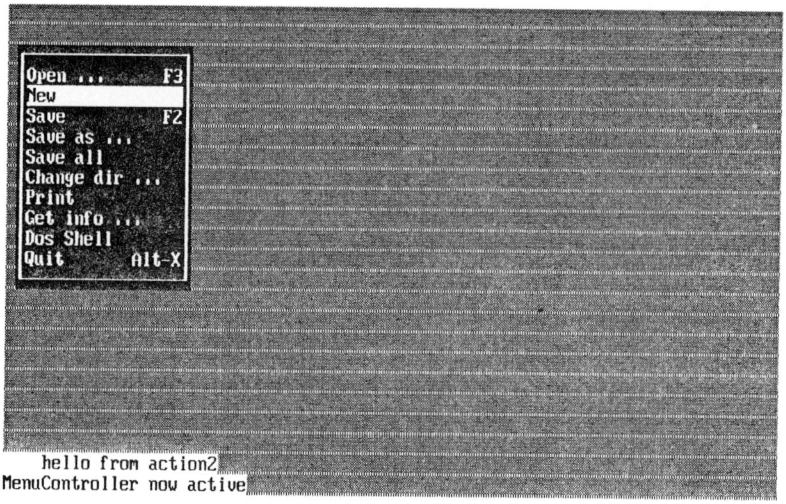

Figure 14-11. *Menu model with window-oriented view for Program P14-6*

Figure 14-12. *Menu model with keyboard controller active for Program P14-7*

actions are specified for some of the menu choices. A window is also used in Program P14-7 for all output, so the program comes closer to simulating a real application. Two different controllers are employed by Program P14-7: **MenuController** and **MouseMenuController**. Note that **MouseMenuController** is derived from **MenuController**. This makes it possible for a pointer declared as

```
MenuController* pController;
```

to point to an object that is either a **MouseMenuController** or a **MenuController**. To run Program P14-7 you need a project file, P14-7 .PRJ, consisting of the following files:

P14-7.CPP
DT.LIB
DTUI.LIB

OFORM.CPP
WINDOW.CPP
MENU.CPP
MVIEW.CPP
MCONTROL.CPP
MOUSE.CPP

When you first run the program, the standard **MenuController** takes control. Try moving the menu bar around and selecting various choices. Any output generated is sent to the window at the right. After selecting choice 1 and choice 2, your screen should appear as in Figure P14-12.

Selecting the "Save as" choice causes the output window to be cleared. Other choices enter loops that send test strings to the window.

Once you select the Quit choice, the program attempts to install a new controller. First the program checks for the presence of a mouse. If a mouse driver is not installed, the program sends a message indicating so to the output window and terminates. If a mouse is present, the positions of the window and the menu are changed, and control is passed to a **MouseMenuController** object. It is possible to move both windows and menus to different locations on the screen without altering the internal data of the window and menu models. This means you can make the same menu appear as either a pop-up or a pull-down menu. Alternately, you could implement a different view for a menu, which causes the selections to be listed horizontally across the top of the screen like the top level menu in the Borland C++ programming environment. The actions associated with each choice in the top level menu could invoke pull-down menus, which in turn could invoke application-specific actions.

Figure 14-13 shows the output of Program P14-7 if a mouse driver is available. The nice thing about having alternative controllers is that you can write programs that adapt themselves to available hardware. A program can test for a mouse, and if one is available it can use a **MouseMenuController**. If a mouse is not available, the program can use a **MenuController**.

If a mouse is available, Program P14-7 will now accept either keyboard or mouse input to control the menu. Mouse control works in two ways: you can either move the mouse pointer to the appropriate menu choice, press and release the left mouse button and the action associated with the choice is selected, or you can move the mouse anywhere inside

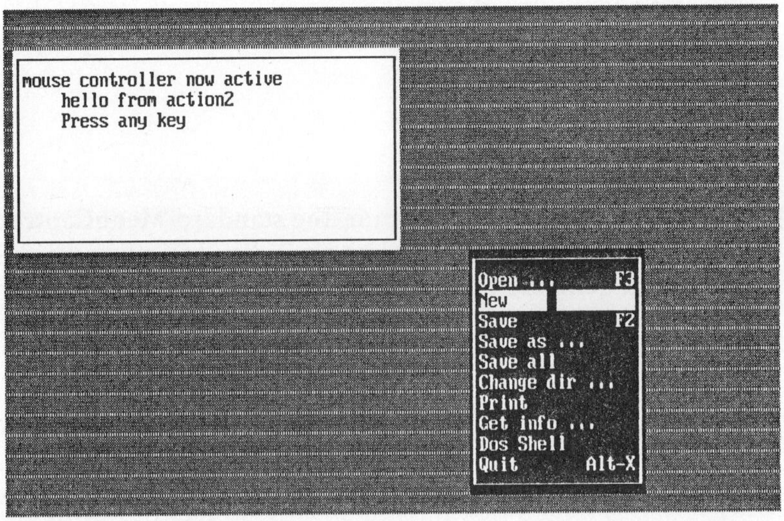

Figure 14-13. *Menu model with mouse controller active*

the menu, and press and continue to hold the left mouse button down. As long as you continue to hold the left button down and move the mouse inside the menu, the highlight bar will follow the mouse. If you move the mouse outside of the menu, the highlight will stop tracking the mouse. If you release the left mouse button with the mouse pointer inside the menu, the choice that is highlighted at the time of release is selected. If you release the left mouse button with the mouse pointer outside the menu, no selection is made.

You might want to try modifying the code for the **MouseMenuController::takeControl** method in P14-7.CPP. This method is responsible for reading mouse input and dispatching the appropriate control message to the menu. For example, try changing the program so that if the mouse pointer is moved inside the menu; the left mouse button is pressed and held; and the pointer is moved outside of the menu and released, then the highlight bar is forced to disappear. The pull-down menus in the Borland C++ IDE disappear if the mouse button is pressed outside of the active menu or if a drag selection (moving the pointer inside the menu with the left mouse button held down) is released outside the menu. There are hints inside P14-7.CPP that show how you can simulate this behavior.

On Your Own

We hope that these programs show that object-oriented programming is more than a theoretical tool. C++ objects and classes are solving practical problems today. As more people get used to thinking in terms of objects and more class libraries become available, applications will get more sophisticated and easier to build. This is only the beginning. It will take time for OOP tools to evolve. Now is a good time to think about how you might use these new concepts and tools. You may want to provide class libraries for others. Or you may be building projects that will benefit from the emerging class libraries. Either way, we hope that the code you find here will give you ideas for further exploration.

Happy OOPing.

Index

G

H

I

K

L

M

N

O

P

R

The manuscript for this book was prepared and submitted to Osborne/McGraw-Hill in electronic form. The acquisitions editor for this project was Jeffrey Pepper, the technical reviewers were John Sieraski and Jim Turley, and the project editor was Judith Brown.

Text was designed by Lance Ravella and Michelle Salinaro using Century Expanded for text body and Swiss for display.

Cover art by Graphic Eye, Inc. Cover supplier and color separation by Phoenix Color Corp. Screens produced with InSet, from Inset Systems, Inc. Book printed and bound by R.R. Donnelley & Sons Company, Crawfordsville, Indiana.

C++: The Complete Reference
by Herbert Schildt

C++ is rapidly winning converts among programmers of all kinds, and Osborne/McGraw-Hill has the book they're looking for: *C++: The Complete Reference* by internationally known C expert Herb Schildt. *C++: The Complete Reference* covers C++ in full detail starting with aspects common to the C and C++ languages. This example-filled book thoroughly discusses those features specific to C++ and includes several chapters on effective C++ software development.
$24.95p ISBN: 0-07-881654-8, 784 pp., 7 3/8 X 9 1/4

C: The Complete Reference
by Herbert Schildt

This renowned reference guide, revised to comply with the new ANSI C standard, is the best and most complete source on ANSI C. C programmers at every level can take adavantage of Schildt's expanded sections on the C language and the ANSI libraries. Comprehensive reference sections are conveniently organized by topic for quick fact-finding.
$28.95p ISBN: 0-07-881538-X, 823 pp., 7 3/8 X 9 1/4

UNIX® System V Release 4: An Introduction
by Kenneth H. Rosen, Richard R. Rosinski, and James M. Farber

This informative introductory text gives you a solid background in UNIX basics before covering the many new features and functions included in AT&T's latest UNIX release. *UNIX® System V Release 4: An Introduction* includes detailed discussions of timely UNIX topics such as running DOS under UNIX, connectivity with other systems, system administration, and UNIX security. The authors include three members of AT&T Bell Laboratories, where UNIX has been developed and improved almost constantly for the past 20 years.
$29.95p ISBN: 0-07-881552-5, 1228 pp., 7 3/8 X 9 1/4

UNIX: The Complete Reference
by Stephen Coffin

Coffin approaches UNIX with a perspective that benefits users of microcomputers, minicomputers, and mainframes. There is special, timely coverage of UNIX on the 80386 micros; all code in the book was run on a 386. If you're just beginning UNIX, this book will help you get started. If you're an experienced user, this is an invaluable reference.
$29.95p ISBN: 0-07-881299-2, 750 pp., 7 3/8 X 9 1/4

Osborne **McGraw-Hill** **Available at local book and computer stores.**

Windows 3: The Complete Reference
by Tom Sheldon

The enormous interest in Microsoft® Windows has generated many requests for a comprehensive reference—and now Osborne has the book you've been asking for. *Windows 3: The Complete Reference* contains detailed information on every feature, function, and aspect of Windows Version 3. Tom Sheldon, author of numerous computer books, also discusses multitasking under Windows, communicating under Windows, and a discussion of Windows utilities.

$24.95p ISBN: 0-07-881679-3, 950 pp., 7 3/8 X 9 1/4

Windows Programming: An Introduction
by William H. Murray, III and Chris H. Pappas

This guide is a down-to-earth introduction to Windows 3, a program that gives users of IBM PCs and compatibles a graphical interface capability. The authors take you from simple windowing concepts to the creation of sophisticated Windows programs. Best of all, you'll learn how to migrate programming concepts from Windows to OS/2 Presentation Manager.

$28.95p ISBN: 0-07-881536-3, 651 pp., 7 3/8 X 9 1/4

Turbo Pascal® 6: The Complete Reference
by Stephen K. O'Brien

The most complete single resource ever published for all Turbo Pascal programmers is now available in a special edition that covers all the new features of Borland's recently released version 6. The revolutionary Turbo Vision application framework is also covered so you can use this new tool to write professional-quality applications. Whether you're a beginner or an expert programmer, you'll find the information you need on every Turbo Pascal 6. feature, command, and programming technique.

$29.95p ISBN: 0-07-881703-X, 1008 pp., 7 3/8 X 9 1/4

Dvorak's Guide to DOS and PC Performance
by John C. Dvorak and Nick Anis

John Dvorak, the world's most widely read computer columnist, and Nick Anis, author and programming ace, offer all PC owners a wealth of knowledge and experience about IBM-compatible PCs and the DOS operating system, plus a collection of top commercially available DOS-based PC utilities. Whether you want to add a command to your AUTOEXEC file or to install a new motherboard, Dvorak and Anis give you the context, examples, and specific instructions you need for peak PC performance.

$49.95p ISBN: 0-07-881658-0, 850 pp., 7 3/8 X 9 1/4, Dvorak*Osborne/McGraw-Hill

Osborne **McGraw-Hill** ■ **Available at local book and computer stores.**

Glossbrenner's Complete Hard Disk Handbook
by Alfred Glossbrenner and Nick Anis

This comprehensive volume covers everything from buying a hard disk to installing, loading, organizing, and "tweaking" it for optimum performance. *Glossbrenner's Complete Hard Disk Handbook* also includes two diskettes packed with tutorials, software tools, and utilities. You'll savor the lively style and amazing ability to organize information that Alfred Glossbrenner has brought to dozens of books and articles on computers and software.

$39.95p ISBN: 0-07-881604-1, 450 pp., 7 3/8 X 9 1/4

Dvorak's Guide to PC Telecommunications
by John C. Dvorak and Nick Anis

Telecommunications just got SIMPLE—all you need is your computer, a modem, and this exciting book and disk package. Internationally renowned John C. Dvorak, the world's most widely read computer columnist joins forces with programming wiz and author, Nick Anis, to present the most compelling reason for discovering telecommunications. Packaged with this comprehensive guide are two disks jam-packed with reliable, easy-to-use utilities, interactive tutorials, communications software, and special discounts from the major on-line services.

$49.95p ISBN: 0-07-881551-7, 1053 pp., 7 3/8 X 9 1/4, Dvorak*Osborne/McGraw-Hill

PC Tools Deluxe™: The Complete Reference
by Hy Bender

Every feature of PC Tools Deluxe, including version 6, is described in detail and accompanied by hundreds of illustrations and examples in this Complete Reference. Simple instructions help you quickly learn the fundamentals of this outstanding DOS-based utility program, then Bender discusses the most important and widely used features, such as managing your files and directories, composing and editing documents, transmitting faxes and electronic mail, and more.

$27.95p, ISBN: 0-07-881648-3, 750 pp., 7 3/8 X 9 1/4, Covers Versions Through 6

XTree® Made Easy
by Mike Callahan and Nick Anis

If you're one of the 3.5 million users of XTree or XTree PRO GOLD, you'll be delighted with this book. Mike Callahan, a.k.a. Dr. File Finder, and Nick Anis complement the XTree documentation by providing you with all the details on this popular DOS shell and utility program. This book includes a step-by-step instruction guide as well as a handy reference. You'll learn everything from basic file management to using XTree on large hard drives and on networks.

$19.95p ISBN: 0-07-881711-0, 352 pp., 7 3/8 X 9 1/4, Covers XTree, XTreePro and XTreePro Gold

Osborne McGraw-Hill ■ **Available at local book and computer stores.**